THE
Reformation

THE
Reformation

Edited by Pierre Chaunu

St. Martin's Press
New York

Copyright © Hermé, 1986
Copyright this edition © Alan Sutton Publishing Limited by
arrangement with Hermé and Desclée de Brouwer, 1989

All rights reserved. For information, write:
Scholarly and Reference Division,
St. Martin's Press, Inc., 175 Fifth Avenue,
New York, N.Y. 10010

First published in the United States of America in 1990

Printed and bound in the Netherlands

ISBN 0-312-03750-3

Library of Congress Cataloging-in-Publication Data

Aventure de la Réforme. English.
  The Reformation / edited by Pierre Chaunu.
      p.   cm.
  Translation of: L'Aventure de La Réforme.
  Includes bibliographical references.
  ISBN 0-312-03750-3 : $49.95 (est.)
  1. Reformation.   I. Chaunu, Pierre.   II. Title.
BR305.2.A94   1990
270.6–dc20   89-37008
                                                                    CIP

Contents

General editor

Pierre Chaunu
Professor at the Sorbonne, Paris
Member of the Institute

Authors

Guy Bedouelle
Professor at the University of Fribourg

Jean Bérenger
Professor at the University of Strasburg

Jean-François Bergier
Professor at the Polytechnic of Zurich

Pierre Chaunu
Professor at the Sorbonne, Paris
Member of the Institute

Jaques Courvoisier
Honorary Professor at the University of Geneva

Olivier Fatio
Professor at the University of Geneva

Alexandre Ganoczy
Professor at the Hermann Schell Institute of Würzburg

Carlos Gilly
Doctor of Philosophy, historian

Hans Guggisberg
Professor of Modern History at the University of Basle

Robert Kingdon
Professor at the University of Wisconsin (Madison)

Marc Lienhard
Professor in the Faculty of Protestant Theology, Strasburg

Georges Livet
Professor at the University of Strasburg

William Monter
Professor at the University of Evanston, Nordwestern

Gabriel Mützenberg
Historian at Geneva

Rémi Taveneaux
Professor Emeritus at the University of Nancy

Bernard Vogler
Professor at the University of Strasburg

Manfred Welti
Professor at the University of Constance, historian

English translation
Victoria Acland
Charles Gordon Clark
Ruth Page
Ros Schwarz
Barbara Snell
Pamela Swinglehurst

Co-ordinating editor
Ruth Page

Foreword

1517: A point of departure

On 31 October every year, from Geneva to Wittenberg, from Edinburgh to Los Angeles, from Amsterdam to Stockholm and Pretoria, the anniversary of the Reformation is celebrated. The Protestant world commemorates Martin Luther on this day traditionally associated with martyrs of the faith, for on All Saints' Eve in 1517 he nailed up his ninety-five Theses against Indulgences on the gates of the castle church at Wittenberg. They remain there to this day, the Latin words and Gothic letters cast in bronze on the huge imperial commemorative monument of 1883. In that year the four-hundredth anniversary of Luther's birth was celebrated in an atmosphere of unquestioned Protestant virtues, a little embittered by the *Kulturkampf*, that 'struggle for civilization' which disguised an outburst of anti-Catholic bigotry in Bismarck's Reich. Richard Stauffer, who would surely have wielded his pen with even more authority and talent today, if God had not decreed otherwise, notes humorously that, 'Even though in the three centuries since the first annual festival of the Reformation audacious critics have rudely questioned the very existence of Jesus, no German theologian would have dreamed of questioning that the ninety-five theses had really been affixed'. Not even good Père Denifle, the pugnacious sub-archivist of the Vatican – who at the beginning of this century aroused the indignation of scholars of Luther and the anger of Lutherans, wounded by those insinuations of his which healthy criticism has since overturned – would have done so.

If the mutual respect born of a true and healthy ecumenism did not restrain them, Roman Catholics could poke fun at all these commemorations, which almost overshadow the unique commemoration of the death and the glorious resurrection of Christ. (At one time the inhabitants of Geneva even questioned the propriety of celebrating Christmas, Easter, Ascension and Pentecost.) Indeed, since each Sunday recapitulates the whole gift of God, why have regular celebrations of a rather minor event which perhaps did not even take place? There is no doubt about the existence of the ninety-five theses, but it is in fact unlikely that they were nailed up on All Saints' Eve, 1517. But posted or not on 31 October, this year we will once again sing *Ein' Feste Burg*, as we have always done on Reformation Day.

1536: A point of arrival

If 31 October 1517 is customarily hallowed, the major event of 1536 is not. Nevertheless, the unanimous decision of the city council of Geneva on 21 May 1536 to adopt the Reformed discipline coincides with a whole complex of convergent events: the little city's pledge to live according to the Gospel for reasons that were complex because they were human (concern for the glory of God not being the only one); Farel's invitation and Calvin's first stay in that lakeside city at war with its bishop (he was devoting himself to the glory of a twenty-five year exile in France); the publication at the end of March by Thomas Platter in Basle of Calvin's *Institutes of the Christian Religion* (that theological handbook which was destined for such a vast success and the instruction of a much larger circle than that of the clergy).

In choosing to highlight 1536 we are choosing the Reformed tradition, which constitutes one of the two major axes of the Reformation. Protestantism, with the great Catholic tradition and eastern Orthodoxy, is an integral part of Christ's Church, which no institution can contain and which the Holy Spirit gathers together from age to age. So too the Reformed tradition stands out as one of the richest dwellings in the great house of Protestantism.

In 1502 Frederick the Wise, Elector of Saxony, founded the University of Wittenberg. This little town on the Elbe became famous fifteen years later when Martin Luther nailed up his 95 theses (as tradition has it) on the door of the castle church.

View of Wittenberg, engraving on copper by Braun-Hogenberg, *c.* 1558.

11

CHRISTIA

NAE RELIGIONIS INSTI-
tutio,totam ferè pietatis summã,& quic
quid est in doctrina salutis cognitu ne-
cessarium, complectens : omnibus pietatis studiosis lectu dignissi-
mum opus,ac re
cens edi-
tum.

PRAEFATIO AD CHRI
stianißimum REGEM FRANCIAE, qua
hic ei liber pro confeßione fidei
offertur.

IOANNE CALVINO
Nouiodunensi autore.

BASILEAE,
M. D. XXXVI.

The publication in Basle of the *Institutes of the Christian Religion* made 1536 a notable year. It was Calvin's principal work, which played a key role in spreading the Reformation and in instructing the faithful.

First Latin edition of Calvin's *Institutes of the Christian Religion*, 1536. Société de l'Histoire du Protestantisme Français, Paris.

Lutheran reform burgeoned; all its major points were contained in the great polemical tracts of 1520 but were given form in Saxony between 1526 and 1529, from where it spread rapidly over the Holy Roman Empire in concentric circles and stirred up a swarm of troubles in nearly all of Christendom through little conventicles of informal evangelicalism. By contrast, the Reformed tradition, more intellectual and less emotional, more political and less detached from city life and the world and its ways, took a little longer to develop. It wavered, hesitated, and found a home in the little mid-European city-states. Then it was consolidated in Church-dominated towns which combined theocracy with a measure of Caesaro-papism to form complete strongholds. Without the help of this protective wall Lutheran Europe would have been marginalized into a gigantic Bohemia embattled like the fifteenth-century Hussites.

Three reasons justify the choice of 1536. Firstly, as I have said, the publication in Basle of the first Latin edition of the *Institutes*. Suddenly the humanist Reforms of Zwingli, Oecolampadius, Bucer and Capito found their guide and reference point. Certainly Luther had come first and given the signal to advance. But although Calvin was bringing up the rear, he was the St Paul of Protestantism. At twenty-seven he was a spiritual leader without knowing it. In this Reformation centred on The Book, this 'salvation by printing alone', the single greatest event was a book.

Secondly, in 1536 Geneva was still hanging back, just as later in Amsterdam the workers preferred to wait until the eleventh hour. Geneva was dragging its feet and hesitating, but in 1536 Calvin came to live there, his young glory seized on by Farel.

Lastly, by 1536 the Act of Supremacy had been passed in England. Even though this was only a stage in a process, it certainly fixed the irreversibility of the Anglican schism and so for the time being England's support of Protestantism.

The eight years leading up to 1536 had been decisive. After the Peasants' War and the double conflict with the lawless mob and Anabaptism's destabilizing activity, there came an end to the short period of evangelical ambivalence and the cohabitation of two forms of worship. On average about five years passed between the last mass and the first Reformed order of worship. Berne changed over in 1528, and with the bear of Berne came the biggest military force in Central Europe. Basle burned its bridges in 1529. The Colloquy of Marburg, in the same year, made three points clear: the solidity of Lutheran Europe; the unshakeable characteristics of the humanist Reforms along the axis of the Rhine and the Alps; the power of the printed word, of the printers and the 10 per cent or so of the population who were literate. Despite the unbridgeable gap over the meaning of *Hoc est corpus meum* in the Eucharist, despite the splits over ritual and over different approaches, Marburg proved that the division lay between Catholics and Lutherans rather than between Lutherans and the Reformed.

The Confession of Augsburg (25 June 1530) lit the torch for a succession of confessions of faith. But this hardening of attitudes led to the unfortunate 'Affair of the Placards' (18 October 1534) and so to the French kingdom, a state with a quarter of the financial and military resources of Europe, inclining from the camp of varied evangelicalism towards a more traditional position, and then to Tridentine Catholicism, without being able to change back. French-speaking Protestantism

could grow only on the fringes, beyond the grasp of a strong political power which had had to make a reluctant political choice constrained by an intransigeance over the sacraments. That was Geneva's greatest good fortune.

In 1536 the future map of Europe was more or less drawn, with islands of Lutheran and Reformed Protestantism in the great mass of traditional Catholicism which was soon to be reinforced and systematized by the work and decrees of the Council of Trent (1545–63).

The unique commemoration

Commemoration, whether of 31 October 1517 or of 21 May 1536, does however pose a problem. And it is certainly not just at Geneva that the surprise lies. For commemoration touches on the sacred, and is in the Judaeo-Christian tradition it is the very essence of the only conceivable religious act. 'As a memorial of the one perfect sacrifice', the Eucharist, the Lord's Supper, the sacrament of all the Christian Churches, is commemoration – the most important of all commemorations. Just as on Maundy Thursday the Holy Spirit makes the Transcendent present at the Eucharist, calling us to the eternity which he bestows on us.

The word itself has separated us for a long time, because Catholics have suspected Protestants of not giving 'commemoration' its total meaning, the one I have just reiterated in terms that Calvin would not have repudiated. Pope Paul VI had the courage to reintroduce the word 'commemoration' into the new order of the mass, which completely conforms to Catholic tradition – and raised a storm of anger which brought the great Catholic Church within a hair's breadth of schism. But in that truly ecumenical act that Church invites us to find again the sense that the great Reformers, and especially Calvin, gave the Lord's Supper: commemoration, the action of breaking the bread and passing the cup from hand to hand, from mouth to mouth. Commemoration is an acted sermon, a 'recital' they would have written in the sixteenth century, which makes the Word of Christ live again. The Transcendent, once present in time, for the totality of space and time is the Word; it is the whole work of the Church within that history which is given meaning by the Word, to keep the memory of that fact.

There is nothing more serious than for that commemoration to be made wrongfully outside the Church or profaned within it. If we were faithful to our traditions we would spontaneously be scandalized by the commemoration of any other Word than that imparted to Abraham and of any other event than the expected coming of the Transcendent and the one perfect sacrifice which the Lord's Supper and the sermon commemorate. Any commemoration which might interfere with that of the Sabbath was rejected by the Reformers as a papist abomination.

This portrait of John Calvin is the only one painted during his lifetime. He was twenty-seven when he arrived in Geneva, but already had a great reputation as a humanist and, thanks to the *Institutes* which had just appeared, as a theologian.

Portrait of the young Calvin, first half of the 16th century. Musée Historique de la Réformation, Geneva.

In 1536 the young Calvin was called to Geneva by Guillaume Farel. In a few years this small town, a commercial and banking centre, had become the 'Protestant Rome'. From the banks of Lake Geneva the Reformed religion spread along the route of the Rhine, to the British Isles, and from there to the New World.

View of Geneva at the beginning of the 17th century, oil on panel by Josse Momper. Musée d'Art et d'Histoire, Geneva.

The obstacle can be overcome if light is shed on it. The impossibility at the time of the Reformation of the whole Church continuing in unity and strength led to the Reformation's choice of the lesser evil of a rupture for the greater good. The Reformation wanted to set the Word of God free, believing it to be buried, betrayed, warped. We do not have to make unfair judgements on the continued medieval order which issued inevitably from the confrontation – mutual respect for our particular traditions beyond our common heritage has served the ecumenical movement well. But we know that the Reformation was lived as a new Pentecost, a re-emergence of the blessed time of the Apostles, a restoration, a Christian restitution of insulted national feelings. As we commemorate the Reformation by tracing this side of the Holy Spirit's work in history, it is to the Word of God and to that alone that we claim to be rendering homage and glory. Only when we have done that do I believe that may we find pleasure and profit in reminding ourselves of the courage and zeal of those men of whom we are not ashamed, even if these attributes were not always used in very inspired ways.

To accept the inheritance of the Reformation does not mean that we have to approve of it all. Émile Doumergue, who was above suspicion, was inspired when, on 25 September 1902, he submitted to the Museum of the Reformation his project for the expiatory monument which stands today at Champel on the place of Michael Servetus' execution. 'We are respectful and grateful sons of Calvin, our great Reformer, but we condemn an error which was that of his century and we are strongly attached to freedom of conscience.' There is no need to emphasize that as exponents of the Reformed tradition we are also capable of discerning the value of other traditions and that we can rightly expect others to discern in our overlapping traditions the mark of the Holy Spirit. That is why we have not separated the history of the Reformation from that of the Catholic Reforms, and why the group of eminent specialists who have generously contributed includes Reformed of all tendencies, Lutherans and Catholics. Even when the confrontation, the arguments, the reciprocal persecutions were at their most violent, John Calvin, in his little treatise of 1543 on *The faithful among the papists*, ends by conceding the status of a church to the foe, and states that it could therefore be lawful to follow the prayers in the parish mass, 'since the people are assembled that day to invoke God and since most of the prayers are better and more holy than those on other days, in so far as they are taken from the early Church'. And again, in the same work, 'The Church can be considered in different ways. I certainly do not doubt that the true Catholic Church is spread through all the countries where the tyranny of the Pope dominates. For just as St Paul concluded that the grace of God would never depart from the Jews because he had once received them into his unbreakable covenant, so we can say that the virtue of God's grace will dwell eternally among all the peoples whom God has once enlightened with his Gospel. Moreover they have baptism which is a sign of God's covenant . . .' These pearls of early ecumenism are too rare to be neglected.

Yes, we are fashioned by the world of the Reformation. These men are our fathers in the faith and the commemoration is justified – to affirm Scripture alone (*sola Scriptura*) when everything is in dissolution; grace alone (*sola gratia*) when we believe ourselves alone and feel disheartened; after darkness, Light (*post tenebras Lux*) when we feel we have been driven into a tunnel of resounding nonsense; *Libertas*, the freedom of creation, of God and of humanity. 'I have set before you life and death, therefore choose life!', and crowning and unifying all these affirmations, 'To God alone be the glory' (*soli Deo gloria*).

In today's shaken world Protestant Europe takes centre-stage. It often feels the tremors before they actually arrive, and exaggerates them when they do. More than any other area of the industrial world, it needs our attention. A serene vision of the past, just and beneficial, frank and true, would enable us to promote optimism.

The Reformation today

Not so much a turning point as the confirmation of a tendency, 1536 introduced a phase of acceleration at the end of nearly twenty years of transition. What was produced during those years of change, invention and richness, at that high-water mark of religious energy, constitutes one of the distinctive features of Christianity. It seems to me that we can be quite uncomplicatedly Reformed and at the same time beneficiaries of more than a century of ecumenical reflection. We can distinguish the leading features of a coherent tradition as one of the main axes of a complex totality; and see that its riches increase even in proportion to the opposition they arouse.

The Reformation is one of the most important epochs in the history of the Church, that Church of Jesus Christ which is drawn together by the Holy Spirit. To have meaning and value beyond the accident of a historical moment, the

Reformation must be seen as part of the continuity of the Church, and also as part of the continuity of the sacred. It is one aspect of the great anthropological phenomenon of religion, that tying of the individual being to the essence of all things, to the sacred, which is what the Latin word *religare* means. The Reformation was certainly, historically speaking, a break; but it was intended to be the correction of a deviation, the appeal to a true rather than a false continuity, to continuity in the main stream. It may not have completely achieved its goal, but it needs to be considered in the context of the whole Christian religious picture.

So we need a double point of departure, general and particular, natural and supernatural, following a distinction dear to nearly all theologians, Catholics as much as Calvinists. We must start both from the first tomb that truly belongs to all mankind, and also from the Word spoken to Abraham whose world-wide significance is no less sure for being less evident. Man knows that he is going to die. The first man Adam signified his presence on the earth with the tomb which bears testimony to the first funerary rite. This rite is the way into the full human game. Modern man has a conviction that there is something beyond appearances and beyond death. On this point personal supernatural revelation only makes more precise, enlarges, and illuminates the natural revelation that can properly be called universal.

No happening, in my opinion, is more important than the one through which we have been living and which has been revealed to us through the implacable agency of opinion polls. Between 1960 and 1965, 70 per cent of Europeans, asked whether they believed in an afterlife, ventured to reply that they did. After 1970 less than 30 per cent in France have made that affirmation, while the 70 per cent who can no longer believe what men and women have always believed, have confessed sincerely enough, 'There is nothing, alas, and that grieves us'. May they find again the remembrance of their past and may that give them a little hope as they await the greater Hope which, with Faith and Charity, can only come from the Wholly Other.

2

The Reformers, and Calvin in particular, insisted on the importance of the re-enactment of the Last Supper: one of the central debates of the 16th century, was it not concerned with the nature of the presence of Christ and thence with the question of Communion in both kinds? Trusting in the gesture of the breaking of the bread, and in the cup which passes from lips to lips, the faithful commemorate the passion of Christ.

1. The Last Supper, wood engraving by Albrecht Dürer, 1510. Bibliothèque Nationale, Paris.

2. *The Lord's Supper*, engraving of the school of Schaüfelein, Augsburg, *c.* 1537. Bibliothèque Nationale, Paris.

1

Revelation and the sacred in Christianity

The Judaeo-Christian tradition began as the history of a Word passed on by Abraham to his descendants. From Palestine to Byzantium, and later among the Reformers, the debate about rites and images could not disguise a fundamental belief in revelation, common to both Jews and Christians.

Religion – as old as humanity

Jean Delumeau reasserts an obvious truth, often overlooked: Martin Luther was led to a belief in justification by faith through his own existential anguish. He would not have aroused so great a response 'if he had not expressed the underlying, unconscious sentiments of great numbers of men and women, and if he had not offered an acceptable solution to their religious problems'. Jean Delumeau, Lucien Febvre and W.L. Langer are agreed on this point: the Reformation, if it is to be explained at all, is to be explained on religious grounds.

There is a relationship between psychological and theological needs, between the tormenting question and the tardy answer. The new historiography concerns itself with the tension between the considerable need in that religious age, and the demand which was not met. Jean Delumeau concludes that this new approach gives a total explanation, or, better, it goes beyond 'moral' explanations concerning the abuses of the Church or Marxist explanations in terms of economic or social evolution. But then, if the new historiography dares to require a religious explanation for a religious phenomenon, the Reformation must now be placed within the entire continuum of the religious sense.

The earliest incontestable appearance of religious belief dates from the first deliberate burials, carbon dated to between forty and fifty thousand years ago. The first tombs are the first cathedrals of history. They signify that after long development humanity had reached the point of civilization where death was not only a door that closed, but also a door that opened. The tombs are common to *Sapiens sapiens*, and to *Sapiens neanderthalensis*. They show signs of a complete funerary rite, with the placing of tools nearby, the traces of pollen and the foetal position of the body observed by C. Reichel-Dolmatoff among the Kogi Indians in Columbia, and which Mircea Eliade deciphered. In fact, the ethnologist comes to the aid of the prehistorian, teaching him that the rite is a mimed complement to a myth which affirms that human destiny is not just to be a prisoner trapped in corporeal existence. The first tomb is the affirmation that there is for humanity something beyond the observable, that destiny is not entirely wedged between the abyss before and the abyss behind; in short, that there is something beyond death, and the visible part of existence is not separable from the obscure side of destiny. Religion is thus as old as humanity, the dowry of the complex brain of which we still know so little, and is manifest in the funerary rite. Calvin notes that burial, like kneeling, is a natural action: we would say that they both belong to the universal cultural inheritance.

Since consciousness of death relates us to time, we may suppose that consciousness of time appeared in our distant ancestor *Australopithecus gracilis* three million years ago. He deliberately split a stone for which he could foresee use as a weapon, working from a memory to a future action. That consciousness of time was again reached forty-five thousand years ago, with the appearance of the first tomb. In 'you will die' one must also hear 'you know that you will die'.

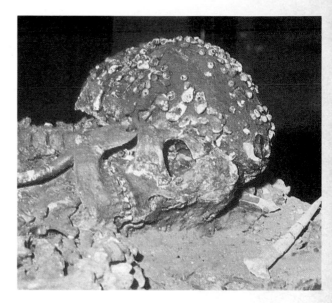

Burial of the dead forty or fifty thousand years ago is the earliest manifestation of religion and of belief in an afterlife. The practice was common to a large number of very diverse and widely separated civilizations. So this skull from the Augignacian period, which is decorated with shells and deers' teeth, is an integral part of a universal cultural inheritance.

Skull of Menton Man, Cavillon grotto.

In the early centuries after the death and resurrection of Christ, Christians made their tombs into works of art uniting aesthetic qualities with religious symbols like the Cross.

Ancient Christian mosaic, Tabarka, Tunisia.

The sacred relates us also to space. The fully developed human, as Mircea Eliade notes, is not only the upright human – 'one cannot remain upright except in a state of watchfulness' – but is also 'the hunter who knows how to hunt', according to the aphorism of Edgar Morin; that is, a hunter in a group which understands orientation. It seems that the most ancient manifestation of the sacred may be this particle of tutelary and protective space which takes on recognizable form and is inscribed on the memory; a tree in the savannah, a raised stone or a rock permits a being who is more and more deprived of instinct to move with assurance in a space which might otherwise give rise to anxiety about what is above or below him, before or behind, to left or to right. Consciousness of space preceded that of duration, but scarcely less than consciousness of time produced mournful existential anguish.

If space is experienced like a fluid, there are in the fluid certain solid particles. The best definition of the sacred which I have read comes from Roger Caillois: the sacred is what stands in opposition to the profane, to the fluid, to the meaningless. It is firm, something which really exists; the sacred is the solid part in beings and things. It helps us to apprehend the field of our consciousness; it is the really Real, beyond the *I*. One could call these particles of the sacred in ambient space 'hierophanies'. The most ancient hierophanies are marked places made tangible by springs, stones, trees. In a region inhabited from antiquity these benchmarks from a distant past have a strange aptitude for enduring. From neolithic times to our own, in all places of ancient western Latin Christianity, there are marked sites whose meaning has changed, but not their position. Thousands of such places continue to exist, even in the centres of our large industrial cities.

This *excursus* into the life of humanity forty or fifty thousand years ago is intended as a caveat against the naïvety of expressing in contemporary awareness of temporal succession the sacred sense which belonged to the flowing, oscillating realities of ancient humanity: 'an element in the structure of consciousness, not a milestone in the history of that consciousness'. Indeed history and the sacred are the components of a latent conflict which came to the surface with exceptional intensity in the sixteenth century.

Christianity as history

The sense of the sacred is as old as humanity. Without it humans could not have survived in the face of death. It may be devalued, but no human society has been able to make it disappear. The sacred is the oxygen of our tragic existence with death forever lying in wait. The sacred, complete, perfect and fully religious, is as old as consciousness of death, but its polymorphic content is elusive. On the other hand Judaism, and Christianity in continuity with it, have their own modality which cannot be reduced to the history of religions. There the sacred has little obvious place to the point where one variety of 'neotheologians going out into the world' have been able to claim that, since in their view Christianity is not, strictly speaking, a religion, the churches offered an area of experience for radical desacralization, like the one brought about by the humanist Reformers, the Zwinglians, the founders of the Reformed tradition. That is clearly a great misunderstanding.

For a comparative history of religions, the emergence of Judaism and Christianity corresponds to the movement from a diffuse to a concentrated sense of the sacred. Pompey at Jerusalem, for instance, was surprised to discover that the Holy of Holies in the Temple of YHWH was empty. For pagans, Christians were, in the strict sense, impious atheists, lay desacralizers who lived without a god, profaners of that holy thing which – in ancient paganism as, often, in African religions – was everywhere. While paganism ground the tension between the sacred and the profane into fine dust which was sprinkled over social and individual life, the Judaic and Christian tradition concentrated that tension on the relationship between the Creator, source of all being, and humans in their world. And as the Wholly Other wished no representation of what in essence cannot be represented, he could be satisfied only with negative definitions. He could however be recognized by means of a Word, not pronounced but heard. He is infinite, without beginning or limit; time cannot contain him and his eternity denies all means of knowing him, all means of existing in time. That is why the Judaeo-Christian tradition desacralizes, removes and ridicules every natural emergence of the sacred, which it considers an idol, or a false god.

The sacred for Hebrew and Christian is concentrated in a Word which one man, Abraham, remembered all his life, which he passed on to his descendants and which was finally incarnated in a 'prophet', a 'Messiah', 'he who should come'. He was the entire Word, the Word of creation, re-creation and salvation. That Word, collected

into Scripture as memory of the lived experience, memory of the history which turned things upside-down, gives history its complete meaning. The specific character of the Judaeo-Christian tradition resides not only in the concentration of the sacred, which it shares with other monotheistic religions which promise salvation, but also in its unique relationship with history. Unlike Islam, Christianity cannot be identified either with a book, a collection of prescriptions or a dogma, which would be a gnosis; what is Christian is contained in the history of a man and a lineage whose unique and specific character gives meaning to all the lives which make up the web of history. Each life is unique, irreducible and specific, like the life of the transcendent, incarnate, which is offered for their cognition.

What is Christian is in the first place a history accessible through historical memory, but it is also a religion among all other religions: it has to do with existence, provides an explanation, implies an interpretative knowledge, hence a dogmatic.

Yet whatever the status of knowledge may be, and whatever the status of the sacred, members of Christian societies and civilizations are always more complete than their non-Christian counterparts in profane societies and civilizations. The threat to the Christian world is deficiency rather than excess. The philosophical foundation of that separation of the sacred from the profane is provided by the unique and irreducible doctrine of creation, the key to all Christian thought. That separation protects Christianity from the transformation of its text into an idol so that it is not esoteric knowledge but a history.

Even when the history of God's steadfast love and his coming is entrusted to a book (the seventy-two or sixty-six books of the biblical canon), a relationship can be established only with history, not with the letter of the text. The Reformers did not rediscover a book which no one had forgotten; rather they learned again to read it simply as one reads a good history.

Since Christianity derives from an event in the past, in the collective memory of a certain people, it is by nature 'historicist'. This is proved by the schism of the sixteenth century, in which quarrelling Christians reinforced their arguments with historical proofs.

At the same time, the access to meaning is central, since all dogmatics flow from that; Christian theology is first of all exegesis and hermeneutic. The humanists, with Erasmus (in the introduction to the *Novum Instrumentum*) at their head, freed exegesis from its indistinct role, for medieval university usage had congealed it into an exercise in high logic. Such exegesis gave pride of place to derived meanings over the clear primary meaning, the historical meaning. Equilibrium was established, the work back in hand; meaning is never exhausted. Each generation needs to rediscover it. The humanist reaction was necessary as a sharp recall to order from the

The whole Jewish and Christian sense of the sacred is concentrated on the Word spoken to Abraham which the patriarch remembered all his life and passed on to his descendants. The mysterious visit of three young men to Abraham is a frequent subject of illustration, as is the symbol of his posterity seated in the lap of the patriarch.

1. *The visit of the three angels to Abraham*, French Bible of Lefèvre d'Étaples, Antwerp, 1534. Bibliothèque Nationale, Paris.

2. *The Generation in the bosom of Abraham*, Souvigny Bible, late 12th century. Bibliothèque Municipale, Moulins.

Baptism changed its character in the 5th and 6th centuries. It was no longer for adults but for infants, and involved sprinkling rather than immersion. It came to be understood as the sacrament which removed original sin.

Baptism of Christ, late 5th-century Byzantine mosaic in the Baptistry at Ravenna.

Word, action and image are all presented in this popular figure of early iconography. In the frescoes of the Catacombs prayer is represented by a man standing to pray with arms outstretched and his face turned towards God.

Man praying, fresco in the cemetery of St Peter and St Marcellinus, Rome.

superposition of commentaries, of high-flying logic and the fragile scaffolding of meaning further and further removed from the text, not to mention the fascination of the letter. The humanists' review was perhaps excessive and unjust, but it was necessary. By its very essence Christianity cannot be static, assured, fixed; its gifts, which are as immutable as they are infinite, have always to be reappraised. Words and gestures too often repeated, having been vectors of meaning, may come to constitute a stumbling block which has to be removed. There is no undisturbed Christian history.

Within cultures, in the course of centuries, priorities change. It is therefore very natural that the Church, the community of Christians, should remember its 'Unique Event' in various ways. In the *Enchiridion Militis Christi* (1504), that first 'best-seller' of Christian humanism, Erasmus, able to read Latin and almost all the native languages of Christianity, envisaged a novel development: personal, silent reading of Scripture, with the eyes alone. But Erasmus' wish was Utopian: at that time less than a tenth of men and fewer women, even in the Rhenish district, could read fluently. Large Bibles in native languages did not really begin to emerge until the very end of the seventeenth century; fluent, silent reading — which was an achievement of the monastic orders of the thirteenth century — was to remain the privilege of a minority until the revolution in learning which began in the second half of the seventeenth century.

Word, action and image

If devotional reading was rather slow to arrive, the case was quite different with preaching. Marcel Jousse insisted that the language of the Gospel was to be spoken and imitated. Father Jacques Guillet was more moderate: 'It remains true, however, that the speech of Christ . . . obeys laws and rhythms which leave their mark.' The Word of the Gospel is living, dense, purified, crystalline in having been spoken and received. It was that Word which preaching reinstated.

Preaching was the iron lance which conquered the Mediterranean world in the first centuries. Thereafter, in a world where the Church was so triumphant that 'Christendom' became a geographical term, preaching yielded its place to more humble practices: the gesture with the hand, the gesture with the feet on pilgrimage to the land where the Lord had walked, to the shore where the Apostle James was reputed to have landed, to the cemeteries where lay the ashes of martyrs and saints whose souls already beheld the face of the Lord. A whole network of such actions came into being, a whole collection of expedients emerged again from the depths of the ages: this was the Christianized inheritance from paganism, which, in default of a more direct way, had to substitute a sense of the sacred for the inaccessible idol in the Church.

Preaching could continue alongside this network of action as a necessary complement. In the thirteenth century it emerged again for the first time, and in the new urban society became the privilege and the *raison d'etre* of the mendicant orders. In the sixteenth century preaching became the new 'royal road' to the point of a positive surfeit of words. Here was a religion of the Word, a clear religion without any other mystery than Christ made present by the Gospel, which was proclaimed, followed, retold and commented on. This religion was perhaps excessive, unjust, simplistic, intransigent and too sure of itself, as if its superiority totally condemned all other ways of access. Geneva is a good instance of these excesses: for the most tenacious there were several hours of sermons there daily. Calvin himself bore witness to an enormous revolution when he recalled on his death-bed the religious state of Geneva in 1536: 'When I first came to this church hardly anything was happening: there was preaching and that was all . . . there was no reformation and everything was in uproar.'

This then was the heart of the confrontation. What has been interpreted as a conflict over dogma was essentially a conflict concerning different liturgical means of access to God. When at the Reformation one of these was imposed as the only one to conform to transcendent, divine majesty, people could not bring themselves to admit that both might coexist.

Moreover, the privileged means of communication remained ritual action. Baptism, which began by being the voluntary participation in the death, burial and resurrection of Christ, lost its primary meaning in a double lapse. Firstly infant baptism was assimilated with circumcision: 'One cannot think that the child God gives to his people should not belong to him.' There was therefore a movement away from the deferred late baptism of the fourth century to the baptism of the newly-born from the fifth and sixth centuries onwards. Secondly, there was a

'The visit of the three angels' was depicted in Christian mosaic long before it inspired painters like Rembrandt and Tiepolo.

Abraham and the Three Angels, 5th-century mosaic. St Mary-the-Great, Rome.

The entire meaning of Christ's words *Hoc est corpus meum* came to be concentrated on the host. So the Eucharist as the sacrament of the one perfect sacrifice became the focal point of Protestant opposition to the Church of Rome.

The Last Supper by Fra Angelico, Museo di S. Marco, Florence.

departure from immersion to sprinkling water on the forehead. From then on, the sacrament of the Passion became that which blotted out the stain, the acquittal of the wages of sin. The power and grandeur of this condensed and miniscule action, which became pure Act, are witness and symbol of the saving power which God delegated to his Church. The Lutherans maintained it intact. Calvin, wishing to uphold the freedom of God and the discipline of *sola Fide*, forbade private baptism to his converts. What counted for children who died before baptism was faith alone, that God had saved them without the liturgical rite.

The Eucharist, which is *par excellence* the sacrament of sacrifice and of the Love of God up to death and which surpasses it, was the centre of the confrontations. It was the focal point of the debate. In this sacrament of divine presence ('I am with you today, every day, to the end of the world'), the ancient Church from the fourth and fifth centuries had been fascinated by the very forceful words of Christ: *Hoc est corpus meum*, 'This is my body'. The emphasis was on the host – but could one recognize familiar bread in that translucent circular wafer which had no use outside the Eucharistic celebration? The wine, 'This is my blood', came to be reserved for the celebrant alone and marked the distance between the cleric, participating directly in the mystery, and those who kept a respectful distance from the inaccessible and unsustaining sacrament. But, evangelically speaking, were they in the worst place?

How dared they approach, knowing their thoughts were scattered, their repentance impure, their regret imperfect? Such people communicated only by looking; shame and reverence kept them at the far end of the nave, at an infinite distance from the grille which separated the people from the officiant. Reinforced by the opacity of its iconostasis, the grille shielded the unsustaining consecration even from sight.

It is understandable, therefore, that mass should have become the central issue of the controversy. Things were not so bad in the parish mass (which retained something of the warm conviviality of the master in the midst of his disciples) as they were in the private mass. Before the evangelical Lord's Supper was even clearly drawn up, the denial of the mass, the 'no' to the mass, became the denial of the ritual action of these Hebrew priests.

It must be remembered that the attitude of the Christian churches in relation to ritual action, whether central or secondary, is coherent and yet oscillates between two poles. The debate concerning the eternal problem of images had already taken place in the eighth and ninth centuries in Byzantium – but it was taken up again in the sixteenth century when Reformation – intransigent, radical – was accompanied by an irrepressible ardour of iconoclasm.

The savage rejection of images found its justification in the strong prohibitions of the Old Testament. It was linked with the historical necessity of learning again that God is really Wholly Other, wholly elsewhere, entirely beyond human conception, totally inaccessible and unimaginable. That was the principal truth from which

22

everything else followed, and which in the end was forgotten. That is what explains the hard teaching of the iconoclasts. Periodic outbreaks of wild opposition, generally in response to excesses, were launched to restrain the sensibility which made the transcendent seem close at hand. Iconoclasts had legitimized the recourse to images and accepted these props which made the Word of God more lively and humanly comprehensible. According to orthodox theologians, the injunctions of the Old Testament texts were no longer justifiable in the era of grace. By becoming incarnate in Christ the transcendent God eliminated distance, making himself flesh, gesture, image, and thus legitimized the use of the senses. The Synodikon of 843 proclaimed: 'Those who confess verbally the incarnation of God the Word, but will not suffer to see him in an image of that act, are not sincere. They pretend to confess in word but they deny our salvation in reality. Let them be anathema!' In a word, let us who are Reformed not be more royalist than God.

The great Churches of the Reformation accepted the depiction of the Passion and a pious iconography of the gospels – the Lutherans without difficulty, the Reformed with hesitation and with some mean actions which may be explained historically but not totally justified. Unlike that sectarian folly, Rembrandt's paint-brush is on the side of reasonable, controlled use of icons. Rembrandt and Bach demonstrate that art may be the humble servant of the true faith.

Revelation

The Christian sense of the sacred, a place in the memory of people who know themselves to be the people of God, implies a conception common to Jews and Christians: revelation. Revelation is the knowledge of the source. 'How shall I understand if no one explains to me?', cried the Ethiopian. Revelation can only be personal. If it were from the start accessible to everyone, even at the cost of great effort, it would only be knowledge (*gnosis*). Revelation is the Word addressed to Abraham and the Apostolic witness to the Promise. Yet how would one ever attain to this additional information which gives meaning to life, death, suffering, anguish and destiny unless something accessible and comprehensible had not aroused us to seek, question and wait? In the Christian conception the cosmos inevitably bears the mark of its creator: 'The heavens are telling the glory of God; and the firmament proclaims his handiwork.' Therefore as well as the Word addressed to Abraham there will be a Word coming from the created world. 'What can be known of God . . . is manifest . . . They are therefore without excuse' (Romans 1). Yet what the universe has to say to human intelligence is at once limpidly clear and insufficient. An address proclaimed above the rooftops cannot reach us; a word meant for all cannot

2

Christian churches regularly have to face the issue of images, just as Islam must in its own way. The question which had split the Byzantine Church was raised again by the Reformers in the 16th century: should the prohibitions on images in the Old Testament be respected, or does the Incarnation make the use of images legitimate for rendering the word of God more accessible? Between the two extremes of opinion there is room for a range of compromise.

1. *The Destruction of Images by Karlstadt*, 16th-century engraving.

2. A scene of iconoclasm in *Von dem grossen lutherischen Narren* (*The Great Lutheran Fools*), by Thomas Murner, Strasburg, 1522.
Bibliothèque Nationale et Universitaire, Strasburg.

1

Lucas Cranach was the friend and painter of Luther as well as Burgomaster of Wittenberg from 1537. In the famous reredos of the parish church of St Mary he depicts the Reformer twice: in the *Lord's Supper* in the character of the knight George, to whom a cup-bearer hands a goblet, and in the *Crucifixion* in which Luther points to Jesus executed like a criminal for the community of the Church.

Reredos by Lucas Cranach the Elder, church of St Mary's, Wittenberg.

communicate unless it is addressed to each individually. That is why the really significant Word, for everyone, was addressed to one man alone, to 'my servant Abraham'.

Within the consensus, at the heart of the universal Church, at the invisible frontiers which the Holy Spirit draws again from age to age, may be found two areas of indecision, and hence of tension. The first concerns the relationship between general or natural revelation, and the revelation which is personal, supernatural, scriptural or ecclesiastical. The medieval Latin tradition had a tendency to inflate excessively the area of natural revelation, even though the *via moderna* of the fourteenth and fifteenth centuries was more restrictive than the *via antiqua* of thirteenth-century Thomism. The Reformers (even Zwingli and Calvin, who were greater rationalists than Luther) held fast to the personal revelation, underlining the irreducibility of the Scriptural message.

The second point of friction came from the manner of hanging on what the Spirit meant to the Churches. For the most part medieval tradition made little distinction between the contents of the message and its vehicle, though certainly the two strands existed. 'It is a common and pernicious error that Holy Scripture has as much authority as the Church on account of the information common to both, as if the inviolable truth of God could be propped up by human imaginings', wrote Calvin in the first book of the *Institutions*. Another expedient was the recognition of Scripture by the Church as the ancient part, the foundation of the Tradition of the Church, but in that case its comprehension depended on the Church. On the other hand, against the evidence of the Church of God is drawn that of Scripture, the word of God, the ancient Apostolic tradition grafted on to the priestly tradition of the Hebrew Scriptures at the time of Christ. That tradition, the treasure of the Church, is also the judge of the Church.

Cardinal Henri de Luback has shown clearly that all theology – the *lectio divina* – is a commentary on the ancient biblical corpus, to which is added the Apostolic tradition of the New Testament canon, the extent of which was largely agreed by the fourth century. The Church makes judgement in cases of serious exegetical divergence. The debate is less on the place of Scripture at the heart of revelation as on the function of interpreting Scripture. But firm on the rock of ancient tradition, on the Word of God to the Apostles otherwise called Scripture, one may appeal to the ancient faithful Church against the modern Church which is unfaithful to its mission.

This was the recourse of Pierre Valdès at the end of the twelfth century (but paradoxically he was rejected by Wyclif and Hus at the end of the fourteenth and fifteenth centuries). So the appeal to Scripture against the unfaithful Church was not a novelty in the sixteenth century. There was already a tradition behind it. The *sola Scriptura*, however, had never been affirmed with as much force as by the Reformers, in solidarity on this point with the humanists. But for *sola Scriptura* to found a new ecclesiology something else was needed: another relationship with God which would take upon itself the anguish of living under the eye of Death and the expectation of judgement: the *sola Fide*.

Rembrandt shows that art may be the servant of faith and thus, like Cranach, contradicts the iconoclasts. The extreme simplicity of composition and the striking effects of the disposition of light and shade make the divine presence visible with extraordinary intensity.

The Pilgrims of Emmaus by Rembrandt, oil on canvas, 1648. Musée du Louvre, Paris.

PART ONE

DAWN OF MODERN TIMES

A long exodus

There is no image that better conveys the history of Christianity than the Exodus. Just as Creation is succeeded by the Fall, which itself leads on to Redemption, so also the Bible, notwithstanding different translations and interpretations which may have changed the actual words, imparts its meaning and provides the building materials for Christendom. The Reformers were to be united in their respect for this tradition which came, from Palestine, to the 'Christian homeland'.

Creation, Fall, Redemption

The transcendence of the jealous God implies on the one hand the entrenchment of the sacred in the cultural memory, and hence the notion of revelation, and on the other hand the transmitting of the Word which gradually becomes written as Scripture. The first account in the written revelation is that of Creation. The world we inhabit and we ourselves are not of our own making; on the contrary, we have received our being from the One who is, who is all-knowing, incommunicable, inaccessible – in a word, transcendent. Of all the propositions in the revelation, that of Creation, which stems from the first three words of the Bible, *Bereshith Bara Elohim*, is the most important; it is the starting point and the foundation, with infinite philosophical and practical implications.

The written revelation also tells of the Fall. Man as he is has not kept all his promises, but the being received from God in his creation is a genuine being, not merely a reflection of being. In giving man his being, God at the same time gave him freedom, which is the capacity to forge his own fate. The Fall is expressed in the story of Adam in Eden, beneath the tree of knowledge of good and evil. It is the story of a being who henceforth will know death; it is also the test of the reality of his freedom. It is only in the Bible that we find a proposition that makes man responsible for death: 'I have set before you life and death . . . therefore choose life!' To appreciate the degree to which God had truly given everything, to the extent that he made man a 'little God', as the biologist Pierre Paul Grasse neatly puts it, it was necessary for man to misuse his freedom. And the Bible shows this misuse of freedom to be responsible for all the misfortunes and tragedies of our existence.

Nothing, however, can really thwart the design of God. The defeat of God, in the Fall, can only be an apparent, temporary defeat. After the Fall, foreseen through all eternity, the revelation tells of Redemption. Whatever the cost, God proceeds, as it were, to another Creation, one which will repair and restore; he comes with 'a mighty hand and an out-stretched arm' to save what has been lost, to make straight what has been made crooked, so that finally the ultimate design of Creation might be reached.

The great neo-Calvinist theologian Herman Dooyeweerd pointed out that the central motifs of most philosophical and religious systems are binary: the world organizes itself around an axis that is form/matter, which is briefly Christianized into nature/grace before becoming, in the nineteenth century, nature/liberty. Christian thought, however, is the only system that is ternary. The Bible says: Creation, Fall, Redemption. It was to be the job of theological reflection throughout the ages to bring out this sequence.

Christian belief is ternary: Creation, Fall, Redemption. To attain Creation's ultimate goal, God came down to earth to save those who had been lost, to bring back on to the straight and narrow those who had strayed.

Christ Pantocrator, Byzantine mosaic of the 11th century, Dafni.

The revelation speaks not only of Creation, but also of the Fall. In this 13th-century psalter, the two essential moments of scriptural revelation are juxtaposed: after the Creation comes the Fall, represented by the episode of Adam and Eve, and then by that of Cain and Abel.

Canterbury Psalter, early 13th century. Bibliothèque Nationale, Paris.

But theological work is of secondary importance: it is far more essential to be aware of the historical aspect. The conscious recollection that invests history with meaning is the very essence of Christian ritual. The Christian cult acts as a memorial, recalling the past and thereby making it present through its symbolic acts, its preaching, its prayer, its sacramental celebration. It leads imperceptibly to the image of the Christ, and the sudden revelation of eternity lived in his presence, beyond the last instant.

'I am'

This is how it seems to me that one can attempt to sum up the whole history of the Church. For, just as one cannot disassociate theology from history, one can no more separate the period of the Reformation from what came before and after. Christian theology is a theology of history. And the whole of Christian history is a long exodus. No image better conveys this than the Exodus itself, that long march which took forty years – the span of a generation – from Egypt, the symbol of purely human efforts and achievements, towards the promised land, Canaan, and an existence beyond suffering and death.

It was in a society of bedouins, linguistically Semites, that there emerged what was by far the most important change in the history of religious thought. It is not illogical to suppose that they were informed by a source outside empirical and rational knowledge, that is to say by a 'revelation' having reference to the existence of a God who refuses to let himself be 'imagined' (translated into images) and who accepts competition from no other god. This gave rise to the monotheistic cult of the Eternal YHWH. He who is alone able to state and be called 'I am', accepts no competition in the hearts of the people with whom he has entered into union.

In effect, the gods of other peoples are not real gods, but only semblances of gods. 'Thou shalt have no other gods before me' becomes 'there are no other gods than thee'. 'Thou shalt not make unto thee any graven image' as other peoples do; no help will be given in attempts to make an image of the one about whom men can only know what he is not – he says 'I' in an absolute way. At the same time, it is said in a way which anticipates the establishment of a personal relationship. He who is called 'I am' has chosen a people who say 'I' when they address God.

No image gives a stronger account of Christian history than that of the Exodus. Under the leadership of Moses, the people elected to leave Egypt, symbol of efforts and successes which were purely human, in order to reach the Promised Land, the prophetic representation of the Kingdom of God.

God sending quail to the Hebrews, Byzantine mosaic. St Mark's Basilica, Venice.

The particularity of this faceless, formless God, behind the veil of the Ark, is that he still says nothing about that which haunts all men, namely what lies beyond death. Early Jahvism, that is to say the old core of the religion of Israel, confines itself to saying that man is responsible for death; God is the God of the living and not of the dead. In Jewish and Christian tradition, however, it is assumed that God's exclusive claims extend also to the realm of the dead. This God, so fiercely jealous of any sharing, is in other respects very undemanding with regard to rites and gifts, which accords well with the theology of no tangible images.

Without philosophy, without cult, through the austerity of the void, of the love demanded by a jealous God, the ancient Hebrews approached (via the competing ideas of the Pharisees, the Sadducees and the Essenes) very close to what Christ, according to Apostolic tradition, meant by the words of Eternal Life. The man who responds to the love of the living God — because that God loves him to such an extent that he sent his Son as a bridge from his transcendence — cannot die but will only seem to others to have died, since he has in fact passed from death into life.

Translation and interpretation of Holy Scripture

This strange religion is merged with the history of a small nation with a long memory — the long memory habitually found in peoples without written records. After the studies of Georges Dumézil on the prodigious Indo-European memory, the objections of the nineteenth-century rationalists lose their point. These peoples remembered, and these events were rhythmically recited in a crude, beautiful, very vivid language. Then these convergent and complementary traditions became superposed and yielded the definitive wording of what was to be the Hebraic canon of the Bible: the Law and the Prophets. The historical memories transcribed in the *Torah* or Pentateuch might indeed have been the work of one man alone: 'for Moses simply meant the world', writes Calvin in his commentary on Genesis. It might also have been the treasure of several men if one admits the theory of Inspiration.

The amazing unity of the biblical text seems to exceed by far the possibilities of chance, even actuated by some obscure necessity — the more so if it is a work of composite origin. As with the universe, so with the Bible; the more we perfect our means of investigation, the more admirable does their architecture appear. It is nonetheless true that, from the seventeenth century onwards, the progressive discovery of multiple authorship, spread out over an extended period of time, has been perceived as a sometimes major stumbling block.

The Bible of the early Christians — which did not yet include the New Testament — was the Greek translation, the Septuagint, itself of great importance. Translation is, perhaps, the best protection against too much importance being attached to the letter, rather than the meaning. The Reformers, helped by the revival of Semitic studies, were careful to go back beyond the Greek translation, beyond the Latin translation (the Vulgate of St Jerome), to the Hebrew text. But they were perhaps wrong to extol the latter to the detriment of the Septuagint which was Scripture accepted by the inspired authors of the New Testament.

The value of the Septuagint in the transition from Judaism to Christianity lies essentially in the rigour of translation, hence the sacrifice of the letter in favour of the meaning. However, one cannot translate without interpreting. 'The Septuagint is a fresh reading of the Hebraic Bible, and it is in this version that the Old Testament was received by the Early Church.' It has been said of this translation that it was 'consciously interpretative'; people have talked of 'philosophical baptism', 'spiritualization in the manner of speaking of God, marked universalism, precisions in the expectation of the Messiah'. It is not self-evident, for instance, that in the first Psalm, *Torah* ought to be translated by *nomos* (the law) and not by *didache* (teaching). Be that as it may, interpreted, annotated, received as the Word of God, the Septuagint was the first of all the translations of the Bible on which Christians were nurtured.

Yes, the first four centuries were the centuries when the great choices were made. The men of the sixteenth century laid claim to them — they made them their own. Michel Meslin sums it up in a sentence: 'It was not by chance that the Scriptural canon was established, that the creeds were fixed and that at the same time a hierarchy of the ministry was instituted.' The great doctrinal debates culminated in

For the Hebrew rebels, the golden calf at the foot of Mt Sinai symbolized the presence of YHWH among them. The synagogue and the Christian Tradition, on the contrary, saw it as idolatry, according to the divine word: 'You will not make graven images.'

Adoration of the golden calf, wood engraving by H. Brosamer, in Luther's *Parvus Catechismus*, 1550. Bibliothèque Nationale, Paris.

The debate on the Trinity, which ran through the great ecumenical councils of the 9th and 10th centuries, inspired exegesis by the Reformers as well as by the Fathers of the Council of Trent. Symbolic representations of it are numerous and varied, from the three angels of Abraham to the triple personage of the medieval illuminaries.

The three persons of the Trinity at a table, Franciscan missal and book of hours, 1380. Bibliothèque Nationale, Paris.

The Trinity in the letter 'O' of the *Sacramentary* attributed to Gellone, second half of the 8th century. Bibliothèque Nationale, Paris.

the four ecumenical councils of Nicaea (325), Constantinople (381), Ephesus (431) and Chalcedon (451), which were to determine the direction of all future Christian thought. The debates on the Trinity and on the dual nature of Christ informed the exegeses of the Reformers, especially Calvin, as they did that of the Council of Trent.

The Reformed tradition solidly supports the theological framework elaborated in those early centuries. Calvin could say: we are the Apostolic Church, as the Augsburg Confession had already done in its first article: 'In the first place, and in full agreement, we teach and we maintain, in the terms of the Nicene Council, that there is only one divine being, who is called and who, in all truth, *is* God, and that in this same divine being there are nevertheless three persons, equal in power, equally eternal, God the Father, God the Son, God the Holy Ghost, all three a single divine being, eternal, indivisible, infinite, having boundless power, wisdom and goodness, sole creator and keeper of all things, visible and invisible. And by the term "person" we mean not a part, not a quality inherent in something else, but on the contrary a being who exists of himself. It is indeed thus that the Fathers used this term in this way.'

Ritual and act

Even before the doctrinal affirmations of the early councils, the Christian choice had been total, radical, and to a certain extent unforeseeable. It was, in imitation of Paul, a rejection of Jewish ritual, which was initially presented as a concession to those who came from the pagan world; then the rejection became more or less total. Even for the Christians of Jewish origin, by the second generation respect for the old rites seemed a lack of confidence in the saving power of the unique and perfect sacrifice of Christ.

The repudiation of Judaeo-Christianity is apparent in the ambiguity of the term. Jean Daniélou says: 'The word may be understood in three different ways.' Firstly, some Jews, the Ebionites, recognized Christ as a prophet but not as the Messiah; at least one branch of gnosticism emerged from this group. Secondly, and this is the most accepted definition, the term designates the early Christian community in Jerusalem, led by James. These faithful Christians continued to put into practice the detail of Mosaic ritual. They were in the strict sense Christian Jews.

Lastly, the term Judaeo-Christian has been applied by extension to areas where there is no link with the Jewish community, but where the framework borrowed

from Judaism is still retained. One thing is sure: the decision to reject Judaic ritual was ruthless and uncompromising – though since one cannot live without rites or observances, by the tenth century the Church had ended up hedging itself round with as much ritual as Pharisaic Judaism had adhered to in its heyday.

As a result of the wholesale rejection of Judaic ritual, the Christians had been left with a distrust of the synagogue. From about 1050 this distrust gave way to open hostility: a persecution of the Jews, hateful and inexcusable, gradually spread across the whole of Christendom. Martin Luther in his own person sums up Christian ambiguity with regard to its Jewish roots: he moved from initial pro-semitism to the school of Reuchlin and a Hebrew-oriented humanism, and then to the anti-semitic ravings of his latter days.

Thus by demolishing a whole package of observances, then by slowly and surely rebuilding it, the Reformation followed once again in the tracks of the Apostolic Church. Like the pagan-Christians at the call of St Paul, the Reformers pruned so much away that it became necessary to graft it on again.

The Puritans – with their dreary Sunday, the new Sabbath – were to rediscover the path of observances, even if, like their punctilious respect for the Sabbath-Sunday, these appear somewhat hollow observances much in the tradition of early Jahvism.

The Church, the Christian homeland

The chief development was still the building of a Christendom. A look at the map of their world reveals a great deal. From Palestine they indeed set forth, as the Master had commanded, down every road. But the churches thickly scattered along the paths of Asia and central Africa did not hold their ground. Only the Roman Empire was won over to Christianity, and even there the southern half was to go over to Islam; the wound has still not healed.

What happened? Is there an explanation for this strange geography of successes and failures? We have seen how much Christianity relies on a long cultural memory, since it does not locate the sacred in space but in memory, which is to say in time. The same was to be true of this 'new Apostolic age' through which the Reformers lived. The map of Reformed Europe, in relation to the areas of high concentration of cultural means of expression, shows the same assymetries as a map of the successful mission of the Church in the early centuries. Christianity depends on the seeds sown in culturally prepared ground.

The spiritual conquest of the Roman Empire differs from the barbarian conquest: the former was accomplished from a position of weakness and culminated in the conquest of the most privileged sections of society and the control of a state at the moment when it was breaking up. The end of the Empire, involving, in the course of three centuries, a decrease in population varying from two-thirds to seven-eighths, was one of the greatest cultural ruptures in history. In the midst of total collapse, the Church establishment – and notably that remarkable protective cocoon that was Benedictine monasticism – defended the last redoubt, a breached rampart around the ruins of the old culture.

In order to preserve the art of reading and writing, necessary for survival, the Church establishment was constrained to take secular society in tow. By providing the primitive barbarian states with writers to draw up such things as their rare charters, the Church saved Western society from total regression leading to the abandonment of writing and a reversion to purely oral records.

This situation had several important consequences. The most significant was the way in which the spiritual conquest of the barbarian world took place. From the eighth century onwards, the idea of mission imperceptibly gave way to a kind of crusade before the event. A colonizing Christianity, a conquest at once cultural, spiritual and at times political and even military, developed in the north and to the east. This form of conquest fashioned the Europe of the large dioceses, the very cumbersome structures of the Church, which was to side *en masse* with the Reformers.

The polycentrism of multiple patriarchates and self-governing churches in the Byzantine Church resolved, in a less tragic manner than in the Latin Church, the tensions between centre and periphery, mother church and missionary church. As for the increasing separation of the Latins and the Greeks which, in 1053, took a sensational turn with the reciprocal excommunication of the Pope and Michel Cerulaire, it stemmed from a process whereby theology took second place to political, cultural and social evolution. There was much bitterness due to the diminished status of the ancient churches, overwhelmed by Islam in areas where the

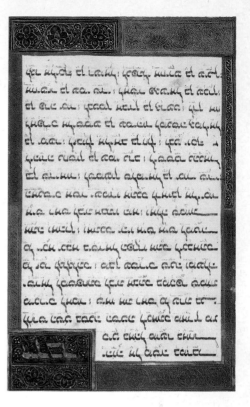

The first five books of the Bible, called the *Pentateuch* by the hellenists, and the *Torah* in Hebrew, takes us from the Creation to the arrival of the Hebrews in the Promised Land. Transmitted orally over the centuries, this historical memory established itself in the Hebrew canon of the Bible.

Pentateuch and Hagiographa, with commentaries by Rachi and Gersonide, Ferrara, 1473. Bibliothèque Nationale, Paris.

After the fall of the Roman Empire, the order founded by St Benoit de Nursie (*c.* 480–*c.* 547) preserved the art of writing and so saved western society from a regression to purely oral transmission of history.

The Albigensians, who threatened both Church and society with their refusal to change their ways, were opposed militarily, but also on a doctrinal basis: the Dominican order was born from predication against the Cathars.

Scenes from the life of St Dominic, from the *Coronation of the Virgin* by Fra Angelico, 1434–5. Musée du Louvre, Paris.

preservation of the Empire had resulted in a slower and more feeble growth compared to the remarkable rise of Christendom and its successes from the year 1000 to 1300.

No more needs to be said about the progressive establishment of the Church in Christendom, that is to say the 'Christian homeland'. This 'Christian homeland' necessarily had relations that were of a political – and, in the event, crusading – nature with the world of the Muslims, the apostates and usurpers of much of Jewish history (as well as of that most authentic of the places of Christian pilgrimage, the empty tomb of the risen Christ). In the same way, the Albigensian heresy in the twelfth century threatened not only the Church but, by its denial of procreation, the very survival of society.

The Church, which alone had the power to define and circumscribe society, then armed itself with a very specific weapon, namely the Inquisition. It was an efficient watchdog of men's consciences. There is disagreement as to whether the Inquisition was active in France in the sixteenth century; if so, it was relatively discreet. Things were very different in Spain and Portugal, where by the sixteenth century the institution of the Church had become the institution of the State, and the Inquisition was in the hands of disinterested, active and intelligent men, and proved remarkably efficient. It is clear that life in Christendom ended by contradicting the evangelical distinction of the two kingdoms. Christianity was threatened by political Augustinianism and was tempted to confuse the interests of the Kingdom of God with the interests of the so-called Christian city.

Late marriage and demographic growth

The homeland of the Latin Christians witnessed an eightfold increase in population in the course of three centuries, and the thirteenth century saw, for the first time in history, the establishment of a fully populated Europe. Almost its entire area was inhabited, with people living at close quarters, in a network of 160,000 parishes, with generally forty inhabitants to the square kilometre. This meant that there was a density of messages and intercommunication truly without precedent or equivalent.

A technical revolution had also made it possible to produce more food and to move men, foodstuffs and chattels rather more efficiently. The *volumen* was replaced by the *codex* – in other words, the scroll by the book; this, together with the introduction of transliteration (small characters) and pages written with margins, meant that reading was done rapidly and silently, with the eyes alone. Such progress was accompanied by a great upheaval of social mores. The demographic explosion, precondition of these advances, was accompanied by a change which appeared to run counter to it, but which in fact favoured it, namely the raising of the marriage age.

In all cultures, the marriage rites were differentiated according to sex; for women, marriage was discriminatory, universal and undertaken at the age of puberty. In the course of five centuries, Latin Christendom established a new kind of marriage, standardized and relatively egalitarian as regards rights and duties. By the end of this period there was a lapse of ten years between female puberty and marriage. Whilst one might expect to find a corresponding fall in fecundity, in fact the reduction of the childbearing time was compensated for by the better standards of food and education and the greater care taken of their children by parents who were not so young.

This change was accompanied by a re-evaluation of marriage, which had been devalued by the asceticism of the total religious commitment of the early Christians and by the mistrust left by the Stoics with regard to the loss of self-control in the course of the sexual act. There was additionally, widespread throughout the whole of society, the concept of a long and rigorous ascesis, an extension of strict observance of pre-marital continence. For almost the entire population this meant ten years living the strict life of chastity. Never in the course of history was such an effort demanded of so many (sixty million souls in twelfth-century Latin Christendom), nor such a total success achieved.

The system of late marriage was not the only possible system in Christendom. However it accorded strictly with the incontrovertible principles of the Christian ethic, which cannot disregard the natural law. It was constrained by respect for the individual: hence respect for the free choice of the other, respect for the person of the other, and complete equality of rights and duties with regard to the marriage bed – even if civil law, on the basis of the need to safeguard inheritance,

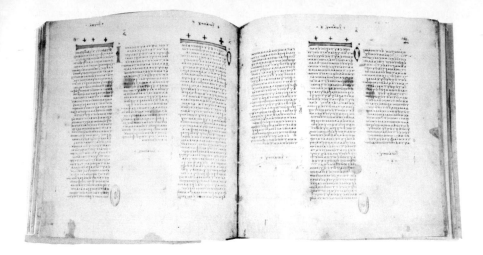

punished more severely the dereliction of one (the woman) than the other (the man).

Finally, we should not forget the change from the most complete endogamy to the most absolute exogamy through the canonical rules of the sixth, seventh and eighth centuries. The endogamy of the old covenant had been designed to preserve a treasure, the covenant of the Eternal God threatened by the competition of Baal, Astarte and other 'feminist' deities worshipped by Canaanites. The son of the patriarch thus married his 'beloved', his sister (perhaps meaning his cousin, daughter of the father's brother who had remained in a far country), for these Semitic languages do not distinguish between sister and cousin. From the time of the establishment of Christendom, where there was no risk of introducing the competition of false gods, exogamy offered a strategy for peace.

Scholastic learning

This cathedral of Christendom was crowned by a great dome, one of the finest constructions of human thought: scholasticism. In the main, through translations from Greek into Arabic and from Arabic into Latin, Greek knowledge was rediscovered, or at least that which had been retained in the Latin transposition. This ancient legacy had already been reconciled with the two canons of Scripture by the Greek and Latin Fathers of the fourth and fifth centuries (in so far as they could be reconciled). The Nicene Creed and the first four councils succeeded in translating into universally applicable abstract formulae the equally universally relevant and concrete substance of Scripture.

The reconstitution of the learning of the ancients during the twelfth-century Renaissance, the progress on all fronts achieved in the thirteenth century, and the development of the network of universities – from three to five thousand clerks completely relieved, thanks to the system of benefices, of all obligations other than the furthering of knowledge – were to lead on the one hand to the transmission of a large body of secular knowledge, and on the other to the creation of an equivalent body of sacred learning: *sacra pagina, sacra lectura*. The study of Scripture through meditative reading gave birth to theology, to the science of the Divinity which, rooted in the bedrock of Scripture, branched out ever faster and further.

Early Christian philosophy had been neo-Platonist in inspiration; by contrast, Christian thinking in the twelfth and thirteenth centuries followed Aristotle, whose realism, respect for the evidence of the senses, and confidence in practical reason suggested the means for real progress. When the Reformers attempted to do without Aristotle, they came back to him, despite Luther's proclamations; Melanchthon's *Loci communes*, an almost canonical work in Luther's opinion, has its natural place in the continuing development of Christian philosophy of Aristotelian inspiration.

Scholasticism reached its first peak with St Thomas Aquinas (1225–74); I shall, however, mention only its rationalist optimism. It seemed to the scholars of the *via antiqua* of the glorious thirteenth century that reason is sure, and that, correctly inspired and with a touch of help from grace, it readily aligns itself along the axis of revelation. Standing on the summit of undivided Christendom and borne up by so many material achievements, scholars ceased to make a clear distinction between the

St Thomas Aquinas, the *Summa Theologica* open on his lap, sits between Plato, who inspired the first Christian philosophers, and Aristotle, whose influence was considerable on the thought of the 12th and 13th centuries.

The Triumph of St Thomas Aquinas, painting by Benozzo Gozzoli, 15th century. Musée du Louvre, Paris.

36

universal revelation and the particular (the promise given to Abraham and incarnated in Christ). The confidence in reason may have been somewhat naïve, but it did allow knowledge a remarkably free rein.

Latin Christendom: a single society of men and states

The Reformation is incomprehensible unless we bear in mind that Europe in the sixteenth century was a swiftly changing world. After the terrible blood-lettings of the late Middle Ages, culminating in the Black Death of 1348–9, the population began to increase again at the end of the fifteenth century, without yet reaching the levels of the thirteenth century. Whereas the countryside had been overwhelmingly predominant, the towns now took over the leading roles, and new men came to the fore, exercising the power given by new weapons: *savoir-faire*, commercial dynamism, movable assets. And it was obviously no coincidence that the Reformation had its greatest successes in the areas where these changes were most marked.

From the sixteenth century to the year 2000

Reformation, Counter-Reformation: the religious movement of the sixteenth century shook Latin Christendom like a hurricane. The winds it raised have never entirely subsided, and to this day let fall on us, like a fine dust, the message of that faith which was then lived so intensely, a faith that would move mountains. Today the 'violence of God' chooses other means than in the century of Calvin and Ignatius Loyola, the Peasants' War and the massacre of St Bartholomew. But let us make no mistake about it: it is still the same violence. It takes us back to the same, the only truth, *Sola Scriptura*. To understand the message promulgated by the men of the sixteenth century, we would have to face, as they did, the demands of a life lived by faith alone, with all that that contains of hope, and also of charity — less evident behind the intolerance of that age as of our own.

The message is rich and also complex. To get to the heart of it we have to take the trouble to decode it, that is to say to get the measure of the century, the physical, intellectual and institutional framework in which it was proclaimed, to take cognizance of the external conditions of the time, conditions which, inevitably, were very different from those that prevail today. The spiritual adventure of the Reformation had its roots in another perception of space and of the physical and human environment. It used other means of cultural expression. It rested on a knowledge of life and a technological mastery which were only at the earliest stages of the astounding advances that have since been made, and which in their approach still made no distinction between the natural and the supernatural, the worldly and the sacred, actual experience and received tradition. It was an adventure lived in a world that had neither the same dimensions nor the same rationale as ours. The key to the message therefore lies in rediscovering the framework of a civilization, of a society — Latin Christendom four hundred and fifty years ago.

The four horsemen

The hurricane referred to above was not unleashed by chance; it was no mere historical accident. It was the outcome of a general loss of direction experienced in different ways but felt collectively throughout Christendom. The consequence of a change — of a connected series of changes, perhaps one should say — which in the last

The dominating emblem of the waning Middle Ages was the sign of the Four Horsemen of the Apocalypse, as if the vision of St John was materializing in a western Europe ravaged by famine, war, plague and omnipresent death. With his series of sixteen engravings of the apocalypse, Albrecht Dürer powerfully conveys the troubled atmosphere in which the Reformation was spawned.

The four Horsemen of the Apocalypse, wood engraving by Albrecht Dürer, 1498. Bibliothèque Nationale, Paris.

two centuries of what we call – God knows why – the Middle Ages, affected men and women in their bodies and souls, in their manner of living or dying, in their material resources, in their relations with each other as well as with the powers that governed them, and in their very perception of nature, of the world and of God.

The instruments of this change were the four horsemen of the Apocalypse: plague, war, famine, death. Historians may ponder – and do – as to whether the high mortality brought about by famine and plague from the outset of the sixteenth century onwards was due to natural causes (climatic changes, hence poor harvests; an outbreak of the Yersin bacillus imported, with silk, from central Asia) or to human error (socially inadequate division of property and food supplies; promiscuity, poorer hygiene); or whether, and this is the more likely, both played their part. They can call to witness Malthus or Marx. But the men and women who lived through those times interpreted the calamities that rained down on them as the visionary prophecies of St John come true.

Famine had raged at the beginning of the fourteenth century, and on a particularly tragic scale in the years 1315–17. It was never a stranger in a Christendom where bread was the staple food, but where crop yields varied from one year to the next, and on average never exceeded three or four grains harvested to one sown. But it became more desperate at the end of the Middle Ages than it had been for previous generations.

In 1347–9, the plague swept down upon the West, carrying off within a few months a good third or more of the population. Henceforth it continued to prowl, plunging cities and provinces into mourning by turn, right up to the threshold of the eighteenth century.

Next, war, war which at the end of the Middle Ages wore a new face, as well as having recourse to weapons and strategies hitherto unknown and far more devastating than ever before. It was no longer a local affair, but was waged between States. It was no longer fought by a few knights followed by their peasants, but by armies of professional soldiers. Such wars were prolonged. They destroyed, they killed. They were fought at appalling cost both to the prince who waged them as well as his subjects, to cities as well as rural communities.

Whether from famine, plague or war, death was an ever-present horror, no longer an individual fate, but blindly striking down whole groups. More than ever, death was at the heart of life, leaving survivors dazed with the fear of death.

The societies suffused with such an atmosphere developed a new sensibility and a new preoccupation with the trappings of death – as evidenced in the fifteenth and even in the early sixteenth century by those 'dances of the dead' depicted almost everywhere, or those books on the 'Art of Dying' (*Ars Moriendi*) which were bedside reading for so many of the literate middle class; or again by the anguish expressed in many wills dictated on the death bed. This preoccupation with death led indirectly to a new appraisal of life, spiritual as much as material. There was a new and

At the beginning of the 16th century, western Europe was dominated by three great powers: the England of Henry VIII, the France of Francis I and above all the gigantic empire of Charles V, which at its high point encompassed 17 principalities, the Austrias and the German domains of the Habsburgs, Franche-Comté, Artois, the Low Countries, part of Italy, Spain and her possessions in the New World, Hungary and Bohemia.

Europe in 1502, detail from the map of Nicolo Caveri. Bibliothèque Nationale, Paris.

War had never been so devastating as it was at the beginning of modern times, due to technical progress and the use of hired professionals to destroy the domains of the adversary. It contributed significantly to providing the 'dancers' for macabre spectacles that were very indicative of the mentality of the time.

How to handle cannon in *The Four Books of Chivalry* by Flavius Vegetus Renatus, 1529. Bibliothèque Nationale, Paris.

Dance of the Dead, wood engraving made for the *Chronicle* of M. Schedel, Nuremberg, 1491. Bibliothèque des Arts Decoratifs, Paris.

Even more than war, famine decimated populations. A freak of climate, a rotten summer or late frosts were enough to upset the precarious balance and reduce hundreds of thousands of men to famine. In the Europe of the 16th century, people knew what it meant to fast.

Lenten fare, detail from an engraving by Pieter Bruegel the Elder, 16th century.

growing awareness of the precarious nature of existence, and a thirst for life, an eagerness to embrace all that life had to offer, without waiting for an uncertain tomorrow. Thus, between the end of the fourteenth century and the beginning of the sixteenth century, developed the social, mental, intellectual and spiritual context that was to lead to the Reformation.

From resignation to resourcefulness

After two or three generations of disarray, reactions set in, at first shadowy, then more concrete. Very different reactions, according to the particular country and its cultural tradition; according to the socio-professional groups and their level of education; according to the degree of awareness of the requirements, chances or means for survival; according to the different degrees of social responsibility. Reactions which affected now the life of the soul, now the life of the body, man seemingly not having realized prior to the sixteenth century to what extent these two aspects of human existence are bound up with each other. In the confusion and contradiction of these attitudes and reactions I see at least one of the sources of the division between Christians at the time of the Reformation.

One of these reactions may well have lain in a rather fatalistic resignation when confronted by a destiny about which men felt they could do very little. This was the commonest reaction in rural areas everywhere and throughout society in the southern, Latin countries. It could lead to two opposite responses: the easier and therefore the most common, that of oblivion and hedonism; the other led to a turning inwards, to contrition or, for some enlightened souls, to a deepening of the inner life, to the *devotio moderna* which was one source of the renewal of spirituality.

The other reaction was, if I dare say so, more practical. Martha compared to Mary. It consisted of assessing the earthly calamities more objectively and, short of being able to get to the root of them, at least treating the symptoms to the best of their ability. In the face of the plague, medicine abandoned its out-of-date books to deal with a reality about which their books told them nothing. Town authorities hammered out and enforced public health programmes: quarantine of suspected cases and of goods brought from infected areas. Hygiene — at least food hygiene — made progress. The plague, as we know, proved intractable despite all their efforts, but another deadly contagion, leprosy, was virtually eradicated.

The struggle against hunger was no less unequal. In the long term, however, it achieved some success. Paradoxically, the huge mortality rate from the middle of the fourteenth century to the first third of the fifteenth century, when Christendom touched the trough of the demographic wave, contributed to this success. There were fewer mouths to feed, but there was also less labour to produce the foodstuffs. Farming was concentrated on the least poor lands; landowners and cultivators conceived various means of rationalizing and increasing productivity. In many provinces of the West, serfdom decreased or disappeared entirely in favour of paid agricultural labour that was less wretched and more efficient. Cereal yields increased, still only by a little (five to seven grains for one sown) but nevertheless enough, taken over the whole of Christendom, to create surpluses, thereby easing the strain between one harvest and the next, and starting to put wheat into circulation between regions and even between countries: wheat from Sicily fed the large Italian towns, and in the fifteenth century wheat from Poland found its way to the northern seaports. The Swiss paid in meat and dairy products for grain from Lombardy or Alsace.

An even more decisive factor in this struggle was the widespread practice of preserving perishable foodstuffs in salt. This made it possible to build up stores, as well as to transport foodstuffs over long distances. From the second half of the fourteenth century salt production and the salt trade grew steadily, whether from the Atlantic and Mediterranean salt-marshes or the salt mines of Austria, Luneburg, Burgundy and Lorraine, and Cracow. In exchange, the great herring-fishing zones (Scandinavia, Holland, England) began to supply the interior of the continent with proteins. From the Alps or the plains of the Danube, a substantial trade in cattle, salted and dried meats, cheeses and butter — which was highly profitable to the stock-breeders — made a considerable contribution to the provisioning of the heavily populated cities.

Around 1500 and beyond, seasonal shortages were not unusual and some years of serious scarcity still punctuated people's lives. All in all, however, people by then had pretty well enough to eat. Better still, they were henceforward to enjoy a less monotonous and better balanced diet than their predecessors. And it is doubtless not irrelevant that the generations of the great humanists and the great servants of God in the century of the Reformation were properly nourished.

Those opposite poles, the art of war and the fight against famine, were certainly motivating forces of the technological inventiveness (in the widest sense) and spirit of initiative – which should not surprise us. However these qualities did not stop at casting cannons or harquebuses, building better ships, improving navigation instruments, producing and selling more bread, meat, salt, spices, wine. They showed themselves in many other fields, all directed towards the same ends, such as in civil engineering: canals for irrigation and transport; rivers made navigable through locks; terracing of mountain land; the clearing of pasture land; the building of roads and bridges. Advances were made in mechanics: for clocks; improved windmills and fulling-mills; the principle of the crankshaft – and in other areas. For the first time in the history of mankind, technology became markedly differentiated, and was the province of specialists – engineers. They drew their knowledge from observation and experience acquired and handed on (by now in writing); although as yet such knowledge had little basis in fundamental scientific principles which were still manifestly lagging behind.

It would be fascinating, but tricky, to chart this inventiveness and analyse the geographical diffusion of technical inventions. We would very probably find that they were more numerous, more strictly practical and spread more swiftly in those countries that were most needy at the outset, namely the countries on the median axis of Europe, from the Alps to Scandinavia, Holland, England and Flanders. Is it a coincidence that, with a few exceptions due to local circumstances, those are the very countries that supported the Reformation? Perhaps the idea of a link between Protestantism and capitalism proposed nearly a hundred years ago by Max Weber might here find new justification: namely the dynamism of necessity?

Technical advances were not solely concerned with machines for killing; in the 16th century scientists and inventors turned their ingenuity to the construction of machines for production and mechanical instruments, such as the mill and the clock. The spirit of enterprise and scientific research were essential components in the climate that fostered the Protestant Reformation.

The Clockmaker, an engraving by Jost Amman, second half of the 16th century.

The Mill, an engraving by Agostino Ramelli in *Le Diverse e Artificiose Machine* . . ., Paris, 1528. Bibliothèque Nationale, Paris.

'There is no wealth or strength without men' – *Jean Bodin*

The *respublica christiana*, the entire community of Latin Christians, was profoundly shaken by the Reformation or its repercussions. All its members were affected, whether immediately or distantly, actively or passively, whether in full consciousness or more dimly through the many screens interposed by tradition and habits, by the vigilance of the Roman Church or national interests. How many did they number, these sixteenth century Christians? Where did they live? In what kind of societies? What picture of their world and of themselves did they reflect in their collective cultures?

Unfortunately, we know little about the overall state of the population of Europe in the sixteenth century. Experts suggest that in about 1500 the population of Latin Europe – excluding, that is, Russia and the Balkans, which would be casting the net too wide – was between 45 million and nearly 70 million. Let us assume that a number close to the higher figure was likely, divided among the principal nations as follows: some 16 million in the Kingdom of France, the most densely populated; a bare 12 million in Germanic Europe including Switzerland (0.8 million for its present territory); about 10 million in Italy, and roughly the same in the Iberian peninsula. Following at a respectful distance are England (3 million), the Netherlands (2 million), and Scandinavia (1.5 million). Setting aside the density of population in France – which in itself may well explain many features of the period – this is not a high number. In fact these levels of population scarcely exceeded the high point already reached by Europe towards the end of the thirteenth century which means that the drain on population of the fourteenth and early fifteenth centuries put back demographic growth by two hundred years. The resurgence began energetically in the second quarter of the fifteenth century, but by 1500 Europe had barely finished catching up.

After that, population growth accelerated everywhere – but not everywhere at the same rate. The Mediterranean countries, with a galloping birth rate, were the first to take the lead. Some provinces (Naples, Sicily, Castille, Provence) doubled their population in under a century, but their growth rate slowed down noticeably after 1550. North of the Alps, population increase was more sustained. England, where the population grew from 3 to 4.5 million before 1570, and the Low Countries which doubled their population during the century, were able to attain these population levels thanks to a remarkable economic growth unmatched in Italy. Population growth in Germany is less clear, but it has been calculated that in the central regions there was an average annual increase of 5.5 per cent. The population of Switzerland reached a million before 1600. In France, already relatively highly populated, there were marked regional differences: the Midi

The portrait of Nicolas Kratzer executed by Dürer in 1520 is lost; the one painted by Holbein eight years later has conserved for posterity the face of the Munich scientist who became watchmaker at the court of Henry VIII. Among the remarkable pieces he made can be seen the sundial with several faces.

Portrait of Nicolas Kratzer by Hans Holbein the Younger, 1528. Musée du Louvre, Paris.

followed the Mediterranean patterns and the Paris basin showed a similar vitality, whereas central and western France lagged behind. Between 1500 and 1600 the population increase barely exceeded 2 million.

All in all, it was a buoyant situation, which ensured that the process of catching up was continued, at least in the early sixteenth century, reflecting the dynamism of a Latin Christendom overcoming its disarray, enthused by the will to live, and to live better. Through good years and bad, these increasing numbers of people had enough to eat, adequate clothing and a roof over their heads. Ever-widening classes of society could spare some of their income, and above all their time, for activities that were no longer exclusively concerned with earning their daily bread, activities which we would call cultural, in the widest sense of the word.

Towards the end of the century, however, they began to run out of steam. In the Mediterranean countries the production of resources seemed no longer to meet demands. In the most developed northern countries, initially in urban environments, new attitudes towards family and children fostered a tendency towards voluntary limitation of the number of children born to each couple. Was concern for the quality of life beginning to take precedence over quantity?

Where did they live, these populations? For the most part, still in the country. It was still the ploughmen or, in mountain areas, the stockmen who formed the masses, the necessarily silent majorites – although every now and then this silence would be broken by uprisings, and even downright civil wars. The proportion of country-dwellers varied from one region to another, but was rarely less than 80 per cent.

The towns nevertheless grew in political, economic, social and cultural importance. Due to events at the end of the Middle Ages and the virtual extinction of the system of power and production based on feudalism, towns were the only real centres of decision-making and management. They were also growing in size. According to the most recent calculations made by Paul Bairoch, the urban population of Europe (excluding Russia), that is to say people living in places with more than 5,000 inhabitants – although many real towns did not reach this figure – in 1500 numbered some 8 million (10 to 15 per cent of the total population), scarcely more than in 1300. But Bairoch estimates the number of town-dwellers in 1600 at nearly 11 million. In general it was the very large towns that grew the most: between 1500 and 1600 the number of cities with more than 50,000 inhabitants increased from about twenty to over thirty, nor were they always the same ones: there was a shift of 'megalopoli' from east to west, from the Mediterranean to the Atlantic seaboard: Lisbon, insignificant in the Middle Ages, had a population of over 100,000 in 1600; Amsterdam, hardly a village in 1300, and still only a small town in 1500, had a population of 50,000 in 1600.

Town and country

In the sixteenth century, the rise of the city came to an end, and was only to continue very much later, with the Industrial Revolution. It had slowly but profoundly modified the traditional order of society. To the three previously existing Estates – the nobility, the clergy and the peasants – was added a fourth, composed of many elements but socially a force to be reckoned with almost everywhere. The towns drew their manpower as well as their food supplies from the surrounding countryside. They even absorbed some of the feudal nobility, or what remained of it. Princes were persuaded to settle in them, or else they set themselves up independently as principalities, seigneuries, republics. They were the seat of executive power, and also of wealth which from now on was shown as much in personal assets as in land. The ruling classes of the towns were able to enter into both the nobility – through marriage, through purchase, or through holding public office in law and finances – and the upper ranks of the clergy in cathedral chapters.

Towns were growing rapidly at the end of the Middle Ages; like Paris, Geneva or Antwerp, Florence acquired considerable power through its commercial and industrial activities.

Goldsmith's workshop by Fei, 16th century. Palazzo Vecchio, Florence.

This all resulted in a reversal of the relations between town and country. The former, so long dependent on the latter, now had the more powerful role in society. The change had taken place quietly and almost imperceptibly, but on the threshold of the century of the Reformation it became obvious, in Florence as in Geneva, in Paris as in Augsburg, in London as in Antwerp. This domination of the towns showed itself in administrative and political domains, particularly in countries where the power of the towns was not held in check by the superior power of a sovereign, as was the case in the Kingdom of France, an absolute monarchy in a league of its own. Neither in imperial Germany, nor in Switzerland, nor in the Low Countries, nor most particularly in Italy was the power of the towns restricted in any way. Nor even in England, in the case of London. Usually this dependence on the towns took the form of a subjugation which denied the rural communities any part in decision-making, even in the exercise of law. The only notable exceptions of rural independence among these communities (in central Switzerland) or of participation (in the Tyrol and the Lombardy valleys) are to be found in the Alps. Such political dependence was to make itself fully felt in the spread of the Reformation and the distribution of denominational differences.

The material dependence of rural areas was even more apparent. The towns were the markets, not only for articles of major international trade and luxury goods

The merchants, whose activities were constantly expanding, held an important place in western society. Under their governance, the towns grew and increased their hold over the surrounding countryside. The traditional relations between the city and the rural areas slowly began to reverse, to the advantage of the former.

1. Engraving from the *Book of Profits* by P. de Crescenzi, 1521. Bibliothèque Nationale, Paris.

2. *Merchants*, an engraving from *Praxis rerum criminalium* by Damhouder, 16th century. Bibliothèque Nationale, Paris.

intended only for the nobility and the bourgeois of the towns, but also for the produce of the countryside, sold on terms and at prices that were established by the merchants, who were city-dwellers, and not by the producers themselves.

The predations of the cities upon the countryside took yet another form: the acquisition of lands, demesnes and country houses by townspeople. They were able to take over seigneurial properties and fiefs that were in escheat, or confiscate fields from peasants who had fallen into debt, or simply purchase land. For them it was a kind of insurance, but above all an investment. This was how they regarded it, endeavouring to obtain the best possible return from their acquisitions: through land development and improvement; through the intensification and diversification of farming; through the preference given to speculative crops, vineyards and market gardening; through the exercise of a healthy rural economy, and often by setting to work themselves: gardening became a sixteenth-century 'hobby'.

It is difficult to discern the social and material consequences of the changes for the peasantry, as there were such marked regional and even local differences. Great domains decreased, especially in western and northern Europe. Peasant property, when it existed, almost disappeared on the outskirts of towns. The majority of peasants were tenant-farmers or share-croppers protected by a lease giving them some security of tenure. Farms of average or large size additionally hired daily labourers whose employment was far from regular. Such unreliable employment, added to the poor earnings of many tenant-farmers and the fact that they were all at the bottom of the social scale, accounts for the impression of poverty which is, on the whole, what emerges from a nevertheless prosperous countryside: a prosperity snapped up by the towns. It explains the presence of those floating populations of paupers on the lookout for work or alms or a spot of villainy, whom the towns either admitted or drove out without scruple, as it suited them.

However we must not focus only on the negative aspects of relations between the towns and the countryside. In many cases the measures taken by the city landowner to improve the management of his estate were of equal benefit to his tenant-farmer. Neighbouring peasants might have been encouraged to follow his example – they could obtain the necessary credit in the town, at interest rates that were not always usurious. Closer ties with the town assured the peasant of a prompt outlet for his share of the harvest, and also – however little, and for better or for worse – made him familiar with the behaviour of townsfolk, their customs and their fashions. The town-dweller, for his part, discovered beyond the city walls a world that was different, but often beguiling, at harvest or grape-gathering time, when he would learn to mix with countryfolk and share in the festivities.

The city of men

The town, however, was a world in itself, its narrow streets full of shops and taverns and houses, and swarming with men and women of every sort, of every level of income, every profession and of different backgrounds: bourgeois of ancient stock, newcomers from the countryside, immigrants from other cities, passing travellers. It would be impossible to paint a picture of a typical Christian city, as they varied so much in situation, size and character, particular customs and institutions.

Most of the cities of Christian Europe nevertheless shared a broadly comparable social organization. At the beginning of the sixteenth century they were also all characterized by a fairly lively social mobility, a sure sign of their dynamism. The barrier separating the *popolo minuto* from the *popolo grasso* was still shifting and fluid, but as the century progressed it became more sharply defined, leading to a social rigidity far more marked at the end of the century than it had been at the beginning.

Each town had its ruling class. The old nobility, who had often come and settled in town at the end of the Middle Ages, had almost disappeared from the towns by 1500, occupied by their duties at court or as officers in the armies. Even when these nobles still resided in town, they evinced little or no interest in local public affairs, and indeed openly distanced themselves from them. Furthermore, many of them regained their lands, or had not left them. Pressed by the need for money, they endeavoured to get as much revenue as possible out of their land, at the expense of their peasants. In the Mediterranean countries, as in Hungary or Poland, the mid-century saw a return to a kind of feudalism, sometimes called 'second serfdom', distinguished however by certain modern economic features, since these lords were becoming wheat and cattle merchants.

Municipal power, extending on occasion to the outlying countryside and villages, was in the hands of the bourgeois or, more accurately, in most towns, in the hands of the trade guilds. The most profitable trades were the wholesale or export trades which

promoted the local speciality and built up the town's wealth and reputation. Almost everywhere the highest offices – syndics, consuls, municipal magistrates – were monopolized in turn by a few families, who also filled the councils. Whilst some towns could boast ostensibly democratic institutions (general councils bringing all the bourgeois together once or twice a year; district assemblies in the very large towns), we should not be deceived: power remained the prerogative of the few, thereby building up an urban aristocracy that was soon to become closed to outsiders.

At a lower level, the bourgeois as a whole formed a kind of middle class, generally quite large. It included all the artisans and tradespeople who served the local community – bakers, butchers, masons, tailors, carriers, timber merchants, apothecaries – as well as the artisans engaged in the export industry but working in humbler premises than their fellow craftsmen, or dependent on piece-work put out to them either by the more established artisans or by a merchant. Such was the system of industrial production that quickly spread in the countries north of the Alps and which is known by the German term *Verlag-System*. This middle class included a very wide range of society from the affluent to what we today would call the proletariat. But it was a propertied class: amost every bourgeois owned at least his own home, his shop, and often a garden, a field or a vineyard outside the city walls. Wills and inventories of the deceased's effects allow us to measure the degree of affluence of these bourgeois. Whilst they were excluded from power in the strictest sense, they nevertheless exerted a certain control, a certain influence. They could form lobbies, and belong to the political support group of the leaders. They assumed

Dürer's engravings bear excellent witness to the way in which the city-dwellers regarded the peasants. In these works executed by a citizen of Nuremberg and intended for an urban clientele, the peasants' slovenly appearance and heavy build are accentuated, but one also feels that these simple robust souls are sympathetically treated by the artist, whose mocking tone is obviously kindly.

Peasant couple dancing, copper engraving by Albrecht Dürer, 1514. Bibliothèque Nationale, Paris.

Living on the fringes of society were groups of beggars, vagabonds and brigands whose frontiers were ill-defined: in times of economic duress, impoverished peasants would leave their lands and the urban poor their houses, and bands of destitute people would take to the roads, living from hand to mouth.

Blind men fighting, painting of the school of Pieter Bruegel. Musée des Beaux-Arts, Basle.

minor municipal responsibilities and, generally through military service, were responsible for the protection of their city against frequent attacks, against fires – the dread of towns in times past – and against the plague. They were very jealous of their few modest privileges and displayed a keen municipal patriotism. They willingly formed their own mutual aid associations, 'brotherhoods' placed under the protection of some saint, and these too, like the guilds, were the scene of frequent festivals. The festival was both a merry-making occasion which broke the monotony of the seasons and the days, and the mark of close bourgeois solidarity.

The ordinary inhabitants, who were not propertied and were therefore deprived of rights and privileges, formed a third strata in society, the extent of which is harder to evaluate and doubtless varied considerably from one town to another, but grew proportionately more than the size of the town. It was composed of all the journeymen and apprentices, the building labourers – there was a great deal of building in the sixteenth century – and all the lowly-paid and the many domestic servants. This strata of society does not appear to have had the same solidarity as that evinced by the higher strata. Nevertheless, driven by poverty or by the working conditions imposed on them, they could be a threat to public and social order. Here and there the journeymen tried to organize themselves at their own level, which tended to break the old hierarchical solidarity of the guilds: in Erfurt in 1509, Ulm and Cologne in 1513, and especially in Lyons, several times, there were echoes of the earlier Florentine revolts. The Lyons episode of the 'great riot' in 1529 was the culminating point which led Francis I, with his statute of Villers-Cotterêts (1539), to forbid 'coalitions' of journeymen as well as of masters.

We come lastly to that class of society that was endlessly on the move: those floating populations, alternately rejected by a countryside that could not feed them and by overcrowded towns that would never keep them for long, if food shortage threatened or jobs were lacking. For the sixteenth century, like the previous

centuries, was an age of intense geographical mobility, with people constantly migrating, either singly or in groups. The roads saw an endless procession of merchants and middlemen, pilgrims, soldiers rejoining their units or returning home, destitute wretches seeking work or succour, monks of every order, students going from one university to another, highway robbers on the lookout for affluent travellers, and so on . . .

Up to now we have made little reference to women. It is impossible to define precisely the situation of women in the towns, as here too attitudes differed so widely. On the whole it does not appear to have been worse than at any other time. They did not have political power except through court intrigues – which bear witness to their prestige and their influence – or else when one of them, exceptionally, was a ruling monarch, such as Elizabeth I or Catherine de Medici. On the other hand, here and there, they did share in economic power: it was not unusual for a widow to take control of her dead husband's business affairs. As the century progressed, and especially towards its end, the growing preference for small families gave greater importance to the mistress of the house, and to the mother educating her children. The woman played a role that was not necessarily passive in marital decisions. A poor and single woman was in a more difficult position. The poorhouse was often the only place for orphan girls, who were exploited as free labour, and the last resort for old women, their final resting place. Prostitution also provided a way out. The prostitute was not always despised, there being little hypocrisy in the male population. She could count on having food and lodging, for a time at least, which was no trifling matter for many impoverished young women. She would also operate within a prescribed area and be subject to police regulations: keep to certain streets, display clear signs of her trade. In Geneva, where no guilds existed, prostitution was, prior to the Reformation, the only organized profession, whose 'queen' negotiated with the authorities on behalf of her fellows.

Half-open horizons

We must not be under a false impression with regard to the fairly intense movement of people, mentioned above: it never involved more than a minority, generally travelling only short distances. For the great majority the horizon was limited, the notion of distance confined to the outskirts of the town, the outlying parishes and neighbouring villages, the nearest fair. Only a narrow élite of those holding high public office, of humanists, artists and businessmen had any knowledge of a wider world, and its different customs, ways of life, cultures. In the course of the sixteenth century, however, distances were conquered in more than one sense: in the literal sense, this was the century of the great discoveries and the founding of the first overseas colonies – but how many, amongst the Christians, really took part in this? In the figurative sense, it saw the conquest of the concept of distances, and the differences these entailed, by simple folk, initially and particularly in urban societies. Sailors and mercenaries may have contributed to this, through the tales they brought back, and through customs they picked up on their travels and introduced on their return – customs both good and bad. (It is said of the Swiss that, at the end of the sixteenth century, they had brought back from their campaigns with foreign armies the vice of alcoholism.) The growing literacy in certain classes of society played its part. On the other hand, the widespread use of the vernacular, even among the upper classes, and of dialects, constituted a sure obstacle to cultural interpenetration at the popular level.

Little is yet known about these matters but they deserve our attention. The multitude of popular sub-cultures (despite a few features they had in common) and the manifestly narrow horizons of perception, and hence of thought, the mistrust of anything 'foreign' ('foreign' began a few hours' ride away) – does not all this help theoretically to explain the contradictions, the misunderstandings, the rejections and the intolerances of the age of the Reformation?

The riches of this world

The age of the Renaissance, of humanism and the Reformation was also a time of remarkable material progress; an age of economic growth, in the sense we give to this concept today, that is to say growth of the 'national' product, if we dare use this anachronism in the absence of fully national economies; growth too of per capita income.

But two reservations must be noted; the growth in question is not measurable, globally, in quantitative terms, since most of the economic indicators (population

In an increasingly complex world where more and more people were acquiring property, in an economic system in which landed wealth was having to yield a part of its monopoly to movable assets, there was a remarkable upsurge in the importance of the legal professions. The written word became as vital in economic affairs as in cultural and religious domains.

Creation of the college of notaries and secretaries of the King and house of France, 16th century. Bibliothèque de l'Arsenal, Paris.

49

There was remarkable progress in the extraction of metals and the metallurgy industry in Germany, which swiftly took the lead in technological advances and the concentration of wealth.

Working in the mines, a wood engraving from *Universal cosmography* by Sebastian Münster, 1544. Bibliothèque Nationale, Paris.

The delights of the ice on the Schelde, an engraving by B. Van de Putte, 16th century. Estampes collection, Antwerp.

census figures, production and consumption figures, average incomes, savings and investments) are not available to us or else are too unreliable. Where it has been possible to piece together a good run of statistics and collect accurate data, these suggest growth but not the full extent of the growth. They also indicate – and this is the second reservation – that the general tendency towards growth was neither steady nor evenly distributed, which will surprise nobody. There were times when growth was arrested, or interrupted not only by crises in food production but also by industrial or financial crises: the amount of money in circulation and credit would rapidly increase or decrease by turn. These fluctuations in circulation became more apparent in the second part of the century, even though at that time Europe was already benefiting from the riches of the New World. These seem to have contributed to the general inflation at the end of the century, but the extent of their influence is the subject of much controversy, as is the fissure through which this gold and silver escaped from circulation in Europe and disappeared without a trace.

With regard to the uneven growth rate in different places, one of the decisive factors affecting the economies of the time, and one which was already in evidence *circa* 1500, was the rapid shift of economic activities and control centred from south to north of the Alps. It was a kind of 'technological transfer', but it affected business technique as much as production techniques. Imaginative freedom north of the mountains brought new life to the broad valley of the Rhine, from the urban states of Switzerland like Basle, Zurich, Berne, Saint-Gall, to the seaports and industrial cities of the Low Countries including Antwerp, Augsburg, Strasburg, Nuremberg, Frankfurt. It established, or at least confirmed, that median axis of Latin Christendom, that artery of the progress of thought and faith.

The commercial vigour of Italy had long dominated the European system of exchange. The Italians had devised its workings and activated its markets. The four corners of the 'urban quadrilateral', Milan, Venice, Florence, Genoa – and Rome too, in its more passive way – had derived profit and prestige from their influential role. The sixteenth century did not bring with it – not at once in any case, and not across the board – any lessening of Italy's creative energy. But it marked the end of her supremacy.

From now on the advanced technologies – the extraction of minerals, metallurgy, the exploitation of energy resources – were developed in Germany; Holland came to the fore in the field in intensive and systematic agriculture. The Italian bankers and great merchants, as though they had run out of steam by the time they reached the fourth generation of Medici bankers, that of Lorenzo, gave way in the business world to newcomers from Nuremberg and especially from Augsburg – such as the Fuggers, the Welsers and many others. Curiously enough these newcomers were little influenced by the Italian models, with which they were nevertheless very familiar. They no longer practised the art of business for its own sake in the manner of the Genoese bankers, but patiently made money, lots of money. They did not juggle with sophisticated techniques of exchange, but negotiated very concrete deals. They speculated, but only on tried and tested commodities like metals or pepper. They were adventurous but calculating, powerful but prudent – although it is true that they were to let themselves be carried away in their turn with massive public borrowing towards the middle of the century and that they were to experience the shock of the huge bankruptcies of Spain and France. Above all they introduced into business an absolutely new dimension with their concept of the long term. Their philosophy was one of duration, delayed profit, savings and reinvestment. Not all of these German financiers such as the Fuggers sided with the Reformation – more out of opportunism than conviction. Yet it is difficult not to see in their professional behaviour a state of mind very close to that expressed by the new Protestantism in Wittenberg as in Geneva.

The European markets, and the great fairs too, soon slipped out of the hands of the Italians. The Geneva fairs, which had long been the Italian businessmen's window on the West, passed under the control of the men of Nuremberg as early as 1480, and had in any case lost much of their importance in terms of the volume of business transacted. Lyons replaced them only as regards providing access to the French market – a vast market all the same, but not the most buoyant. Further away to the north, the Germans favoured Antwerp rather than the old market of Bruges, and too late the Italians realized the outrageous trick that had been played on them: the new market was already in other hands. Antwerp was to remain the most important market in Europe until the dislocation brought about by the Dutch revolt after 1570.

The rise of Antwerp, then of Amsterdam, and lastly of London, represented an even more significant change: the main focus of trade had shifted from the Mediterranean to the Atlantic. The long-standing good fortune of the Italians had

With the voyages of discovery, the Atlantic became the main route for reaching not only the New World but also the Far East via the Cape of Good Hope. The decline of the Mediterranean caused Italy to lose her monopoly of the spice and silk trade, and the centre of gravity shifted to Antwerp. Between 1530 and 1560 that great northern city dominated the European economy, and merchandise came streaming in from the four corners of the world to the banks of the Schelde, before being redistributed throughout Europe.

Extract from *Universal Cosmography* by Guillaume Le Testu, *fo.* 32, 1555. Bibliothèque du Ministère de la Guerre, Paris.

been to monopolize the silk and spice trade with the Levant. We might be surprised at the economic and political importance of these spices, seemingly disproportionate to their use, but it must be remembered that spices, which still included sugar, and which nearly all originated from around the Indian Ocean, formed the base materials of the pharmacopoeia, as well as seasoning and flavouring food. They were not merely a fashion, but a sign of affluence, a status symbol, a mark of distinction, which is why they had long been keenly sought after by those classes fortunate enough to afford them.

Now, however, the opening of the route to the Indies via southern Africa (1498) short-circuited the usual route, to the obvious profit of the Portuguese. In the longer term, the colonization of America was to strengthen the Atlantic seaboard of Christendom. However the heroes of these great voyages, the Iberians, with their ports of Lisbon and Seville, were by no means the only ones to benefit from their enterprises. They were remote from the major concentrations of consumers, nor sufficiently well organized to handle the distribution of the famous spices and so had to hand them over to the northern European distributors who were based in Antwerp and much better equipped to do the job.

At the time of the Reformation, Europe was therefore busy drawing the maps of a new economic geography. The centres themselves had changed, and the major trade routes followed new itineraries. Between Italy and the northern countries, the Gibraltar sea route was still important, but used principally for trade in heavy goods. Swifter, safer, but more costly, and so hitherto reserved for luxury goods that were not too cumbersome, the route over the Alps through the Alpine passes was henceforth more or less abandoned. At the same time, the central Alps, where the Swiss Confederation had been born in the affluence conferred by trade, found

Antwerp found its ideal painter in Quentin Metsys. This great Flemish master, with his impeccable technique and often satirical realism, depicted a prosperous society with a high level of culture and predominantly commercial resources. In this town where middle-class ladies read religious works, money was the basis of power. Capitalism and literacy were, in accordance with the analysis favoured by Max Weber, two elements favourable to the Reformation.

Money lender and his wife by Quentin Metsys, 1514. Musée du Louvre, Paris.

themselves by-passed: wealth, together with political power, shifted to the towns on the Alpine borders. From now on the main overland thoroughfare for trade was the Rhine corridor, from Antwerp and Amsterdam to Basle and Augsburg.

It was along this same corridor that profits were henceforth concentrated and capital amassed. It became the centre of credit. It had its outposts in Genoa, Lyons, Castille, Vienna, Prague, but it was the German businessmen who became, throughout the two or three generations spanned by the Reformation and the Counter-Reformation, the masters of international finance, lending money to princes, repaid by revenues of State: that State to which this all too rapid overview of the century of the Reformation has brought us.

States, powers, territories

At the time of the Reformation, nothing was more ambiguous than the concepts of State, power, territorial sovereignty, and nothing more nebulous than national feeling.

Firstly, a word or two about the latter. The feeling of belonging together in a community was essentially what united the inhabitants of the same village, even perhaps of the same lordship, the same mountain valley, the same town. For the more educated classes, sharing a common language and hence a common culture could lead to a diffuse form of nationalism: not very marked in Spain and Italy, but stronger in Germany. However nationalism remained clearly subordinate to other interests, showing itself chiefly in the face of interference by forces perceived as absolutely foreign: the Low Countries under Spanish rule felt very strongly the 'foreign' nature of the power to which they were subject. The peoples living on the boundaries of Latin Christendom, Poles or Hungarians, found an identity in their

resistance against other forms of civilization like the Russian or Turkish. Only in those provinces that had long been subject provinces of the King of France, however, was a real feeling of patriotism forged by the Hundred Years' War, the Burgundian threat and the occupation of the northern part of the kingdom by the English. As for the English themselves, they seem to have acquired only gradually an awareness of their island identity.

The Renaissance State was thus not the institutional expression of an identity, still less of a consensus. This has some relevance in the present context, as it underlines the fact that denominational choices, in so far as they were free, did not correspond to national or state boundaries. The adage *cuius regio, eius religio* so often invoked was thus only an intellectual construct of the prince's jurists, used to strengthen his power when it was threatened with division or to justify one or other denomination being imposed on his subjects. The only notable exception, whose fate still seemed problematical up to 1609, was the United Provinces of the Netherlands who of their own free will and with widely popular support made themselves a Calvinist republic. Everywhere else, and even in Geneva in 1536, it was the ruling classes that took it upon themselves to make the choice.

A trend that had begun as early as the Middle Ages was now becoming very apparent on the threshold of modern times: namely, the definition of power and the State in terms of territory. The State thus lost its rather abstract character. Whereas it had basically signified a combination of rights and privileges held by the suzerain, but not interfering with the prerogatives of the lords within the feudal system, a new concept of the areas over which the power of the sovereign and his administration extended now came to the fore. This encouraged princes to round off and bring together these areas into one homogeneous whole: the kingdom.

In Tudor England this had been achieved. Peace and unity had been brought to the peoples of the island, apart from Ireland, which remained untameable, and Scotland, which was to be brought under the same crown in 1603. England withdrew once and for all from the continent, keeping her *pied-à-terre* in Calais only until 1558. It was still, in short, a country of only middling significance, having a quarter or one fifth of the resources in manpower or production of France. But it was a soundly structured, skilfully administered country, whose agriculture and industry led the field, so much so that one can discern the beginnings of an earlier 'Industrial Revolution'. In such a country the Reformation was to find fertile soil, and a lasting success due to its being adopted by the State — the unique outcome of a compromise between the faith of the faithful and the interests of the monarchy. Spain, another great kingdom, regained possession of its territory and became formally united around the Castilian heartland. However, the sense of identity of the old autonomous kingdoms remained strong and contributed to the violent rejection of the new religious ideas which were alien to the tradition and temperament both of the upper classes and of the masses.

1

Swift economic growth was accompanied by urban growth in many regions of Europe, but this widespread phenomenon entailed paradoxical situations. Seville, the great Spanish port into which sailed galleons laden with gold and silver, profited less by it than did distant Antwerp.

1. Artisans and merchants, from the *Book . . . of the institution and administration of public affairs* by Patrizzi, Paris, 1520. Bibliothèque Nationale, Paris.

2. Detail from *The Town and Port of Seville* by Sanchez Coello, 16th century. Museo Americano, Madrid.

2

The two Scandinavian kingdoms, Denmark and Sweden, remained unstable. In the end it was the French monarchy which was able to bring the most coherence to a territory that was already vast, stretching from the Atlantic to the valleys of the Rhône and the Saône and henceforward including the Dauphine and Provence, thanks to a centralization of government taken to the highest degree. It was because it was up against this all-powerful concept of the State, founded on unity, that the Reformation was to come to grief, after the well-known struggles.

Various territorially smaller states, such as the duchies of Savoy, Milan and Bavaria, attempted to follow these prestigious examples which held out so much promise. They made little progress, however, being pulled this way and that by the interests of the great princes, the King of France and the King-Emperor of Spain, and impeded by excessive diplomatic intriguing which was forever hatching new military or matrimonial schemes. The ambitions of the two great rival powers, France and Spain, were not confined to the territory that in terms of geography and culture was obviously theirs. For a long time they contended for lands and influence in Italy and the Netherlands. Spain won at this game, seizing power over a good half of the Italian peninsula and holding on to her power in Flanders and the county of Burgundy; on the other hand, she lost too, by spreading herself too thin, exhausting her wealth and milking her subjects. By the end of the century the long match ended in a nil-nil draw.

The trend towards the territorial State was also apparent at the less far-reaching but nevertheless significant level of the city republics and principalities. Aware of the danger of being suffocated and absorbed by their more substantial neighbours, they took precautions by seizing the surrounding area, as far afield as circumstances and competition allowed. This moreover gave them a greater measure of material security in the form of extra supplies and revenue. Florence had already long extended her *contado* to almost the whole of Tuscany. Venice pushed the boundaries of her terra firma as far as the crest line of the eastern Alps. Many autonomous cities of Germany and Switzerland similarly procured a hinterland, a territorial base which bolstered their confidence and provided them with food. Not all were so fortunate, however: Geneva was still wedged on a narrow strip of gardens between Berne, their bearlike ally, and Savoy, their fanatical adversary. In 1530 Geneva had to raze her suburbs to contrive an open space between her city walls and the boundaries of her territory.

This trend towards territoriality was however to take several centuries before it came to completion. The large well-established kingdoms were in the west or – albeit less clearly defined and less stable – on the eastern marches: Poland, Bohemia, Hungary. Between them there was still that same median axis where we have noted the concentration of the imagination and dynamism of modern minds or entre-preneurs: that axis which follows a broad line between Rome and the Hanse towns and which in the main belonged to the Holy Roman Empire. The Empire may be called many things – an echo of antiquity, an ideological relic of the Middle Ages, a prestige crown – but it was neither a State, nor a confederation of States, nor even an alliance. It was at best a common denominator, quite the most incongruous assemblage of territorial or religious principalities, dynasties, proud cities, diverse communities embedded one within another, which might set its combined weight against outside threats – such as the Turk – with some success, but which nevertheless was constantly torn by inner discord. The Emperor had no real power other than the prestige of his person or his Habsburg line, and the importance of his patrimonial estates. Whereas everywhere else in Latin Christendom centripetal forces were triumphing, the forces at work in the Empire were primarily centrifugal.

That such a conglomeration, held together only by contrast, should have become the chosen ground for all kinds of confrontations and experiments, economic as much as religious, social as much as cultural, should not surprise us. It was the country of Erasmus and the Fuggers, of Luther and Bruegel, of Albrecht Dürer and Thomas Muntzer. Driving ambition, the enquiring mind and the questing spirit were not blocked by the intransigence they encountered in the absolutist States of the West nor by the threats that weighed on the eastern States. The least modern part, in political terms, of the Christian world became the most innovating in terms of wealth, thought and faith.

The great loser in the economic changes at the end of the Middle Ages and the beginning of modern times was Venice. The monopoly of trade with the East which had hitherto safeguarded her prosperity was steadily eroded in the decades following the voyage of Vasco da Gama. Monopoly gave way to oligopoly. Henceforward, in spite of occasional resurgence and her wealth of artistic achievements, the decline of Venice was inescapable.

View of Venice from *Pilgrimage in the Holy Land* by Bernard Breimenbach, 1490.

The pre-Reformation climate

In the course of the hundred and fifty years preceding the Reformation, the Church strengthened its temporal authority and, through the expedient of Indulgences, monopolized a power which, it believed, was its God-given prerogative. Even more than the rifts opened up by the great schism in the West, the work of the Englishman Wyclif and the Czech Johann Hus gave clear warning of the upheavals of the sixteenth century.

Beyond the grave

All things considered, the great turning point was not in the sixteenth century itself, but in the combination of changes from which Latin Christendom had emerged and which came to a head in the sixteenth century, such as population increase, the growth of communications and trade, and the changes in people's attitudes towards each other, to their spouses, to themselves, to fate and death. A society tells us much about itself in its attitude to death. More than any other epoch, the Christian fourteenth and fifteenth centuries dared to express the horror of putrefaction through the transis, the living dead, that symbol of the human condition. This surge of horror has often been attributed to the experience of the Black Death (a third of the population wiped out in the space of five months), with the spectacle of huge expanses of rotting corpses, the dwindling hope of life, the sword of Damocles of that lightning-swift death. In fact it would make more sense to see it in the light of the enormous shift towards individualization evinced by late marriage, autonomous and less hierarchically-run families, the free choice of marriage partner, the slackening of bonds of lineage in favour of a territorial State bidding fair to become nation-State, the growth of individualism and, as Philippe Ariès so admirably put it, the incoercible need of an extra biographical chapter when the urban middle classes no longer died 'full of days'.

All cultures resolve the contradiction between death and the memory which the living retain of it, whether through the hypothesis of another shadowy world which extends the world of living to infinity, without great suffering and without joy, or through the philosophically more elaborate hypothesis of the Cycle of Rebirth, the Indian *Samsara*, or indeed the Platonic theory of the immortality of the soul. But the Eternal Being taught the ancient Hebrews that nothing good was to be expected of modest human – all too human – knowledge, and that life within the covenant of God the creator, the jealous God, with his all consuming love, was of such worth that it could not be extinguished. Life after death is not an attenuated but a fuller life, as the Resurrection expresses so well. It was precisely these disconnected ideas that the apostolic witness collected in Christ's teachings about eternal life, through which he revealed the long hidden meaning of human destiny.

It seems that around the year one thousand the pagan masses, rapidly converted, had a fairly untroubled view of death. On the one hand, the Carolingian religion was a hard religion, associated with the harsh ascesis of the contemporary codes of penance. For men as tough as these, there was comfort and consolation in the voluntary chastisement of the body, together with periodic privations of a nourishment that was in any case minimal. To this was added the fundamental function of reconciliation, the recovery little by little of a complement of peace. All these were stabilizing factors in a torn world, as also was the enormous power of the Church in the matter of indulgences: the Church guaranteed forgiveness and would reduce, on simple request, the punishment it had decreed.

The Last Judgement is not too worrying to those who have taken precautions. It is the Judgement of Matthew: on the one hand those whom Christ receives, on the

After the Black Death of 1348 which killed a third of the population, Europe looked the physical aspects of death squarely in the face. Painters and engravers did not hesitate to depict the effects of disease, the decrepitude of old age, even the putrefaction of corpses. One may wonder whether such relish signified preoccupation with the after-life or on the contrary nostalgia for the comforts and pleasures of the flesh.

The Three Ages of woman and Death, painting by Hans Baldung Grien. Kunsthistorisches Museum, Vienna.

55

other hand those he sends away. Now, the spiritual conquest of Europe was still recent enough for there to be a strong feeling of belonging to God's people. What mattered, as Philippe Ariès realized, was to die *ad santos*, to be laid to rest in consecrated ground protected by relics or, better still, in the floor of the church, close to Christ present in the Host. After that, sheltered by the mantle of Christ, nothing more could endanger the destiny of a Christian.

In any case, resurrection and life in a celestial Jerusalem were not an immediate prospect so one would have time to get used to it. Between death and the Resurrection the void would be filled by pagan reminiscences, the survival of which is attested by many Merovingian tombs, and by ordeals on the sites of sins that cried out for vengeance and demanded retribution. The love and prayers of those one had left behind were concrete signs of the solidarity of generations. Did those men have any notion of an eternity other than an extension of life in a city where the sun no longer marks the hours? It is difficult to know. Everything suggests that things did not go too badly and that the Word of God was nevertheless broadly understood. God does not ask the impossible of us for he knows the clay of which he made us.

Time and eternity

This balance was altered in the twelfth and thirteenth centuries, which culminated in Dante's *Divine Comedy*, the finest text ever written by human hand about life after death. I shall dwell on the approach of Judgement rather than on purgatory. God is no longer content with membership of the flock, to which by now everyone belongs. So he is going to look more closely; under such scrutiny, who can still believe himself to be righteous unless justified by pure grace?

Moreover, there were fewer now who seemingly approached their end like the patriarchs and Job, truly 'full of days'. So everything combined to transform eternity, the moment dilated to infinity, into a further duration of time that purgatory makes official by measuring it into days, weeks, years, centuries. Yet it was the biographical extra, that need for more information on *post mortem* happening and activity, which unbalanced their concept of life after death, paganizing it, transforming the untroubled waiting into anguish, phantasms and terrors. It was this added chapter of existence that made purgatory, and by contamination also heaven and hell, extensions of time. And it was this construct pushed to the absurd that Luther was to be tempted to overthrow – at the risk, as so often in the course of history, of swinging the pendulum too far in the opposite direction, notably by rejecting prayers for the dead in anticipation of Judgement, although these made perfect sense in the perspective of the distinction between time and eternity.

The mediating power of the Church

With the system of Indulgences, everything rested on the Church, to which God had delegated his power. The letters which the money changers dispatched to Avignon (1305–78) and Rome, and which in exchange for tinkling florins came back receipted with the pardon and the passport to heaven, bear witness to it. The Church had the key to Scripture which it alone knew and which it scarcely troubled itself about any more. It alone knew, it alone provided, it alone saved. That might have been comforting, but it was dangerous: you should never pull too hard on a single rope.

For a long time the Church gave reassurance. Its majesty was evident in its very buildings and the order and quality of monastic life bore witness to the goodwill of God. At the moment when nothing was threatening it, the theologians of the *via antiqua* gave assurance that what the Church said, Reason confirmed. Saint Thomas, in this respect superficial in his reading of Aristotle, committed the great imprudence of linking God the creator, and individual immortality of the soul to Reason, and thus to the universal Revelation. But these are truths which belong only to the Revelation of Scripture, to the word entrusted to Abraham and incarnate in Christ.

Now, it was on the point of the conformity of Revelation to Reason that the university philosophers and theologians suddenly pulled back. Ockham and the nominalists no longer believed that reason could prove the great tenets of faith. These can only be taught by personal revelation. But for them, personal revelation was what the Church says, and only what the Church says.

The religion of the people unreservedly accepted the mediation of the Church, which was an accepted transfer, marked by tangible consoling gestures. In the upper ranks of a lettered élite, a personal religion centred on meditation over wooden engravings of the Passion became established in counterpoint to the religion of the

The quarrel over Indulgences was the cause, or at least the detonator, of the religious upheavals of the 16th century. The possibility of a man's buying remission of his sins for hard cash led Luther to oppose the papacy. Even if the money collected was devoted to the grandeur of the Church – notably the rebuilding of St Peter's in Rome – many contemporaries could not accept the confusion that seemed to be arising between the salvation of the soul and financial transactions.

The Traffic in Indulgences, a satirical engraving of the 16th century. Kharbine collection, Paris.

Unlike the Italian Renaissance, characterized by charm and *joie de vivre*, the painting of the German masters expresses the raw sensibility of the regions won over to the Reformation. There is no majesty in Grünewald's Christ, no restraint in the distress of Mary Magdalene; the body of Jesus is already putrefying, and the suffering of the saint is at its height.

Detail from the *Issenheim altarpiece* by Matthias Grünewald, *c.* 1512–16. Musée d'Unterlinden, Colmar.

Few writers approached the enigma of the after-life with a passion and dramatic intensity comparable to the genius of Dante. So many agonies and hopes are brought together in the hollow of this 'P' for Purgatory, an illuminated letter from that masterpiece of medieval literature, the *Divine Comedy*.

Detail from a medieval manuscript of Canto X of Dante's *Purgatory*. Biblioteca Nazionale Centrale, Florence.

masses. The *devotio moderna* of this slender urban élite did not fundamentally need the mediation of the Church, but the big battalions of ordinary Christian folk did.

Never had the Church's power of mediation been so fully and profoundly accepted. At the end of an evolution that stretched over a thousand years, the delay of marriage and the widespread practice of celibacy, together with fasting, combined to produce a deep awareness of the intrinsic value of the Christian life of the laity. Thus are explained the urgency with which baptism was sought, the awe in which the sacramental rites of the Church were held, the symbolic actions in imitation of the Eucharist (blessed bread) for the humble, who did not take communion but would gaze upon the elevated Host destined for manducation by the clergy. Everything converged on the Church which united, assured and controlled – even magic whose only place now was in satanism, otherwise known as sorcery.

The consequences of the schism

The concentration of powers at the top stemmed from the way in which the Church itself was run. As it was the Pope of Rome who authenticated through canonical investiture, there was a tendency to bypass the intermediate ranks. It followed that this concentration, this congestion at the top, weakened and exposed the Church to a thrombosis.

The great papal schism in the West was the first serious circulatory disorder in a system by now too perfect to be viable. For half a century Christendom was torn apart between two Popes. The failure of the Council of Pisa took the Church from schism (1376–1409) to chaos (1409–14). Finally the Council of Constance (1414–17) ended the schism, but the price was heavy. After two, and then three, popes, the Church was to taste the worst of tyrannies, that of committee rule. The

The Great Schism in the West which saw two, then three popes dispute the succession to the throne of St Peter, came to an end in 1417 at the conclusion of the Council of Constance. Rome regained her supremacy at the expense of Avignon, but henceforth power within the Church was disputed by two supreme authorities: the Pope and the clamorous machine of the council.

The Council of Constance, wood engraving from an early printed book by Ulrich von Reichental, Augsburg, 1483. Bibliothèque Polonaise, Paris.

Council did not solve the problem of too much power being concentrated at the top, but aggravated it by itself taking the place of the Pope; it was this collective tyrant that was responsible for burning Johann Hus on 6 July 1415, and Jerome of Prague on 30 May 1415, going back on its given word.

Following Constance a long conflict developed between the two supreme authorities, the papacy and the conciliar body. The second schism that resulted (1438–49) was not as far-reaching as the first, but the papacy was diminished by it.

Thus weakened, its resources reduced to less than a third of what they had been before, the papacy attempted to recover its power and independence. In the face of the rise of the territorial States, it tried to endow itself with a modern State by unifying a total area of 42,000 square kilometres, whose population was to reach 1.5 million towards 1550. But it is questionable whether the effort required and the methods employed, most especially by Julius II (1503–13) were compatible with the spiritual leadership of Christianity. There is legitimate cause to doubt it. In his condemnation, Erasmus expressed the feelings of all Christendom.

John Wyclif

By the end of the Middle Ages, virtually nothing had survived of the heretical and sectarian assault of the twelfth century (Albigensianism and Waldensianism). Confined to a few Alpine valleys and an area at the foot of the Luberon, the Waldenses had lost all but a historical significance. In the fourteenth century, the Latin Church rebuilt its unity through strength of conviction and the preaching of the mendicant orders, and the very real strength of the instrument of the inquisition.

However, with Wyclif and Johann Hus the possibility of a different ecclesiology, a different way of understanding the Church, began to take shape. Its cornerstone was the physical link, 'from hand to hand', from Christ right down to the College of Bishops presided over by the Pope of Rome, Peter's successor, *de facto* president of the College of the Apostles, in a Church which exercised the power God had delegated to it on earth.

In 1378, when the great schism erupted in a period of sharp conflict between the papacy and the English throne, which was increasingly resentful of the burden of tributes and controls, Wyclif was at the peak of his influence. Born, it is thought, in 1324, this secular priest was acknowledged at Oxford as one of the most brilliant canon lawyers of his day. From 1365 to 1375, the King made use of Wyclif's skills, employing him to defend the rights of the crown. A historian through his duty to the state, Wyclif came to doubt the basis of pontifical jurisdiction. The reconciliation of the King and Gregory XI, in 1377–8, thus plunged him into a crisis of conscience. He was being asked to draw back just when he was beginning to believe in the task entrusted to him.

His first great treatise, which contains the germ of his whole argument, *De dominio divino* (1376), came too early. It questions the keystone of medieval ecclesiology, the power delegated by God to the Church. On reflection, it appeared to Wyclif that this conception was not very compatible with what Scripture has to say about Transcendance. The true God alone is *Dominus*. It did not seem to Wyclif

John Wyclif is regarded as one of the precursors of Luther. In the last quarter of the 14th century, that is to say a hundred and fifty years before the Reformers, he was already questioning the authority of the ecclesiastical hierarchy, the Dominium delegated by God, the doctrine of transubstantiation and the justification of indulgences.

Portrait of John Wyclif, English school of the 17th century. Société de l'Histoire du Protestantisme Français, Paris.

that it was seemly to imagine that God could unburden himself of this *dominium*. The *De civili dominio* carries certain implications for the government of the Church: the priest has no power at all; the sacrament only attests the presence of grace, it does not procure it. His *De officio Regis* flatters the power of kingship; *De veritate Scripturae Sanctae* and *De ecclesia*, both of 1378, use the authority of Scripture to complete what was destined to become the ecclesiology of the Reformation. Almost everything that the Reformers were to build on is potentially present, albeit without the powerful inspiration, in the work of Wyclif.

In 1378 the legist became a pastor. Retiring to Lutterworth, he devoted himself to preaching, evangelizing the peasants, and to the huge task of translating the Bible into English. Wyclif, like Hus and later Luther, suffered as an Englishman from the frustration of being on the fringes. He now spoke out against the privileged position of the clergy and the power of the Pope in short incisive treatises that were particularly well received in Bohemia. Wyclif came finally to conceive of a universal priesthood which would remove the barrier between the laity and the priesthood. He criticized the Mass for being alien and unfaithful to the Last Supper. The Sacrifice was unique, perfect, unrepeatable. It would be sacrilege to imagine that God could abdicate his power to the whim of man.

But the social disturbances of the years 1381–2 did a disservice to Wyclif much as the Peasants' War was to do a disservice to Luther. Poor priests, *idiotae* and *simplices*, who were soon to take the name of Lollards, took up his ideas and were opposed by the Crown and the mendicant orders. Condemned in 1381, Wyclif died three years later without having been personally molested, for the King was mindful of his zeal. But by a decree of the Council of Constance his remains were ordered to be exhumed and burnt, and his ashes scattered.

Johann Hus

Wyclif's true descendants are to be found in Bohemia rather than among the Lollards. Johann Hus, born probably in 1369, and tragically put to death in 1415, lived through the drama of the great schism in an outlying country crushed by the weight of the Church. The Church owned a considerable share of the lands of Bohemia and skimmed off enormous wealth. The Archbishopric of Prague alone absorbed about a third of all the revenues in coin paid by the peasants to the prelate. It was a colonial situation.

In June 1412, relying on an already powerful reformist climate, Johann Hus publicly condemned 'the suspect and fallacious indulgences of a modern Pope'. Prague resounded with shouts and songs vituperating against the legates, whose coffers were smeared with excrement, while Czech students were burning bulls of indulgence a hundred and five years before Luther.

After the executions of Hus and Jerome of Prague, those who henceforth in honour of the martyr called themselves Hussites lit an iconoclastic blaze that destroyed statues and images. The first revolutionary commune took possession of Mount Tabor, in southern Bohemia, in February 1420.

1

The Czech Johann Hus (1371–1415) was the link between Wyclif, many of whose doctrinal themes he took up, and the Reformers of the 16th century, who took inspiration from his struggle against the hierarchy and against abuses. Twice excommunicated, he was finally condemned to be burnt at the stake during the Council of Constance.

1. *Portrait of Johann Hus*, 16th-century engraving.

2. *Johann Hus burnt, his ashes scattered to the wind*, wood engraving from an early printed book by Ulrich von Reichental, Augsburg, 1483. Bibliothèque Polonaise, Paris.

2

Among the obsessions and new riches that characterized 15th-century Christendom, fear of Judgement, now seen as more immediate, was by far the most dominant. For some, the best way to prepare for the after-life was to buy the Indulgences sold by the papacy; for others, opposed to a practice they considered scandalous, only faith could save. Christ did not die for nothing, they said with a fervour sublimely illustrated by the *Pietà* of Enguerrand Quarton.

The Last Judgement, from Saint Augustine's *City of God*, manuscript of the 15th century. Bibliothèque Sainte-Geneviève, Paris.

Pietà of Villeneuve-les-Avignon, painting on wood by Enguerrand Quarton, *c.* 1460. Musée du Louvre, Paris.

The *Four Articles* of Prague, presented in 1419 and promulgated in 1421 by the Diet of Caslav, formulated the basic demands of most of the Bohemian Church, while the left-wing Pikharts and Adamites began to make wide-ranging demands, from purely ecclesial radicalism to total, and particularly sexual, anomie. The country was ravaged by attempts to reconquer it after the manner of the Albigensian Crusade. They failed until the day when the moderates and Catholics joined forces.

Precursors of the Reformation, Wyclif and Hus set an example to future generations. And whereas we might hesitate to describe Hus unreservedly as pre-Lutheran, we must remember that Luther himself once said: 'We are all Hussites'.

'Sola Fide, Sola Scriptura'

So at the two extremities of Christendom, in the England of Wyclif and the Bohemia of Hus, there were two aggregates that lacked the essential element needed to produce a general precipitation. Intellectually less structured, the Hussite challenge had more fertile politico-social soil; Bohemia, attached to the right flank of the Empire, was like a continually aching abscess which was to make Rome exceptionally sensitive to the echoes from Saxony, a small, rather out-of-the-way electorate of the Empire, where recently a university had been established at Wittenberg.

In a word, Christendom was both obsessed by new fears and endowed with riches. Firstly, the fear of Judgement. How could one prepare oneself for the dread face-to-face? The great *Ars Moriendi*, one of the five or six best-sellers in Christendom, which could be bought at fairs, is probably the work of a Dominican of the priory of Constance (1415–17). Of the 234 manuscripts that have survived, 126 are in Latin, 75 in German, 11 in English, 10 in French, 9 in Italian. The predominance of German and Latin versions (Latin was more widely understood in Germanic countries) locates the epicentre of the anxiety. The obsession was with everything concerned with the judgement of the individual at the hour of his death and the struggle between demons and angels contending for possession of the dying man. That is why the Church was tempted to increase the supply of indulgences: it was more in order to meet demand than to raise money for the rebuilding of St Peter's. But plentiful supply leads to devaluation. With the rising tide of religious waters, people's fear increased. What if God is not to be fooled by our book-keeping? What if redemption really has a meaning? Fear of Judgement paved the way to the most fantastic shortcircuit in spiritual history, the Lutheran *Sola Fide*.

But this route to free salvation would have been totally inconceivable without the shortcircuit of the *Sola Scriptura*. Humanism, which we can say started with Petrarch, Boccaccio, Lorenzo Valla in the incomparable city of Florence, is an aggregation of a number of philosophical techniques, a discovery of language as a subject of study and an object of history. Once again the magnificent heritage of antiquity had been allowed to become corrupted. Scholastic Latin was an abstract technical language that could not be used to speak of morning dew, a woman's love or the scent of a rose. Since all essential knowledge had been entrusted to the writings of antiquity, what was the point of accumulating commentaries if their sediment obscures the meaning, the simple, the natural, the obvious meaning to those who read with fresh eyes? The whole history of culture consists of these 'achievements' that smother the rising sap of life beneath the encrustation of unnecessary refinements. Humanism was one of those necessary shortcircuits in the history of humanity.

We know that the Reformation can be summed up in two propositions: *Sola Fide* and *Sola Scriptura*, which are also the two axes of its history. It is difficult to say which is of greater importance. The Lutheran Reformation started from *Sola Fide*. Based on the experience of the Saxon Church, it was the response to the refusal to admit a truth that was both liberating and confirmed by Scripture. But without the *Sola Scriptura* it is hard to see how the Lutheran Reform could have taken hold. The reformed doctrine, which called for the Church to be remodelled on the hard core of Holy Scripture, was able to evolve in the humanist milieu, akin to and yet distinct from the university milieu. The axis of the *Sola Scriptura*, from Zwingli onwards, was the solid axis of all the cultural successes of Europe – through mid-Europe, from the Rhine to the Alps – a Europe in which society had not yet been herded by the territorial State into solid masses that were difficult to manipulate. But where, without the *Sola Fide*, would have been the emotional charge that enables us to die joyfully (should God call us to witness) since all is grace and since he loves us?

PART TWO

FRAGMENTATION

From humanism to Reformation

Between 1490 and 1540 humanism spread throughout Europe, creating intellectual milieux and producing admirable achievements. A whole series of favourable conditions made this advance possible. With the technological revolution of the printing press, and under the protection of wealthy patrons, exceptional men used a 'return to the sources' to give free rein to their curiosity in all domains of the human spirit. But when the Reformation arrived, humanism had to face hesitation, inner conflict and then harrowing decisions.

A lively reaction

After the magnificent Gothic synthesis of the thirteenth century, which was theological, canonical and literary as well as architectural, Christianity seemed to have lost its *élan vital*, draining its energies in national quarrels and rival interests. Nevertheless, even in the shadow of the Avignon papacy – so indicative of spiritual decline and dependence on a secular power – dawned the new poetry of Petrarch (1304–74), who came from Tuscany and travelled all over Europe. Is he the last scion of the medieval humanism made famous by Dante, or the first modern humanist? He is clearly at least a precursor on account of his taste for classical Latin and his Christian dialogue with pagan authors. His contemporary Boccaccio (1313–75) was much more clearly inclined to neo-paganism, the natural temptation of humanism, always denounced by its adversaries.

Petrarch and Boccaccio, with their literary vitality, lived during the great plague, the most devastating of a whole series of epidemics which for over a century created a vivid sense of death's attraction and repulsiveness in western consciousness. The magisterial works of J. Huizinga, J. Toussaert, A. Tenenti and F. Rupp have described 'the autumn of the Middle Ages' with its taste for the macabre, its emphasis on merit and the harshness of life – to be compensated in the next world. In reaction humanism, in full flower by the end of the fifteenth century (and earlier than that in Italy), displayed a vigorous return to the vital powers of humanity and society.

It was a matter of a will for rebirth, for coming back to life, which was later justly entitled Renaissance. Humanism believed in the recreation of man by man, almost as if death, so recently omnipresent, did not exist; as if civilizations – especially Graeco-Latin antiquity – were not mortal, or at least could be resurrected. The humanist age therefore includes an aspect of avowed reaction to the preceding period. Its first expression appeared in Lorenzo Valla (1405–57), who belonged to 'critical' humanism, which Augustin Rodet has distinguished from 'enthusiastic' humanism. Dazzling in his capacity to detect sensitive areas which he probed with his scalpel, Valla expressed two humanist convictions in his *De libero arbitrio* (and *De Voluptate*. First, human free will does not preclude divine fore-knowledge; second, spiritual pleasure, a foretaste of future life, is the true good to be sought. What had to be done was to clarify the relationship between, on the one hand, revelation with its doctrine of original sin and redemption, and on the other the morality of pagan antiquity.

In his most 'critical' works Valla introduced into knowledge a sense of distance. He scandalized his contemporaries by showing that the 'Donation of Constantine' to Pope Sylvester was not authentic, although the temporal sovereignty of the papacy

Lorenzo Valla, founding father of critical humanism, was the venerated master of Erasmus. He understood that a language like Latin had a history. Among other achievements he refuted the Donation of Constantine and denounced the False Decretals.

Portrait of Lorenzo Valla, 16th-century engraving. Bibliothèque Nationale, Paris.

Elegantiae Terminorum . . . an alphabetical lexicon published in 1491 at Deventer, drawing on the *Elegantiae* of Lorenzo Valla among others. Bibliothèque Nationale, Paris.

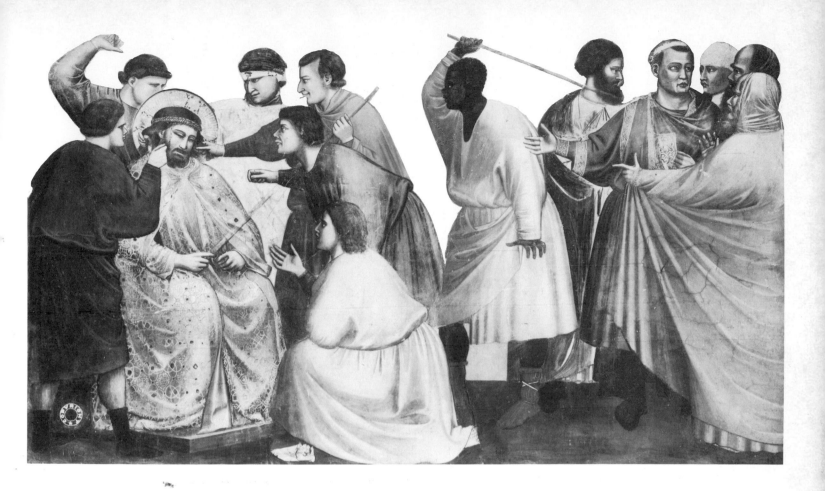

was based on it, and he demonstrated historical stages in the development of the Latin language in his *Elegantiae*. But above all he compared the Latin Vulgate translation with the original Greek text of the New Testament in his *Collatio* (1442) which, in its later form *Adnotationes* (1455) was printed by Erasmus in 1505. Thus Valla broke with the illusions of contemporaneity and introduced the historical dimension which humanism required for its development.

The use of perspective

There were historians in the Middle Ages, so the change which came about in the fourteenth and fifteenth centuries was not a 'discovery' but an understanding of the past *as past*. Methods did not change but judgements, even when they were inexact, presupposed a perspective distinguishing between epochs and contexts. Leonardo Bruni, in his *History of Florence* (1420), and Macchiavelli and Guicciardini at the beginning of the next century, in fact made history secular, arguing that it is from the qualities or the ambitions of people rather than from providential action that one may see what lies behind the events of this world.

Historical distance was acquired soon after the invention of perspective in painting, which, as a matter of technique, is attributed to Paolo Uccello, although historical comprehension in representation goes back to Giotto. He was the first to individualize characters in a scene in a realistic manner. In his fresco *The flagellation of Christ* at Padua, Pontius Pilate is clearly represented as a Roman and is distinguishable from the Jews around him. This shows an awareness on the part of the painter, and hence on the part of the spectator, of their own position in space and time.

Only this preoccupation with distance could have given rise to the humanist watchword: *ad fontes!* One had to realize how distant one was from philosophical, biblical and patristic sources in order to attempt a return to them. The aim was not only to rediscover the great authors but to read them with pristine classical eyes, avoiding the spontaneous or deliberate apologetic preoccupation of the medieval commentators, for whom all that counted in ancient texts was their *praeparatio evangeli*. Thus unless Virgil's *Aeneid* was an allegory of the soul's ascent to God, unless Stoic morality prefigured Christian ascesis, why should one read these books? But the rehabilitation of the text and its plain interpretation were to win the day.

Humanism was accompanied by a real revolution in art brought about by the Italian masters. Before Masaccio laid down the laws of perspective in the 15th century, Giotto introduced realism and individuality, thereby breaking with the conventions of Byzantine art and Gothic painting.

The Flagellation of Christ, fresco by Giotto di Bondone, painted between 1303 and 1305. Scrovegni Chapel, Padua.

65

Certainly an erudite priest like Marsilio Ficino was not going to renounce the ideal of *Plato Christianus* since the whole tradition had pointed in that direction. Likewise Reuchlin and his followers were interested in the Jewish Cabbala through wonder at the integration of Jesus' name in the divine Tetragrammaton. But all of them, conscious of the distance separating them from the texts they studied, disengaged themselves from the screen set up by earlier commentators. Thus the textual corpus of the great philosophers of antiquity was reconstituted. Marsilio Ficino in Italy dealt with Plato, Lefèvre d'Étaples in Paris with Aristotle and Johannes Reuchlin in Germany with Pythagoras. These three names were often linked by contemporaries to pay homage to their labour in restoring the sources, even though in the case of Lefèvre it was rather a matter of more exact translation of Aristotle from Latin, though with the help of Greek professors who abounded in the West.

Greek sources

Rare contacts between Latin- and Greek-speaking humanists took place during the Council of Ferrara-Florence (1438–9) and were continued thereafter. Thus Bessarion, Archbishop of Nicaea, partisan and artisan of the union with Rome, later came to live in Italy. On the Latin side some learned men like Cardinal Nicholas of Cusa were clearly interested in Greek manuscripts and thought.

The fall of Constantinople to the Turks in 1453 sent educated Byzantines into exile in the West. They brought with them some of their manuscripts and, more importantly, their knowledge, which enabled them to decipher the Greek treasures hidden in Latin libraries. Many of them earned a living by teaching their language. Thus they freed the Greek sources for the humanists and gave them access to the Septuagint for the Old Testament, the original language for the New and primitive Christian literature, as well as Church Fathers like Origen, the Cappadocians and many others up to Pseudo-Dionysus. At last there was direct contact with philosophers known previously only through interpreted translation. The scientific knowledge of antiquity, such as the work of Archimedes, was learned the same way.

Demetrios Cydones, Manuel Chrysoloras at the beginning of the fifteenth century, then George Hermonyme, Theodore Gaza and Demetrios Ducas, all eminent persons of the Hellenic diaspora, introduced a knowledge of Greek – at first modest, later profound – into Paris, Italy and Spain before the foundation of humanist colleges where the language of Plato and the Gospel played a major role. Love of Greek led sixteenth-century humanists to create pseudonyms by translating their German or French names (Capito, Melanchthon, Oecolampadius): a rather pedantic notion.

The printing press – mistress and servant

The printing press could become the instrument of a cultural revolution, enacted and vouched for by humanism, only because it had benefited from techniques already invented and assimilated. 'The revolution of the book is first a revolution in paper.' That Chinese invention had been known in the West since the twelfth century through the Moors in Spain, and the analysis of the process permitted its diffusion throughout Europe. The fragility of paper counted against this future tool of the printer, but in its favour were its lightness and modest cost, for in Gutenberg's day parchment was six times dearer.

In spite of their attachment to the symbolic solidity of parchment, the universities progressively resigned themselves to using paper. After all, it took almost 300 sheepskins to copy a single Bible. In France, Champagne originally distributed Italian-made paper at its fairs, but in time became itself a producer of paper. Yet there was still no effective means of production in quantity, so technical ingenuity once again preceded the definitive invention.

Universities had the astute system of the *exemplar*, which was a basic manuscript authoritatively attested as authentic. This was an effort to remedy the numerous faults due to successive errors accumulating from copy to copy. Much greater security was attainable through the model manuscript controlled and lent out only for a fee. The system persisted with the first books, which were themselves very costly. In the second place another process from China was introduced, the useful but cumbersome xylography. One could multiply words or pictures on an engraved block of wook smeared with ink. Card games and almanacs were made, and there are hundreds of instances of religious images suitable for popular piety made this way. From the loose leaves one could in fact make small books which sold well and reinforced the popularity of the *devotio moderna*. Xylographic reproduction preceded the printed book by about seventy years.

A factor in the development of the printing press was the spread of the paper-making process, for though paper was fragile it was much less troublesome than parchment. It was a Chinese invention, transmitted by the Moors in Spain, which spread through Italy and throughout all Europe.

Papermaking, 16th-century engraving by Jost Amman. Bibliothèque Nationale, Paris.

The woodcut, another Chinese invention, preceded print and the printing press with its system of movable individual characters corresponding to the letters of the alphabet. By means of print, however, humanism could expand into all the cultivated milieux of Europe.

1. *Biblia Paulerum*, 14th-century woodcut. Bibliothèque Nationale, Paris.

2. Facsimile of a page of the oldest woodcut *donat* (Latin grammar) printed in Mainz by Gutenberg and Fust, *c.* 1450.

3. *Inside a printing works*, engraving after Jost Amman, 16th century. Bibliothèque des Arts Décoratifs, Paris.

In that case, what was the invention of the printing press, properly so called? It has been attributed to three people whose relationships are not clear: Johannes Gutenberg, Johannes Fust, who seems to have been the source of funding, and Peter Schöffer, the son-in-law of Fust, once a student at the University of Paris. Mainz, rather than Strasburg which claimed the honour, was the location of the discovery around 1450 of a complex system of movable independent characters corresponding to the letters of the alphabet. A character placed in a hollow metal matrix could be reproduced. Certainly the invention of the printing press was allied to improved metallurgical techniques. Then, with ink adequate to the new process of composition, the printing press could begin its career.

Although a thirty-six line Bible preceeded it, the first major printed work was achieved in 1455, a Bible of agreed Latin text with forty-two lines which, like all the first printed books, looked like a manuscript of impeccable regularity. In August 1457 Fust and Schöffer published the first dated and signed book, a magnificent Psalter printed in red and black letters. These first *incunabulae*, as the books printed in the fifteenth century are called, disseminated Latin texts (77 per cent of the total), both religious (45 per cent) and literary (30 per cent), which already indicates the kind of public to whom they were addressed. In fact one can draw a precise map of the expansion of printing from Strasburg, Augsburg and Nüremberg to Italy in 1467, to France and Holland in 1470, then to the rest of Europe. It corresponds exactly to the growth of urban population and the increase in literacy among the laity since the beginning of the Middle Ages. By 1500 the printing presses had brought out six million books and about forty thousand editions – probably more

exemplars than all those which were copied in the West during the entire Middle Ages.

One might expect the Church to welcome the new invention, as indeed it did, yet it could also see danger in the diffusion of books contrary to the true faith alongside so many useful publications. That was the positon of Pope Alexander VI in a Bull of 1501, and also of the fifth Lateran Council in 1517, the very year in which Luther was aroused. The Council rejoiced in 'the new art of printing books', but counselled the faithful 'to be watchful' that poison was not mixed in their medicines, and they instituted *de facto* a preliminary censorship which was to develop in both Catholicism and Protestantism as they grew in opposition.

Thus the book began its formidable career which can be traced in a number of ways, such as through the inventories of monastic, capitular or royal libraries, or by the numbers of Testaments studied in different places; for instance in Amiens in the sixteenth century, one house in four possessed one or more books, most of them extracts from the liturgy. The printing press even changed the manner of learning, freeing the memory and liberating the pedagogue from the need for encyclopedic information. The manuscript memorandum, full of glosses and insertions, lost the role that it once had, for it used to be only through glosses and successive afterthoughts that one might reach the theological arsenal of commentaries on the Bible or the *Sentences* of Peter Lombard. Now one could enjoy freedom of research which set new ideas and hypotheses in motion, and that made the printing press redoutable. A striking example is Copernicus, the Polish savant who worked in obscurity and silence for the first forty years of the sixteenth century. After 1543, the year of his death, his heliocentric theory was discussed among the intellectuals of his time, who took it up with or without caution. Giordano Bruno, Campanella and then Galileo drew diverse conclusions from it which, one way or another, were made known through publication.

Hypotheses which in the Middle Ages would have remained the property of a very narrow circle were now within reach of a much larger public, lessened only by the varieties of national language. Although the printing press was made to be a tool, it

The *Vision of St Augustine* by Vittore Carpaccio is one of the first representations of a Renaissance humanist's study, in which each object has symbolic value. The picture is also remarkable in that the features portrayed as those of St Augustine are those of Cardinal Bessarion (1403–72), a Byzantine theologian who became a member of the Roman curia. He gave patronage to many humanists and bequeathed six hundred precious Greek manuscripts to Venice.

Vision of St Augustine, Vittore Carpaccio, 15th century. Scuola di San Giorgio degli Schiavoni, Venice.

could be tyrannical in necessarily posing problems concerning freedom of expression and the extent to which ideas could be spread – problems which characterize the modern age. That is why the age of Luther, Erasmus and Servetus is so different from that of Hus or Wyclif. Humanists found themselves constrained by the rhythm of the Frankfurt book fairs. Moreover, what use would they make of this marvellous instrument since they themselves depended on patronage for their living?

Protection and patronage

In the Middle Ages intellectual research was carried out in clerical institutions, especially monastic ones, or in universities and funded by the students. That was no longer the case in the sixteenth century except among the Carthusians, who, especially in Cologne, made up a humanist group, as did the Maurists later. The universities, except for recent foundations like Wittenberg and Alcalá, were unwilling to admit humanists, who therefore created their own parallel institutions under the protection of the sovereign in Paris or Louvain.

Following the magnificent example of the Medicis in Florence the princes protected their humanists, as they did their artists and sometimes their astrologers. Henry VIII, Francis I and the Emperor Charles V attached humanists to their courts as almoners, teachers or librarians, while the Popes had an even greater selection of functions to offer throughout Christendom. Humanism occurred at the same time as the emergence of national or even absolute monarchy. The centralization of royal power had been hastened not only by war but also by the invention of gunpowder and the need to deploy infantry troops. The position of humanists like Ariosto, Thomas More or Erasmus, all in one way or another pacifist, shows their independence of spirit in the age of Machiavelli.

Men of subordinate but independent power were numerous enough to constitute an efficient source of patronage to many eminent humanists. Erasmus has left a piquant catalogue of his receipts, from the 'Cardinal of Sion' (Schiner), 'lots of promises and not a penny', to the sparkling generosity of Clement VII, 'a true Medici'. He lived on payments from Lord Mountjoy and then on pensions from the Emperor. Lefèvre d'Étaples owed much to the protection of Margaret, the sister of Francis I, Duchess of Alençon and later Queen of Navarre. Vivès went from the patronage of Catherine of Aragon, while she was still Queen of England, to that of Charles V, her nephew. Italy, with its many sovereign states, was for a long time the home of patronage.

Although the relationship between a humanist and his printers was close and intimate, even to the point of sharing his house (Erasmus stayed with Manuce in Venice and with Froben in Basle), or to the point of friendship, like Lefèvre and Josse Bade, it could not take the place of financial help from a patron, who could also provide effective protection during academic or religious disputes. Moreover, the printers themselves were often humanists, like the Amerbachs and the Estiennes, while young humanists such as Beatus Rhenanus often began life as proof-readers. The presses paid their artisans better than their authors.

With the use of the printing press, and under the protection of the powerful and wealthy, humanists felt their moment had come: at the beginning of the sixteenth century they had not yet despaired of creating a new golden age.

An intellectual élite

Humanism *per se* never existed; there were only humanists. The concept comes from the nineteenth century, while the word *humanista* was coined in the fifteenth century and became common in diverse vernaculars. It designated a member of a distinct intellectual group dedicated to *studia humanitatis*, the humanities. Synonyms abounded: *humanae artes*, *artes liberales*, *studia litterarium* and *bonae artes*, all of which can be translated as liberal arts.

The humanists formed what one might call an 'international intellectual club'. They professed a noble ideal, which was sometimes compromised by their internal quarrels and the ridiculousness of their mutual and therefore biased admiration. These small faults ought not to hide the greatness of this intellectual élite, a group well represented by two people whom we shall cite often since they symbolized the splendour of humanism during the forty years before they both died in 1536. Posterity ratified the judgement of their contemporaries: Desiderius Erasmus (1469–1536) is indeed the prince of humanists. Both his devoted work and his genius merit the first place among them all. Through his immense correspondence he became a kind of arbiter of style, while behind his taste for paradox and the

In the 16th century printers were often humanists as well, such as the famous dynasty of the Estiennes. Their mark was an olive tree in memory of the mother of Henri Estienne, the first of the line, whose maiden name was Montolivet.

The mark of Charles Estienne, printer in Paris, on the first edition of *Proedium rusticum*.

The Dutchman Erasmus was the prince of humanists on account of his erudition, the depth of his thought, the elegance of his style and his biting irony. Holbein, Dürer and Quentin Metsys all painted that good friend of ancient wisdom and modern knowledge, that master of thought who declined a cardinal's hat but remained a Catholic while preaching tolerance towards the Reformed. A notable year in many ways, 1536 was also the year of his death. And so another page was turned.

Portrait of Erasmus by Hans Holbein the Younger, 1523. Musée du Louvre, Paris.

ERASMI ROTERO-
DAMI ADAGIORVM CHILIADES QVA
TVOR, CENTVRIAE'QVE TOTI
DEM. QVIBVS ETIAM QVIN
TA ADDITVR IM.
PERFECTA.

Adagiorum Chiliades Quatuor . . . the title-page of
Erasmus of Rotterdam's *Adages*, published by Aldo
Manuce in Venice in 1520. Bibliothèque Nationale, Paris.

The gap between innovators and upholders of the
established order widened over the Reuchlin
affair concerning a German savant who studied
Jewish sources. On one side were ranged
Erasmus, Lefèvre d'Étaples and all humanists
opposed to 'obscure men'; on the other were
theologians concerned at the dangerous
consequences of the new ideas. In fact these
were two cultures, two modes of knowledge
which were opposed. In this engraving Reuchlin
is portrayed with a double tongue, the symbol of
duplicity, while Pfefferkorn, his implacable
enemy, kicks away his chair to reveal Reuchlin's
imposture to his assembled disciples.

A satirical anti-Reuchlin engraving by Johannes
Kapnion, 1516.

ferocity of his humour or irony lurked an acute perception of people and ideas. Both the particular qualities and the limits of the humanist movement seemed to be set by Erasmus.

Lefèvre d'Étaples (1455–1536) was older before he came to public recognition, and his name is best known in French-speaking countries. A professor at the College of Cardinal-Lemoine in Paris, his interests were at first diverse. Then, through a kind of intellectual conversion, but without restriction, he concentrated on Holy Scripture alone from around 1508 or 1509, translating and commenting on it. Lefèvre was much more in tune with the Reformers than Erasmus ever was, and at the end of his life he took refuge in an enigmatic, and no doubt painful, silence.

The high point of the humanist movement can be dated from the peak of the influence of Erasmus and Lefèvre, between 1510 and 1525. By that time a humanist élite could be found all over Europe, but its Italian birthplace never lost its attraction as both reference point and home. After it had spread through France there appeared 'an Oxford-Louvain-Strasburg-Basle axis linked to the new geography of the book', which grew steadily more dominant and more intransigent. Finally humanism had networks in Spain and Portugal and even in more distant countries like Hungary, Poland and Bohemia, carried there by students influenced in Paris or Oxford and burning more ardently in their isolation.

The humanists collected in their train a whole entourage of cultivated men and women. Some were glorified by a simple mention in the correspondence between great men which served as an almanac of the well-connected or a gazette of the 'republic of letters'. Others made collections of books, like Peter Fälk at Fribourg who enjoyed the reputation of being a humanist essentially on account of his reading room full of well-chosen texts.

A matter of conscience

As often happens, humanism discovered itself to be a movement rather than an attitude of mind when it was suddenly attacked from without in the Reuchlin 'business', to use the exact word of Erasmus *(negotium)*. The German humanist Johann Reuchlin (1456–1522) had written an introductory manual to Hebrew and was closely interested in the Talmud and the cabbala. He made no secret of his desire to direct research into Jewish sources. The Dominicans of Cologne, who were competent and powerful theologians in the city's faculty, had been stimulated and even excited by the Christianization of a Jew, Pfefferkorn. They dragged Reuchlin into a long theological polemic in 1509 which degenerated into a bitter and sometimes vulgar confrontation between the two camps. Its most important feature was less the doubtful matter dragged before the universities and then the Pope, than the call to arms among the humanists supporting Reuchlin's cause against the 'barbarian' theologians, whom Rabelais was soon to call 'theologasters'.

When Reuchlin published in his defence authentic letters of support which he had received from his literary brethren under the title *Epistles of famous men*, Hutten, the German humanist who was soon to be a partisan of Luther, composed a biting collection of imaginary letters from the theologians, *Epistles of obscure men* (1515). That was the divide: the *illuminati* versus the obscurantists. It is hardly surprising, therefore, that the Reuchlin affair brought into the open the suspicion of the theologians, especially of the Sorbonne, towards Erasmus and Lefèvre, the two principal defenders of the Hebraist. Yet the quarrel gave humanism an identity, and allowed it to predict the victory of its ideal.

At that time, around 1510 to 1525, it was still possible to believe that a golden age would come again. Its condition was described at length in a letter from Erasmus at Antwerp, dated 26 February 1517, to Wolfgang Capito, the future Reformer of Strasburg. In the apparent arrival of peace in Europe and in the renewed study of the three biblical languages, Erasmus saw two signs of a return to piety and culture. 'Not only are honest habits and Christian piety going to shine again, they will be joined by ancient literature in its original purity and also all the finest disciplines.' The truly wise would triumph over the 'barbarians'. But Erasmus indicated the possible danger of a parallel renaissance of paganism, or rather that, under cover of the golden age, 'it may try to raise its head, for even among Christians there are those who know Christ only on the surface . . . while more deeply they aspire to paganism'.

That is why Lefèvre d'Étaples, as if to avert the danger, insisted that the new golden age had to be inspired by the early Church, that primitive Church which was the purest source. In the preface to his commentaries on the Gospels, he wrote: 'The light of the Gospel has come again . . . so that there has been no other age since the

end of the primitive Church's decline under Constantine when there has been such great knowledge of languages, or such a wide and complete discovery of the whole world.'

So this golden age disdained the past. Lefèvre explained the humanist presupposition of the decline of the Church after the conversion of Constantine. Like Erasmus, he counted on the renewed knowledge of biblical languages to make the Word of God better known and therefore more convincing and more whole-heartedly lived.

A pedagogical ideal

Humanists were teachers through their desire to instruct and their optimistic conviction that everything could and must be learned and taught, including religion and piety. Modelled on Cicero's translation of the famous Greek term *paideia* by *humanitas*, humanism gave rise to positive dynasties of pedagogues and always put concern for education among their priorities. The precursor was undoubtedly Peter Paul Vergerio the Elder (*d.* 1444), who was to influence the whole sixteenth century with his *De ingenuis moribus*. His inspiration is visible in the development of the school at Strasburg; it is illustrated by Wimpfeling and Sturm and incorporated into the Protestant heritage through Mathurin Cordier, with Claude Baduel and Peter Ramus, who was killed in the massacre of St Bartholemew's Day.

Juan Luis Vivès (1492–1540), who remained a Catholic, was also an educational reformer. He came from a converted Jewish family and left Aragon in 1509 for the great humanist centres of Paris, Louvain and Oxford where he became famous for several large pedagogical treatises. He became the tutor of the future Mary Tudor and championed the ideal of education for women (an ideal he shared with most humanists), the fine and gracious fruit of which was to be seen in Margaret Roper, the daughter of Thomas More. *Utopia* (1516), the enigmatic work of More, future Lord Chancellor of England, could bear the interpretation – among many others – of the paradoxical life of the island's inhabitants as a model pedagogy. There would be Socratic irony in that. More's great friend Erasmus was also, and especially, a teacher. His *Enchiridion* (1505) is a manual of Christian instruction; it was followed by the *Institution of a Christian Prince* (1516) for the young Charles V. He sought through his *Adagia* and *Colloquia* to instruct through pleasure and humour.

Lefèvre d'Étaples used more austere methods directed towards the users of the texts which he presented. He edited, commented on and divided up the Aristotelian corpus, along with his friend and disciple Clichtove, for the convenience of students at sea among the distinctions and glosses of the latest medieval scholasticism. He did the same for his biblical commentaries. His *Quintuplex Psalter* was clearly designed for monks to give them better comprehension of the offices they recited. Then, bit by bit, after his commentaries on the New Testament, Lefèvre wanted to instruct all the people of God through his biblical translations and to give them access, in Meaux and elsewhere, to Holy Scripture.

The epoch was a turning point. Some great spirits like Pico della Mirandola and Leonardo da Vinci could still think of mastering all knowledge, the former by speculation and the latter by experiment. Some, like Agrippa of Nettesheim or Paracelsus, hoped to succeed by occultism or alchemy. These are the last representatives of that ideal. Certainly the taste for encyclopedic learning was still present in Rabelais, who expressed it comically in the letter Gargantua sent to Pantagruel (1532), significantly dated from Utopia. The junior giant had to acquire in Paris an 'abyss of knowledge'. But even then the humanists had to divide out the domains of knowledge.

Humanists found that they had a teaching vocation. The Spaniard Juan Luis Vivès, teacher at Louvain and then at the English court, was the friend of Erasmus. He favoured education for women as well as for men and became tutor to the future Mary Tudor.

Portrait of Juan Luis Vivès, engraving taken from Reussner's *Icons*, 1587. Société de l'Histoire du Protestantisme Français, Paris.

The provinces of the 'republic of letters'

As we have seen, the return to languages was both a method and a praxis for the humanists. In 1517, the year in which he announced the golden age, Erasmus founded at Louvain the 'College of the three languages', which the theologians opposed, as they did the 'College of royal readers' established by Francis I in 1530. Erasmus was urged to organize this but he declined. Instead Guillaume Budé (*d.* 1540) resisted the Sorbonne's effort to hold on to all disciplines which might have a bearing on theology and was able to choose the most competent men for its various chairs. These were augmented far beyond strict philology, for instance Oronce Finé , a mathematician from the Dauphiné, was appointed to astronomy, and they formed the non-university structure of the future *Collège de France*. Guillaume Budé, 'restorer of Roman Law' and Hellenist of repute, is a good example

of the return to the original language in juridical matters. His knowledge of Greek allowed him to bypass the accumulated glosses of centuries on the famous *Pandectae* of Justinian.

The philological method was applicable to all the works of ancient authors who in the sixteenth century ruled the diverse provinces of the 'republic of letters', including philosophy and law, mathematics and medicine and above all grammar and rhetoric, the art which profoundly shaped thought. The philological method disdained medieval constructions like *summas* or *quaestiones* and went to the heart of theology, to its source and its foundation – Holy Scripture in company with the Church Fathers. Thus a good number of humanists concentrated on exegesis, biblical commentaries, textual emendations and especially new translations into Latin or a contemporary language.

The instruments

Humanists understood themselves to be endowing the world with 'instruments' in all domains, but particularly in relation to the Bible. The concept behind creating instruments is necessary in order to understand the gigantic, incessant work to which they gave themselves. They had to use good tools to make progress. Thus they rediscovered Aristotle's notion of the *Organon*, which was translated by *Instrumentum*. So when Erasmus published, somewhat precipitately, his Latin translation of the New Testament in 1516 he gave it the unprecedented but very significant title of *Novum Instrumentum*. The Word of God, which itself uses the image of a sword (an instrument), allowed theology to be built on a new base or, more exactly, to find the bases which had been buried.

Everyone then went to work. The most spectacular of these instruments, because it issued from a lengthy collective scientific enterprise, was certainly the *Polyglot Bible* of Alcalá, called the *Complutensian* from the Latin name of that young university founded by the Spanish Cardinal Ximines de Cisneros, regent of Castille. De Cisneros financed the venture by buying or borrowing Hebrew manuscripts which were deciphered by Hebrew-speaking Christians, including converted Jews like Alphonso de Zamora who also provided a Hebrew and Aramaic lexicon. The six volumes appeared between 1514 and 1517, but the six hundred copies of the *Polyglot Bible* were not distributed until 1522. Although the Latin Vulgate appeared central, and not only typographically speaking, it was illuminated by the Greek Septugint, the original Hebrew for the Old Testament, the Targums for the Pentateuch and a Latin translation. The dedication to Pope Leo X is a vibrant eulogy on the role of the original languages in improving knowledge of all Scripture.

Having cited the two greatest contemporary achievements in the *Complutensian* and the *Novum Instrumentum* of Erasmus, mention should be made of other humanist work aimed at a better establishment of the sacred text. First the *Quincuplex Psalterium* of Lefèvre d'Étaples, not so much for its properly scientific value as for its early date (1509, with a slightly revised version in 1513), its success and the admiration it aroused. It contained and commented on the Psalms in Latin, first the three successive versions edited by St Jerome, then an older and very rare version, and finally an attempt to reconcile them all, which at least in theory was meant to be closest to the Hebrew.

Erasmus took Jerome as his model and patron and all the humanists rallied to the saint's ideal of *Hebraica veritas*. Therefore access to the original text of the Old Testament became urgent and necessary. It was a great occasion when the 'rabbinic' Bible, with Hebrew text and Jewish commentary, was published in Venice in 1516–7 by Daniel Bomberg and edited by Felix de Prato, a baptized Jew who became an Augustinian monk. Its second edition of 1524, incorporating Jacob ben Hayim's work on the Masoretic text, was even more important.

Finally one may point to the Latin translation from the Hebrew of Sanctus Pagninus (*d.* 1531), a Dominican from Lucques. It may be called a 'matrix' since it inspired, stimulated and supported later texts, especially translations into contemporary vernaculars where its influence may be seen. This translation, which appeared in 1528 in rather rough Latin, had the immense advantage of being very literal and on that account valuable. Pagninus, who was a technical exegete rather than a humanist, was also the reputed author of a Hebrew dictionary published in 1529. Indeed the humanists, with their model of instruments, multiplied works intended to facilitate the reading and the study of the Bible. All sorts of dictionaries, grammars, lexicons and glossaries appeared either on their own or as appendices to editions of the scriptural text. Thus Sebastian Münster devoted himself in the cause

NOVVM IN
ſtrumentū omne, diligenter ab ERASMO ROTERODAMO recognitum & emendatum, nõ ſolum ad græcam ueritatem, uerumetiam ad multorum utriuſq́ linguæ codicum, eorumq́ ueterum ſimul & emendatorum fidem, poſtremo ad probatiſſimorum autorum citationem, emendationem & interpretationem, præcipue, Origenis, Chryſoſtomi, Cyrilli, Vulgarij, Hieronymi, Cypriani, Ambroſij, Hilarij, Auguſti.
ni, una cū Annotationibus, quæ lectorem doceant, quid qua ratione mutatum ſit.
Quiſquis igitur amas ue-
ram
Theolo-
giam, lege, cogno
ſce, ac deinde iudica.
Neq́ ſtatim offendere, ſi quid mutatum offenderis, ſed
expende, num in melius mutatum ſit.

APVD INCLYTAM
GERMANIAE BASILEAM.

CVM PRIVILEGIO
MAXIMILIANI CAESARIS AVGVSTI, NE QVIS ALIVS IN SACRA ROMANI IMPERII DITIONE, INTRA QVATVOR ANNOS EXCVDAT, AVT ALIBI EXCVSVM IMPORTET.

1

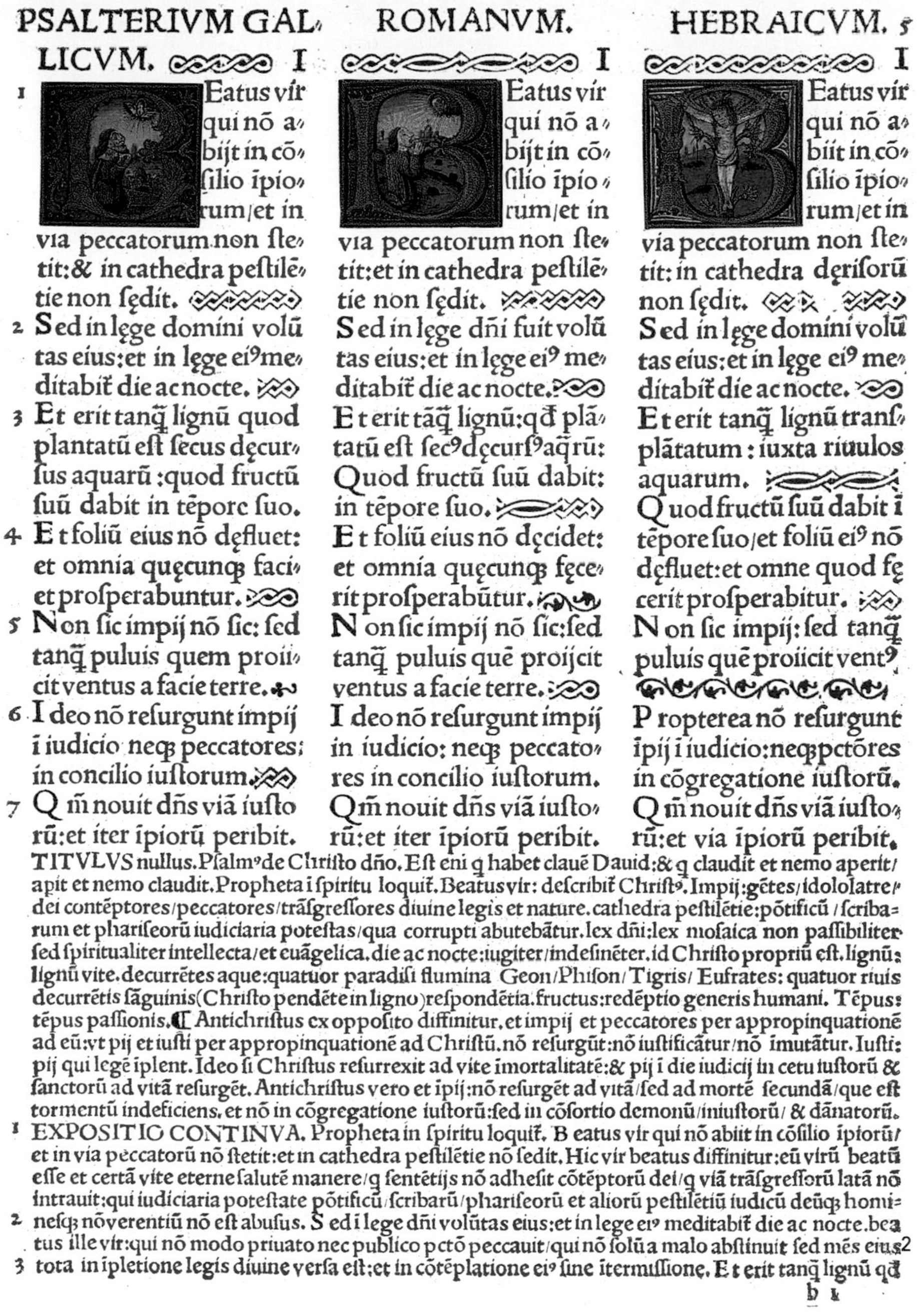

Column 1 (PSALTERIVM GALLICVM):

1 Eatus vír qui nõ a, bíjt in cõ, filio ípio, rum/et in via peccatorum non fte, tit:& in cathedra peftilẽ, tie non fedit.

2 Sed in lege domíni volũ tas eius:et in lege eí⁹me, ditabĩ die ac nocte.

3 Et erit tãq̃ lígnũ quod plantatũ eft fecus dẽcur, fus aquarũ :quod fructũ fuũ dabit in tẽpore fuo.

4 Et foliũ eius nõ defluet: et omnia quẽcunq̃ faci, et profperabuntur.

5 Non fic impij nõ fic: fed tãq̃ puluis quem proíí, cit ventus a facie terre.

6 Ideo nõ refurgunt impíj i iudicio neq̃ peccatores: in concilio iuftorum.

7 Qm nouit dñs víã iufto, rũ:et íter ípíorũ peribit.

TITVLVS nullus. Pfalm⁹ de Chrifto dño. Eft eni q habet claué Dauid:& q claudit et nemo aperit/ apit et nemo claudit. Propheta i fpiritu loquif. Beatus vir: defcribiĩ Chrift⁹. Impij:gẽtes/idololatre/ dei contẽptores/peccatores/trãfgreffores diuine legis et nature. cathedra peftilẽtie:põtificũ /fcriba, rum et pharifeorũ iudiciaria poteftas/qua corrupti abutebãtur. lex dñi:lex mofaica non paffibiliter fed fpiritualiter intellecta/et euãgelica. die ac nocte:iugiter/indefinẽter. id Chrifto propriũ eft. lignũ: lignũ vite. decurrẽtes aque:quatuor paradifi flumina Geon/Phifon/Tigris/ Eufrates: quatuor riuis decurrẽtis fãguinis(Chrifto pendẽte in ligno)refpondẽtia.fructus:redẽptio generis humani. Tẽpus: tẽpus paffionis.¶ Antichriftus ex oppofito diffinitur,et impij et peccatores per appropinquationẽ ad eũ:vt pij et iufti per appropinquationẽ ad Chriftũ.nõ refurgũt:nõ iuftificãtur/nõ imutãtur. Iufti: pij qui legẽ iplent. Ideo fi Chriftus refurrexit ad vite imortalitatẽ:& pij i die iudicij in cetu iuftorũ & fanctorũ ad vitã refurgẽt. Antichriftus vero et ipij:nõ refurgẽt ad vitã/fed ad mortẽ fecundã/que eft tormentũ indeficiens, et nõ in cõgregatione iuftorũ:fed in cõfortio demonũ/iniuftorũ/& dãnatorũ.

1 EXPOSITIO CONTINVA. Propheta in fpiritu loquif. Beatus vir qui nõ abiit in cõfilio ipiorũ/ et in via peccatorũ nõ ftetit:et in cathedra peftilẽtie nõ fedit. Hic vir beatus diffinitur:eũ virũ beatũ effe et certã vite eterne falutẽ manere/q fentẽtijs nõ adhefit cõtẽptorũ dei/q viã trãfgefforũ latã nõ intrauit:qui iudiciariã poteftate põtificũ/fcribarũ/pharifeorũ et aliorũ peftilẽtiũ iudicũ deũq̃ homi,

2 nefq̃ nõuerentiũ nõ eft abufus. Sed i lege dñi voluãtas eius:et in lege ei⁹ meditabĩ die ac nocte.bea tus ille vir:qui nõ modo priuato nec publico pctõ peccauit/qui nõ folũ a malo abftinuit fed mẽs eius2

3 tota in ipletione legis diuine verfa eft:et in cõtẽplatione ei⁹ fine itermiffione. Et erit tãq̃ lignũ qd

b i

Column 2 (ROMANVM):

1 Eatus vír qui nõ a, bíjt in cõ, filio ípio, rum/et in via peccatorum non fte, tit:et in cathedra peftilẽ, tie non fedit.

2 Sed in lege dñi fuit volũ tas eius:et in lege ei⁹ me, ditabĩ die ac nocte.

3 Et erit tãq̃ lígnũ:qd̃ plã, tatũ eft fec⁹dẽcurf⁹aq̃rũ: Quod fructũ fuũ dabit: in tẽpore fuo.

4 Et foliũ eius nõ dẽcidet: et omnia quẽcunq̃ fẽce, rit profperabĩtur.

5 Non fic impij nõ fic:fed tãq̃ puluis quẽ proijcit ventus a facie terre.

6 Ideo nõ refurgunt impíj in iudicio: neq̃ peccato, res in concilio iuftorum.

7 Qm nouit dñs víã iufto, rũ:et íter ípíorũ peribit.

Column 3 (HEBRAICVM):

1 Eatus vír qui nõ a, biít in cõ, filio ípio, rum/et in via peccatorum non fte, tit: in cathedra dẽriforũ non fẽdit.

2 Sed in lege domíni volũ tas eius:et in lege ei⁹ me, ditabĩ die ac nocte.

3 Et erit tanq̃ lignũ tranf, plãtatum : iuxta riuulos aquarum.

Quod fructũ fuũ dabit i tẽpore fuo/et foliũ ei⁹ nõ defluet:et omne quod fẽ cerit profperabitur.

5 Non fic impíj: fed tãq̃ puluis quẽ proiicit vent⁹

Propterea nõ refurgunt ipij i iudicio:neq̃pctores in cõgregatione iuftorũ.

Qm nouit dñs víã iufto, rũ:et via ípíorũ peribit.

---

of Hebrew to translating the works of Elias Levita, one of the greatest Jewish grammarians of the sixteenth century.

Works of the kind known since antiquity were revived by re-editing or by new elaboration. The production included concordances in the different languages, 'harmonies' to give a synopsis of the gospels, summaries, atlases and also what were called *claves*, the 'keys' or critical portions of Scripture which were soon to reflect confessional orientation. These were in effect rules for the interpretation of Scripture – different rules according to the theological perspective they represented.

Humanist exegesis

All the instruments invented or rediscovered had as their sole aim the better comprehension of Scripture. Contrary to common belief, sixteenth-century human-ism was not simply concerned with pure erudition but sought a life-giving, saving reading of the Word of God. In that age when unbelief and atheism were regarded as deviations and incomprehensible provocation, the need for faith to be effectively nourished remained the impetus of intellectual work.

In opposition to what it considered a 'middle' age between antiquity and itself, the Renaissance repudiated the categories and methods which had been current among the 'gothic' theologians. Thus in different degrees they departed from medieval hermeneutics which had kept the four senses of Scripture, for they were not

Since they founded their thought on the study of the Bible and the philosophers of antiquity, humanists had to provide themselves with intellectual instruments. Thus the first half of the 16th century was marked by an enormous scientific output: translations of the Bible, like the *Novum Instrumentum* of Erasmus, presentations of the Psalms, such as Lefèvre d'Étaples' *Quintuplex Psalterium*, grammars, dictionaries, lexicons and glossaries were duplicated by means of the recent invention of the printing press.

1. The title-page of Erasmus' *Novum Instrumentum*, Basle, 1516. Bibliothèque Nationale, Paris.

2. Page from the *Quintuplex Psalterium* of Lefèvre d'Étaples, published by Henri Estienne in 1509. Bibliothèque Nationale, Paris.

3. Title-page of J. Depautère's *Prima pars grammaticae*, published by Robert Estienne in 1550. Bibliothèque Nationale, Paris.

4. Title-page of Robert Estienne's *Dictionary of the Latin language*, 1531. Bibliothèque Nationale, Paris.

Prima Pars Grãma-
TICAE IOANNIS DESPAVTE-
rii Niniuitæ diligentiff.recognita.

Index copiofiffimus omnium dictionum, quæ
hic explicatæ reperiuntur.

3

LVTETIAE.
Ex officina Rob. Stephani Typographi Regii.
M. D. L.

DICTIONARIVM,
feu Latinæ linguæ Thefaurus,
Non fingulas modo dictiones continens, fed integras quoque Latinæ & loquendi, & fcribendi formulas ex optimis quibufque au-
thoribus accuratiffime collectas.

Cum Gallica ferè interpretatione.

PARISIIS.
Ex officina Roberti Stephani.
M. D. XXXI.

Cum priuilegio Regis.
Ipfius priuilegij exemplum in calce operis perfcriptum inuenies.

4

attracted by that rather symbolic number. Since patristic times theologians, who were not yet distinct from biblical scholars, read Scripture according to a certain key. First was the literal sense which simply explained the text, particularly historical accounts; second came the allegorical sense which referred to the truly spiritual meaning; the tropological indicated the moral content; the anagogical spoke of eschatology and heavenly realities. That made a marvellous instrument, as Henri de Lubac has shown, giving a different tonality according to the needs of the commentary. The best medieval authors knew how to give priority to the essential in the divine message through the certainty of theological sense, which was sometimes little different from ordinary good sense.

But from the fourteenth century the system of quadruple senses deteriorated through over-systematization. Exegesis became mechanical in an age when literary symbolism bordered on over-refinement, when Gothic styles were flamboyant and nominalism flourished. Tremendous efforts were made to find an application for each of the four senses not only in each passage of Scripture, but soon in each phrase and even in each word. The harp of the four-fold sense became discordant when it was used for everything.

The artificiality of the exegesis was then logically doubled by the accumulation of commentaries which were either contradictory or in reply to each other. Even at the beginning of the sixteenth century, one glossed Bible comprised the gloss itself (interlinear and marginal), with notes by Nicholas of Lyra (*d.* 1349), commented on by Matthias Doering to whom Paul of Burgos (*d.* 1435) replied . . . The revealed Word was certainly there typographically, but it was almost choked by annexed commentary which drew on a thousand things from patristic tradition, but also from more recent authors of very unequal worth.

Humanist exegesis sifted that mass of decoration to find again the 'pure' word of God. That instinctive decision is not to be confused with the Protestant claim of the *sola Scriptura*, but one can see that at least technically the two movements began in the same way and that Luther could find support in the humanist ideal of a return to the purity of the text. In fact, ever since the difference between Antioch and Alexandria in the early centuries of the Church, exegesis has been drawn both to the spiritual sense and to the literal, and the latter has too often been assimilated to 'the flesh' or to 'the letter that kills' in Pauline vocabulary. The four senses could be reduced to two which do not have to be in opposition. Such was the synthesizing tendency of humanist exegesis of which the following are some examples.

Evolution is visible in Lefèvre d'Étaples' method, though not in the precious base he studied. In the *Quincuplex Psalterium* he used a model presentation he was to employ again. Through continuous exposition, theological concordance (not of words alone) and annotation he sought, so to speak, a literal-spiritual sense by means of which he found Christ in every biblical statement. Medieval exegesis had subdivided the word too minutely; Lefèvre's exegesis endeavoured to unify it and to centre it round the Incarnate Word himself, and yet both still suffered from the same over-systematization. Therefore Lefèvre made his method gentler in his commentaries on Paul and the evangelists while maintaining the Christocentric intention which makes his work so remarkable. 'The Lord Christ is the spirit of all Scripture', he wrote in a 1524 preface to the *Psalter*. The letter that kills is the Scripture without Christ. That established a true perspective beyond all quarrels over method.

Oddly enough, Cardinal Cajetan (*d.* 1534), that great theologian anxious to safeguard the faith, a faithful and also original Thomist, took some daring positions in the matter of exegesis for which the Sorbonne reproached him posthumously. Cajetan desired a return to the literal sense, 'the foundation of all the others', in a phrase he took from Aquinas. He wanted, especially for the Psalter, to arrive at the exact meaning even if 'the torrent [of Fathers] and doctors' had directed tradition towards a different, more mystical meaning. This independence of spirit which led him to make distinctions within the canon of Scripture and to reject the Johannine comma (I John 5.7–8) as Erasmus did made him a critical humanist on biblical matters.

Erasmian exegesis is subtle and difficult to systematize, like all the thought of the 'prince of humanists'. He certainly has a critical spirit which would put him in the school of Valla. He wished to arrive at the most exact text possible and provided one for the New Testament after belatedly learning and mastering Greek. But what made him a real force in the humanist biblical movement was the privileged place he gave to the Church Fathers whose works he edited, thereby providing an *organon* of the tradition of the first centuries. In 1512 Erasmus wrote: 'Among all theologians none is better than Origen, no one is more subtle and agreeable than Chrysostom, none more holy than Basil . . . Ambrose is extraordinary in his allegories, Jerome in

Jacques Lefèvre d'Étaples (*c.* 1450–1536) is the only 16th-century humanist who is to some extent comparable to Erasmus in his total output. Like Erasmus he defended a new conception of biblical exegesis and a less dramatic piety – on account of which he often had to flee from persecutors. His studious life was likewise disturbed: he took refuge at Meaux, then at Strasburg, but came back into favour with Francis I before finding a secure retreat with Marguerite de Navarre at Nérac.

Portrait of Lefèvre d'Étaples, engraving from the 16th century. Bibliothèque Nationale, Paris.

his practice on Holy Scripture.' He could have added Augustine to the list. As André Godin has shown, the work of Origen was the most influential on Erasmus. On account of the great Alexandrian he rehabilitated allegory (which he distinguished from allegorism), which allowed language to find its deeply moving quality again, and through that under God to be adapted to our condition. Origen lead him back to the original source of the medieval senses of Scripture in the tripartite division of biblical anthropology, where the soul came between the spirit and the body as the principal mediator. In following this tradition Erasmus saw the presence of Christ not only in Scripture but also in the Church and in the human soul.

Thus the patristic perspective and the best of medieval tradition were reintegrated through the genius of Erasmus. The other humanists certainly knew the fathers but Lefèvre, for example, cites them rarely. Erasmus, on the other hand, even in the midst of philological straits, rediscovered a kind of hermeneutical plenitude. He made all interpretation gravitate to Christ, but he was also able to extend it in an ecclesiastical and personal direction. For him the Church was not primarily a rule-bound institution, but the mystic reality of the body of Christ.

Scripture in the common tongue

There was a profound desire in the common claim of the humanists and the Reformers to be able to put the Bible within the reach of the people of God so that each labourer, each weaver might have access to the Word. Before Luther, or at the same time as him, it was the ideal of Erasmus and Lefèvre that all Christian men and women might pray in a language they could understand, a matter put into practice with the help of Bishop Briçonnet in the diocese of Meaux. That desire was consonant with the ever alert pedagogical instinct of the humanists.

In France Lefèvre, the 'evangelical' humanist, progressively put together the first complete translation of the Bible into French, which was printed in Antwerp in 1530. It did not have great repercussions, but after various turns of fortune and a complicated genealogy it passed into the Catholic tradition of Louvain and inspired the Protestant version by Olivetan, especially for the New Testament.

During the sixteenth century, in France as elsewhere, Latin translations from the Hebrew and Greek played an intermediate role between the original texts and the common languages. Although Spanish translations came later, Antonio Brucioli published the first Bible in the language of Tuscany in 1532 with the help of Pagnini's version and the counsel of Elias Levita. In England in 1535, Miles Coverdale edited an English Bible incorporating the translations of Tyndale. On the orders of Henry VIII the Great Bible which appeared in English in 1540, was to be accessible to every parishioner in the realm. It was a composite work inspired by Pagnini, Münster and Luther's famous German translation.

In this way the Word of God was popularized by humanists using the work of humanists, the case of Luther proving the most complex. For him the perspective always had to be theological, involving the universal priesthood of believers and his great theme of justification by faith alone, which challenged Church structures and scholastic edifices and even, for his opponents, the very doctrine of the Church aided by the Holy Spirit. The debate began in the 1520s. On many points humanists agreed with the Reformers' claims and appeared to have facilitated, if not to have consciously prepared, the denunciation of the decadence of university theology. This was done by operating a kind of short circuit between the primitive patristic Church and the contemporary one, through preaching a return to the gospel alone and putting it into the hands of the simple, or at least of the laity, in the common tongue.

The shock of the Reformation in Germany, and then in France, shows that humanism cannot be dogmatically defined. Each humanist had to choose his allegiance. Even if through peaceableness, wisdom or feebleness he refused, he was still torn inwardly. Thus from the 1520s humanism was confronted with a choice.

Living is more important than disputing

Contrary to what one might expect from an intellectual movement, humanism was not primarily speculative or dogmatic. But even that was an intellectual choice. In reaction to the medieval *disputatio* the humanists pleaded for a Christianity which was first of all a way of life, an involvement of the whole being. *Vita magis quam disputatio*, a motto proposed by Erasmus, represents the spirit and ethos of humanism. In 1523 Erasmus described the history of the Church as a slow asphyxiation of faith by reason which engendered controversy and submission to

Origen, writing in the third century, was the greatest theologian of Christian antiquity, along with St Augustine. Erasmus turned to the Latin translation of Origen in order to appreciate the mystical sense of Scripture.

Tertius tomus operum Origenis, 1512 edition. Bibliothèque Nationale, Paris.

When the Vaudois in Piedmont decided to join the Reformation in 1552 they gave Robert Olivetan responsibility for printing a French Bible. He used earlier work and translated part of the text himself. Calvin lent his support to the project by contributing two prefaces.

Robert Olivetan's French *Bible* published at Neuchâtel by Pierre de Wingle in 1535. Library, Lausanne.

philosophic systems. 'In the old days faith rested on a way of life rather than knowledge of articles of belief.' The Church had been compelled to define the faith in its struggle against heretics, but that, he believed, was to the detriment of love. 'Faith began to be in texts rather than in souls.' This anti-intellectualism, which only intellectuals could uphold, is understandable in an age which had seen many sterile debates, but it would prove dangerous when the religious confrontation took on a theological character. At the beginning of the sixteenth century it had a positive role in encouraging evangelical behaviour and Christian experience – morality in its widest meaning.

Humanism highlighted 'true nobility' and exalted personal virtue and merit while playing down the importance of birth and even knowledge. In Stoicism humanism found the taste for antique models and the cult of great men – as is witnessed by the success of Plutarch's *Parallel Lives* which was often translated (for instance by Amyot, into French), and led to imitation and pastiche, such as Brantôme's. This admiration for great men made humanists aware of the new classes which were emerging through their ingenuity, talent or *savoir faire*, but it also conditioned their attitude to themselves. Most of them were, or had, disciples: Humanism had a natural tendency to gather in circles or coteries around a master or within the orbit of his genius. Lefèvre d'Étaples had the gift of grouping men of talent round him at different times in his life, in the College of Cardinal-Lemoine, in St-Germain-des-Prés, at Meaux and even, when obliged by circumstances, in Strasburg or Nérac. As for Erasmus, he had a *familia* composed of secretaries or collaborators, but through his correspondence and his controversies all Europe seemed to want to be of his

school. In Spain, a country in which Erasmus never set foot, his influence was decisive, as Marcel Bataillon has shown in his magisterial study.

Over and above the honour given to Erasmus by great men in the service of the Emperor, such as Gattinara, Maurique and Archbishop Fonseca of Toledo, an Erasmian movement sprang up which after 1530 was difficult to distinguish from illuminism (the *Alumbrados*). It moved too easily from the recommendation to return to the gospel and ritual simplicity to a form of quietism. People took too literally the Erasmian 'variations' on the paradox of the Cross in his *In praise of folly* (1511), one of the greatest successes of humanist literature.

Humanism had the faults of all élitism even when it turned pedagogue and instrument for spreading the truth. It had blind spots in its vision, lack of comprehension and far too hasty rejections. We have already seen its rather allergic reaction to medieval values. With its emphasis on action and engagement in the world it had little sense of the graciousness of monastic life with its ideal of contemplation at leisure *(otium)*, just at the moment when the Reformers, coming at the matter from a different angle, condemned religious vows as pretension to merit which would deny grace alone.

Although very modern in their gospel-inspired pacifism in a century saturated with violence, Erasmus and Thomas More (and even more the men of lesser personality) found themselves unprepared and powerless at the time of religious rupture. They had to make choices, and choosing would sometimes be carried to extremes.

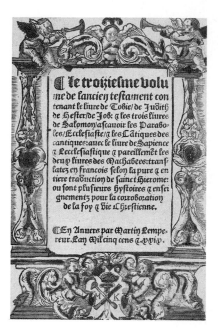

Olivetan's *Bible*, particularly his New Testament, was inspired by the first complete translation by Lefèvre d'Étaples, published at Antwerp, the pivot of European trade and a privileged place for the diffusion of new ideas.

The port of Antwerp, painting attributed to Sebastian Vranck, early 17th century. Massey Museum, Tarbes.

The Third Volume of the Old Testament, French translation by Lefèvre d'Étaples printed at Antwerp by Martin Lempereur in 1530. Société de l'Histoire du Protestantisme Français, Paris.

The Reformation was an insurmountable hurdle for the humanist movement, which was divided like the rest of society. Although most made a definite choice for one side or the other a few endeavoured to preserve the possibility of reunion by defending the middle way. That was the case with Vatable, one of the principal followers of Lefèvre d'Étaples.

Portrait of François Vatable, engraving from *True portraits of illustrious men* by Theodore de Beza, 1580. Bibliothèque Nationale, Paris.

The rupture

When Luther first appeared, the humanists judged in his favour for a few months. The monk of Wittenberg invoked great truths and denounced abuses so flagrant that they had instant sympathy with him. Men as different as Martin Bucer and Huldrych Zwingli, both of whom may be called humanists, welcomed the Reform of the Church. But after that first period came a time of hesitation: the news and the books out of Germany were questioned. There followed time of interior conflict and choice. Two pupils of Lefèvre during his Parisian period exemplify this stage. Josse Clichtove (1472–1543) and Guillaume Farel (1489–1565) took opposite paths. Clichtove rejoined the ranks of Catholic orthodoxy and without giving up the notion of Church Reform worked with a will within the reviled Sorbonne. Farel, after a short stay in Meaux, became a famous, ardent Reformer. Neither of them developed the humanist leanings of their youth. Disciples of Lefèvre like Vatable and perhaps Bovelles, who were more profoundly humanist, sought a *via media* of Catholic character like their master himself. In Germany Melanchthon, who was undoubtedly a humanist, remained one in proximity to his master Luther.

So humanism was confronted with a choice. Sir Thomas More, encouraged by his sovereign, declared himself an adversary of Luther's, argued with him and entered into controversy. Yet in an attitude which transfigured the motto *vita magis quam disputatio*, in the name of the inviolable right of conscience (that Pauline phrase so dear to humanists) More resisted his sovereign's pretensions to replace the Pope himself as supreme head of the Church in England. Even though Henry VIII was not doing anything unheard-of in claiming a national Church, More detected the moment when the king arrogated rights which were not his according to traditional ecclesiology. The Lord Chancellor paid for his lucidity with his life.

As for Erasmus, in spite of a certain doctrinal indeterminacy which made some eighteenth-century thinkers claim him as one of their own, and in spite of his bitter criticism of churchmen and superstitions, when he was called upon by the Pope and the Emperor he did not shrink from battle. He carefully chose his terrain to fight for a humanist theme *par excellence* – human free will, a notion which had been decried by Luther as incompatible with *sola gratia*. In the great polemical writings of 1524–6 humanism was constrained to follow her presuppositions as far as they would go in pursuit of the optimistic vision of humanity and creation.

Human dignity

One of the fundamental themes of humanism was expressed by Pico della Mirandola in 1498 in his famous discourse *On human dignity*. He held that the greatness of human creatures consisted in the liberty which the Creator had given them, which allowed them to choose between animal being and transfiguration, and like Proteus, a figure dear to Erasmus, to achieve their definitive appearance. This position seemed to reduce the role of grace unless the place of Christ was emphasized. According to Pico, 'Prince of Peace' in search of harmony and reconciliation, Christ the redeemer, the Way and the Truth, was the sole principle of synthesis and unity. The 'face' of humanity made in the image and likeness of God was restored by the divine face of Christ. The brilliant Pico della Mirandola personifies one form of optimistic humanistic conviction. The Middle Ages were very aware of the 'philosophical' unity of human nature. The Renaissance, the age which affirmed the individual, tried to restore a lost harmony through symbiosis among individuals.

Lefèvre d'Étaples, whose affinities with Pico della Mirandola have not been sufficiently emphasized, and whom he admired explicitly in his writings, exalted this ideal of harmony and reconciliation. On the same grounds as the Refomers he endeavoured to reconcile faith and works when he wrote a commentary on the Epistle of James.

For Erasmus that reconciliation was in the name of tolerance and charity in constant recourse to the name of Christ: *omnia ad Christum referere*, to refer everything to Christ. The true 'philosophy' is the philosophy of Christ, the eternal wisdom who teaches us love. Thus the Abbé Brémond could say in the following century: 'Humanism wanted us to be saints as a matter of logic.' That attitude of discipleship led Erasmus, who once cried, 'St Socrates, pray for us', to personal humility before the consequences of the Lutheran 'tragedy': 'I will support this Church until I see it to be better and the Church must support me until I become better.'

There we have at the same time the greatness and the limitations of humanism in religious matters. Its approach was primarily moral in the deepest sense of that term, looking at things from the side of conversion. For Luther what was at stake was a

secular misapprehension of redemption and its ecclesiological consequences. The God of the 'Christian philosophy' in the end spoke more through the Sermon on the Mount than the cry of dereliction on the Cross. But Church tradition has never separated these and humanism, through its optimistic rehabilitation of free will, provided many elements of what was to be called the Catholic Reformation.

Humanism and the Catholic Reformation

Historiography has not done justice to humanism in its confrontation with the Protestant Reformation. It is true that it appeared feeble, disabled and disarmed for a while, and was even suspected by the Catholic theologians at the time of connivance with the Reformation. A characteristic example in our own time is the Catholic historian Joseph Lorts, who he came to a measured appreciation of Luther at the expense of Erasmus whom he blamed for all the evils. Thus across the centuries he joins the Sorbonne theologians for whom Protestant teaching was only the predictable fruit of Erasmian and Fabrisian ideas.

It is only recently that value has been placed on humanist continuity, which through crises and upheavals maintained Catholic continuity. It prepared the way for the Reform of the Roman Church, the Counter-Reformation, to expand spiritually at the beginning of the seventeenth century. The heritage of 'pious humanism', to use a phrase of Brémond, belonged to François de Sales, Bérulle and the French school.

Modern historians are coming to a less partisan appreciation of the work of the Council of Trent. 'The Tridentine position is more moderate, traditionalist and centrist than it appeared at first sight. It borrowed from Thomas More and the English . . . taking its circumstances into consideration one can only be struck by its moderation,' writes Pierre Chaunu. As soon as one studies minutely the editing of the different decrees, it is obvious that the definitive decisions never represent extreme positions. At Trent there was 'a desire not to go beyond a balanced mean'. Some examples will illustrate the humanist component in Tridentine decisions.

The first two periods of the Council were devoted almost exclusively to elaborating dogmatic responses. The issue of justification was central in the debate with the Reformers. It concerned the relationship of humanity with God, for the nub of the controversy of the sixteenth century was probably anthropological. The free will defended by Erasmus was therefore foremost of the problems which confronted the conciliar churchmen at the end of 1546. The working out of the texts was slow and difficult. It was a matter of finding a formulation which did not concede too much to Luther nor to Pelagianism, of which the humanists were often suspected by the Reformers. Nor was it enough to give a purely negative reply without any positive definition.

After having sifted several texts provided by Seripando, who was thought to concede too much to Luther, the Council reaffirmed both the grace of salvation and the co-operation of free will with that grace, and thus the possibility of 'merit', the touchstone in Catholic doctrine of a sound doctrine of the communion of saints. The decree and canon on justification did not arrive at a truly definitive synthesis, which was not after all the aim of the editors. All the debates on Molinism and Jansenism in the seventeenth century give ample proof of that. But beyond the technical formulation it preserved the humanist intention of confidence in humanity on account of God's goodness.

The work of the humanists on the return to Holy Scripture and true tradition bore some fruit in the Council. That is proved by the traditional yet open character of the decree on Scripture and tradition, which calmly reaffirmed the list of inspired books without closing the door on distinctions within the canon. It declared the Latin Vulgate 'authentic', which simply meant 'officially received' and adequate for controversy in particular. The Council thus paid attention to various humanist requests and followed their example by ordering a revision of the Vulgate which had become infested with faults in the medieval process of copying. That had to be undertaken twice under Sixtus V in 1590, then two years later under Clement VIII, which is a good sign of critical strictness after the manner of humanist exegetes from the beginning of the century.

Finally emphasis should be given to the importance the Council placed on teaching, especially in drawing up Reformed pastoral methods. In that it shows itself the disciple of humanism. One of the masterpieces of Catholic Reform is the organization of seminaries for the training of priests. Even though the programmes of these institutions were not automatically inspired by a return to the sources, and even less by *bonae litterae*, their intention was basically humanist – as was the

It is often said that humanism marked a break with medieval thought by giving humanity back its rightful place. No one maintained that idea more eloquently than Pico della Mirandola (1463–94), the famous Italian scholar whose name became synonymous with universal knowledge.

Portrait of Pico della Mirandola, engraving from Thevet's *Chronicle*, late 16th century. Bibliothèque Nationale, Paris.

Title-page from Lefèvre d'Étaples' French translation of the *New Testament*, printed at Antwerp by Martin Lempereur in 1530.

teaching of the Jesuits, in which could be seen 'the birth of modern humanism'.

Concern for the schooling of élites and the moulding of Christian people was active at all levels of Catholic Reform. It can be found in the composition of the famous catechism of the Council of Trent. The Council, following the Protestant Reformers themselves, expressly demanded a brief account of the faith in the medieval tradition which would be within the grasp of all Christians, mediated to them by their pastors. The editors of this work were designated by the Pope and clearly demonstrate the influence of Carranza (*d.* 1576), the great Archbishop of Toledo who had been imprisoned for many years on a charge of Erasmianism. It is not the least of paradoxes to see, as has now been shown, the Erasmian inspiration of Carranza's *Catecism Christiano*, the book which made him suspect, in the instrument *par excellence* of the Catholic Reformation.

There were no doubt errors, failures, *faux pas* and rigidities due to the circumstances of the age, but the great Catholic Reformers, men like Ignatius Loyola, Sadoleto, Reginald Pole, Charles Borromeo and François de Sales, clung to the humanist ideal absorbed through their culture and even more perhaps through their deepest intuitions.

The humanist paradox

In the second half of the sixteenth century, and especially its last decades, humanism was refined, purified and decanted from its rather narrow, polemical and over-

Among the inheritors of humanism on the Catholic side were members of the French school of spirituality, particularly François de Sales and Cardinal Pierre de Bérulle (1575–1629).

Cardinal de Bérulle, painted by Philippe de Champaigne, early 17th century. Seminary of St Sulpice, Paris.

literary positions. It had been tried by fire, rupture, combat and decision. It had had to evolve from the dream of the return to a golden age to a realism full of disillusionment. Basically it could apply to itself the paradox of *In praise of folly* – it could not avoid the Cross because the folly of God is wiser than the wisdom of man. Yet the crisis made the serious optimism which is the best of humanism emerge even more shining and more credible. The fine smile of Erasmus painted by Holbein, the wit without bitterness displayed by Sir Thomas More a few seconds before his beheading and the incisive humour of Rabelais are all in the same vein. Even stripped of its illusions, humanism was fundamentally gay, joyous and free.

But humanist optimism was not psychologically or sociologically deficient. It did not deny feebleness or sin but was rooted in confidence in God, and hence in humanity which is by nature theological. After the discourse which Erasmus attributed to Folly one could cite in their defence Thomas More's *Utopia*, a kind of parable on the *City of God* and a recognition of natural wisdom culminating in the gospel which he presented in the guise of an enjoyable and mysterious entertainment. Then there is the paradoxical description which Rabelais made of the Abbey of Thelima, a name which evokes free will conforming to the divine, in that Christian liberty of which the motto is 'do what you will' but where one loves 'with devotion and friendship'. It is an evangelical Utopia putting into practice the famous phrase of Augustine's: *Ama et fac quod vis*.

After the confrontations of the Wars of Religion, after the bloody and tearful testing, a more serene, peacefully smiling humanism flourished again, but now it knew the cost of a smile which was neither roguish nor ironic. Before it developed or was sidetracked into baroque, Catholic optimism could show in the simplicity and sweetness of François de Sales, one of the great architects of Catholic Reform. In his *Introduction to the devoted life* (1608), written for Christians of all kinds, he described evangelical humility and his own sound realism: 'I would not like to play the wise man on account of what I may know, nor on the other hand would I like to play the ignoramus . . . I wish to play neither the fool nor the wise man, for if humility keeps me from airs of wisdom, simplicity and plain-dealing prevent me from playing the fool.'

In the balance of de Sales one can see the maturity and the transcendence of the humanist movement with its paradoxical integration of 'learned ignorance' according to Nicholas of Lyra or its Erasmian 'wise folly'. Humanism, touched by the grace of the imitation of Christ, teaches humility but equally lives humbly. Thus one may justify the immense hope its followers entertained in the sixteenth century to bring about the interior transformation of believers and hence of the Church, without which neither of the two Reformations would have echoed the gospel.

Humanism raised fundamental questions concerning human destiny. Their answers were serious and founded on extraordinary erudition, but they were also based on optimism, humour and *joie de vivre* – visible in the works of Erasmus, More and Rabelais.

1. Frontispiece of Rabelais' *Pantagruel*, 1557 edition. Bibliothèque Nationale, Paris.

2. Engraving from Thomas More's *Utopia* in the 1516 Louvain edition. Bibliothèque Nationale, Paris.

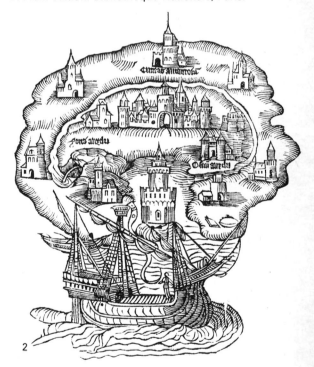

Luther and Europe

Martin Luther's life was passed in the very heart of Germany: he died in 1546 in the town of his birth, Eisleben, in Thuringia.

The house in which Luther died, photograph taken *c.* 1925.

The Protestant Reformation was a shock which turned Europe upside down. Obviously, it cannot be reduced to Luther's personal history; its course nevertheless depended closely on what the leader from Wittenberg did and wrote. Everything was contained in the Lutheran *Sola Fide*: faith and faith alone, not the learning of the humanists, however religious, moved mountains. We cannot reduce the Reformation to Luther, but without Luther it may only have been a passing episode in intellectual history. He breathed into it life and vigour and so it partook of spirit and flesh.

Landmarks

Luther was born in 1483 at Eisleben, in the very heart of Germany. In 1505 he entered the Augustinian monastery at Erfurt. According to his own testimony he passed through a serious inner crisis there, from which he emerged by discovering justification by faith. The traditional paths of University and Church were easier to follow. His orientation was towards teaching and in 1512 he became a doctor of theology at Wittenberg, where he lectured successively on the Psalms and the Epistles to the Romans, the Galatians and the Hebrews. At the same time he presided over important academic disputations. In 1517 the debate over Indulgences placed him in the public eye. The conflict with Rome led in 1521 to the excommunication of this monk who would not yield his position – but in the end nearly half of western Christendom went with him in his break with Rome.

Writing the history of Luther: four centuries of confrontation

Luther is one of the most studied figures in history. There are still nearly a thousand studies published on him each year world-wide. We must bear in mind that the story of Luther itself has a history, because of the effect on us of past approaches to him – even if in the twentieth century we stand back from them.

From the beginning, the history of Luther is written into the confrontation between Catholics and Protestants. The *Commentarii de actis et scriptis Martini Lutheri* by Cochlaeus (1549) set for centuries the tone of the Catholic approach: Luther was depraved, a heretic with nothing Christian about him. This attitude was still taken by Denifle in his *Luther and Lutheranism* (1904): for him Luther's 'reforming' activity was only a cloak for his moral failings. And as for his teaching, only his ignorance or his habit of lying could have prevented him from seeing that his conception of the 'righteousness of God' was well known to theologians of the Middle Ages and therefore that the theme of justification by faith was hardly novel.

On the Protestant side, the first 'biographies' (by Melanchthon (1546), Mathesius and Spangenberg) and even the first 'histories' of the Reformation (Myconius, Spalatin, Sleidan) were apologetic works. But, as Protestantism evolved, so the images of Luther changed. Orthodoxy saw him above all as the 'doctor' and preferred his teaching to his person. At the end of the seventeenth century, Seckendorf, author of a *Commentarius*

historicus et apologeticus seu de Reformatione, put the emphasis more on the first years of the Reformation and on Luther the man, an emphasis Pietism echoed. Pietism also criticized the way the Reformation had developed, particularly the hold established by the princes on the territorial churches. In the eighteenth century, the Enlightenment saw Luther as the agent of a decisive emancipation of mankind with respect to Rome, and as the herald of the liberty of conscience. In the nineteenth century, Romanticism underlined the heroic dimension of Luther's progress. Neo-Protestantism, notably in the person of Troeltsch, rediscovered the degree to which Luther was still rooted in the Middle Ages by his conception of the Church as the general institution of salvation, his supernaturalism and his conception of the sacraments. But, 'by the direct and powerful character of his religious experience', Luther had transcended his times and would have a permanent validity.

Other points of view have also been expressed, particularly since the nineteenth century. Engels and Marx placed Luther in the great movement of socio-economic struggle which stretches from the Hussite wars to the revolutions of the contemporary era. Luther arose in a world where feudalism was on the wane. He contributed to its downfall by criticizing the principal feudal force of the period, the papacy. But he halted there and became the herald of the *Frühbürgerliche Revolution* (early bourgeois revolution), which supported nascent bourgeois capitalism, while Müntzer and the peasants would have wanted to change things much more radically.

Luther was also identified, favourably or unfavourably, with Germany. 'He is the new Arminius who for the second time has chased the Roman legions from German territory,' it was said in the *Revue de Metaphysique et de Morale* in 1918. For Madame de Staël, 'Luther has the most German character of all the great men Germany has produced.' She was thinking of his sincerity, his devotion to his faith, his zeal for work, his sense of duty, his taste for meditation. Others saw rather his faults, such as his coarseness: his taste for obscene jokes led Paquier to dub him in 1926 'the German Rabelais'. Germanists like Vermeil have tried to explain the history of Germany in terms of the influence of Luther. They claim that he was content to free the inner self without progressing to an individualism which could be critical of the social and political stratification, and without opposing the subjection of the Church to the territorial State. According to Vermeil, Luther encouraged that divorce between the rules of personal and public morality which prepared the ground for the strong state of Bismark and even that of Hitler.

The Franco-German wars, particularly those of 1870 and 1914–18, refurbished various images of Luther. Many German preachers and even some historians, such as R. Seeberg, virtually amalgamated the Reformation and Germany. Luther, they claimed, must have been fighting with Germany in 1914–18 to defend the German spirit against atheist, decadent, or Catholic France! On the French side, Claudel

Luther's character is one of the themes most frequently dealt with in the 19th century, with Romanticism insisting on the Reformer's heroic nature. His life is also the subject of an extremely rich iconography.

The Monument of Worms, raised in homage to Martin Luther, 19th-century lithograph.

Luther and the Legate, 19th-century watercolour. Société de l'Histoire du Protestantisme Français, Paris.

claimed in 1914 that France was defending Christ with the aid of the Virgin against 'that apostate Luther who sides with the devil'. The Protestant Henri Monnier reacted by establishing that Luther's God was the God of grace and forgiveness and not the God of Teutonic battles; in his *Luther and Germany*, Vienot claimed that Luther had given a value to the rights of conscience while German nationalism was collectivist and totalitarian. More curious was the step taken by G. Pariset who attempted to prove in 1916 that Luther was as much a Slav as a German. The 'amalgam' of Luther and Germany also explains the attempts made by French Protestant historians between 1850 and 1930 to underline the purely French origins and characteristics of the Reformation in France.

New perspectives in the twentieth century

Notable changes have taken place in the twentieth century. The Catholic approach underwent a Copernican revolution with the authoritative book by Lortz, *The Reformation in Germany* (1939–40), which acknowledges the reality of abuses in the Church and also the strictly religious nature of the steps which Luther took. More recent works, like that of Otto H. Pesch, are concerned with Luther's theology rather than his personality. They judge that Catholic theology can accept the existential way in which he proceeded, in particular that justification is by faith, but still see difficulties over the problem of the papacy. On the Protestant side, theologians have accomplished an immense amount of theological interpretation since the beginning of the century, from Karl Holl and his school to the most well-known contemporary student of Luther, Gerhard Ebeling, who thinks that

Much more valuable for the story of Luther are contemporary works, particularly those of Lucas Cranach, who was his friend for many years and devoted himself to the cause of the Reformation. This great master of the German Renaissance has passed on to us Luther's appearance and that of his wife, Katharina von Bora, and pictures of the Reformer's activity as a preacher.

Portrait of Luther at the age of 43, by Lucas Cranach the Elder, 1526. Nationalmuseum, Stockholm.

Portraits of Luther and Katharina von Bora, by Lucas Cranach the Elder, 1529. Galleria degli Uffizi, Florence.

Luther in the pulpit, the predella of an altar-piece by Lucas Cranach the Elder. Church of St Mary, Wittenberg.

Luther's novelty lay essentially in his hermeneutic, that is to say the way he interpreted Scripture. Protestant students of Luther, generally more interested in his theology than his biography, recognize that Luther's action was limited during the Peasants' War or the establishment of territorial churches, or again in his violent moves against the Jews from 1540.

Publications associated with the five hundredth anniversary of Luther's death demonstrated nationalist and Marxist approaches. The first seems on the way out: in France as in Germany the old 'amalgams' of Luther and nationalism are no longer taken up. As early as 1928 Lucien Febvre rose up against the nationalistic and ethnic approach in his magisterial book *A Destiny: Martin Luther*. Although Luther was a member of a particular people and country, observed Febvre, he nevertheless thought not of Germans but of Christians in general. The Marxists, on their side, have not abandoned their traditional scheme of explanation, but they underline Luther's positive role against feudal forces more than his reactionary role at the time of the Peasants' War.

Today, explaining Luther by the defects of the Church seems to be coming back into vogue. It is convincing in so far as polemic against certain abuses is certainly present in Luther's writings and where the anticlericalism of the period contributed to the success of Luther's message. But we must make no secret of the limits of this explanation. Erasmus was violently opposed to abuses in the Church but remained faithful to Rome. The Catholic reforms did not bring back the Protestants. Besides, explanation in these terms favours the moral dimension over faith and its theological expression. To some degree this explains Luther's 'success', but it does not explain Luther himself!

From Febvre to Jean Delumeau, French historians have placed Luther in the context of the collective thought of his times, setting him 'in the atmosphere of the expectation of the end of the world which was then dominant in Europe and especially in Germany . . . Luther was obsessed by the thought of the Last Days' (Delumeau, *Fear in the West*). We must acknowledge that this is a fertile approach which sets us free from economic reductionism. It also avoids reducing the Reformation to Luther the man or to a theological system. It has a great deal to contribute towards explaining the impact Luther made. But certain questions arise: was everybody afraid in the sixteenth century? Did individuals express only common feelings? Could they not also react against them? The theological advance sometimes seems rather marginalized. Luther was after all a student of Holy Scripture and a theologian, and that must be taken into account in analysis of the Reformation.

Many works have touched on Luther's personal psychology, reminding us that he was not an impersonal theological system but a man of great sensitivity, easily angered, capable also of great gentleness, and that often this man and his actions interested contemporaries and posterity more than his ideas. In the twentieth century psychoanalysis has given a new impetus to this type of approach. Some have discerned an identity crisis through which Luther passed, due in particular to conflict with his father, a conflict reinforced by the fears which the 'arbitrary' God of Occamism inspired in him. Any such crisis must finally have been resolved by the

Luther's breach with Rome originated in the affair of Indulgences, a matter which aroused great public attention. Spiritual excitement was added to peasant claims and the *'Bauerkrieg'* was the touchstone of Luther's life. He has not been forgiven for having openly condemned the peasants' excesses.

A seller of Indulgences hung by peasants, 16th-century engraving.

Portrait of Luther, anonymous German painter, 17th century. Église des Billettes, Paris.

trust that he put in the Divine Word and by his belief in the emancipation of the individual from the institution in an exclusive attachment to Christ.

This useful insistence on Luther's human nature, sometimes neglected by theologians, also reminds us that the Reformer was a particular individual. But there are limits here too. Firstly with available sources: too little is known about Luther's youth, let alone his struggles in the monastery, to lead to conclusions which would satisfy a psychoanalyist. Besides, what set his followers in motion was not simply Luther's actions and character, but undoubtedly a certain message drawn from Scripture. People other than Luther, and with different psychologies to his, have also found that message

There remains the theological approach, or, in other words, the study of Luther's ideas in their relation to the Bible and tradition, taking into account the simultaneously traditional and innovative nature of Luther's intellectual progress. This will bring back into view the Luther who is considered solely as a theologian and a doctor of the Church. He became a Reformer, it will be said, neither because of his own psychological needs nor because of the institutional and moral abuses in the Church, but because he thought that the Church's message was flawed and that an erroneous theology weighed down the preaching and teaching of his time. Luther and the Reformation are thus another way of studying theology, and another way of preaching and believing.

But the historian cannot restrict himself to the theological approach, which does not suffice to explain the impact of Luther. His message and also his attitudes encountered expectations which historians of ideas and of institutions can pertinently identify. And it must be remembered that the history of the Reformation and of Protestantism is not always in line with Luther's great theological intuitions, particularly since their subsequent history is marked by diverse influences such as humanism, which Luther fought against in the person of Erasmus.

Luther's development

It is not easy to grasp Luther's truly religious concepts in depth, nor to understand why justification by faith was such an important article of religion for him, to the point that he wrote in 1537: 'On this article rests everything that makes up our life, everything that we teach against the Pope, the devil and the world. So we must be absolutely sure about it and have no doubts, or else everything is lost.'

Luther shared with his contemporaries the conviction that all mankind would appear before the Judgement seat of Christ. From auricular confession to the numerous preparations for death, the Church helped the individual prepare for this moment. Far from weakening this conception of things, Luther radicalized it. Man would one day have to face God. This prospect of the Judgement of God breaks into his life at the present moment and determines his existence. Luther also felt strongly the imminence of the Last Day. The perspective of Judgement is never softened in Luther's theology, even after he discovered the way of Reform. It is precisely in connection with the Judgement, or with the holiness of God, that the message of justification freely given to the sinner, takes on a weighty and liberating reality.

Luther's advance implied a certain way of talking about sin. It is a question of seeing people no longer as they tend to see themselves, with virtues that can be illusory, but in the light of the holy and radical demands of God. From this perspective the permanence of sin in human life becomes clear, it being understood that sin (Luther's term is concupiscence) is not a matter simply of the senses or the instincts, but rather a fundamental orientation engraved in the heart of human beings, driving them to shrivel up within themselves. The human being shuts itself up in the self instead of making a connection by faith with the Word and abandoning the self to God. This tendency is also shown, on the one hand, by libertinist anti-nomianism, advocating life without reference to a law, and, on the other, by the good works through which people try to affirm the autonomy of the self. From this angle too comes Luther's violent opposition to scholastic theology. He reproaches it for minimizing sin, for fostering the illusion that 'the totality of original sin, as well as actual sins, can be taken away, as if it were a matter of things which can be forgotten in a moment, in the way that darkness is chased away by light'. Since sin affects the totality of our being, the idea is equally excluded that human beings can put themselves on the way to God through their own capacities: *'Facere quod in se est'* said theology at the end of the Middle Ages; Luther goes back beyond that theology to Augustine: only the intervention of God can overcome the depths to which mankind has fallen.

Luther, we must also note, had problems over the words 'righteousness' and 'righteous'. In the early years he felt constant anguish over certain texts: 'The righteous shall live by faith', 'Free me in thy righteousness'. Luther began by understanding 'righteousness' or 'justice' primarily in the Aristotelian sense, that is as human conformity to a certain norm and as God's judgement recompensing people according to their deeds. Was that the 'righteousness of God . . . revealed by the Gospel'? In 1545 Luther described the interior drama which this questioning posed for him: 'Despite the irreproachable character of my life as a monk, I felt myself a sinner before God; my conscience was extremely unquiet and I had no certitude that God was appeased by my satisfactions. And I had no love, indeed I even hated the just and vengeful God.'

The breakthrough which freed him came when he examined the sequence of words: 'The righteousness of God is revealed in the Gospel, as it is written: the righteous shall live by faith'. Luther commented on this: 'I began to understand that God's righteousness is that by which the righteous lives through God's gift; to know about faith and that the meaning was this: the Gospel reveals to us the righteousness of God; to know the promised justice by which God in his mercy justifies us by faith, as it is written: the righteous shall live by faith. So I felt myself to have been born again and to be entering by the wide open gates into Paradise itself.'

Was this as new in comparison with the traditional teaching as Luther claimed? It seems that, at least in Luther's experience, the image of God the Judge and the concept of an active justice controlled by grace and mediated by human agency must have predominated in the theology and spirituality of his time. Some notable discussions have taken place in the last few years regarding the exact moment of Luther's discovery of 'passive justice'. It seems best to place it in 1513 or 1514, while admitting that we are talking of an event which actually occurred over a period of time. It is more important to know how the 'righteousness of God', understood in this way, determines the message Luther gives in his first writings and thereafter.

The Reformation began on 31 October 1517, when Luther nailed up his 95 theses, or so tradition has it, on the door of the church of Wittenberg. In condemning the system of Indulgences he was defying the papacy and opening up a quarrel which in a few years was going to provoke the break-up of Christendom.

Luther writes on the door of the church of Wittenberg with a large pen, satirical Swiss engraving, 16th century. Bibliothèque Nationale, Paris.

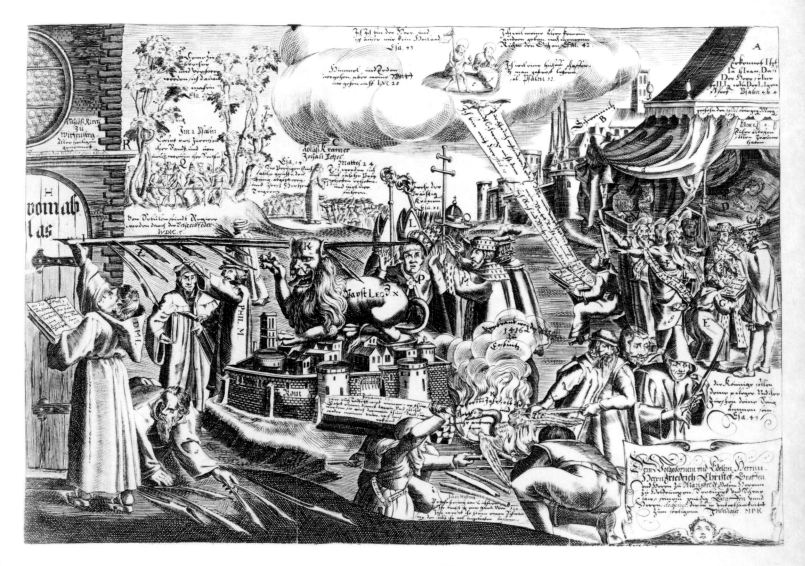

The message of justification by faith

God recognizes sinful human beings in so far as they are children of God, and admits them to communion with him despite their unrighteousness. This is the non-imputation of sin or forgiveness. At the same time, positively, God recognizes in man a new righteousness which is that of Christ. God sees him united to the one who is righteous *par excellence*: Jesus Christ. This is righteousness from without, because not created by the Christians themselves, and it is by this righteousness that Christians are called to live before God all their life. But this divine Judgement declaring a person righteous is not a mere fiction – God acting 'as if' the person were righteous. God is also the creator of righteousness, and begins in baptism to attack sin and in a real manner to fill a person with the righteousness of Christ – a process which will be consummated only at the end of time.

How does the righteousness of God reach a human being? How is that person justified? The answer is clear: by the Word and by faith. Justification is not seen in terms of a sacramental infusion of grace into a person, but in terms of personal relations. The new righteousness is attributed to the person by a Word which is not simply what is written in the Bible, but is the message of the Gospel under various forms like absolution and preaching. People must attach themselves to this Word by faith, while achieving detachment from self – which includes their own piety.

The Word in question is not simply information about redemptive events in the past or about the otherness of God. For Luther it is identical with the very coming of God in the person of Jesus Christ. That is also to say that justifying faith is not simply the recognition of sin on the one hand and of righteousness from without on the other, but is union with Jesus Christ. Luther insisted a great deal on this union: not a mystical fusion of the soul with Christ, but the implantation of Christ in us by faith (*fides apprehensiva Christi* or simply *fides Christi*), producing 'the admirable and marvellous exchange' by virtue of which my sin becomes that of Christ who discharged it on the Cross, and the righteousness of Christ becomes mine.

To reiterate: only faith tied to the Word and to Christ allows someone who has been given the grace of the new righteousness to stand before God. Was that misunderstood in the sixteenth century because different people understood different things by the word 'faith'? The medieval tradition, Aquinas in particular, placed faith at the level of human reason and defined it as the acceptance of the truths of the faith, while the relation between God and a person was defined rather in terms of love. In fact, Luther made a parallel distinction: faith that is merely an acceptance of historical facts, cannot justify because demons can have that too; the faith which saves is trust. It encompasses the whole of a person. Thus Luther did introduce a new definition of faith. But is it so far removed from what Thomas Aquinas meant when he defined the relation of a person to God as love?

Another misunderstanding which arose in neo-Protestantism was the idea that faith could be a human work which a person had in some way to produce in order to be saved. Faith is not, however, human activity providing the conditions for salvation. It is God himself who through the Holy Spirit offers salvation by arousing faith. The passivity of faith must thus be stressed, faith that renounces all works before God, in order to give itself over to God alone and to his righteousness.

'Simul iustus, simul peccator'

Luther has a famous phrase which Catholic sensibility finds very difficult: he defines Christians as 'at once sinners and righteous'. This phrase has three different meanings in different writings of Luther, as the work of O.H. Pasch has clearly shown. First, it underlines that on earth the struggle between a person and sin is never finally won, a concept which all churches share. In the second sense, the formula underlines that it is only at the end of time that a person will be entirely righteous in their own being: now we are so in hope. The third meaning sheds light on this enduring state of sin. It is difficult to conceive of a man as a subject made up of various properties: just as a body cannot be at the same time hot and cold, so the same person cannot be at the same time a sinner and righteous. In scholastic terminology they are either in a state of sin or in a state of grace. According to Thomas Aquinas, one is justified, that is freed from sin, 'in an instant'. But Luther does not conceive of human sin and grace in terms of the self-exclusive properties of a subject, but in terms of relations. Sin is the relation of enmity or rupture with God; grace and righteousness that of friendship and communion with him. This perspective of seeing these terms as a matter of relations does not exclude the simultaneity in question and takes account of human experience. The Christian does

The episode of nailing up the 95 theses quickly took on a symbolic value for Protestants, who chose the year 1517 to commemorate the birth of the new faith.

Luther nailing his theses to the church at Wittenberg, painting by Hugo Vogel, end of the 19th century.

not cease sinning, even in doing good. For instance, while we may be tempted to justify ourselves by doing good, we do not in the end escape the grasp of sin. However, at the very heart of this harmful relation, and despite the sin which attaches to it, we do receive the pardon of God. We are called to believe this and affirm it in the face of sin.

Because the believer does not escape the grasp of sin we remain penitents all our lives. This is important for Luther, especially at the time of the debate over Indulgences: 'Our Lord and Master Jesus Christ has willed that all the life of the faithful should be a penitence' (Thesis 1 of the ninety-five Theses). That is to say that faith is at the same time confession of sins and confidence in forgiveness.

We must lastly consider the question of the certainty of salvation. Perhaps it was only in 1518 that Luther came to a clear view of this subject. He certainly stigmatizes 'scholastic fables' for denying that Christians can be certain whether or not they live in a state of grace. It is not for Luther a question of future salvation or the possession of grace understood as a human quality, but of the favour of God, announced to the sinner now by the Gospel. Here is the existential and relational perspective so typical of Luther. It means that the believer receives the certainty of salvation by their own faith in receiving the pardon of God. Luther distinguishes this from a false security which would do away with the struggle against doubt and sin. He sees it no longer as an inalienable possession, for faith is always threatened. Lastly, he distinguishes it from the psychological experience of consolation, a subjective experience which can weaken or even disappear, and which does not necesarily involve any connection with faith and grace.

The breach

In essence, these themes are already found in Luther's writings before the debate on Indulgences, but it was that affair which from 1517 set in motion the process which led to the break. Luther's first commentaries, only recently printed for the first time, are above all theological in nature. Practical criticism scarcely went beyond what was already in the air, and ecclesiological problems were not prominent. But it is fair to say that a certain type of Church, based above all on the simple preaching of the Gospel, flows naturally from what he affirms about justification by faith. This is what was to become clear between 1517 and 1521. The key question is whether the break was inevitable. Luther's aim was to recover the original Gospel as it had been before it was hidden by the deformed theology of the medieval tradition. But when confronted by the ideas which Luther conceived in connection with the business of Indulgences, representatives of the traditional Church considered that these ideas would lead, as Cajetan suggested, to 'the building of a new Church'.

The unfortunate business of Indulgences need not detain us too long, since so much has been written about the abuses they engendered. It is more important to consider the affair in the light of Luther's central intuitions. He affirmed that the practice he denounced bore upon 'the sincerity of contrition' (Thesis 40) and upon permanent penitence, which enveloped the whole of the life of a Christian since they were 'at once a sinner and righteous'. It also obscured 'the Church's real treasure', the Gospel, the only basis of faith. Luther did not question the authority of the papacy in the Church, but he considered that only those penalties imposed by the papacy or those that were canonically in order could be remitted by the papacy; by contrast the theory of Indulgences claimed that Indulgences could also remit divine punishment. Luther acknowledged that priests pronounced pardon and did not minimize their role as agents of God in this. But he put Indulgences into perspective: 'Full remission of penalty and fault is due to any repentant Christian, even without a letter of Indulgence' (Thesis 36). The ethical significance of justification by faith is also shown by a new scale of values: 'Those who give to the poor or lend to those in need do better than if they bought Indulgences' (Thesis 43).

Many Catholic theologians today say that none of these theses are heretical, that some could and should be the subject of debate, and that the whole constitutes a justifiable critique of the abuses connected with Indulgences. Nevertheless, a process had been set in motion. Luther's first opponents, Tetzel and Eck, did not keep the debate on the level of Indulgences or that of Christian life in general. They raised the problem of the authority of the papacy and that of the sacraments in the Church, trying particularly to show that Luther was reviving the heresy of Johann Hus.

Towards the end of 1517, Luther was denounced to Rome by Archbishop Albert of Mainz. The investigation turned into a charge of heresy and offence to papal dignity. But instead of summoning Luther to Rome, the Pope ordered Cardinal Cajetan to hear the case and obtain a retraction from this Augustinian monk. This

Erhart Schön joined in the struggle for reform through his pictures. He attacked the Roman clergy in this engraving showing a monk whose nose serves as bagpipes for the Devil.

The Devil with bagpipes, a satirical wood engraving by Erhart Schön, c. 1525.

The quarrel about Indulgences issued very quickly in a widespread questioning of pontifical authority and of the sacraments. This enlargement of the debate was as much the work of the Lutherans as of their opponents, such as the Dominican Johannes Tetzel, whose preaching of Indulgences had aroused first Luther's indignation and then his revolt.

Portrait of Johannes Tetzel, 17th-century engraving.

The Quarrel about Indulgences, wood engraving by Hans Holbein the Younger, first half of the 16th century.

was the famous interview at Augsburg of 12 to 14 October 1518, the importance of which cannot be overstressed, even though there are considerable gaps in our knowledge of the affair. The debate turned first on Indulgences and in particular on the Pope's powers in this matter. Luther restricted these powers to the domain of the Church and its discipline, making a firm separation between the actions of the Pope and the merits of Christ. These latter act directly on the inner man without the mediation of the Pope. Instead of withdrawing his objections, as Cajetan demanded, Luther pressed on to enquire about the doctrinal and particularly the scriptural basis for the theory of Indulgences and the powers accorded to the Pope. The scriptural basis was very suspect: that the 'treasure' mentioned in certain parables (Luke 19.20 and Matthew 13.44) must have been confided to Peter! Only the notion that the magisterium could interpret Scripture and even add to it in an infallible way could give any authority to the doctrine of Indulgences. Luther wished to eliminate neither the ministry nor the magisterium in the interests of the sole authority of Scripture, any more than Cajetan wished to eliminate Scripture in the interests of the sole authority of the magisterium. What was in question was the principle of accepting Scripture as the critical norm which the doctrinal judgement of the magisterium had to take into account. Luther resisted Cajetan in the same way that he resisted the injunctions served upon him at Worms, that is to say in the name of the authority of Holy Scripture, that truth which is 'mistress even of the Pope'.

The confrontation with Cajetan bears on another point too: the certainty of salvation. Was it necessary, asked Cajetan, as a good Thomist denying that one could be sure of being in a state of grace, to have the certainty that God pardons one personally, in order for the sacrament of penitence to effect salvation? Luther answered passionately: how could one be content with a general faith in the efficacy of the sacraments while everything pointed to the requirement of personal certainty? Could the Church and the magisterium put in question this certainty, which was tied to the very Gospel of grace? Luther saw a great gulf between the Word of God transmitted by Scripture and proclaimed by the Church, and the Church itself as an institution, at least its magisterium. To revoke his theses would be to abandon what had made him a Christian. Sadly he discovered that salvific communion with God was not identical with communion with a visible Church unless it depended on the very Word of God transmitted to us by Scripture.

The breach widens

Everyone knows how Luther, with this perspective, became more and more critical of the Papacy. Appealing to a General Council on 28 November 1518, he affirmed that the primacy of Rome was merely 'of human law', established in the course of history. The obedience owed to the Pope was of the same kind as that owed to temporal authorities. In 1520, especially after the bull *Exsurge Domine*, the suspicion, implicit in his earlier writings, was clearly expressed: since the institution

of the papacy is subservient to Holy Scripture, it must be regarded as the Antichrist predicted in Holy Scripture.

Luther was not impressed by Councils either. At the disputation at Leipzig with John Eck in July 1519, he came to the conclusion that General Councils could also err, so that the only infallible authority for Christians was Holy Scripture.

The pattern of events between 1518 and 1521 is well known. There were political reasons behind Rome's slowness to act, and, besides, it took time to become alarmed about Luther. On the theological level his opinions were first condemned by the theological faculties of Cologne and Louvain in 1519. On 15 June 1520 Rome promulgated the bull *Exsurge Domine*. Forty-one of Luther's propositions were condemned, and he was ordered to retract within sixty days under pain of excommunication. Some of the propositions condemned were: 'To deny that sin dwells in an infant after baptism is to trample under foot both Paul and Christ' (2); 'In every good work, the Christian sins' (31); 'Free will, after sin, is nothing but a phrase; and when it acts in its own power it commits mortal sin' (35); 'The Roman Pontiff, successor of Peter, is not the Vicar of Christ, established by Christ himself in the person of Peter over all the churches throughout the entire world' (25); 'It is certain that it is in no way in the power of the Church or the Pope to establish articles of faith, and even less laws about behaviour or good works' (27); 'The remission of sins and the gift of grace are not enough: there must be belief that sin

There were two ways into Christ's sheepfold: through the roof, the illegitimate way, after having kissed the Pope's feet; or through the door, where believers are received by Christ and by a layman holding the keys, signifying the priesthood of all believers. Behind, the Good Shepherd assembles his flock around the Cross.

Christ's Sheepfold, an allegorical wood engraving, 16th century.

Caricature against monks and papists, wood engraving, 16th century.

At Augsburg, in October 1518, Cardinal Cajetan tried to obtain Luther's retraction. This important interview, in the course of which the two men confronted each other over the question of the powers of the Pope, ended with Luther's refusal to close ranks. The breach had begun to open and would soon become permanent.

Luther and Cajetan, wood engraving taken from *Historien der Heyligen Ausserwaehlten Gottes Zeugen*, by Ludwig Robus, Strasburg, 1557.

has been forgiven' (10). The affirmations were certainly made by Luther, but the bull was hardly satisfactory. It qualified propositions as heretical or scandalous, but did not make clear what was considered heresy, what scandal, and what scholastic opinion. However, the process that had been set in motion concluded on 3 January 1521 with the excommunication of Luther and his supporters by the bull *Decet Romanum Pontificem*.

Between 1963 and 1971, in line with the very positive way many modern Catholic historians and theologians have judged Luther, the question of lifting the excommunication of Luther was considered — and cut short by Rome with a negative. Luther's intentions may have been pure and he may not have been properly listened to by the Church of his time. But, in fact, beyond the person of Luther there is a whole theological controversy (made worse by writings of Luther's that appeared after *Exsurge Domine*), which does not seem to be really settled, even if many of Luther's affirmations are considered by Catholic students of Luther today as compatible with the Catholic faith. The hierarchy of the Catholic Church has not really progressed beyond the position of Lortz: Luther is considered as an important person in the history of religion who 'has kept a considerable amount of the riches of the ancient Catholic faith. . . . and can be considered as our common master' (Willebrands). But his 'subjectivism' is regretted. His ideas about the Church, the ministry, and above all the papacy continue to be rejected, quite apart from the way in which Luther's heirs have, in the eyes of Rome, dug the trench even deeper, at least until the twentieth century.

The Reformation treatises of 1520

Several works written in 1520 express in classic fashion Luther's great themes, for the attention of not only theologians but also the general public. As Luther had been reproached for devaluing good works and calling people to faith alone, he brought out in June of that year one of his best monographs, a treatise entitled *On Good Works*, which went through eight editions in the course of that year.

It is a good work, Luther affirmed, if an act is accomplished in faith, that is to say when people give up seeking their own interest, or even their own salvation, in order to conform solely to the will of God whom they love as a child loves its father. The first commandment — to have no other gods — is the basis of all the others, and 'the first and supreme good work, the most noble of all, is faith in Christ'. Faith alone makes a work specifically Christian, 'for all other works can be accomplished also by a pagan, a Jew, a Turk, a sinner'.

Faith, that is to say, the heart's confidence in God, can be present in the most humble acts of daily life. The Christian has no need to take up extraordinary works or specific religious acts such as pilgrimages but should not neglect what in accordance with the will of God serves to promote the life of one's neighbour. In the context of faith every work is good 'even if it is as little a thing as picking up a wisp of straw'. According to Luther, the Spirit of Christ present in the life of the believer renders him capable of discernment and frees him from exterior constraints, whether those of an ecclesiastical magisterium, a social contract or some moral code. 'A

Christian who lives by faith has no need to be taught good works: on the contrary, whatsoever is presented to him, he does.'

Continuing through the other commandments, Luther shows how the Christian fulfils them in the spirit that has been thus enunciated. Only the believer truly honours God (second Commandment) by acknowledging that all they have and are comes from him. God's honour is defended by the affirmation of truth and justice over heresy and injustice, even though that can lead to martyrdom. In connection with the sanctification of the day of rest (third Commandment), Luther insists on participation in belief at the Eucharist, characterized by 'being thirsty for divine grace and wishing to be freed from one's sins', on preaching which makes one aware of sins and arouses the desire to be forgiven, and on prayer which needs few words. The prayer of the community is 'precious and efficacious'. He also legitimizes fasting as a personal discipline for the believer in the struggle against one's own flesh. Obedience due to parents (fourth Commandment) is extended to ecclesiastical and civil authorities, but in the case of 'intolerable excesses committed in the name of God . . . we have in truth the duty of resisting in all righteousness as far as we are able; and in this case we must act like upright children whose parents have become mad or insane'. His commentary on the other commandments is more summary. A positive orientation predominates: faith in God, who is gracious, leads the believer to be merciful to his neighbour. A Christian must not only avoid bearing false witness, but must also witness to the truth.

In August 1520 another of Luther's writings appeared, certainly one of the best known: *To the Christian Nobility of the German Nation*. It was in some degree the agenda for a Council which Luther was summoning. In the first part, Luther wanted to act like Joshua before Jericho: to sound the trumpet so that the enemy walls should crumble. He takes his stand first on the distinction that was established between the ecclesiastical state and the lay state, and affirms that the only differences between Christians are functional ones. He then criticizes the Romanist pretensions 'to be the sole masters of Scripture' and to make people believe 'that the Pope cannot

Evangelical preachers truly work in God's vineyard, while Catholic clergy only exploit it: such is the moral of this work by Cranach, which shows Luther with a rake and Melanchthon, anxious to go back to the right sources like every good humanist, occupied with drawing water from the well. Meanwhile Christ is addressing the Pope, the bishops and the monks to try to persuade them to change their way of life.

Luther in the Vineyard, painting by Lucas Cranach the Elder. Church of St Mary, Wittenberg.

93

err in the domain of faith'. 'Since we are all priests and have only one faith, one Gospel, one set of sacraments, how could we not also have the power to appreciate and to judge what is true and what is false in the domain of faith?' Finally, on the basis of this universal priesthood which he has affirmed, Luther appeals to the general body of Christians, and in particular to the temporal authorities, to work for the calling of a General Council.

In the rest of the treatise Luther sets out a certain number of reforms which he would like to see tackled by a Council, taking up the traditional idea of a Reformation of the Church 'in its head and in its members'. It would involve a commitment to restore the Pope and the prelates to the simplicity of apostolic life, to reject the theocratic pretensions of the Papacy, to reduce the number of religious orders, to abrogate life vows, to abolish the obligation of celibacy for the secular clergy, and to suppress institutions such as masses for the dead, interdicts, patronal festivals, the different dispensations and letters of Indulgence issued from Rome, and the excrescences on the cult of saints, in particular their canonization. The last propositions preach reform of the schools of public assistance and of the universities. The emphasis on Aristotle must be reduced, but that on Latin, Greek, Hebrew, mathematics and history should be increased. Canon law should be suppressed. At all levels of teaching it should be Holy Scripture that is taught above all. Luther also criticized the Germans' fondness for luxurious clothing, their taste for feasting and drinking bouts, and the sinister role played by the large commercial companies.

Not all in this treatise was new. But as far as it took up ideas that were in the air and touched on very concrete problems in the Church and society of his time, Luther could count on having a great success. Not everyone, however, perceived the vision of the Gospel and the faith which lay behind this writing and all that came from Luther's pen.

Another study was more theological in tone and was, moreover, written in Latin: *De captivitate Babylonica*. It too dealt with freeing the Church from the pernicious domination of false teaching, particularly the grip which Rome exercised over Christendom regarding the understanding and practice of the sacraments. Luther pleads for the laity to have access to both kinds of Eucharist, and criticizes the doctrine of transubstantiation, but without questioning the real presence of the body and blood of Christ. Finally, he castigates the impious way in which he thinks 'the mass is considered a good work and a sacrifice'. The Eucharist is not something that humanity brings to God, but it transmits to man the gift of God in the form of the promise of salvation and the sign attached to that promise, that is to say the body and blood of Christ present in the bread and wine. So it is faith which is needed in order to participate in the mass in a way that saves: personal faith, which excludes votive masses but not intercession for the living and the dead. Luther would root out of the canon of the mass everything that implies the concept of sacrifice, without however excluding the idea that the believer ought to respond to the gift of God with prayer and personal action.

The baptism of children is considered efficacious in so far as it expresses 'the truth of God which will guard (the believer), so much so that if everything else was to break down this promise at least would not fail'. Christians must always come back to their baptism and not rely on penitence as a kind of second plank of salvation. But baptism only works if there is faith. It signifies death and resurrection. To believe is to enact for the whole of one's life what baptism signifies. Luther talks of the mysterious attribution of faith to children by the Holy Spirit, and also of the role of the intercession of the Church to bring this faith to birth.

It must be stressed that Luther recognizes the legitimacy and utility of private confession as a remedy for an unquiet conscience which opens up to a Christian brother or sister, not necessarily to a priest, and receives in return the Word of salvation. But this is not strictly a sacrament, and this restriction of the term goes also for the other ceremonies considered by traditional Catholicism as sacraments. Ordination is a certain way of entrusting a ministry to certain people, it being understood that the principal task of the priest is to preach and not to hallow churches and bells or to confirm children.

A new vision of the Church is thus sketched out here. It is no longer a sacramental organism enclosing Christians from cradle to grave, but the communion of believers who share in the good things dispensed by Christ, by means of the Gospel which is proclaimed, and of baptism and the Eucharist. The Church has not been suppressed in the interests of individualism nor disincarnated in favour of some invisible reality: it has been redefined and reinstated.

In October of the same year Luther recapitulated some of these ideas, in a non-polemical fashion, in *On Christian liberty*, addressed to Pope Leo X. It is extant

in a German and a Latin version. It is certainly one of his most famous writings, but there are some problems in its interpretation. How does a person become a Christian or how are they one? Once more this is Luther's basic preoccupation. The answer is, whatever makes a person 'righteous, free, and truly Christian, that is to say a spiritual, new, inner man'. That refers neither to exterior practices nor to a given social or personal condition, but to the Word of God. 'The soul can do without everything except the Word of God.' Faith comes in at the point when the soul becomes incandescent like iron heated on the fire. The person becomes a new creature. Luther also describes faith as union with Christ, using the traditional image of the link between husband and wife, and says that the union permits a 'happy exchange': man gives Christ his sin and receives from him righteousness.

He next describes what the liberty thus received by the believer means existentially: a royal liberty in so far as the Christian is master of all things, including suffering and death. 'There is nothing, from the best to the worst, which does not conduce to my happiness, if only I believe.' It is a priestly liberty too, allowing each believer to approach God directly and with confidence, as priests do.

But at the same time as faith makes people totally free, so they also freely consent to put themselves under constraints. That is the purport of the second part of the treatise. First there is the whole domain of the personal discipline of the believer. Christians are not totally spirit here below, but contend with the weaknesses of the old Adam, and so must submit themselves to fasting, watches, and bodily discipline. Salvation is not thereby attained, because that has already been gratefully received, but they make the outer man conform to the inner man and fit the body for the service of one's neighbour. That is in fact the other form of submission, the service of other people after the example of Christ whose love we must pass on ('we are Christ for one another'). From this perspective Christians will even submit to laws and ceremonies which they do not need themselves, but which they accept in order to show solidarity with others and to give an example.

Luther certainly insists on faith as the only source of justification and gives a relatively small place to good works, but he urges that there be no confusion between liberty and licence. 'Faith in Christ, in fact, does not free us from good works, but from our opinion about them: from the foolish presumption that we can seek to be justified by doing them.'

The spread of the message in Germany

The relationship between Luther's message and printing is well known, and the Reformation has been dubbed 'the daughter of printing'. Until then, what was written, practically always in Latin, was reserved for the élite. Now it was going to mobilize the crowd. It was not that the number of those who could read had risen sharply, but that writings acted on the crowd through the mediation of preachers. Moreover, some printed works, such as pamphlets, were read aloud to groups of listeners.

Luther's writings are undoubtedly the most important printed texts associated with the evangelical movement. Even in his own lifetime there were about 4,000 editions or further impressions of his different works. A third of the German literature of that time came from his pen. His first great success was the *Sermon on Indulgence and Grace* (1517), which went through twenty-two editions between 1518 and 1520. Thirty writings in similar vein, published between 1517 and 1520, were reprinted 370 times in total, which means about 250,000 copies. *The Address to the Christian Nobility* was reprinted thirteen times in 1520 alone. As a rule there were between 1,000 and 1,500 copies in each impression, but the first edition of the *Address* saw 4,000 copies sold out in a week! Obviously Luther's role must not obscure the literary activities of the other 'evangelical' authors: Zwingli published his first evangelical writing in April 1522, Bucer his in 1532, and the *Christian Apology* of the Strasburg preacher Matthew Zell appeared in 1523. Even before that other authors were at work, publishing mainly pamphlets: one of the first in support of Luther came from the pen of Spengler of Nuremberg and dates from 1519. The anonymous *Karsthans* appeared at Strasburg in 1521, praising what Luther had done for the laity, and went through several editions.

However important the role of printing, the preachers played a more decisive part. They certainly attracted the crowds. The Reformation could be defined as the emergence of a new sort of preaching. Most often they were former monks who left their monasteries and found work as preachers. Pellican, who preached at Basle, and Myconius, at Gotha, were former Franciscans; Bucer, who worked at Wissenburg and then at Strasburg, was a Dominican; Brunfels from Strasburg, a Carthusian; Ambrose Blaurer, a Benedictine. Augustinians provided their contingent of

3 ¶ Getruckt zu Leypßgk durch Wolffgäg Stöckel im iar.1520.

'evangelical' preachers like Zwilling at Wittenberg or Prugner at Mulhouse. But there were members of the secular clergy too, incumbents or preachers established in a parish before the emergence of Luther, like Matthew Zell at Strasburg. These 'evangelical' preachers were above all at work in the towns, being particularly numerous in the south, at Nuremberg, Augsburg, Constance, Nordlingen, Ulm and Strasburg. But the evangelical message also resounded in the halls of knights: thus Bucer worked for a time at the castle of Franz von Sickingen.

The evangelical movement

Between 1521 and 1525-6 the Empire was thrown into agitation by what historians call in general 'the evangelical movement'. It was not yet the Evangelical Church, but it was already more than a simple movement of opinion. Changes took place at the level of worship and even of institutions. But it was after 1525 that the breach with the traditional Church really institutionalized itself into the territorial churches which were being set up almost everywhere.

About 1521, the evangelical movement definitely cristallized around the message and person of Luther. He was clearly responding to a number of aspirations diffused through the society of his country and his time. Around 1519 the humanists had already let fly with superlatives: 'inspired angel of God', Melanchthon said of him in that year; Crotus Rubeanus described him as *pater patriae*, worthy to be represented in statues of gold; Hedion called him 'saviour and guide'. A pamphlet which appeared just before the Diet of Worms likened his history to the passion of Christ.

In 1521 Luther was summoned to the Diet of Worms, where he was to meet the new Emperor Charles V. The almost triumphal journey that Luther made to Worms and the story of his appearance before the diet on 17 and 18 April are well known. But the exact words of the declaration he made, which showed so well how far he had travelled, bear repeating: 'Unless I am proved wrong by the witness of Scripture or by evident reason – for I believe neither in the infallibility of the Pope nor in that of Councils, since it is established that these have often made mistakes and contradictions – I am tied by the biblical texts which I have cited. I am a prisoner in conscience to the Word of God, and so I cannot retract and I will not retract. To go against the conscience is neither safe nor right. God help me. Amen.'

Luther's proclamation reverberated through the testimony of eye-witnesses and then pamphlets and kindled many spirits. A man had claimed to be attached to the authority of the Word of God alone and had in public asserted the relative unimportance of all who claimed to come between God and the believer's conscience.

In 1521 Luther was summoned before the Imperial Diet at Worms, where he again refused to retract. In the Lutheran consciousness this famous episode, where one man on his own, at peril of his life, stood up to the power of the Pope and the world, took on a heroic character.

Luther before the Diet of Worms, painting by Anton von Werner, 19th century. Staatgalerie, Stuttgart.

The Edict of Worms, promulgated on 26 May, exiled Luther from the Empire and all his writings were ordered to be burnt. But that was not going to stop the evangelical movement spreading.

But what was it really all about? Was it a sectarian attachment to the personality of Luther or was it a vast movement of religious and even social and political reformation of which he was only the most conspicuous spokesman? John Eck was already talking of 'Lutherans' in 1520, and Jerome Enser, another of Luther's adversaries, spoke in 1522 of 'Martinians'. This was certainly a case of particularizing and personalizing the movement by employing a sectarian perspective. Luther defended himself over this in 1522: 'I beg people to have the goodness not to use my name and not to call themselves "Lutherans" but "Christians". For what is Luther? This doctrine in no way belongs to me; I have not been crucified for anyone . . . It is the papists who rightly bear a partisan name, since they are not satisfied with the teaching and name of Christ, but wish to be also the Pope's disciples. As for me, I am no one's master nor do I wish to be. I share with the whole community this common and unique teaching of Christ who alone is our Master.'

The sources show that evangelical preachers were constantly striving to say that they were not simply partisans of Luther, but that they were announcing the Gospel, basing themselves on Holy Scripture, without thereby denying that Luther had rediscovered the Gospel in a convincing way. All through the century the Churches which issued from the Lutheran Reformation refused to call themselves 'Lutheran', seeing this as a term of abuse emanating from their opponents. For instance, the *Defence of the Confession of Augsburg* of 1530 says: 'Our opponents describe this dear and holy Gospel as 'Lutheran' because it is concerned with true penitence, with the fear of God, with faith and its nature, with the knowledge of Christ, with the righteousness which comes from faith.' The term 'evangelical' was accordingly preferred, qualified from 1530 by the title of the confession of faith which expressed 'Lutheran' convictions, the Confession of Augsburg. It was only in the seventeenth century, the era of orthodoxies and confessionalism, that hesitations about speaking of 'the Lutheran Church' fell away.

Soon, however, Luther was not fighting alone: his message was heard and taken up by numerous preachers, the most celebrated of whom are represented here by Cranach. From left to right, Paul Eber, J. Forster, John Bugenhagen, Erasmus (who of course remained faithful to Rome!), Justus Jonas, K. Kruziger, and Melanchton.

The Group of Reformers, copy of the painting by Lucas Cranach the Elder. St Blaise, Nordhausen.

Luther's disciples and collaborators

However predominant Luther's role may have been, other men must be mentioned. In Luther's immediate entourage the roles played by Nicolas von Amsdorf, Justus Jonas, Bugenhagen, Spalatin, and above all Melanchthon, were not negligible. The

This caricature taken from a pamphlet written by Luther and Melanchthon symbolizes the papacy. The ass's head is as out of place on this body as the Pope is at the head of the Church. The left foot alludes to the rapacity of the Catholic clergy, the elephant's arm to the crushing domination of souls, the old man's face turned backwards to the coming end of the Pope who looks to the past. As for the tail in the form of a dragon's head, it spits fire in the same way that Rome spits out bulls, edicts and condemnations.

Wood engraving taken from *Concerning Two Monster Prodigies, to wit an ass Pope . . . and a calf monk*, Geneva, 1557. Bibliothèque Nationale, Paris.

last named published the first Protestant dogmatic work in 1521, the *Loci communes*, and did much thereafter to try to reconcile humanism and the Reformation. He was also a link with the Swiss Reformation, particularly with Calvin.

Beyond Wittenberg itself there was a crowd of evangelical preachers, some of whose names have already been mentioned. Martin Bucer from Strasburg stands out especially among them, a theologian who gave importance to the Holy Spirit and to the new Law and obedience incumbent upon the Christian, a man very keen on organizing the evangelical Church well and establishing its discipline. At the cost of a certain amount of manoeuvring he made efforts to reconcile the positions of Luther and Zwingli. So he too constitutes a link between the Lutheran type of Reformation and the Swiss Reforms, even more so because Calvin spent three years in Strasburg between 1538 and 1541.

There are differences of emphasis among the evangelical preachers between 1521 and 1525. Certainly the main themes of the Wittenberg master were taken up: justification by faith, the priesthood of believers, the authority of Holy Scripture. But each writer had certain specific emphases; for instance the urban Reformers underlined, more than Luther did, the changes that they thought would promote communal life. Men like Zell and Bucer showered less abuse on legalism than on the attitudes and institutions which worked against love. Divergences also appeared on the subject of the sacraments, which men like Carlstadt understood in a more spiritual manner than Luther did, and on the images in churches, whose destruction was advocated in some sermons.

Lay preachers also emerged between 1521 and 1525, often untrained, but full of zeal since Luther had preached the universal priesthood and because they had a great deal to say. Thus Clement Ziegler, the market gardener from Strasburg, did not hesitate to claim the direct inspiration of the Holy Spirit to justify his preaching in the city, as he had among the peasants in the Obernai region. He denounced the veneration of images and the cult of the saints, rejected the baptism of infants, and gave a relatively low status to the Lord's Supper. He also criticized the system of tithes and preached a more fraternal society where men and women would be truly free and share equally in the world's goods. The fuse had thus been lit which would explode in the peasant uprising.

The first changes affected the mode of life and the status of the clergy. Monasteries emptied after 1521, above all those which had been brought back to their proper observances. Many of the clergy married. Once they became possessed of civil rights they took over from the civil authorities. There were changes in worship too: in places like Strasburg baptism and the Lord's Supper were celebrated in German, and in 1524 the Lord's Supper was received in both kinds. At Wittenberg and elsewhere the Eucharistic liturgy was purged of everything which could evoke a sacrificial concept of the mass.

Here Jesus is baptized in the Pregnitz at the gates of Nuremberg. Present are Johann Hus, Luther, Melanchthon, Justus Jonas and Erasmus. To the left, Frederick the Wise and John the Constant, Electors of Saxony.

The Baptism of Christ and the Evangelical Preachers, 16th-century engraving. Bibliothèque Nationale, Paris.

These changes excited a debate which was often difficult, even among the followers of the evangelical movement. Carlstadt, Luther's colleague at Wittenberg, thought that progress should be rapid, just as a knife is seized out of a child's hand. At Christmas 1521, in Luther's absence, he celebrated a German mass which was considerably truncated and had no preliminary confession. Luther wished to go less far and less fast, and above all considered that it was first necessary to preach and to convince intellectually. There was also discussion about who should give the lead to the changes: was it to be the impatient voice of the multitude, ready to destroy images and even to lay the blame on certain clergy? And should the preachers act with the temporal authorities or on their own initiative?

The question of violence and revolt emerged in 1521 in a number of places. Clearly Luther's message was putting a light to powder. There were outbursts of iconoclasm, at Wittenberg for example at the beginning of 1522. Another fire broke out the same year in the form of a revolt of the imperial knights, a social class which was losing importance. Led by Franz von Sickingen, they thought the way to respond to Luther's appeal to the nobility was to fight for freedom and justice for Germans. Their foe was above all the Roman Church, and particularly the princes of the Church with their properties and territorial power. But Sickingen's invasion of the lands of the Archbishop of Trier failed pitifully. Besides, Luther had distanced himself from the use of violence by the evangelical movement when he published his *Sincere Admonition to all Christians to keep themselves from all uprising and revolt* in 1522.

German society and the message of Luther

The success of Luther's message can be explained in various ways. At first he took up criticisms made of the traditional Church for decades, stigmatizing its abuses with a new perspective and new vigour. But then he had to go further. His message was also a response to genuinely religious reflections concerned with assurance in the face of death and judgement, and was concerned with a more direct access to God and with investing the world with a sense of the sacred. Luther's progress attracted attention due to the forms of religious living which it proposed and which seemed to correspond to certain desires: the upgrading of preaching, worship in the common tongue, a certain questioning of exterior elements of the faith, together with an insistence on inner piety, and new attention paid to the Bible.

There is an evident correlation between the mentalities of different layers of society and the message in question. This holds true, in the first instance, for the towns. In more than fifty of the eighty-five free cities of the Empire, the Reformation took root. It was here that printing and reading took place, that humanists went about their business and that the evangelical preachers gave their sermons. There was

It is possible that Dürer's *Knight* represents Franz von Sickingen, the former mercenary who protected Luther at the Diet of Worms and then headed the revolt of the imperial knights.

The Knight, Death and the Devil, copper engraving by Albrecht Dürer, 1513.

a more or less latent conflict between the burghers and the traditional Church, which seemed like a foreign power in the cities. Luther's message incited lay people to take church affairs into their own hands, since they were in a position to judge the teaching given and to employ or dismiss the clergy. Once the distinction between clergy and laity was abolished, and the Church integrated into the city, the clergy became burghers subject to the municipal taxes and jurisdiction.

At the bottom of the social scale, the journeymen and their mates and the poor artisans were alive to the social resonances of the evangelical message, and to the critique of clerical immunities. They welcomed the reorganization of public assistance undertaken in towns like Strasburg (1523) and Nuremberg, which offered a certain security to the urban poor. Members of the middle classes agreed with the value put on work by Luther, with desacralization of begging and reduction in the number of holidays. They were caught by the idea of diverting the resources of secularized convents or monasteries to the common weal and to schools of public assistance, while they also called for a different use of tithes, which they proposed to devote directly to the upkeep of the pastors, instead of seeing them disappear into what they considered the over-full coffers of chapters. As for the members of the upper classes, not all were eager to change the traditional Church institutions, to which many links bound them. But even if they were not won over by the evangelical message, they were anxious for social harmony and were not displeased to see political power extended over the whole of a city, rendered possible by the new religious message.

Outside the towns, the knights, prey to an identity crisis, heard with interest the appeal addressed to the nobility. For some of them the interest lay in the possibility of getting hold of clergy possessions and secularizing them, and for others it was in recovering a leading role in the Empire. As for the peasants, in so far as they had access to the new message, they seemed to take hold of two themes in particular: on the one hand the autonomy of the laity and the local community, and on the other the idea that new rights had to be established, based above all on Scripture. Their charters, such as the *Twelve Articles*, are liberally peppered with biblical quotations.

Clerical reactions were very diverse. The dignitaries were on the whole reserved about the new movement. Among the parish clergy, assistant priests and preachers, there were some which joined, and others who would not. The regular clergy rallied to Luther, notably those of his own order, the Augustinians, as well as many other orders, especially those in monasteries that had not been Reformed. The evangelical movement offered them a new vision of the religious life, and a new social status, making possible marriage and civic office. Once more it became necessary to make an effort to take on the functions of preacher or teacher, something that appeared to have been neglected by some of the clergy of the period.

The attitude of the authorities

The Edict of Worms exiled Luther from the Empire and condemned his writings, but the Prince-Elector of Saxony took care to shelter him in the Wartburg. The authorities in the various imperial towns and territories carried out the Edict of Worms in very different ways, rigorously enough in Albertine Saxony, more leniently elsewhere. The towns of southern Germany were slow to publish the edict. Strasburg only did so on 30 September 1521, with transitory effect. In 1522 almost all the writings favourable to the evangelical movement appeared there without any indication of the printer's name. Between 1522 and 1524 the magistrate had the most violent writings issuing from both sides seized, including the *Great Lutheran Madman* by Murner (1522) and the *Apologia* by Catherine Zell defending clerical marriage (1524).

From 1522 to 1524 three diets met at Nuremberg; none took any measures which might have held up the expansion of the evangelical movement. The second diet ordered in 1523 'the preaching of the Holy Gospel according to the writings approved and accepted by the Holy Christian Church'. This edict was reissued, often in a diluted form, in towns like Zurich, Worms, Basle, Berne and Strasburg. In 1524 a sitting of the Diet of Nuremberg on 4 April insisted that the Edict of Worms was observed 'as much as possible'. It suggested the meeting of a national German council, but that was forbidden by Charles V in July.

A number of towns, such as Nuremberg, Ulm, Reutlingen, Memmingen, Constance and Strasburg, protested and concerted their opposition, particularly in a meeting held at Ulm from 6 to 12 December. Changes which conformed to the views of the evangelical movement were undertaken in the towns during the year, which the civic authorities allowed or endorsed, although they rarely took the initiative themselves. That would have

meant exposing themselves to retaliatory measures from the imperial authorities. The diets may have been of little efficacy because they were so divided, but the *Reichsregiment*, a kind of executive authority taking the place of the absent Emperor, was animated by princes hostile to the evangelical movement such as Archduke Ferdinand and Duke George of Saxony. But the fear of popular uprising and revolution seems to have restrained their desire for repression.

A number of territorial princes showed sympathy with the evangelical movement: Frederick the Wise, the Prince-Elector of Saxony, who, however, ceased only in 1522 to enlarge his collection of relics, and who waited till his deathbed in 1525 to communicate in both kinds; his co-regent, Duke John; Albert of Brandenburg, the Grand Master of the Teutonic Order and Duke of Prussia; the Landgrave Philip of Hesse; Ernest of Luneburg; and several others. Up to 1525 they merely turned a blind eye and did not come out openly in favour of the new movement. Other territories, however, such as Bavaria, the episcopal territory of Salzburg, and some bishoprics, decided to repress the new faith and made common cause.

The Habsburg territories

The fire kindled by the Augustinian monk from Wittenberg did not remain confined to Germany proper. Other countries in Europe were affected early on, beginning with territories depending directly on the Habsburgs such as Austria, the Tyrol, and the Low Countries. In 1521 a reformist writing by Vadian was printed at Vienna, where the Lutheran preacher Speratus advocated marriage rather than clerical celibacy. Sympathies for the evangelical movement appeared at the same period at St Polten and at Waidhofen. Caspar Tauber, the first evangelical martyr, was burnt at the gates of Vienna in 1524, but the sympathies of the citizens of Vienna and Lower Austria for the new movement remained alive. This was obvious in the support given in 1525 to the peasant uprising. In Upper Austria it was particularly the upper classes who were influenced. The son of the *Landeshauptmann*, Christoph Jörger, and a friend were won to Lutheranism in 1522 by reading Luther's translation of the New Testament. From that followed the employment of an evangelical preacher, Michael Stiefel, to work in Lower Austria from 1525 to 1527. Many descendants of the nobility attached themselves to the new faith, whose first martyr in Upper Austria was the assistant priest Leonard Kaiser in 1527. In the towns the bourgeoisie was also attracted, particularly at Steyr where 'Lutheran' preachers are mentioned in 1520 and 1525, and at Linz where Freisleben edited in 1524 one of Bugenhagen's writings. In Styria and Carinthia the movement had adherents in all circles. In 1526 an evangelical preacher was installed at Villach. In

2

1

Without the support of the German princes, the Reformation would undoubtedly have been nipped in the bud, as the Hussite revolt had been in the previous century. But Luther could count on the unyielding support of the joint Electors of Saxony, the two brothers Frederick the Wise (1463–1525) and John the Constant (1468–1532).

1. *Portrait of Frederick the Wise,* from the studio of Lucas Cranach the Elder. Kurpfälzisches Museum, Heidelberg.

2. *Portrait of John the Constant,* from the studio of Lucas Cranach the Elder. Kurpfälzisches Museum, Heidelberg.

There were many close links between the Reformation and humanism. In many cases, the same men took part in the two movements and the same ideas were taken up on both sides. The German translation of the Bible by Luther, a real monument of the German language, was written in the context of a return to the ancient tradition contained in the canon of Scripture. Its principal aim was to put Scripture, as the infallible authority, within reach of all believers.

Frontispiece of the *Old Testament* translated into German by Martin Luther, Wittenberg edition, 1523.

Title of the *New Testament* translated into German by Martin Luther, first edition, Wittenberg, 1522. Weimar Library.

the Tyrol the preacher Jakob Strauss exercised great influence until 1522, and was replaced for a time by another evangelical preacher, Urbanus Rhegius. In 1524 a pile of books and Lutheran treatises was discovered in the monastery at Stams. In the Tyrol also, the connection between social claims and religious ideas emerged in the peasant uprising. As for the territory of Salzburg, the archbishop succeeded with great effort in re-establishing the unity of the traditional faith.

In the Low Countries, the Lutheran movement had been prepared for by the *devotio moderna*, by humanism, and by the influence of Erasmus. Around 1520 Luther's writings were studied and reprinted in the southern provinces. In 1520 a mandate imposed by the papal legate ordered the writings of the Augustinian monk to be burnt. This was done at Louvain, and then, after the Edict of Worms, at Antwerp, Ghent and Utrecht. A circle with reformist ideas existed at Antwerp in the Augustinian monastery which had become observant and whose prior, Jacques Probst, was a former cellmate of Luther's. All the monks were imprisoned, but some were able to escape; Henri Voes and Jean Van Eschen endured martyrdom on 1 July 1523, which strengthened the new faith. As a contemporary observed: 'Should one not say that the new Religion is thereby rooted out? But the facts have shown quite the reverse, because by the constancy of the aforesaid two who have been executed at Brussels that doctrine is in the said city so planted that it will never cease.'

The work of the Antwerp printers spread remarkably: 176 different Bibles issued from their presses. In 1524 the French translation of the New Testament started by Jacques Lefèvre d'Étaples appeared there. Two years later, Jacques Van Liesvelt published the first Bible in Dutch which was strongly inspired by Luther's still incomplete translation. But the Antwerp printers also distributed Bibles in Danish, English and Spanish. And between 1525 and 1530 five writings of Luther, including the *Treatise on Good Works*, appeared in a French translation from the workshop of Martin Lempereur.

France

According to a letter sent on 14 February 1519 to Luther by the Basle printer Frobenius, '600 [copies of the works of Luther] have been sent to France and Italy; they are being bought in Paris and even the Sorbonne professors are reading them.' On 1 November 1520, a Paris student informed Zwingli that, 'at Paris there are no books sought after with more eagerness than those of Luther'.

Most of the books came from Basle, Strasburg and Antwerp. In Paris, Conrad Resch, the Basle bookseller, was active in this field until 1526. There was also the bookseller from Lyons, Jean de Vaugris and the Parisian printers: Simon du Bois, who not only printed in 1525-6 the *Epistles and Gospels*, which came out of the Meaux circle, but also works of edification by Luther, translated into French, like the *Exposition on the Magnificat* and the *Expositions on the Lord's Prayer, Creed, and Ten Commandments*. And c. 1525, Simon de Colines printed the *Prayer of Jesus Christ* in which writings of Luther figure.

Until Luther's condemnation by the *Determinatio* of the Sorbonne on 15 April 1521 his polemical works circulated freely enough, it seems, in Paris, and then gave way to works of piety. So W. Moore concluded in 1930. Higman's recent work has filled in the picture. He has shown that, as well as works of piety, 'certain fundamental theological writings of Luther were available in France much earlier than has been believed'. This was particularly the case with the famous preface to the Epistle to the Romans, completed by Luther in 1522, published in Latin at Strasburg in 1523 and in French at Paris c. 1525. French readers who were ignorant of Latin and German could then discover the essentials of Luther's thought.

Other publications including excerpts from Luther's writings must also be mentioned, such as *The Lord's Prayer and the Creed in French*, published by Farel in 1524, extracts of which were included by Louis de Berquin in his translations of Erasmus. The text by Farel and Luther is reprinted with other writings in *The Prayer of Jesus Christ* in 1525. *The Book of True and Perfect Prayer* (1528) repeats some of the passages in a condensed form.

Frenchmen like the Franciscans François Lambert and Guillaume du Moulin and the knight Anémond de Coct familiarized themselves with Luther's thought in 1523–5 while staying in Wittenberg. They helped to spread his writings in France by translating some of them and, with Farel, writing themselves some works of Lutheran inspiration. But who read these writings in France? Preachers were naturally to the fore. At Lyons a Dominican, Aimé Maigre, preached a course during Lent 1524 which expressed Luther's doctrine, in particular justification by faith. Pierre de Sébiville acted in the same way at Grenoble. According to a decree of the

Parliament of Paris in 1525 there were other propagators of the 'errors and doctrines of Luther' at work at Rheims, Orléans, Châlons, Angers, Sens and Bourges. The case of Meaux is the best known, and the beliefs of the circle gathered round the bishop, Briçonnet, still intrigue historians. The most celebrated, Lefèvre d'Étaples, has attracted most attention, but there were also men like Gérard Roussel, Michel d'Arande, Pierre Caroli and Vatable. The evangelical nature of the group at Meaux has been variously judged: does the silence of the writings emanating from the group on important points of Catholic doctrine signify a breach, or is it that the members of this evangelical tendency were resolved to remain within the Gallican Church at all costs and to renew it from within? Whichever it was, Lefèvre d'Étaples and Roussel had to take refuge at Strasburg, while Bishop Guillaume Briçonnet, Matthieu Saulnier and Martial Masurier were arraigned.

But other areas seem to have been contaminated, including the Court and the king's sister, Marguerite de Navarre, courtiers such as his doctor and his 'readers' Guillaume Cop and Pierre du Chastel, Guillaume Bude, and members of the Council like Louis de Berquin. Even the populace seems to have been touched by 'Lutheran' evangelicalism at Meaux, Noyon, Amiens, Metz, Bar-le-Duc, Châlons-sur-Marne, Vitry, Alençon, Lyons and Grenoble.

Even before 1530 the accusation of Lutheran heresy had led men to the scaffold: Jean Vallière, the Augustinian from Normandy, burnt at Paris on 8 August 1523, Jacques Pauvent from Meaux, burnt on 28 August 1526, found guilty of translating books inspired by 'Luther's sect', and Louis de Berquin, who was executed in 1529. The executions and other measures mark clearly the limits of the spread of the Lutheran movement. Having failed to win over the leading bodies of the Sorbonne and the parliaments, it was fatally wounded by the hostility of these powerful institutions.

Italy and Spain

Lutheran writings circulated in Italy from 1519, while ideas of reform were passed on by foreign students at the Italian universities. But the Lutheran movement affected certain élites rather than the mass of the people. At the beginning of the 1520s Lutheran writings were available in Pavia, according to the printer Frobenius. A letter from a German gentleman, Burchard von Schenck, to Spalatin on 19 September 1520, attests to their spread in Venice. The *Loci communes* of Melanchthon were known in the Po region, and a number of regular clergy in Venice were interested in Luther's message, such as the Franciscan martyrs Girolamo Galateo and Bartolomeo Fonzio. In 1530 an Italian translation of the New Testament appeared, the work of Bruccioli, and after that the best known adherents of the evangelical movement emerged: the Augustinian Zanchi, Peter Martyr Vermigli, and Bernardino Ochino Vergerio. The Spaniard Juan de Valdès arrived at Naples in 1532 and stimulated evangelicalism in certain circles among the nobility. In Piedmont, students of the University of Turin, such as the Frenchman Anémond de Coct, Celio Secondo Curione, Jacopo Bonello and Francesco Guerino were influenced from 1523 on. Two French students, friends of Farel, arrived there in 1528: Jean Canaye and Émile Perrot. From that date the court at Ferrara welcomed evangelicals of various tendencies.

In Spain the evangelical movement, for which the way had been prepared to a certain degree by the mystics and by humanism, did not succeed in gaining a real foothold. Some Spaniards observed the Diet of Worms and shared the German sympathy for Luther, including Juan de Vergara, later accused of Lutheranism, who had been to Worms. As in Italy, the spread of Lutheran writings is attested in the 1520s. In 1521 Luther's commentary on the Epistle to the Galatians became the first reformist writing to be translated into Spanish. At Antwerp the treatise *On Christian Liberty* was translated and published, as were other writings including Luther's small work *That Jesus Christ was Born a Jew* (1523), which was spread by Spanish Marranos. These writings at first made their way to Spain by sea, principally through the interest of the bookseller Peter Vilman of Antwerp who had branches in Medina del Campo and Seville. But later a watch on Spanish ports meant that they had to be transported by land, by way of Lyons. Little is known about the appearance of evangelical circles, notably in Seville, which were later wiped out. After 1530 there were Spaniards such as Francisco de Enzinas and Juan Diaz who were influenced by the new message outside Spain.

DETERMI

natio Facultatis Theologie Pari- *a De qui-*
fienfis, fuper aliquibus propofitio *bus Ptolo-*
nibus, certis è *a* locis nuper ad eam *meus 19 t.*
delatis, de ueneratione fanctorū, *bula Africe*
de canone miffæ *b* deque fuftenta= *b Expoli-*
tione miniftrorum altaris, & *c* cete *tio.*
ris quibufdam: cū familiari expo- *c Accli-*
fitione, in qua Hereticorum ratio *matio. & ē*
nes confutantur. *phrafis M.*
N. ceteris
quibufdam
p alijs qui-
bufdam.

M. D. XXIIII.

In France Luther's works were fairly freely available until the Reformer was condemned by the theologians of the Sorbonne in their *Determinatio* of 15 April 1521. They were read and commented on by Lefèvre d'Étaples and the other humanists of the circle at Meaux grouped round Bishop Guillaume Briçonnet (1472-1534).

Title page of the *Determinatio Facultatis Theologiae Parisiensis*, 1524 edition. Société de l'Histoire du Protestantisme Français, Paris.

Portrait of Bishop Briçonnet, 16th-century engraving. Bibliothèque Nationale, Paris.

England and Scotland

On 12 May 1521 Luther's books were burnt near St Paul's Cathedral in London, although they were being studied at Oxford and Cambridge. We need only mention the names of such readers as Robert Barnes, Thomas Bolney, John Frith, Thomas Cranmer, Matthew Parker, Hugh Latimer, and Nicholas Ridney. Above all there was William Tyndale, who studied at Wittenberg in 1524/5 and began there his English translation of the Bible. He incorporated into his preface to the Epistle to the Romans the famous one by Luther. Henry VIII's opposition to Luther is well known, and humanism tended to strengthen attachment to the traditional Church. Among the common people, however, the persistence of Wycliffite and Lollard ideas prepared the ground for the evangelical movement.

In Scotland the Frenchman de la Tour was condemned to death around 1525 or 1527 for having spread Lutheran writings. All through the 1520s these penetrated Scotland through the east coast ports, particularly Aberdeen, despite the interdiction imposed by Parliament in 1525. Tyndale's translation of the New Testament, which appeared at Worms in 1524, and was then reprinted at Antwerp in 1526, was widespread. The spread of the Reformation through preaching entered an active phase in 1525 through the efforts of Patrick Hamilton, who was executed in February 1528. The Scottish Reformation, still restricted to university and aristocratic circles, drew its inspiration from Luther for twenty years.

North-east Europe and Scandinavia

Thanks to the interest shown by the Grand Master of the Teutonic Order, Albert of Brandenburg, the Lutheran movement won over Prussia. The Bishop of Samland (East Prussia) was also favourable towards Luther. The preachers Johann Briessmann and Paul Speratus established the Reformation in 1523 in the diocese of Königsberg, after which the Baltic region was affected by what went on in the towns of Danzig, Thorn, Kulm, Elbing, and above all Riga. The bourgeoisie of German origin, first to be won over, then spread the word to the Baltic populace. At Riga, however, iconoclastic excesses, for which the furrier Melchior Hoffman was reponsible, slowed down the movement, together with the archbishop's resistance and the changing of sides by the Provincial of the Teutonic Order.

In Scandinavia also the Lutheran movement made itself felt during the sixteenth century in a fairly typical symbiosis of religious and political advances. A first attempt at reform was put in hand in 1520 by King Christian II of Denmark, with the aid of Carlstadt. But, as it was directed against the clergy and nobility, it aborted, and the king lost his throne. One of his companions in exile, Hans Mikkelsen, who had taken refuge with him at Wittenberg, produced there the first Danish translation of the New Testament. The new King of Denmark found himself able, slowly it is true, to give free rein to the Reforming activity of his chaplain Hans Hausen. A diet which met at Odensee in 1526 declared that all religous teaching should be subordinate to the Scriptures, and decided that bishops should in future be consecrated by the Archbishop of Lund and not by the Pope. In the following year another diet, meeting in the same place, made the clergy dependent on the State. The evolution of the Reformation in Sweden and Finland came about in the same way. Former students of Luther at Wittenberg, the brothers Olaf and Lars Petersen (or Petri), as well as the archdeacon of Strängnas, Lars Andersen, collaborated with Gustavus Vasa, the new king of a Sweden which had become independent. Their aim was to fight against the bishops, to secularize a certain amount of ecclesiastical goods while preaching the 'pure' Word of God and keeping the traditional liturgy and the episcopate.

Eastern and south-eastern Europe

After the disputation of Leipzig, when Luther had revalued the positions taken up by Hus, all kinds of relations were established with the *Unitas Fratrum* (the Bohemian Brethren). Writings by Luther were translated into Czech and Czech students were trained at Wittenberg (twenty-nine in 1520, eighty-eight in 1530). At Iglau, in Moravia, Paul Speratus preached Lutheran doctrine in 1522, but later Zwinglian and Anabaptist influences proved stronger.

In Hungary the Archbishop of Estergom had ordered, no doubt out of necessity, that the bull exiling Luther should be read in the main towns of the country. The first propagandists of the movement were foreigners, between 1518 and 1525, but there were also some indigenous clergy. One of them, at Buda, was Simon Gryneus, who had lost his post of professor at Vienna. The royal Court at Buda showed

sympathy with the Lutheran cause to the point of making Hungarian Reformers like Conrad Cordatus and Johann Henckel Court preachers. Merchants who frequented the markets of Cracow, Vienna, Breslau, Leipzig and both Frankfurts spread the new ideas and the writings of the Lutheran movement. Even before the fateful battle of Mohacz (1526), the German bourgeoisie of certain towns like Sopron and Leutschau took up the cause of the Reformation. Twenty Hungarian students matriculated at Wittenberg between 1522 and 1530, including Matthias Biró Dévay, a former Franciscan who won the name of 'the Hungarian Luther'. But the Magyar population, particularly the nobility, showed considerable reserve about this foreign influence, which they considered to have a pernicious effect on the young king. After the defeat of Mohacz and despite the hostility of the two rival kings and of the hierarchy of the traditional Church, the Reformation continued to spread, thanks to the appointment of itinerant preachers and the burgeoning of a whole literature of evangelical inspiration.

Opposition to Luther

The wide stream of the evangelical movement was composed of very different currents. Between 1521 and 1525 certain of Luther's adherents distanced themselves because they wished to go faster and farther than their master. They are often known as 'radicals', 'Dissenters', 'Nonconformists', 'Anabaptists', or even as 'the left wing of the Reformation', but none of these appellations are totally convincing, for the steps taken or proposed by Carlstadt, Müntzer, or the Anabaptists did not overlap at all points, not to mention those like Sebastian Franck and Schwenckfeld who held a 'spiritual' interpretation of Christianity and who became noticeable at the end of the 1520s.

After the troubles at Wittenberg and Luther's return, Carlstadt left the town for Orlamünde. Calling for the priesthood of all believers, he affirmed the faith of simple folk there and their place in the common life. He was opposed to Luther both in his rejection of images in churches and in questioning the real presence of Christ in the Eucharist. Generally he preached an immediate experience of God through *Gelassenheit*, ascesis, and meditation on Christ crucified, but gave only a relative value to exterior means of grace. Carlstadt was opposed by Luther and, after many wanderings, finished his life as a professor at Basle.

More serious was the conflict between Luther and Thomas Müntzer, who had been a partisan of the evangelical movement from its first days, but who was led by the 'illuminati' of Zwickau, those who had 'seen the light', towards the notion that God speaks directly to people through dreams, visions, and ecstasies. He became a preacher at Allstedt, and opposed Luther more and more violently, reproaching him particularly for preaching too mild a Christ (the Christ of justification by faith), for establishing the rule of the scribes instead of that of the prophets and for not allowing the authorities to move, if necessary by force, against the impious. In his last writings Müntzer preached that only socio-political changes could make the work of God possible. It was necessary to liberate simple folk from cultural oppression by doctors of the Church who 'wished to say that they were themselves the sole judges in matters of faith, with their usurped Scripture'. This liberation implied that the simple folk should learn to read. In the second place, they should be freed from the political oppression instituted by the princes who were on the side of the scribes. Finally, it was necessary to fight against usury, taxes, and dues which confined the poor so much to the material life that they had no leisure to give themselves to the things of the Spirit.

In the spring of 1525 Müntzer saw the Day of Judgement in the peasant uprising. He took an active part in what he considered the struggle of the servants of God against the impious, signing his inflammatory calls to arms 'Müntzer, armed with the sword of Gideon'. But for him the Peasants' War ended in death.

More peaceable protests came from the Anabaptists, at least from the little group in Zurich who in 1525 proceeded with rebaptisms and who preached a variety of Christian community strictly separated from society. Christians should not take part in politics, nor go to war, nor take oaths. This type of Anabaptism, no doubt appearing at the same time in different centres, spread through the Empire between 1525 and 1530; it was attacked by Luther when he wrote against rebaptism in 1528, and harshly repressed by imperial laws and by the actions of the territorial authorities.

Alongside these different dissident groups there is the unique event of the Peasants' War which entered its final phase in the spring of 1525. Karl Marx called this 'the most radical fact in German history', a tragic episode which left nearly 100,000 dead. In the middle of 1524 peasants in the south of Germany banded together to demand a lowering of various dues, the abolition of serfdom, the

The climate of opinion engendered by the imprudent preaching of Luther's disciples had an unforeseen and unfortunate consequence: the peasant uprising of 1524–5. Luther, regarded by some as the sorcerer's apprentice, condemned the movement, but without however underwriting the bloody repression exercised by the princes. Many of the partisans of the Reformation lost their enthusiasm, but it then entered a phase of consolidation and institutional organization.

Peasants in arms, 16th-century German engraving.

Luther was not spared by his adversaries, who used the same weapons as he did to make their ideas triumph. When he is not decked out with a pair of horns, he is endowed with seven heads, an allusion both to the contradictions imputed to him and to the dragon of the Apocalypse.

1. *Luther with seven heads*, wood engraving taken from *Lutherus septiceps* by Johannes Cochläus, 1529. Staatliche Kunstsammlung, Weimar.

2. Caricature of Luther taken from an anti-Lutheran pamphlet, 16th century. Société de l'Histoire du Protestantisme Français, Paris.

re-establishment of ancient rights of pasturage and game, and the right of the local community to choose its own pastors. The movement was at first peaceful, but turned into an uprising when it was resisted by the ruling classes; it spread to Alsace, the Palatinate, Hesse, Thuringia, and Saxony, and devastated a number of towns. Destruction and massacres followed before it was finally crushed in May 1525.

Scholars still debate the causes: were they socio-economic or juridical? The impact of the evangelical movement is also still a matter of discussion. There had been similar risings before the sixteenth century; Gunther Franz has counted eighteen between 1423 and 1517. But Luther certainly acted as a catalyst: without meaning to, he blew on a smouldering fire, shaking the traditional authorities who until then had suppressed peasant uprisings. In certain writings like the manifesto *To the Christian Nobility* he touched on socio-economic problems such as the tithe, criticized usury as much as monopolies, and preached the secularization of the Church's possessions. His habit of referring to the Bible alone gave the peasants norms for conceiving a 'divine justice' and, finally, he gave value to the rights and duties of lay people within Christian society. The peasants therefore could feel themselves encouraged to take things in hand.

However, Luther condemned the uprising. At first he attempted to reason with both parties and to promote peace. This was in vain. Then he hardened against the peasants and argued mainly in two ways. First, he turned down the idea that the peasants' fight was a Christian one. Christian liberty alluded to in the Gospel was something other than liberation from serfdom. As for the social rights claimed by the peasants, they did not as such follow from the Bible and from the Christian faith. 'Suffering, suffering, the cross, the cross, those are the rights of Christians and there are no others.' Secondly, Luther rejected the notion that subjects could rebel against authority. Only when one had conscientious objections could one resist – with passive resistance. Luther saw in the peasant revolt the work of the devil, who wished to destroy God's good creation and stifle the Gospel.

However, during the repression Luther abused 'the tyrants thirsting for blood' and

In the Peasants' War, misery, memories of previous uprisings and anti-clerical feelings, exacerbated by the imprudent preaching of Luther's disciples, all combined to bring about the devastation of a whole region of Germany.

Pillage of the Abbey of Weissenau, engraving taken from the *Chronicle of the Peasants' War* by Abbot Murer, 1525.

asked the victorious princes to show clemency. Undoubtedly Luther's attitude, often badly misunderstood, was going to cool the ardour of some of those who had followed him from the beginning. Things certainly became clearer. Luther had saved what was essential in his eyes – the Gospel as he understood it – but there were people who had expected something else, a Reformation which affected the whole of society. Moreover, after the Peasants' War the evangelical movement was channelled into territorial churches. The time had come for pastoral inspections and ecclesiastical ordinances, and also the time for princes and civic authorities to take a definite part and actively assist in the organization of evangelical churches.

The Lutheran movement confirmed and consolidated

Until 1525 Luther and the authorities let 'the word run its course'. Finally, at Luther's request, the princes began to organize parochial inspections in their territories. This was an assumption of episcopal functions, but the hold that lay authorities had gained over certain ecclesiastical institutions before the Reformation had prefigured this kind of operation. So commissions composed of lawyers and theologians made tours of inspection from 1525 in Prussia, and from 1526 to 1530 in Hesse and Electoral Saxony, where an 'Instruction for Visitors' detailed the object of the inspection: to examine the pastors and see whether they had really shaken off 'papism', whether or not they were teaching error, whether they led an irreproachable life, and whether they were suitable for the ministry. It was necessary also to settle the question of their stipends by using existing prebends or by arranging for contributions from the faithful. Those who intended to escape from the 'Christian instruction' given by the authorities, and from the norms of evangelical doctrine, were invited to leave the territory. As Karl Holl has written, 'the regime of the territorial church was established through this instruction'. To fix catechetical norms the theologians edited doctrinal texts, including the *Little Catechism* and *Greater*

Catechism, put together by Luther in 1529, which were to transmit the Lutheran faith to many generations through to our own today. The inspections were regularly repeated but were not however permanent institutions. That is why superintendents were installed after 1530 to supervise an ecclesiastical area, and at the territorial level consistories were nominated by the prince. The superintendents were regarded by Luther as provisional bishops and indeed acquired a preponderant influence.

Besides the large territories that have been mentioned, a series of towns in northern Germany joined the Reformation camp between 1525 and 1530: Magdeburg, Stralsund, Celle, Goslar, Brunswick, Göttingen, Hamburg, Lübeck. Unlike the towns of southern Germany which had already been won for the movement, these were not imperial towns, but the link with the territorial authorities was sufficiently relaxed for the town authorities to yield to pressure from below and install churches of an evangelical type.

In the Empire a certain latitude was shown after the Diet of Speyer (1526), which no longer referred to the Edict of Worms, and authorized the States of the Empire 'to bear themselves in religious matters as they believed they could justify before God and His Imperial Majesty'. This was an open door for the advance of the Reformation. But matters became worse after the second Diet of Speyer in 1529, which was dominated by a Catholic majority. The Emperor, freed finally from the anxieties of war, insisted on the application of the Edict of Worms, on a halt to any extension of the Reformation until the next Council, and on the tolerance of Catholic worship in territories won for the new faith. The 'evangelicals' protested, which earned them the nickname of 'Protestants'.

From 1 to 4 October 1529 they strove within the framework of the Colloquy of Marburg, but without any obvious success, to overcome the disagreements which had arisen between Luther and Zwingli on the subject of the Eucharist. In June 1530 the Diet of Augsburg was held. Zwingli sent a *Fidei ratio*, but the Swiss, theoretically still members of the Empire, were absent. The representatives from Strasburg, torn between Luther and Zwingli, together with three other towns of Upper Germany, presented their own confession of faith, the Tetrapolitan. The territorial states, such as Electoral Saxony and Hesse, and also a certain number of towns, presented what was thereafter called the Confession of Augsburg, composed of twenty-six articles. This text, edited by Melanchthon, was to be the principal charter of Lutheranism – the classic expression of the evangelical faith, even – to this day.

The Confession of Augsburg (1530) constitutes the first great profession of faith of the Reformation. Inspired by the work of Luther and drawn up by Melanchthon, it keeps to a middle way, opposing the 'sacramentarians' while resisting the injunctions of Charles V, who was endeavouring to re-establish religious unity in his Empire.

The Confession of Augsburg, engraving taken from a Protestant Bible of 1620.

Zwingli

After questioning the authority of the Pope, Luther was in his turn opposed by other Protestant theologians, in the front rank of whom was Huldrych Zwingli. Although they agreed on many points, the German and the Swiss disagreed on the question of the Eucharist. As the Zurich Reformer who was very close to his people, and a deep spirit who had very decided ideas about the State as well as the Church, Zwingli is a link between the two great moments of the Reformation, between Luther and Calvin.

'Armour – that should not be feared.' Zwingli

A humanist clergyman

Huldrych Zwingli was born at Wildhaus, in the Toggenburg valley of the canton of St Gallen, on 1 January 1484. He came from a family of note, among whom the ecclesiastical state was highly revered. Life was rough in this mountain village among the alpine meadows and forests, where the winters were long – conditions which favoured a very personal culture. Young Huldrych lived in a patriotic atmosphere. 'From my earliest days', he was to write, 'I had a great love for them (his compatriots) and I always set myself to be industrious and useful in order to serve them.' The countryside impressed him and later he recalled, 'the mountains, that tragic, crushing, mysterious mass . . . which proclaims the immovable power and majesty of God while maintaining and affirming the earth as the bones do the flesh.' Later, during his ministry, he was to evoke as a countryman 'the shepherd who strikes certain sheep, pushes others, hitting them or kicking them, whistles to others, attracts them with a handful of salt, but also carries the weak ones or leaves them in the stable until they are strong enough.' Zwingli was, in short, a peasant: 'Since the beginning of the world it has been among those who work on the land that peace and virtue have flourished.'

Huldrych Zwingli was born in 1484 at Wildhaus, in the canton of St Gallen.

Zwingli's birthplace, 19th-century engraving. Bibliothèque Nationale Suisse, Berne.

Between the ages of six and ten, young Huldrych lived at Wesen, on the shores of the Lake of Wallenstadt.

This countryman, who displayed the qualities of shrewdness and intelligence often found among such people, began his studies early. At the age of six he was sent to an uncle, the dean of Wesen on Lake Wallenstadt to start his schooling. At ten, he was sent to Basle to receive instruction in the *trivium* there (in Latin, music and dialectic). After two years by the Rhine he finally went to Berne to finish his studies. There Lupulus, a high-standing humanist, helped him discover the treasures of the ancient world and perfect his Latin. He continued his studies at Vienna and then at Basle (1502–6), took his degree, and frequented humanist circles where he met Frobenius, Erasmus and Thomas Wyttenbach, from Biel, who delivered him from 'the sterile chatter of the sophists'.

On 29 September 1506 Zwingli was ordained by the Bishop of Constance and celebrated his first mass in the village of his birth. At the end of the year he became parish priest at Glarus. He was a parson in the classic tradition: one summer he could be seen at the head of a procession with the consecrated host because fine weather had come after rain. He was faithful to his calling, even though as a man of strong temperament there were deviations from his course. He wrote in 1523, 'Although I was so young, ecclesiastical functions inspired more fear than joy in me, because I knew, and have remained convinced, that I would be called to account for the blood of the sheep which would perish if I were negligent'. He was indeed a classic parson, but also a cultivated one, unlike the majority of his colleagues. At Glarus as at Einsiedeln, where he spent two years from 1516, he divided his time between his pastoral ministry and his studies, for he was an enthusiastic humanist.

Humanism had not yet become Reformation, for those who espoused it were men of study rather than men of action. What interested them in the Christian religion was less the revelation of salvation in Jesus Christ than the discovery of a religious truth concerning the human spirit in general. The humanists saw Christ as the Master and the model of morality, while the Reformers saw him as the Saviour who pardons, the one through whom eternal life is attained. *Christianismus renascens* had different meanings to the two groups.

As a humanist, Zwingli copied out for his own use the epistles of Paul in Greek. In his first parishes he kept in constant touch with the group of humanists in Basle. He was on excellent terms with Erasmus and hailed him as the man 'to whom we owe most from the point of view of the sciences and mysteries of holy scripture'. Erasmus wrote back that he 'congratulated the Swiss people . . . on what you and your friends are doing to strengthen and ennoble yourselves by serious studies and perfect behaviour.' In Zwingli's library were Erasmus' *Enchiridion*, *Colloquies*, *Complaint of peace* and *In praise of folly*. However, the paths of life of the two men had to diverge: disagreement came when Ulrich von Hutten, one of the poverty-stricken knights who had had to flee Germany, sought refuge in Basle in 1522. He was denounced by Erasmus who was affirming more and more strongly his attachment to the Roman communion. Zwingli however provided him with a refuge on an island in the Lake of Zurich, where he died after a final sad year.

Portrait of Huldrych Zwingli by Hans Asper, early 16th century. Kunstmuseum, Winterthur.

The shepherd of the Swiss people

For Zwingli politics and the Christian life went hand in hand. If the God who created the heaven and the earth, and so also Switzerland, was the first person of the Trinity, Jesus Christ, his Son, was the second, but it was all one and the same God. God who had created the Swiss also wanted them to be saved, which led to a policy of alliances with the Pope against France. Zwingli agreed with that for a time – following Cardinal Schiner.

These alliances involved the transfer of mercenary troops from one country to another as funds dictated, and the Swiss, good soldiers as they were, were very much sought after. Such a state of affairs necessarily involved the play of influences with no touch of morality about them, while foreign princes maintained recruiting agents on Swiss soil who of course worked on commission. Zwingli fought as hard as he could against these customs which, he said, were bound to demoralize the country. He had to leave his first parish, Glarus, because of this attitude. On the other hand he did go to the wars as chaplain to the Swiss troops at the battle of Marignano. Influenced by Erasmus' *Complaint of peace*, he professed pacifist ideas. An opponent of foreign wars and a war veteran, Zwingli was an advocate of a defence force to guarantee the integrity of the homeland. In 1522 he wrote a letter to his compatriots in Schwyz to denounce the evil work of engaging mercenaries, a work 'which ruins that of God to which we owe our unity, a work of which the Devil is the author'. 'The situation is grave; we are already contaminated. Religion does not exist among us. We despise God as we would a drowsy dog.'

Zwingli took up the same theme two years later, when the Reform of the Church was already under way in Zurich. Then he invoked the memory of Nicholas of Flüe, the hermit who had brought peace to the confederates in 1481. 'You are wise enough to know what good brother Nicholas of Flüe, from Unterwalden, said weightily about the Confederation. It has no oppressor to reject but *Eigennutz* (egoism or personal interest). *Eigennutz*, that is the enemy.' This appeal to the hermit of the Ranft valley shows how closely love of country and religious faith are tied in Zwingli's thought. Oskar Farner, Zwingli's biographer, described the Swiss Reformer excellently when he wrote, comparing him with Luther, 'Where Luther put the question: How shall I be saved? Zwingli said: How shall *my people* be saved?'

A thought leading to Reform

Luther's spiritual crisis is well known; Calvin's 'conversion' is obscure. What we know about Zwingli lies in between. At the beginning of his ministry in Zurich, during the summer of 1519, while he was in the Grisons, he was called back to his parish where an epidemic of plague had broken out. Devoting himself to his parishioners' needs, he caught the disease and was brought to death's door. Careful nursing cured him, and he wrote a poem, the *Pestlied*, where he paints a spiritual journey paralleling the course of the illness. His healing inspired him to write this prayer to his Lord: 'Thou hast decided that I shall not sink in the power of sin.' He understood himself to have received the pardon of God through Jesus Christ. Arthur Rich suggests this spiritual development in Zwingli went along with a new understanding of his vocation. From a humanist he had become a Reformer.

Zwingli had command of the language of philosophy and showed it on occasions,

notably in the *Treatise on God's Providence*, a sermon preached at the Colloquy of Marburg before the Landgrave of Hesse. But he is principally what might be called a theologian of revelation. 'We know who God is as little as a beetle knows who man is'. To know who God is, God must reveal himself. Where does he reveal himself? In his Word. This Word that the Bible bears witness to, is above all an event, just as Luther had found. 'Do not put yourself in opposition to the Word of God, because truly it will follow its course as surely as the Rhine. With an effort you can hold it up for a moment with dykes, but it is impossible to arrest its course. An eternal power flows from it.' The Gospel is the apprehension of this power. The power of the Word of God is shown in what it accomplishes for humanity in Jesus Christ.

The first disputation in Zurich (January 1523) had to decide about the introduction of Reform into the Church. Zwingli prepared sixty-seven theses, where he stated that those who yield themselves to the proclaimed salvation are as sure of that salvation as if they had a sealed letter; those who resisted the Good News would be ground to dust. Such is the power of God's word – the sign of Jesus Christ from the moment that the destiny of a man is sealed in union with him by faith.

All through the sixty-seven theses runs the Christological axis of Zwingli's thought, as Fritz Blanke and Gottfried Locher have shown. Christ is 'the only door open towards salvation; nothing can be compared with him or placed beside him'. He is the centre of humanity and of Christianity. In his *Commentary on true and false religion*, his principal work along with the sixty-seven theses or *Schlussreden*, Zwingli defined religion in general in its relation to the Christian religion in particular: 'Religion begins where God calls to himself man who is fleeing . . . man acknowledges his nakedness. He recognizes his faults as so important that he doubts the possibility of a return in grace to God. But God is merciful . . . as a father hates the follies or impertinances of his child, but cannot hate the child itself. He calls softly: Adam, where art thou? . . . And he calls him in order to reveal to him his faults, for man no longer knew where he was . . . Well, I say that it is there that religion, or rather loving confidence (*pietas*) is born.' Religion, then, is this: God leads man to recognize his disobedience, his treachery, his misery, as Adam did.

Although this is a description of religion in general, there is no difficulty in recognizing that in such a definition Zwingli has the Christian religion in view. The merciful God who calls Adam, the God who detests the wrong but not the wrongdoer, the God who reveals man's state to him and convinces him that what he has said before is true, this God is only understandable in Christ, because, and Zwingli ends with this, 'Just as God created man through his Son, so God decided to save by his Son man who had fallen and was being delivered to death.' Creation and restoration are in one and the same hand. Given all this, all religion makes sense because of what God once accomplished in Jesus Christ.

Zwingli gives the same message in his *Exhortation to his Schwyz confederates*. God has created men in his image 'so that they should live a peaceable life after the example of the three persons, Father, Son and Holy Spirit. You see from that that the Eternal Wisdom has not only desired from the beginning that concord should reign, but has also desired it as part of the new birth which Christ has conferred on us. If fleshly birth acknowledges itself powerless to unite men, spiritual birth succeeds.' Such a definition is addressed to his confederates, by definition baptized people. The conclusion is that life in society is unthinkable without Christ, who alone makes social life possible. From that it follows that when two men live in peace together, it is because Christ is with them, whether they know it or not.

Zwingli, who served as a chaplain to the Swiss troops at the battle of Marignano, stood out against the custom of his compatriots serving as mercenaries in foreign armies. In his view they should only use their military ability to defend their own homeland. In this he was following Nicolas de Flüe, and henceforth he advocated pacifist ideas which were, however, quickly forgotten when it became a question of helping the Reformation triumph.

Brother de Flüe, medallion by Jakob Stampfer, Aurich, *c.* 1550.

The Swiss lansequenet, illustration taken from *Costumes of different peoples* by M. Sluper, Antwerp, 1572. Musée des Arts Decoratifs, Paris.

The Battle of Marignano, drawing after the bas-relief on the mausoleum of Francis I. Bibliothèque Nationale, Paris.

Two Alsatians who had rallied to the Reformation from the early years backed up Zwingli in Zurich: Conrad Pellican (1478–1556) was professor of Hebrew and Greek there, and Leo Jud (1482–1542), pastor of St Peter's church and professor of Greek, who let Bullinger take the lead after Zwingli's death and undertook a Latin translation of the Bible which Pellican completed.

1. *Portrait of Conrad Pellican*, 16th-century engraving. Zentralbibliothek, Zurich.

2. *Portrait of Leo Jud*, 16th-century engraving. Zentralbibliothek, Zurich.

The Discription of the severall Sorts of Anabaptists, English engraving of the 16th century.

That, then, is the Christological axis. If the Reformer would rather be seated with the sages of antiquity in the kingdom of God than with the prelates of Rome, it is because they have been saved by Christ, even without knowing it here below.

The 'Prophezei'

The basis of the Reformation is Holy Scripture. Zwingli was already forming his church by his preaching, but it was necessary to give a biblical education to priests and train future preachers. So the *Prophezei* was created in 1525 especially for the study of the Old Testament. It consisted of a colloquy which met daily in the Cathedral choir. Zwingli opened the meeting with prayer, then one member, generally a young one, read the daily text from the Latin Vulgate, another read it again in Hebrew and explained it, a third read it in Greek from the Septuagint, a fourth returned to Latin and presided over a discussion on the text. The exercise closed with prayer.

Everyone in Zurich who could be considered educated came to the *Prophezei*: clergy, former canons, chaplains, advanced students. Among others two Alsatians were to be found there, Conrad Pellican, an Old Testament specialist, and Leo Jud, Zwingli's chief collaborator. The accomplishments of the *Prophezei* resulted in the publication in 1529 of the Zurich Bible, a Bible for the Swiss people, with country phrases. You read in Matthew 9.16 that you did not put a *Blätz* of new material on to an old garment! The *Prophezei* is the ancestor of our theology faculties, the base on which the Zurich school and the Reformed scholarly tradition in general was established. Its traces are found in the ecclesiastical convention of Strasburg as in the 'congregations' of the Company of Pastors in Geneva. Later, the Puritans took up the expression 'Prophesyings' for their meetings for study and edification.

Zwingli and the tradition of the Church

Parallel to the peasant movement and an echo of happenings in Germany, but with less dramatic consequences, Anabaptism had appeared. It has been called the radical wing of the Reformation, but this judgement needs qualification. The Anabaptists who, it is true, based themselves on the Bible, distinguished themselves from the mainstream Reformers on other fundamental points. They had anarchist elements who denied all authority to the State and openly preached disobedience to it, sometimes identifying it with Satan. Basing themselves on the 'Let your Yea be Yea' of the Gospel, they refused to take any oaths. Leaping across the centuries, they interpreted Scripture as if nothing had happened since the ancient world. On their side, the Reformers respected the traditions of the Church just so far as they conformed to what was given in the Bible. The Anabaptists declared that the church of the Roman communion was dead, while the Reformers pronounced that it was sick, but still living. So Zwingli refused a pension from the Pope but never, as far as is known, renounced his ordination in the Church of Rome. For the Anabaptists the Church had to be recreated; for the Reformers it had to be reformed. The difference is so great that it could reasonably be said that the break was between the Roman church and Zwingli on one side, and the Anabaptists on the other. These folk, who would not baptize infants but rebaptized adults who wished to be converted, were considered enemies in a society where Church and State were united in 'Christendom'. They were persecuted in Zurich until their teachings were rooted out; Zwingli, who published several writings against them, approved this measure.

Against the Anabaptist communities, therefore, the Church asserted its continuity with what had gone before. According to Zwingli, the Church was founded on divine election, a doctrine which has nothing to do with what is sometimes meant by predestination considered as a metaphysical doctrine. This election is the work of God, who, in Jesus Christ and through him, chose man to make him his child. It is an internal doctrine of the Church and has no significance outside the Christian revelation.

The Church is prefigured in the Jewish people which is its first stage, for there is only one covenant of God. It is the community of those who share one faith in Christ and whom God alone knows. Although its members are visible on earth, it is, as a Church, invisible. So it is the gathering of those who, across the world, profess Christianity, that is the Catholic Church. Finally, it is the local community constituted by these same Christians forming a parish.

These different ways of envisaging the Church are related. The Church as a community of the elect must become incarnate in the sociological reality of the parish, and must show itself by the mutual recognition of its members as such, through its public confession of faith and participation in the sacraments. As a sociological reality the Church requires a ministry subdivided into preaching on the

114

one hand and oversight on the other, which implies a discipline. Discipline though, although indispensable to the Church on earth, is not a 'mark of the Church', something reserved to the preaching of the Word and to the sacraments. The goal of discipline is not the exclusion of the guilty but the means, sometimes extreme, of bringing the sinner back into the right way – like the kick directed at a sheep. It was following that line of thought that the matrimonial tribunal of Zurich was created.

Zwingli against Luther

In reaction to the progress of the Reformation, the Swiss cantons who remained loyal to the old faith persuaded the diet to convoke a disputation. This took place at Baden in 1526. As a result Zwingli was banned in a document which reproduced the terms of Luther's condemnation, with the difference that he had been condemned at Worms in 1521 by an imperial diet, while at Baden it was only a disputation. What had had a legal dimension within the Empire did not have one in the Confederation. The Zurichers were not intimidated by it.

The name Anabaptists was given to those who took the reformation to its furthest limits, recognizable by their refusal to baptize their children. They caused an upheaval by re-baptizing adults who wished to be converted. Born into a context of misery and violence, Anabaptism constituted a sort of left wing of the Reformation by its real or imagined excesses and its wish to establish on earth the primitive communism referred to in Scripture. The condemnation by the most extreme members of the sect of personal possessions and the traditional family structure brought numerous persecutions upon the anabaptists.

The Society of Anabaptists, engraving by Solis and Aldegraver, 1536. bibliothèque Nationale, Paris.

Onn dem Nachtmal
Christi /widergedechtnus
oder Sanckfagung Huldrychen Zuinglins meynung/
yetz im Latinischen Commentario beschriben/ vnnd
durch dry getrüw brüder ylends in tütsch
gebracht. Ob Gott wil zü gü=
tem ouch tütscher Na=
tion.

Christus Matth.vj.
Kummend zü mir alle die arbeytend vnd beladen
sind/ vnd ich wil üch rüw geben.

The Eucharist was at the centre of the debate dividing not only Protestants and Catholics, but also Zwingli and Luther. The former saw an exclusively spiritual presence of Jesus Christ in the bread and wine, while the latter was convinced of the material presence of the Saviour in the two forms.

Title page of *Christ's Last Supper* by Huldrych Zwingli, Zurich, 1525. Zentralbibliothek, Zurich.

Communion cup bearing the hallmark of Simon Leclerc, made in Lausanne in 1484.

The success of the Roman Catholics stemmed in large part from the theological situation. It is well known that Luther and Zwingli differed on their interpretation of the Eucharist. Where Luther saw the Body of Jesus Christ joined with the elements, and so a real presence of this Body in a material sense, Zwingli saw an exclusively spiritual presence. Where Luther took the words 'This is my body' literally, Zwingli took them in the sense 'This *signifies* my body'.

Erasmus was asked to be one of the arbiters in the dispute. He prudently refused, but said all the same that 'the words of Holy Scripture have forced Luther to confess what the Catholic Church says'. As for Eck, the doctor from Ingolstadt, the most celebrated opponent of both Zwingli and Luther, he declared not only that Luther's conception was nearer his own than Zwingli's, but that on this point, if not on others, he could even feel in sympathy with Luther.

A deep wedge was driven between the Lutherans and the Zwinglians, given the importance of the sacrament and its significance in the struggles of the era. As a result of Eck's manoeuvre, the Zurichers were isolated from those who were ranged behind Luther, with all the political consequences that necessarily followed.

The situation became more and more difficult as the years passed. The Landgrave of Hesse, who has other claims to fame than his bigamy, had understood that reform of the Church was necessary, and that even if only from the political point of view the divisions between the partisans of Luther and Zwingli had to be healed. He had the idea of a meeting between the two Reformers and easily convinced Zwingli of its advisability. Luther, at first treating the idea with reserve, finally accepted his invitation. This meeting, known as the Colloquy of Marburg, took place in October 1529.

Luther disliked Zwingli. He felt towards him the superiority of the subject of a prince towards a peasant who had only magistrates to obey in his own country. Their respective languages were also a bone of contention. Where Luther was one of the founders of the German language, Zwingli held on to his own dialect, as rough as his country. Luther punningly said that the Swiss language made him sweat (from *schwitzen*, to sweat, and *Schwyz*, Switzerland).

Zwingli's idea of the Eucharist, in line with realist doctrine, claimed that a body, even that of Jesus Christ, could not be in two different places at once. If the body of the Lord had ascended to heaven at the Ascension, it could not be in, or with, the bread – an argument Calvin was to take up. On the other hand, his spiritual, divine body was everywhere, and so as much in the bread of the Communion as anywhere else. Besides, since, according to Scripture, faith was the necessary condition of salvation, the believer was saved by the very fact that he believed. But this salvation had to be accomplished among and in communion with other Christians. It was only possible to be a Christian in the bosom of the Church.

The Lord's Supper still has a very particular meaning. The spiritual body of Christ may be found everywhere, but it is especially, sacramentally, in the Communion. Comparing the sacrament to the royal ring round the sovereign's finger, Zwingli wrote that it was not the value of the gold which made the ring precious, but the fact that it was the king's ring. 'We do not value these signs for the cost of the materials they are made of, but for the great and lofty nature of what is signified.' The sacrament thus has a high value. It is there so that I may affirm my faith to my brothers. By its nature it is a sacrament of the Church, and even more necessary to the Church than to the individual believer. This could be called the ecclesial dimension in Zwingli's thought. The ecclesial dimension and the Christological axis stand out as the two columns holding up Zwingli's theology.

In a letter written to Luther's follower Matthew Alber, Zwingli said that 'to eat the bread and drink the cup is to unite oneself in one body with the other brethren, and that body is the body of Christ', namely those who *together* 'believe in the sacrifice of Jesus Christ for their salvation.' Believers form one body together: 'This body is the Church of Christ, and that is why, since we are one body, we are also called one bread, because in eating this bread we confess before our brethren that we are members of the body of Christ.' As Julius Schwiezer writes, that implies a change, a transubstantiation, of the community of Christians in Zurich assembled in the Grossmünster – a change into the *verum corpus Christi*. The equation reads bread = body of Christ = Church.

The Colloquy of Marburg examined the whole range of the Christian faith and agreed on a common text; but the chapter on the Lord's Supper showed where the two parties agreed to differ. They separated without taking Communion together, and Luther said to Bucer, the Strasburg Reformer who had tried to find a formula of agreement, 'Our spirit and your spirit don't agree . . . It is clear that we don't have the same spirit.' From this Colloquy dates the division between the Lutherans and those who, from c. 1570, were to be called Reformed and who represented the traditions of Zwingli and Calvin.

116

A concept of the State

The relations between Church and State played a big part in Zwingli's thought and life. In 1523 he preached a sermon, which later he turned into a treatise, called *On divine justice and human justice*. The relations between Church and State are seen in terms of these two aspects of justice. One acts in accordance with divine justice in loving God and loving neighbour. Since that is sufficient its accomplishment saves the practitioner. But given the existence of sin, another justice – human justice – is needed (although it is weak in many respects), the accomplishment of which renders life in society possible, but which does not save a man. It exists so that order may reign, and, indeed, so that the Gospel may be preached. These two forms of justice interpenetrate, after the manner of the visible and invisible churches; divine justice gives meaning to the prescriptions of human justice – essentially the Ten Commandments – and human justice draws its resources continually from divine justice – essentially the Summary of the Law. So the magistrate is like a schoolmaster who teaches children with rod in hand. His aim is not to strike them, but he knows that if he does not show his pupils the rod they will not work. The magistrate who bears the sword does not seek to use it, but nevertheless he must keep it in his hand in case he has need of it. The Christian will not obey him out of fear of chastisement, but for conscience's sake. The magistrate, for Zwingli and later for Calvin, is considered a minister of God. Such a doctrine clearly involves strong links between the minister and the magistrate, as does the role which the latter is called to play in the reform of the Church.

Zwingli also stood for clear ideas about international politics. In a letter to Conrad Som, the Reformer of Ulm, he wrote: 'The Papacy and the Empire are both Roman.' In his view, a power wishing to dominate Europe had necessarily to be allied with the Papacy or to use it, even if, as was the case at that time, these two powers were arguing about their pre-eminence. He also conceived and discussed with the Landgrave of Hesse a plan for European politics aimed at resisting Habsburg power. The plan proposed a political union of Zurich with Hesse, to which would be associated Strasburg, then Saxony, the cities of southern Germany, and Württemberg. Finally, there would be an attempt to bring in Denmark, the Republic of Venice, and France, where Francis I was reputed to be a friend of the humanists and where his sister Marguerite of Angoulême was favourable to the Reformation.

In 1526 the Catholic cantons had the Diet of the Swiss Confederation convene at Baden. At the end of the disputation, Zwingli was condemned in almost the same terms as Luther had been at Worms in 1521.

Meeting of the ambassadors of the Confederation at Baden, 17th-century engraving after a 16th-century painting. Musée National Suisse, Zurich.

In this way a kind of wall would be built, dividing Europe in two. To the west Gospel liberty would reign and so check the power of the Empire. This is recognizable as a forerunner of the policy of the balance of power, as far as it was a Protestant policy established in European history under the aegis of England.

The 'reformed Reformation'

Zwingli's ideas were by no means all realized. The situation in Switzerland was precarious because some cantons resisted reform out of loyalty to the old faith, and so the Reformation proceeded very jerkily. In fact the situation became so tense that civil war broke out. Zwingli took part as a chaplain, despite his people's pleadings, and was mortally wounded. So died one who in his treatise *The shepherd*, had written: 'The greatest honour that the heavenly Father can confer on one of his sons is to permit him to die for him.'

Was Zwingli's reform a humanist one? Yes, up to a point – because of his methods, because of the seriousness with which he studied texts, because of the importance he attached to pagan antiquity. Has it not been said that Zwingli was the most cultured of the Reformers? Examples drawn from antiquity are frequent in his work. Up to *De providentia Dei* humanism can be felt throughout his argument.

However, from his earliest writings, particularly the *Auslegung des Schlussreden*, something quite different can be seen coming to light, something which would run right through his work and which we have called the 'Christological axis'. Everything derives from that. With Calvin we take part in the blossoming of the Reformation, but with Zwingli we witness its spring, rich in promise. In Zwingli's writings we find the seed – and sometimes it is more than the seed – of the great options lying before Reformed theology on which Calvin would expand. Matters are developed and sharpened with Calvin, brought to the most accomplished intellectual and spiritual construction in history, but they are already sketched out with all the freshness of novelty by Zwingli.

In his work we find this sovereign authority of the Word of God, even when he uses philosophical language, as when for example he declares that reason is what conforms to what Scripture says. In his theology we also find this spiritual notion of the sacrament

A cruel irony destined Zwingli, the keen defender of pacifism, to die in battle on 11 October 1531. He was actually accompanying the Protestant troops as a chaplain after taking leave of his family, and he participated in the tragic battle of Kappel where the Reformed cantons fought against those who remained faithful to the traditional religion.

Zwingli's Farewell to his wife before Kappel, 19th-century lithograph after Ludwig Vogel. Musée Historique de la Réformation, Geneva.

which Calvin understood less well than one might have hoped, together with the notion of visible and invisible forms of the Church, by virtue of which there are not two churches but one whose two aspects interpenetrate in a dialectic. Zwingli already defends the diversity of ministries (absent in Luther), in which besides the preacher there is also the superintendent, the *Wachter*, a ministry sometimes filled by the magistrate. Bucer, influenced by Zwingli, developed this idea in 1536 with the theory of four ministries: pastor, teacher, elder and deacon – a theory taken up by Calvin and applied by him in Geneva. Zwingli thus made a distinction between minister and magistrate, Church and State, even if in reality there was often confusion between them. With Zwingli as with Calvin, discipline is necessary to the Church even if it is not an actual 'mark of the Church' and does not by itself assure the salvation of the believer.

Lastly, in opposition to Luther's 'Christ is not interested in politics', Zwingli developed for his country and for Europe a political thought centred on his faith. Echoes of this can be found in Calvin, especially in his letters, but it is much less pronounced. Unlike the Lutheran Reformation but strictly in line with Calvinism, Zwingli's reforms can be called 'reformed Reformation', giving to this term the definition accepted throughout history.

Portrait of Regula Zwingli, anonymous peinting, 16th century. Zentralbibliothek, Zurich.

The Reformers were also great teachers, as much of children whom they felt they had to mould from their earliest years as of adults whom they had to put on the right path. The parallel is particularly close with Zwingli's teaching about the magistrate, who as a minister of God was comparable to a schoolmaster among his pupils.

Frontispiece to the 1524 German edition of the *School manual* of Huldrych Zwingli, which had appeared the previous year in Latin.

Calvin

John Calvin's biographers usually divide his life into three quite distinct periods: a privileged and studious youth; a proscribed existence when he could only count on uncertain hospitality anywhere; and finally a quarter of a century at the head of the Genevan Church hierarchy. These useful divisons are justified so long as they do not obscure the remarkable unity in the life of this fighter and thinker. From Paris to Basle, from Strasburg to Geneva, he elaborated on his teaching, the importance of which has remained undiminished to this day.

Formation of an intellect

We know little about the childhood of the future Reformer of Geneva. He was the grandson of artisans and son of a property agent in the service of the canons of Noyon in Picardy. There is evidence for his father's authoritarian character and for the retiring and devout personality of his mother, whom he lost very early, as well as for his acquaintance with the aristocratic Hangest family, who were influenced by humanist culture. A significant detail is that of the four nephews of Charles de Hangest, Bishop of Noyon, the two who had been fellow pupils with Calvin entered religious orders, while the two others, who had not been in such prolonged contact with him, joined the Reformation. His father originally destined him for an ecclesiastical career and he was sent first to the Collège de la Marche in Paris in 1523, at the age of fourteen. Here he had as 'regent of grammar' Mathurin Cordier, a priest of radiant faith and a pioneer of modern teaching methods.

As an adolescent he spent four years (1523–7) in the famous Collège Montaigu, in the section reserved for well-to-do students, before studying law at Orléans and Bourges. At Montaigu his studies probably consisted of logic, metaphysics, ethics, rhetoric and science, all of which were taught on the basis of Aristotle with the teachers drawing inspiration from authorities like Ockham, Buridan, Scotus and Thomas Aquinas. These studies were intended as prolegomena to theology and Calvin finished them at eighteen without having been able to begin the sacred sciences which consisted of a commentary on the Bible and the *Sentences* of Peter Lombard. He thus

John Cauvin or Calvin was born in the little town of Noyon, in Picardy, in 1509. The son of a leading citizen, he received the tonsure as early as 1521 and left two years later to continue his studies in Paris. He led a wandering life thereafter until he settled by the shores of Lake Geneva.

The town of Noyon seen from Mont Renaud, engraving by Claude Chastillon, 1591.

Portrait of John Calvin, Swiss school, 16th century. Musée Historique de la Réformation, Geneva.

NOYON.

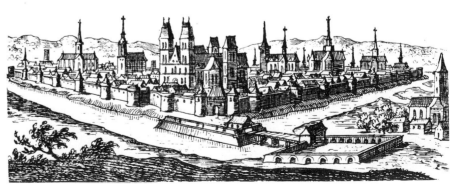

escaped the scholastic strait-jacket and kept his intellectual virginity for a humanist and soon a Lutheran interpretation of Catholic tradition. The ecclesiastical masters of Montaigu had no opportunity to inculcate in Calvin the art of abstract speculations, as remote from life as from concrete language, and quite alien to the Gospels, in which the nominalist theological masters, such as Gregory of Rimini, Thomas Bradwardine, or John Major (their interpreter at Montaigu) excelled. I do not think that any influence of Major on Calvin's thought has been established, despite the claims of researchers as eminent as F. Wendel and K. Reuter.

Calvin acquired his theology by drawing on the more spiritual and accessible springs of the new historical methods. Not only the austere clerks of the college, but also a good number of followers of Erasmus and Lefèvre who were open to new ideas, passed on to him the *devotio moderna* – mysticism for everyman with its ideal of the 'imitation' of Christ and its ardent meditations. All the theological camps had members who practised this concentration on the person of Christ, both as Lord and as Saviour. But only the devout humanists of the period, like the celebrated circle around Briçonnet, the Bishop of Meaux, or the more Platonizing one at the court of Marguerite of Navarre, felt the affinity between this piety and Luther's passionate Christocentrism. It was in the company of such believers that the young Calvin found his spiritual home. There too he learned how to apply the force of his personal faith to a Church and a Christendom in need of reform. In so doing he was to go much further than the reforming tendencies of Erasmus or Lefèvre d'Étaples, and became a greater agent of social change than Luther, his Saxon senior.

Besides this devotion, with its extension into criticism, the young man from Noyon also enriched himself by acquiring the methods of studying the traditional texts with a historical perspective. These texts were not only the Bible, the Fathers and the philosophers of antiquity, but also, on account of his legal studies, the Roman and medieval juridical collections. To make such studies it was essential to know the original languages. Despite the efforts of the Sorbonne to decree that the Vulgate was the only text that theology could use, a textual criticism had developed going back to the Hebrew and Greek originals, which inevitably revealed certain faults in the Latin version. Calvin learnt the two biblical languages at Orléans and at the Collège Royal which Francis I had founded as a counterbalance to the conservative and inquisitorial Sorbonne. He shared the passion for *hebraica et graeca veritas* of men of letters like Wolmar, his friend from Orléans days, Vatable and Danès, his teachers in Paris, as well as Erasmus and Lefèvre d'Étaples. This was not an academic passion, but that of an ardent believer seeking better understanding for his faith. He could not be satisfied by purely historical studies: he wished to know God and himself in the light of a Word freed from all deformity. And so piety and learning together determined the way he would take.

Towards the Gospel

Calvin's quest for personal salvation was never divorced from a lively interest in public affairs. He had after all mixed enough with the privileged circles where riches, culture and political influence fed ambitions for the reform of Church and State. The ancient philosophers like Plato and Aristotle, and especially the Stoics like Cicero and Seneca of whom the young humanist lawyer had soon acquired a good knowledge, reminded him of what it cost to sustain the common good. So too did Augustine's *City of God*, which he frequently quoted with strong agreement in his very first work, a commentary on Seneca's *De Clementia,* that reminder to Nero of the needs of political ethics. This work shows how the young author felt for society in all its forms, and in it he puts social order at least as high in his scale of values as the virtues of mercy and equity, backed by force, which Stoicism preached for the sovereign. But the order in question becomes disorder if it is imposed by tyrannical means. The civic sense of the twenty-three-year-old future Reformer is quite admirable as he develops his criticism of all persecuting regimes: he did the same three years later in his letter to Francis I, which is a preface to the first edition of the *Institutes* and takes the form of an apology from the French partisans of the Gospel after the wretched 'Affair of the Placards'. No, they are not adversaries of the established order. Those, by contrast, are the Anabaptists, whose doctrine of the sleep of souls after death is criticized by Calvin in his work *Psychopannychia,* almost certainly published in 1534. These sectarians are not only breaking the unity of the Church in holding this fantastical doctrine about an essential point of dogma; they are also showing themselves breakers of the civic law. The author tries to show this with the help of scriptural and patristic arguments. Moreover, this little treatise does

not have any of the earlier polemical allusions to the deformations of 'the Church under the papacy'.

A remarkable thing is that the anti-Roman accent does not appear either in the academic sermon of Nicholas Cop, which Calvin probably helped to prepare and which unleashed the thunders of the Sorbonne Inquisition in November 1533. In this sermon, the Erasmian theme of 'Christian philosophy' is preached alongside Lutheran themes: *solus Christus, sola gratia,* the opposition of Gospel and Law, disinterested love of God, justification by faith alone. Out of this theological context there arises, with the 'Blessed are the peacemakers' of the Sermon on the Mount, a vibrant appeal to those in responsible positions in the State that they should conduct their argument against the party of the Gospel with the word rather than with the sword. While waiting for that peaceful dialogue, there is the reminder that, 'Blessed are those who are persecuted for righteousness' sake.'

Was this the beginning of the decisive break? Bringing together the Gospel, justification by faith alone, and the defence of the persecuted (which meant Lutherans, of course): does this signify a position for Luther and against Rome – even if it is expressed in a roundabout way? The hypothesis must not be lightly dismissed. Some researchers have even built it into a thesis. But a deeper understanding of the situation makes it rather less clear-cut. The preacher was Nicholas Cop. He was one of those followers of Erasmus who continued to read Luther's writings despite the latter's condemnation by the papacy in the bull *Exsurge Domine* in 1520 and by the Sorbonne in 1521, but without feeling the need to cut the links with the established Church. Their hesitations are explained by their goal: they wished to reform the Church and not found a new one. Cop, recently elected rector of the University of Paris, was defending the Queen of Navarre from the Sorbonne's attack on her reformism and not the monk of Wittenberg arraigned for his theological radicalism. Certainly the theses which figure in his address had probably been drawn from Luther's *Kirchenpostillen* in their Latin translation by Bucer. But the context and the tone of Cop's words are very close to humanist reformism. Calvin's support for a person in Cop's position in the autumn of 1533 does not imply that he himself was considering breaking with the Church. But nevertheless the inquisitors of Paris suspected him of belonging to 'the accursed Lutheran sect', and he had to flee the capital. The defender of the persecuted submitted to persecution for the first time.

He was given sanctuary by a churchman of impeccable loyalty, Louis du Tillet, curé of Claix in Saintonge, a member of the chapter of Angoulème. For some months he provided Calvin with a haven of tranquillity favourable to theological study, and with free use of his library, which was rich in biblical and patristic works. Thanks to his prodigious memory, the future Reformer rapidly assimilated the texts of the Catholic tradition. This amount of knowledge needed a principle of interpretation, and Calvin found it in the writings of Luther which he read at Basle. He arrived here with du Tillet in January 1535, after leaving his native country.

'The Institutes of the Christian Religion'

Basle was a centre for humanists who had been won over to the Reformation, and there Calvin gave free rein to his penchant for expressing in writing ideas which he had only recently read about. He was a student as well as a writer, and Luther gave him his first real instruction in theology. The *Institutio religionis Christianae* which appeared in 1536 owes a great deal to the *Parvus catechismus*, the *De captivitate Babylonica* and the *De libertate Christiana*. The material is laid out on the whole in the same order as in the shorter Wittenberg catechism: law, faith, prayer, sacraments — that is to say, commentary on the Decalogue, the Apostles' Creed, the Lord's Prayer, baptism and the Lord's Supper. As for the two other Lutheran writings, Calvin sets out their ideas in the chapters which bring his work to a close: *De falsis sacramentis* and *De libertate Christiana*.

Was that mere reproduction without any originality? Was the pupil content to formulate the master's thoughts in better Latin? Certainly not. The *Institutes*, to begin with, enlarge the biblical material, strengthen it with good exegesis, and so furnish a more solid basis for the argument. Where Luther affirms and judges, Calvin reasons and argues. And he has more nuances. This personal re-reading of Luther's theology also owes much to other sources and other masters: to Melanchthon's *Loci communes*, which appeared in 1521, to the *Commentarius de vera et falsa religione*, which Zwingli published in 1525, and to the *Enarrationes* on the four gospels, whose second edition Martin Bucer produced in 1520. So we may conclude that the author of the *Institutes* was drawing on theologians influenced by humanism in order to reformulate Luther's ideas.

While living in Paris, the young Calvin published his first work (1532); in it he sought to find points in common between Seneca's stoicism and the Gospel.

Frontispiece of *Commentary on Seneca's 'De Clementia'*, by John Calvin, 1532. Société de l'Histoire du Protestantisme Français, Paris.

What of scholastic theology? The highly technical speculations on God and man in which the masters of the Sorbonne excelled, notably the famous Scot, John Major, left no evident trace in the first edition of Calvin's *summa*, and only on the subject of ecclesiology in that of 1559. It is true that the young man from Noyon had only had to attend courses on philosophy at Montaigu. It would have been astonishing if Calvin had at the same time familiarized himself with the scholastic dogmatic which drew essentially on the *Sentences* of Peter Lombard. In fact the first *Institutes* reflects only a very incomplete knowledge of that manual, being limited to the fourth book. Besides, Calvin had no respect for that sort of theology. Its method was to cut texts up and mishandle them in order to make them easier to refute. His reaction is understandable. Scholastic aridity and abstraction could not survive the discovery of the vital, prophetic, biblical theology of Luther, especially for someone who was now able to draw directly on the sources of the Bible and the Fathers.

This intellectual and spiritual experience was reinforced by the persecution inflicted on the sympathizers of the new theology by the holders of a superannuated one. We must take account of all these factors in explaining the change of orientation or 'conversion' which Calvin lived through while he produced his manual of dogma for educated readers. Orthodoxy – intolerant, repressive, refusing all discussion – was compromising the credibility of its formulas and theses. This was especially so for a keen, critical and enlightened mind coming from a background of law and the humanities which had just become open to theology. The political and ecclesiastical dimension of this tension – the two aspects being inseparable at that period – equally provoked the lawyer in Calvin. The *Institutes*, the first important fruit of his researches, made him side with the evangelical Reformation and against the papacy.

But curiously, the now explicit anti-Roman trend of his writings went side by side with protestations of loyalty towards the King of France, who even before the 'Affair of the Placards' did not object to his parliament burning 'heretics'. His prefatory letter addressed to Francis I is a plea in defence of evangelicals, to show that they are good Christians in no way opposed to the political order, having nothing in common with the 'fantastical sect' of Anabaptists. What is the meaning of this fidelity to a monarch who, after having sympathized with reformism, had turned

In the opinion of the French Reformers, the attitude of Francis I would determine the success of their movement. At first the monarch was favourable to the new ideas, but he then adopted a more critical position, and finally passed to open repression after 'placards' against the mass had been fixed to a door in the Château of Amboise (October 1534) – aggression which, if not condemned, would have put the kingdom to fire and sword. Calvin nevertheless did not despair of winning him to the Reformed religion.

Portrait of Francis I by Jean Clouet. Musée du Louvre, Paris.

Procession formed by Francis I in 1528 in reparation for the mutilation of a statue of the Virgin, French school, 16th century. Bibliothèque Nationale, Paris.

himself into a powerful ally of the Inquisition, that baneful watch-tower which Rome had erected after the Catharist crisis to make any dogmatic and disciplinary deviation impossible? One possible answer would be to put a high value on Calvin's hopes of winning over the King himself, and thus all France, for the Gospel. Winning over power to his side? But does that not mean taking account of the sword rather than the persuasive word? The tragic end of Michael Servetus in Geneva was later to throw light on the contradiction with which Calvin seems to have been confronted from the beginning.

Geneva, Basle, Strasburg

The success of the *Institutes* encouraged Calvin in the pursuit of his studies, and he sought to join Martin Bucer in his church-city of Strasburg. But Guillaume Farel, who had not been able to establish the Reformation in Geneva, begged him to help build the Reformed Church 'according to the Word of God' in that city. Calvin agreed. He became the reader in Holy Scripture, expositor of the Epistle to the Romans, a participant in the Disputation of Lausanne where his patristic learning and his skill in argument – that inheritance from Montaigu was real enough! – drove his Roman adversaries to capitulate. This new success made him appreciate the need to have well trained pastors, so he willingly tackled the task of producing *Ordinances* for the community of Geneva which gave the pastors a weighty influence even in the civil domain. Presiding frequently at Holy Communion, they also exercised a judicial function thereby admitting only the worthy, and excluding and excommunicating the unworthy. 'Worthiness' was judged primarily by adherence to the *Confession of Faith* which Calvin produced and wished the magistrate to impose on all citizens under pain of exile. He also wrote a catechism to initiate all into the faith.

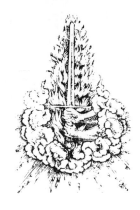

The emblem of Guillaume Farel, Calvin's friend and protector, was 'the sword of the true word', surrounded by flames.

Frontispiece of *Commentary on the Epistles of St Paul*, 1548 edition. Société de l'Histoire du Protestantisme Français, Paris.

Like Luther before him, Calvin was at the same time an academic and a preacher, a very subtle theologian and a popularizer who could communicate with children and uneducated people, as his *Catechism* proves.

Title page and last page (in Hebrew) of the *Catechism* by John Calvin, edited by Robert Estienne in 1553.

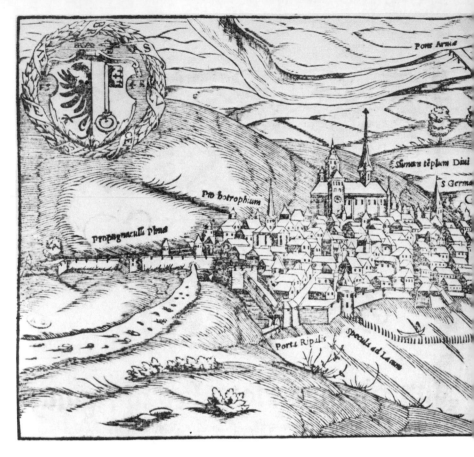

In 1536, Guillaume Farel (1489–1565) from
Dauphiné called Calvin to Geneva. A disciple of
Lefèvre d'Étaples, the first Reformer of Geneva
understood the advantages he could gain from
the genius of the younger man. Furthermore,
after their expulsion in 1538, Farel once again
persuaded Calvin to rejoin him in Geneva in 1541.
They were followed by thousands of exiles who
came from all over Europe to take refuge in the
'Protestant Rome'.

The Town of Geneva, engraving from the *Cosmography*
of Sebastian Münster, 1544. Bibliothèque des Arts
Decoratifs, Paris.

The Last Meeting between Farel and Calvin, painting
by Joseph Hornung, 19th century. Musée d'Art et
d'Histoire, Geneva.

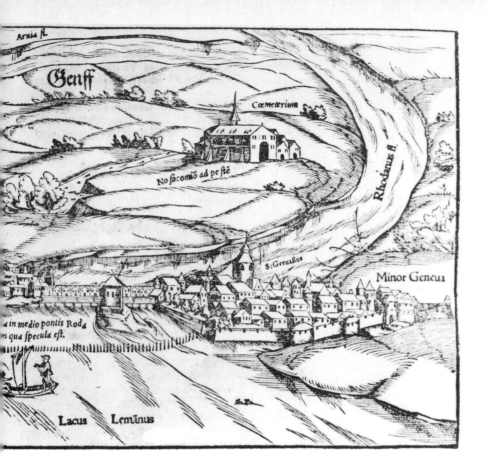

But the magistrates were not happy under the tutelage of pastors whose political influence was helped by a rather vague definition of their duties. It is significant that it was on the subject of the Easter Communion that the conflict broke out in 1538 and Calvin and Farel were expelled.

Once again the author of the *Institutes* took refuge in study and established himself in Basle. But he was now possessed by doubts about his vocation. He was a layman who had received no ordination, neither in the Church of his childhood nor in any Reformed community; was God really calling him to a ministry? To a responsibility that was at once pastoral, educational, governmental, and prophetic? Should he not be content to serve the Church of God with thought and pen? His faithful friend, du Tillet, urged him to renounce his ministry and return to the bosom of the Established Church. Bucer on the contrary, inviting him to Strasburg, confirmed him in his vocation and also had the sense to find the ideal employment for his French protégé: pastoral responsibility in the French-speaking parish. This gave him enough leisure to study and participate in talks between the evangelical churches of various persuasions at Frankfurt, Haguenau, Worms, and Ratisbon. In Bucer's insistence, as in Farel's at Geneva, Calvin recognized again 'the hand of God' so that he no longer doubted his vocation. Fortified by this new assurance, he deployed his talents as an advocate and a controversialist as never before. His reply to Cardinal Sadoleto demonstrates this.

Sadoleto, the Bishop of Carpentras, was one of those prelates whose faithfulness to Rome and to Catholic traditions was equalled only by an evangelical and reformist spirit. His open-mindedness was accompanied by tolerance. In March 1539, taking measure of the chaos into which Geneva had relapsed after the expulsion of Calvin and Farel, he wrote a letter attempting to bring the Genevans back to the bosom of the Church under papal authority, the 'true Church', the only one which had the universal consensus of all teachers and all ages in its favour. Calvin, alerted by his bereft followers in Geneva, agreed to reply to Sadoleto. What he wrote was a little *summa* of ecclesiology, showing his ready fluency. The true Church was not primarily that which was recognized by teachers and secular traditions, but the one where the Word of God had unshackled reality. The Word alone constituted the Church. But its human condition was such that it was in need of reform. It authenticated its claims to be one, holy, catholic and apostolic, by accepting as sole criterion the *verbum Dei*. That Church still existed and evangelicals had never left it. They were not deserters, but, rather, good soldiers of Christ, who raised His standard and

127

With the influx of refugees, the town of Geneva, of which this is the earliest picture, developed considerably, although its citizens felt themselves submerged by the newcomers.

View of Geneva in a painting by Conrad Witz, 15th century. Musée d'Art et d'Histoire, Geneva.

Calvin in his study, anonymous work of the 17th century. Société de l'Histoire du Protestantisme Français, Paris.

brought back order to a confused army. They did not want schism. They wanted ecclesial communion on all truth. And this truth was on their side, even if they were in a minority. Had not the prophets and Jesus himself been right, although rejected by a majority of priests and academics? The open letter to Sadoleto had its desired effect. Geneva did not yield but recalled Calvin in September 1541.

Return to Geneva

The Reformer's second settlement in Geneva was like a laborious harvesting of the seed sown by the first edition of the *Institutes*. Theory and practice joined together, and theory was exposed to verification by the prosaic realities of daily life in a city which the Reformer wished to make into a church. Calvin produced new *Ordinances*, established the fourfold ministry of pastors, teachers, elders and deacons, and also reformulated his catechism. The *Ordinances* of 1541 make the rights and duties of pastors more precise, as ministers appointed essentially to preach and administer the sacraments. They were grouped into a 'company' and charged with weekly meetings

LES
ORDONNANCES
ECCLESIASTIQVES
DE L'EGLISE DE GENEVE.
ITEM
L'ORDRE DES ESCO-
les de ladite Cité.

A GENEVE.
Pour Michelle Nicod.
M,DC,IX.

Calvin returned to Geneva in 1541 and, in the years that followed, organized a new Church governed by 'ecclesiastical ordinances'. The pastors, instructed by the doctors and assisted by the Elders, had the tasks of administering baptism, celebrating the Lord's Supper, and teaching the catechism. The weekly meetings, monthly synods, conferences and colloquies amounted to collegiate direction of the daily life of the Genevans. Calvin and his friends kept a strict control of all sectors of activity: education, relief of the poor and ill, entertainments, dress, justice and so on.

Title page of the *Ecclesiastical Ordinances* published by John Calvin in November 1541, 1609 edition. Bibliothèque Publique and Universitaire, Geneva.

Religious colloquy held in Geneva in 1549 (Calvin, de Beza, Colladon, Farel, Froment, Viret, Grenault, Lafontaine), 19th-century engraving after D.A. Labouchère.

Letter from Calvin to Michael Varro, procurator of the hospital. Archives d'État, Geneva.

where biblical texts were expounded and practical matters deliberated. Four times a year, the 'company of pastors' was convoked for mutual censure, recalling in some ways the monastic use of the *culpa*. At the same time, the college of clergy was to examine new candidates for the pastorate, to establish whether or not they could be ordained.

The ministry of teachers remained less clearly drawn. In principle they were equally set aside for the service of the Word; in fact the teaching of theology fell to them although they shared this responsibility with certain pastors. The Elders, on the other hand, had a very wide field of action. Their presbyteral service consisted of a sometimes punctilious surveillance of public and even private morality. For in the city-church one should have nothing to hide! The consistory, where pastors and Elders sat side by side and whose presidency was entrusted to a syndic of the town council, was a veritable tribunal for questions of faith, manners and discipline. The methods which it was led to employ sometimes recalled those of the Inquisition.

From today's viewpoint, it seems that the emphasis on lay participation in the conduct of the Calvinist presbyteral college was a revival of the style of government established by Paul in the communities at Corinth, Ephesus and Rome. As for the diaconate, Calvin wished to give it back its erstwhile purpose of social action. The deacons of Geneva were charged with the care of the poor and the sick. As the 'hands of God', stretched out towards those who suffer, they were not to be content with giving material help, 'distributing soup', but must also manifest the Word of God in their actions. It is as if the Old Testament concept of *dabar Yahweh*, at once Word, event and palpable thing, found here its rightful expression. On account of this theological slant the Calvinist deacon found himself entrusted with the symbolic task of distributing the bread and wine at the Lord's Supper.

To understand the context in which the new Genevan catechism was conceived, we must note that Calvin's dogmatic thought, during his stay in Strasburg and the elaboration of the second edition of the *Institutes*, gained much in originality, to the point of becoming an autonomous theology. To take one example: he no longer followed the Lutheran model which treated of Law before faith, with the intention of showing the contradictions between the two. Indeed, Calvin denied that the Old Testament Law was the source of a legalism which insisted on observances and works to the extent that it lost all its meaning with the coming of Christ and his Gospel. He strove, instead, to integrate the Law into the sphere of evangelical faith as order transfigured by the new covenant and as the necessary stimulus of all ethical progress. So also obedience to the Law of Christ represented in his eyes a notable act of faith. The continuity of the two covenants and their 'substantial' if not 'economical' identity, is an idea which clearly illustrates the theological freedom which the French Reformer won for himself from Luther's tutelage.

The dangers of intolerance

Calvin's doctrinal assurance went on growing in the wake of his controversies. So did his intolerance, at least in regard to adversaries who provoked him on the spot and whom he did not consider as members of the great evangelical family. Three cases illustrate this fact. First, in 1543, there was the confrontation between the Reformer

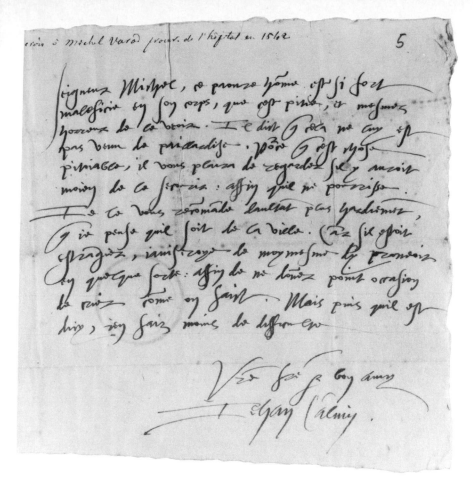

INSTITV
TION DE LA RELI-
GION CHRESTIENNE: EN LA-
quelle est comprinse vne somme de pieté,
& quasi tout ce qui est necessaire a congnoi-
stre en la doctrine de salut.

Composée en latin par IEAN CALVIN, &
translatée en françois, par luymesme.

AVEC LA PREFACE ADDRES-
sée au Treschrestien Roy de France, Françoys
premier de ce nom: par laquelle ce present liure
luy est offert pour confession de Foy·

Habac. 1:
IVSQVES A QVAND
SEIGNEVR:

M. D. XLI.

The *Institutes of the Christian Religion*, a real *summa* of Calvinist thinking, was almost certainly sketched out in 1534 and then published in Geneva in 1536. The definitive edition, after a quarter of a century of reflection and doctrinal disputes, dates from 1559.

Title page of *Institutes of the Christian Religion* by John Calvin, 1541 edition. Société de l'Histoire du Protestantisme Français, Paris.

and Sebastian Castellion who questioned the canonicity of the Song of Songs and criticized Calvin's interpretation of Christ's descent into hell. Calvin perceived in this opinion danger for the authority of Scripture and did everything in his power to stop it spreading. He went as far as preventing Castellion's ordination as a pastor, and finally had him expelled from the city. By an irony of fate the author of the commentary on *De clementia* had attempted to silence a man who went on to become in his turn an advocate of tolerance and freedom of conscience with his work *De haereticis, an sint persequendi*, which was published in Basle and thus also on Reformed soil.

The affair of Jerome Bolsec had a similar outcome in 1551. It was provoked by the severe and even injurious criticism that this former Carmelite had made about a particularly sensitive and also very personal point of Calvinist theology: the doctrine of double predestination. Melanchthon and the church of Berne tried in vain to intervene: the Reformer of Geneva would not tolerate within the city's walls a man who contradicted him and would not be swayed. The explanation lies probably in Calvin's prophetic consciousness, in his certainty that he was simply delivering the words of God in suitable form. This sometimes gave his decisions the air of divine judgement.

Calvin's intolerance reached its height in the implacable way in which he hunted down Michael Servetus, whom he considered quite justifiably as the destroyer of Trinitarian dogma. To hold that the Father, the Son, and the Holy Spirit are simply three modes of action of the one unitary God seemed a falsification of all that Paul, John and the Fathers, from Nicaea to Chalcedon, had taught in creating a universal creed. It opposed divine majesty and its truth: the death penalty was appropriate for such a crime of lese-majesty. The Inquisition set up by Innocent III had already made use of the comparison between heresy and capital offences against the sovereign. Calvin had long discussions with Servetus in his prison in Geneva to try to make him change his belief, but finally demanded the death sentence for him. Basle, Berne, Schaffhausen and Zurich all agreed (eventually Melanchthon consented also) and the 'heretic' was burnt alive on 27 October 1553.

Standard-bearer of a new civilization

Quite a different spirit guided the Reformer in the controversies between the sister Churches of the Reformation over the doctrine of the Eucharist. On this field of battle, he showed himself less defensive and more creative, as well as more desirous

Title page of *Supplex Exhortatio* by John Calvin, with the author's signature. Société de l'Histoire du Protestantisme Français, Paris.

The academy at Geneva trained numerous European Reformers, such as the Scot John Knox and the Dutchman Philip de Marnix. Marnix (1540–98), diplomat and burgermaster of Antwerp, divided his literary activity between translating the scriptures and anti-Catholic satires.

Portrait of Philip of Marnix, engraving by J.-J. Flipart, 16th century. Bibliothèque Nationale, Paris.

John Calvin, like all the great Reformers, passed on his message by both the written and the spoken word. For years believers flocked to this chapel to hear him preach.

of peace. Two instances may be given: the Synod of Berne in 1537, before Calvin settled in Geneva, and the *Consensus Tigurinus* signed in 1549.

The meeting in Berne had as its goal the examination of the Eucharistic doctrine developed by Bucer, in order to establish whether he had gone too far, in the eyes of the Swiss churches, in the concessions he made to Luther. The debates reached a satisfactory conclusion after the Confession of Faith, which the young author of the *Institutes* had specially drawn up for this discussion, proved effective. From that time on Calvin gave evidence of a consummate art of discovering a middle way which went beyond simple compromise. This was marked more by creative intelligence than by theological diplomacy, and led him in the direction of the thesis on Christ's spiritual presence at the Lord's Supper. Between the two extreme positions – Luther's, which got tangled up in a realism resembling the scholastics', and Zwingli's, which followed the exigencies of rational thought to the point of mere symbolism – Calvin proposed an interpretation oriented entirely towards the operation of the Holy Spirit. The Spirit was described as the vehicle of the heavenly Christ in his desire to communicate himself in his entirety to believers. Theologians today must, if they are to be objective, recognize that Calvin had the genius to take up a doctrine strongly attested by the eastern Fathers and conforming with the Pauline and Johannine tradition. This result then is rather more significant than a simple defence of Bucer.

The role that Calvin's pneumatology played in the Zurich Agreement of 1549 directs us to specific features of the *Institutes*. But before coming to that, the significant events in the rest of the Reformer's life must briefly be mentioned. The *Consensus* of 1549 did not bring any peace between the churches which had sprung from the Reformation. Quite the contrary: it reinforced the divisions between orthodox Lutherans like Joachim Westphal or Tilemann Hesshusen and the Swiss who had learnt how to integrate part of Zwingli's legacy into their sacramental doctrine – a doctrine to which Bucer, Bullinger and Calvin had each made their contribution without it becoming diffuse. As a result, Calvin became the long-term spokesman of the Reformed. At the same time, he continued to consolidate and to construct. He was in contact by letter with important people, including the King of Poland and the Duke of Somerset, protector of the young King of England. Calvin expected to win these countries for the Reformation from on high. He also, in genuinely pastoral letters, upheld the French Reformed whose little congregations often grew only at the cost of real heroism.

The opening of the academy in Geneva in 1559 was the event, the consequences of which were to be decisive for the strengthening and internationalizing of the Reformed movement. Calvin consulted Johannes Sturm, the eminent educationalist from Strasburg, and drew inspiration from the *Leges scolae Lausannensis*. He brought the best teachers to Geneva: Antoine Chevalier, François Bérauld, Jean Tagaut, Jean Randon and Theodore de Beza. This *alma mater*, consisting of a *schola privata* giving elementary education to children and a *schola publica* designed for higher studies in the liberal arts, biblical languages and theology, assured continuity in its pupils' education. Its library is witness to a desire to make available the thought of ancient and modern writers on philosophy and theology, including the teaching of both evangelicals and Catholics: Thomas Aquinas, Cajetan, Catharinus, Pighi, Erasmus, Lefèvre d'Étaples, Vatable, Bude, Bembo, Sadoleto. The influence of this school was widespread. Many future French pastors emerged from it, but also standard-bearers of the Reformation like the German Caspar Olevianus and the Scot John Knox, and even organizers of the Reformation in Holland such as Philip Marnix de St Aldegonde. The Geneva academy contributed greatly towards the town's status as the 'mother church' for a whole series of Reformed churches in Europe, and also, indirectly, in the New World. In this way the Reformed Church became much more international in character than the Lutheran. It was aided in this by the activity of famous editors and printers: Henri and Robert Estienne, Jean Crespin, Conrad Badius, Jean Rivery.

Calvin, a churchman who had never received ordination, remained a great preacher and theologian, marching at the head of a new civilization, and an intellectual master possessed by a faith at once Christocentric and ecclesial. Indefatigable, despite fragile health, he eventually wore himself out with the enormous task which he had imposed on himself. He died on 27 May 1564 at the age of fifty-five. By his own wish he was buried in an unmarked grave. The prophet of the glory of God did not wish to be glorified on earth.

OPERVM DIVI AVRELII AVGVSTINI HIP/
PONENSIS EPISCOPI COMPLECTENS
τὰ διδακτικὰ hoc eſt,quæ proprie
ad docendum pertinent.

Imprimé par Conrad Badius.
2 M. D. I. XII.

3 BASILEAE APVD IO. FROBENIVM M·D·XXVIII

IN LIBRVM PSALMO
rum, Iohannis Caluini commen
tarius.

1

Oliua Roberti Stephani.
M. D. L V I I.

In his immense body of writings Calvin makes
use of the inheritance left by the early Church
Fathers, but he reads St John Crysostum or
St Augustine with a critical eye: for him,
Scripture is infallible interpreted by itself. This
understanding was soon aligned to St Paul's
phrase (Romans 12.6): 'according to the
proportion of faith'.

1. Frontispiece of *Commentary on the Book of Psalms*
by John Calvin, edited by Robert Estienne in 1557.
Société de l'Histoire du Protestantisme Français, Paris.

2. Frontispiece of *Commentary on the Epistle of St Paul*
by John Calvin, edited by Conrad Badius, 1562. Société
de l'Histoire du Protestantisme Français, Paris.

3. Title page of the third volume of *Work of St
Augustine* edited at Basle by Frobenius, 1528.
Bibliothèque Nationale, Paris.

Calvin's system

An important feature of Calvin's heritage and a decisive factor in its effectiveness
both within the church and without, lies in the systematic nature of his theology.
The essentials are to be found in the arrangement of the *Institutes*. Its contradictions
are rare and for the most part secondary. The last edition (1559) of this work, which
its author had conceived as a compendium of doctrine, is presented synthetically. It
is the fruit of a long evolution during which Calvin learnt how to integrate what he
had acquired through numerous controversies. Luther, the prophet, was never able,
and doubtless never wished, to give such a scholastic formulation to his thought.
Melanchthon had proposed one, but at the cost of a quasi-scholastic domination by
technical Aristotelian categories. By contrast Calvin devised his system in a far more
concrete way. With the Bible and the Fathers on the one hand, and on the other the
practical problems of the life of faith, he reflects, compares, confronts, argues, and
proposes solutions. He acts as a mediator between his contemporaries and a tradition
whose norm is given by the Bible, both Old and New Testaments, and which is
interpreted by a judicious reading of the 'ancients': Tertullian, Cyprian, Augustine,
John Chrysostom, Leo and Gregory. The patristic argument plays a much more
important part with Calvin than with Luther, for he endeavours to shore up their
conclusions. Certainly here as in other areas of argument Calvin makes a clear
hermeneutic choice which determines his selection of witnesses, and none of them,
even the 'most profound' Augustine or the best exegete, John Chrystostom, is
considered above criticism. All have to submit to the judgement of the Word,
incarnate in Jesus Christ, in the form Calvin understood it. The witnesses are tested
and legitimized in the light of this criterion of criteria, and then make their
contribution to a doctrine which has to be as faithful to the original norms as it is
'accommodated to the needs of the times'.

What is fascinating about the system is the encounter between the past that is
remembered and the present that is lived. The latter, after the first edition, is condensed
into three postulates: *pietas, vera religio* and *spiritualis cultus. Pietas* is the humanist term for
the faith that leads to trust. The *pii* are the believers who adopt the only interior
disposition towards God which corresponds to his divinity. This disposition is filial, not
servile like those who 'under the papacy' give themselves to a calculating and superstitious
religiosity. So a return to *pietas* is a programme of Reform. This 'reverence for God tied to
his love in view of the benefits duly received from him', must, as Calvin wrote in 1559, be
entreated and fostered by all available means.

Knowledge of God, reverence for him, and love for him, are the three elements
which necessarily make up *vera religio*, the ethical concretization of *pietas*. Once one
has known God as he really is — that is, not avid for works of satisfaction, but a
Father as just as he is merciful — the loving impulse which carries us towards him is
tempered by all the seriousness of reverence. The pious man or woman, who believes
in God by loving him, takes on the obligation at the same time to observe the divine
commands and to behave within the limits they determine. So *religio* has nothing in
common with the delirium or enthusiasm of those who have 'seen the light', nor
with the isolation of the individual soul, for the *pii* adhere spontaneously to the

community of the Church. The term *pii* first appears in Calvin's dedicatory epistle to Francis I, where it is readily applied to evangelicals. They are gathered by the one Father into the society of the Church, and called to exteriorize their faith by a 'spiritual worship', by liturgical acts purged of all the muddled collection of superfluous ceremonies. These are enlightened and meaningful acts of adoration and thanksgiving, which are inspired by the Holy Spirit, the supreme guarantee of authenticity. Calvin is here referring not to the Spirit of wild charismatic behaviour, but to the Spirit who creates order, the order which supplants chaos in the individual soul as much as in the Church or society.

That is why *pietas, vera religio*, and *cultus in Spiritu* are not confined to the strictly existential dimension, but call for a healthy, solid, simple, clear teaching, purged by criticism of all equivocation. That then is the aim of the theological system proposed in the *Institutes*.

What are its principal contents? The narrow compass of the present study does not permit a complete description, but it should be possible to say briefly how its dogma and doctrine differ from the Lutheran heritage. Like Luther, Calvin insists in the *Institutes* on the radically sinful condition of mankind, on Christ as its only saviour and the only revealer of the true God, on grace which brings about salvation to the exclusion of all 'works', on faith which is the only adequate means of receiving this gift, on the Word of God which is to be heard, listened to, studied, and followed everywhere at all times. But Calvin's system differs from Luther's in that it integrates this patrimony into a context determined by a more developed doctrine of the Holy Spirit, the visible Church, the sanctification of the justified, and the political dimension of Christian existence.

Pneumatology is present everywhere in Calvin's thought. As early as the Eucharistic interpretation which the Reformer developed for the *Consensus Tigurinus*, the Holy Spirit appears as the one who 'joins earth and heaven' to make possible contact with Christ elevated into his eternal glory. Christ's glorified humanity, and so his body and blood, like his whole incarnate being, does not in the Eucharist condescend to a new 'humiliation' as at the moment of his conception in the Virgin's womb. It is not 'enclosed' in the elements of the bread and wine nor tied to them in an ontological way, whether by 'transubstantiation' as imagined by Aquinas or by 'consubstantiation' as proposed by Luther. It is the Holy Spirit who brings about the meeting between the heavenly Christ and the earthly communicants. Through his 'virtue', Christ presents himself to the faithful in his totality and in all reality. The difference between Christ and the elements subsists, without any confusion, at the very heart of the Communion; nevertheless this Communion brings a real and not merely symbolic union between the Lord and those who believe in him. Thanks to the mysterious but efficacious operation of the Spirit, there is a real meeting between them.

Pneumatology also plays a determining role in the verbal, non-sacramental meeting with Christ. Calvin insists that the Spirit is not only the inspirer of the canonical books but also their inner interpreter. No one apprehends the true meaning of a biblical text other than through the 'inner witness' of the divine *Pneuma* (Spirit). Neither the text nor the reader's faith are sufficient: there must be a correlation between text, faith and the mediating Spirit.

But is this enough to ensure that the Bible will be interpreted without any grave error? If so, then did the Anabaptists and Spiritualists practice this inadequately when their reading of the texts ended in contradictory and fantastical interpretations? The Calvinist system gives a negative reply. The Bible must be read and interpreted in the church, in the community of believers assembled in the name of Christ and under the guidance of the Spirit. Individualism is inconceivable. Sharing of charismata is an essential constituent of being Christian. Believers are only truly Christian if they operate in a spirit of mutual support and co-operation through a network of meetings, colleges and councils. Christianity is essentially synodical. So its nature is lost wherever a hierarchy freezes all free flow between Christians, and also in anarchic groups. On the other hand, it expands in a 'congregation' which listens only to the Word of God and under the guidance of the Spirit discovers in its voice the call of God. Such a congregation will certainly not look for the visibility of its Church in the way the contemporary papacy did, in the power and pomp of its prelates. Rather, it would prefer an 'invisible' existence to such a state, that is to say the knowledge of being seen as a Church only by God who elects and calls 'in secret'.

But the true Church must have another sort of visibility; Calvin insisted on that, especially after his stay in Strasburg. This will be the shining torch of evangelical witness, whose first bearers will be ministers, 'organs' of the Spirit, set apart for those services of preaching, sacraments and discipline, which answer the needs of the time. The institutions of such a people of God will even have the value of a *media salutis*.

One of the most lively testimonies to Calvin's appearance is this series of sketches made during a class by a student, Jacques Bourgouin of Nevers.

Calvin, pen drawings by Jacques Bourgouin. Bibliothèque Publique et Universitaire, Geneva.

135

Through them the Church makes explicit her role as mother (an idea Calvin borrows from Cyprian), parenting and raising the children of God, acting as an enlightened teacher, in turn a 'sober disciple' of the Word. The model of that ecclesiology, with its implicit balance between ministry and laity, is found in the Church of the Fathers of the first five centuries; but its ultimate foundation, in so far as it is the great brotherhood of the elect, comes, according to Calvin, from its eternal predestination by God.

Many people nowadays associate the Calvinist doctrine of predestination with an arbitrary, terrifying God who from all eternity wills some to be damned and some to be saved. That was certainly not the Reformer's intention. It seems to me legitimate to regard the theory as an attempt to connect the temporal origin of the Church with the sovereign will of God. The Church is thus seen, not as the product of some evolution in the religious history of humanity, but as the creation of the Almighty. While God alone can transform corrupt sinners into children of God, only one who has freely received this gift of free adoption is a child of God. This filiation is of a supernatural nature, being dependent upon election: it can be neither seized nor bought. Of course, such a belief in an eternal, prevenient election, constitutive of the Church of God in a world which often refuses him, is a concept which requires the existence of a non-elect body. Otherwise election would be neither a real choice nor a sovereign act, exempt from constraint or necessity. But that is only the theoretical basis. In practice, Calvin refused to consider any particular individual or group as reprobate. To those who asked whether they were elect he replied by indicating the precise signs which could give assurance of salvation. But he offered no universal criteria by which a judgement could be made about divine reprobation. Even the excommunicate had the right to a *iudicium caritatis*, to be considered capable of conversion if God gave them grace. From the pastoral point of view, then, Calvinist predestination loses much of its purely negative, terrifying, inhuman, or determinist character and becomes susceptible of an interpretation within the understanding of the Church.

That is all the more possible because Calvin's dogmatic system attaches a primary importance to the sanctification of the justified. The justifying act of God, accomplished once for all, is not enough. It is only intelligible if, with the Apostle Paul, we recognize the beginning of a process, whereby the justified sinner is, as it were, carried by the Holy Spirit. Once again it is the Spirit who helps one to follow the way, make progress, seek the things of heaven, bring forth the fruits of *metanoia* (repentance), and be perpetually renewed. The goal of this process is the restoration of the image of God in every justified soul. It is in this way that I suggest the principle of 'progress' can be established theologically. Men and women exist in history and only fulfil themselves little by little. It is by making our way with the aid of the grace which elects us and calls us that our own works, sacred or profane, become possible and agreeable to the Sovereign Judge. Faith which justifies without works raises up works and is expressed in them. It is in the sanctity of the sanctified person that their good works are brought into a unity.

The Reformer's dogmatic system did not stop at the Church. He spoke also about civil government. While mankind is on the march to a heavenly country, it needs to be organized in political communities. That is also the Creator's will, since it makes possible the fulfilment of his project of training men and women in a culture and a justice which gathers them together and makes them worthy of the eternal Kingdom. The different forms of society are the places where the great work of spiritual training takes place. So the temporal institution corresponds to a real ministry willed by God. It is vowed to 'organize our behaviour into civil justice, to bring us into accord one with another, to bring about and maintain peace . . .' Princes and governments have the responsibility of freeing the oppressed and punishing the guilty, thereby accomplishing an 'external service of God' which tolerates neither the subjection of man nor the establishment of injustice or violence.

By joining his political theology to his pneumatic ecclesiology Calvin helped the Reformation to survive and spread. The evangelical movement found in him its organizer and system builder and so survived the Roman Counter-Reformation as well as the Catholic Reformation. Paradoxically, this same Calvinist inheritance is today a source of ecumenical possibilites, significant similarities having appeared between the ecclesiology of Calvin and that of Vatican II.

Bust of John Calvin, anonymous limewood carving, 17th century. Musée d'Art et d'Histoire, Geneva.

The consolidation of the Reformation in Europe

A glance at the map of Europe in the sixteenth century is all that is needed to understand that the Protestant Reformation, despite numerous exceptions, was above all a phenomenon of the north, of the world of city-states, of cantons and little principalities, of modern Europe, dynamic and literate.

The political geography of the Reformation

What happened in the sixteenth century is unique in the history of Christianity and of religion in general. Such a mutation, fifteen centuries after the founding act, appeared like a new age of the Apostles. The Reformation could not be classed as a heresy. The Confession of Augsburg (25 June 1530) and Calvin were on the side of the orthodoxy of the great councils from Nicaea to Chalcedon, against the heresiarchs from the first centuries onwards. It was a turning point after which there were to be in the Church two ways of linking with the common origins, of living the same continuity in a different fashion.

The Reformation was essentially a break and a new start produced by the meeting of two distinct currents, humanism and the Lutheran doctrine of salvation. The Reformation, then, was the authority of Holy Scripture, justification by faith, and the consciousness of a renewal (and thus a modification) in the understanding of endurance. Without printing to multiply and standardize, without the proliferation of pamphlets in the vernacular, without the threshold of 10 per cent literacy, the Reformation would have been possible but its success would not, nor would it have lasted.

In the West, and especially in the areas which adopted the Reformed ways, Reformed worship emerged as a new religious movement, without the Lutheran transitional acts of the German mass. Between the last mass and the first Lord's Supper there was on average about five years. All was fluid for twenty-five years and then was fixed. Just as there was only one true Apostolic Age in the history of the Church, so to this day there has been only one Reformation. Between 1550 and 1560, 90 per cent of the decisions were made. Only adjustments of detail followed.

Its sudden development was associated with a maturity and heightening of individual awareness and so an anxiety about the Judgement. Therefore by its nature the Reformation could involve only a minority, who brought along with them, if conditions were favourable, the new pagans of traditional Christianity. That is why the map of the Reformation's spread reflects accurately the social make-up of the State.

With one exception – England – which confirms the rule, the Reformation caught on for good only in the area of the city-states of the Rhine and the Alps, and so long as Rome was not near enough to condemn the enterprise to failure. Italy, at the heart of the system of Indulgences, could not deny the traditional Church without cutting its head off. In the Iberian peninsula, the phenomenon of the *Reconquista* over Islam and the presence of Judaism made an effective barrier.

The Reformation succeeded in the area of little territorial states, in Saxony and in the east of the Empire, in a less radical form, with the transitional stage of the German mass. There was no success in the great territorial states when they were hostile: they were influenced by the need for peace and so resisted upheavals which aroused discontent among peasants shocked by head-on attacks on their religious habits – peasants who needed a religion of which physical acts integrated their lives and which conformed naturally to their way of being, feeling and believing.

The two super-states of France and England always dominated the political

The success of the Reformation was directly tied to the invention of printing and the noticeable rise in numbers of those who could read and write. A movement founded on the preponderant place of Scripture could not have taken off without the rise of literacy.

Detail from the *Life of St Remy*, French tapestry of 1531. Musée St Denis, Rheims.

On the night of 17 October 1534, French Protestants posted up an anti-Catholic tract about the mass, inspired by Marcourt and brought in from the Swiss Jura, inside the Château of Amboise, and this provoked a violent reaction from Francis I. After the 'Affair of the Placards' the King of France, who until then had adopted a moderate attitude towards the Reformation, chose the way of repression.

Text of the famous *Placards* of 1534. Musée Calvin, Noyon.

Reformation and Counter-Reformation in Europe at the end of the 16th century, map taken from the article on 'The Reformation' by Bernard Vogler, *Encyclopaedia Universalis*.

make-up of the West. Charles V needed seventeen crowns to balance the French super-power. The 'Affair of the Placards' in France in October 1537, and the Pilgrimage of Grace in England in the same year, were proof that any game against these colossi would be lost. So the world-wide nature of the Reformation and its ability to take hold in any country depended on how far it could insinuate itself into the structures of power in these states. In France, the King and one party of his councillors were won over to gentle reform: a Reformation which would hold together a straightforward religion of the Word and the Christ of the Gospels, as Lefèvre d'Étaples and Marguerite of Navarre had wished. This required traditional forms which would be respected for the time being, even though their scope would be progressively reduced as a result of a sustained effort of education. Considering the large area of the kingdom, only a *via media* even more gentle than that which assured the transition in England would suffice.

France was four times stronger than England in the sixteenth century, and was a much more complex state. The Court might incline towards a very moderate evangelicalism, but the majority of the parliamentarians and administrators who ran the State opted for the camp of continued and reinforced tradition. They were, really, calculating the danger and the difficulty of making such a massive body change. State control over the Church, reinforced by the Concordat of 1516, extinguished any desire for reform. Two other reasons made the most powerful territorial state in christendom less tempted than was the brilliant second power, England, to solve problems by adopting the Reformation. These were the degree to which the lawyers and civil servants had the Church of France well under control, and the fact that a much smaller proportion of land was immobilized under Church ownership.

Kingdoms are not turned upside-down like cities. Zurich had 7,000 inhabitants, the French kingdom 15 million. The spark which lit the fuse in England was Henry VIII's remarriage; the red light in France was the 'Affair of the Placards'. The marriage divorced England from Rome; the Placards remarried France. Even without them, Francis I's choice was the result of a careful weighing up of the risks. Lucien Febvre has described the Placards' illegal introduction: they were like fireships sailing into France from the Swiss canton of Vaud and the surrounding areas which had been won over to a hard, aggressive, culture-forming proselytizing variety of the Reformation, relying on preaching and simply sweeping away ritual for a purified evangelical Lord's Supper. Marcourt, the pastor at Neuchâtel, is presumed to be the author of the Placards. It was a good business proposition for the Swiss cantons and towns; but what a mistake to stick up these violent writings on the French King's door! How could 15 million people be asked to proclaim that the prayers of their parents and the heart of worship for a thousand years were only make-believe and satanic snares, 'papistical abominations' in a country where the Pope's power had always been kept on a tight rein? To follow the unrealistic Marcourt was to put the whole kingdom to fire and sword. More than Saxony, France needed a 'French mass'; and if a transitional position were turned down the parliamentarians would be strengthened in choosing to defend the traditional religion by force with no concessions. Once the State had chosen, the geography of the Reformation had to be worked out with the inverse of social logic. It was not the centre, Paris with its high officials, which would swing over, but the south and the west where the Swiss pattern of winning over people of middling power could be followed.

To the south was the old Latin Christendom: Italy with its little bishoprics, Spain with its 'frontier' between Christendom and the infidels. In Italy and in Spain among Marrano Jews, theoretically converted to Catholicism, there appeared little hyper-reformed congregations, often anti-trinitarian, which would provide cells for a radical diaspora to the extreme east, such as Poland.

Further north was the Europe of the French mass and the cloudy area of cantons, city-states, and little principalities. It was a patchwork of radical choices. There also the weighty influence of the powerful centralizing states of France and England affected their high level of culture and economy.

There remains the largest part of the Empire: Hungary, Poland, Scandinavia. One factor played an almost mathematical part: the distance from the centralizing element. Beyond a certain distance Roman tutelage was intolerable: 'What's the use of these folk called cardinals?', demanded Luther. To drain and to suck dry! The ancient Roman *limes* re-emerged. What was beyond that frontier in 400 BC swung away decisively: Britain and the Empire.

Canterbury confirmed Ireland's refusal to join the Reformation but Wittenberg attracted Scandinavia. Poland was split between the most radical reforms and far distant Rome but chose the second, perhaps to counter the Byzantine world of Moscow and the Tartars.

SCOTLAND
Aberdeen
Glasgow ■St Andrews
Edinburgh

IRELAND
Dublin ■
York
ENGLAND
Cambridge □
Oxford □ London ■
Canterbury ■

NORWAY
Oslo
Uppsala
Stockholm
SWEDEN

Riga
COURLAND

DENMARK
Copenhagen
Königsberg
Rostock
Hamburg Greifswald
Pultusk □
Brème
Poznań □
Varsovy
Leyde ■
LOW COUNTRIES
Hildesheim
Magdeburg Frankfurt-on-Oder
Rotterdam
Münster
Wittenberg ★
Breslau
Antwerp
Leipzig ■
St Omer ■ Brussels Cologne
Marburg Wartburg Erfurt Mühlberg
SAXONY
Cracow
Louvain ☆
Herborn ■Iéna
Smalkalde ■
Olmutz □
Cambrai □
Frankfurt
Fulda □
Prague □
HOLY
Sedan ■
Mainz ■Heidelberg ■
Meaux
Trèves
Speyer Worms
ROMAN
Vienna □
HUNGARY
Paris ■
Haguenau
Dillingen □
EMPIRE
Strasburg ■
Ingolstadt □
Molsheim □ Tübingen ■
Augsburg ☆ Munich
Ofen □ Pest
FRANCE
Basle ★
Salzburg □
Nantes
Saumur ■ Zurich
Innsbruck □
La Rochelle ■ Poitiers □
Geneva ■
Lucerne □
Trent ☆
Angoulême ■
Lyons ■
Chambéry □
Milan □
orthodox region with
Billom □
Padua □
muslim minority
Bordeaux ■
Mauriac □
Genoa □
La Coruña
Santander
Montauban ■
Bologna □
Orthez ■ Orange ■
Montpellier
Toulouse
PAPAL STATES
Valladolid □
SPAIN
Avila ☆
Alcalá de Henares □
Escorial ■ Madrid □
Rome ☆
KINGDOM
Barcelona □
Naples □ OF NAPLES
Lisbon

MUSLIM COUNTRIES

Palermo
Messina

▨ Lutheran region		□ Catholic region	
□ Reformed region (Calvinists, Zwinglians)		▦ Catholic minority in Protestant region	
▒ Calvinist minority in France		☆ centre of Catholic Counter-Reformation	
▨ Anglican region		□ principal Jesuit college at end of 16th century	
★ important centre of Reformation		▨ area regained by Catholicism at end of 16th century	
■ important Protestant university		▭ mission region dependant on the congregation for spreading the faith	
▒ area of mixed religion (Catholics, Protestants)			

scale: 1/15,000,000

Reformation and Counter-Reformation at the end of the 16th century

The Confession of Augsburg of 1540 is the first Protestant confession of faith in which the dogmatic elements of the Christian faith are clearly defined. In this 17th-century painting, a number of German princes kneel before Charles V, surrounded by typical scenes from the cultural life of the Lutheran churches, particularly communion in both kinds.

The Confession of Augsburg, German painting of 1617. Church of St George, Eisenach.

In other words, the geography of the Reformation and of the Counter-Reformation depended as much on brakes as on impetus. Thrusts and buffers interacted to produce the essential lines of the topography; for the rest, human action and the invisible hand of mysterious divine grace gave it its character.

Reformation chronology

The Reformation introduced a new sense of time. Even if it only rejected 'errors in recent tradition' in the name of the more ancient tradition, it did bring about at least a break in continuity if not a rupture. It followed that the rhythm of the Protestant world was shorter, jerkier, more rapid. Protestant Christianity deprived itself of the cushioning provided by the religious orders and the separated clergy which made things seem less harsh and more balanced.

This all-or-nothing in the hand of God was shown in the tenets of 'Faith alone', 'Scripture alone', and in a clear and simplified Church ritual. And then, as life goes on, the

rebuilding of what had been destroyed gradually began: thickets of 'discipline' next to the forests of canon law, the *Formulas of Concord*, the *Loci communes*, the *Confessions of Faith*, added to the authority of Scripture correctly interpreted in the spirit of the Reformers. In a word, to look after 'Faith alone' and 'Scripture alone', a form of orthodoxy arose with its network of universities, its statutory professors, and its Latin folios, all hardly less weighty than the ancient orthodoxy.

In the case of grave crisis, the traditional Church had a recourse: the council, which had for example allowed schism to come to an end at the Council of Constance. Historians rewriting history and impelled by the best intentions have imagined that a council in 1520 would have avoided schism. But a council cannot be improvised, and it can happen that the remedy is worse than the evil.

Between 1519 and 1546, the Christianity that came out of the Reformation was cast in the bronze of an alternate ecclesiology, proud of its spiritual apostolicity and its conformity to the scriptural model. On the Protestant side, it can be said that the first council was held in Augsburg and ended on 25 June 1530 with a clear definition

of the dogmatic elements of the Christian faith. In that sense, the Confession of Augsburg filled a void. On the Catholic side, the slowness of the reaction was due initially to the massive size of the Roman Church: still, in 1530, comprising nine-tenths of western Christendom.

Despite the quantity of documents at its disposal, not because of them, the Church of Tradition lacked a clear and complete definition of the Christian faith. Ten years would be needed to absorb the shock of this contagious dissidence and, going beyond brutal and ineffectual recourse to force, to form in 1529 the scheme for solving the crisis by calling an ecumenical council. Only in 1536 was the process begun which issued in the meeting of a handful of bishops – between fifty and a hundred – at Trent on 13 December 1545.

This council was not the conciliatory one expected by the Emperor. This was the Pope's council, prepared in the Italian laboratory of the Counter-Reformation, which chose a frontal assault over all the controversial questions: dogma, reform of institutions and customs, the ecclesiology of the apostolic succession by the laying on of hands, Scripture and the tradition of delegated authority, and from that the sacraments, ideas of heaven, purgatory, and hell, prayer on behalf of the dead linking them solidly with the living in the continuum of life across the ages.

Whatever the cost of these dual Protestant and Catholic responses, they enriched the Church. The further we travel from the 'second Pentecost', the clearer it becomes that division, although a thorn in the flesh, is also the opportunity which God in his goodness gives to his people precisely through the complementary ways of faithfulness which the Holy Spirit offers us in the midst of anguish.

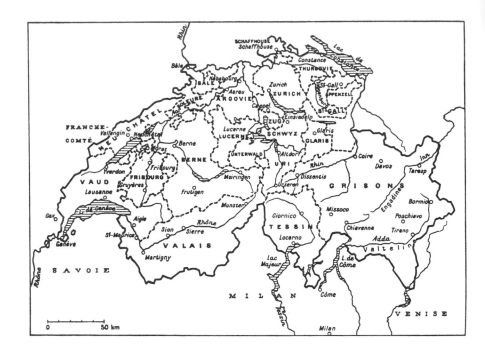

Switzerland at the time of the Reformation, map taken from the *Histoire générale du protestantisme* by E.C. Léonard, PUF, 1961 and 1982.

The establishment of the Reformation in Switzerland

In Switzerland as elsewhere the Reformation could only be established by a desperate struggle waged on theological, political and military levels simultaneously. Among the reasons for its success, the leading roles were undoubtedly played by two men whose names are intimately associated with two cities: Zwingli in Zurich in the 1520s and Calvin at Geneva from 1541 to 1564.

The work of Zwingli

It was at Zurich, a town of 7,000 people and the capital of one of the thirteen cantons which made up the Swiss Confederation, that the reform of the Church began in Switzerland. Its principal author was Huldrych Zwingli, a priest of thirty-four who had carried out his ministry at Glarus and Einsiedeln before answering a call to the post of common preacher of the Cathedral (Grossmünster) of Zurich in 1519, about a year and a half after Luther posted up his Theses at Wittenberg. Zwingli's reputation had preceded him, and it was obvious that things were going to change when he began daily following through the Gospel of Matthew in his preaching, instead of giving homilies based on the readings in the lectionary for the Church year. He had big audiences for his preaching and did not mince his words in denouncing those who did not come.

At first, small reforms were undertaken, like diverting a fund earmarked for chanting the *Salve regina* to the sick and poor. In 1522 some printers had a meal of sausage in Zwingli's presence during Lent, which annoyed the Bishop of Constance. Zwingli's response was a treatise on the freedom to eat any dishes. Then came a booklet addressed to the Bishop demanding the possibility of clerical marriage, and next his 'First and Last Word' to the Bishop (*Apologeticus Archeteles*). On 10 October 1522 the break with the Bishop became final. The magistracy then engaged for the mission of bringing the Gospel to the people Zwingli: the first Reformed minister was appointed.

At the beginning of 1523 a theological disputation took place, convened by the magistracy, for which Zwingli prepared sixty-seven theses directed towards the Reform of the Church on the basis of Holy Scripture. Hugo von Landenburg, the Bishop of Constance, refused his invitation, but sent a delegation led by his Vicar-General, Faber.

Institutional Reform was then instigated. Nuns were allowed to leave their convents and were granted compensation for their secularized possessions. Priests came to ask for their marriages to be blessed. The chapter of the Grossmünster was Reformed and the distinction between canon and chaplain abolished. The tax on ecclesiastical services was removed. Sinecures were no longer filled after their holders died. To instruct the clergy, Zwingli founded the *Prophezei* in 1525. From 1523 the old Latin school was rejuvenated: the masters were better paid and the students better lodged. Zwingli expounded his views on education in a letter written to his stepson Gerold Meyer von Knonau – he had by now married, his bride being a widow.

By and large there was a desire for radical reform, so long as this disturbed the general populace as little as possible. There were those, however, who complained that the reforms were going too slowly. There were scenes of violence; images were removed and crucifixes torn down. A second disputation, convened for the end of 1523, brought no apparent change. Zwingli was given the task of producing a treatise called *Brief Christian instruction for clergy*, which contained regulations for ordering worship, expounding the faith, preaching and general behaviour.

Title page of *How Unity and Peace are Attained*, pamphlet by Huldrych Zwingli attacking radicals and Anabaptists, Zurich, 1524. Zentralbibliothek, Zurich.

143

In 1524 images were removed where they were objects of a cult. There was no more baptism *in extremis* and extreme unction was no longer administered. At the end of 1524, the Abbess of the Fraumünster made a solemn gift of her convent and its goods to the town of Zurich. Finally, by an ordinance of the following year, all the religious houses were closed with the exception of two, one for men and one for women who desired to remain in the monastic state. It was only in April 1525 that the evangelical Lord's Supper replaced the mass. Zwingli had prepared a suitable liturgy. The altars were removed and replaced by a wooden table. The cup and plate were also of wood, so that everything should be very simple. Similarly, the organs were taken out and chanting forbidden in worship. However, until 1529 the citizens of Zurich were still able, if they wanted it, to go to mass outside the canton. On the social side, begging was forbidden, but needy Zurichers were cared for by a daily distribution of hot soup to the poor in front of the Dominican church.

About 1526, the work of Reformation was more or less achieved and things became fairly stable. It was at that time that the matrimonial tribunal was created. Marriage, being no longer a sacrament, became a civil matter, and the Church had the function only of giving a blessing. A new matrimonial law was created and every marriage was entered in a civil register. The matrimonial tribunal enlarged its scope in the next year into a body watching over conduct in general. Composed of four lay people and two pastors, it kept an eye on the behaviour of the citizens, to such a degree that around 1528 Zurich had something of the character later to be found in Strasburg, and above all in Geneva from 1541.

The struggle against Anabaptism and Catholicism

The Peasants' Revolt which ravaged Germany had repercussions in Switzerland, but only of short duration. As a true countryman, Zwingli understood the basis for the peasants' demands. He therefore obtained the abolition of serfdom and so avoided in Switzerland the tragic fate of Germany.

The Anabaptist crisis was a very different matter. People of that persuasion felt that the Reformers were not going as fast or as deep as they should in the reforms they advocated. Conventicles established themselves on the margins of the Church, even the Reformed parts of the Church, and the Lord's Supper was celebrated outside its organization. A fervent desire arose for disassociation, not only from the Church but also from the State. The magistrate attempted in vain to hold discussions with the movement's leaders, and then issued an order to baptize children within a week of birth, and a ban on private meetings. These were also in vain. Some of the leaders were thrown into prison, others fined and expelled from the territory. Finally, in despair over the matter, the city resorted to the death penalty, and the Anabaptist Manz was thrown in chains into the Limmat, Zurich's river.

The other great adversary of the Reformers was Roman Catholicism. In this respect, Switzerland soon divided into two camps. One gained the area around Zurich, the other organized itself for resistance and had its centre in the primitive or forest cantons: Uri, Schwyz, Unterwalden, Zug and Lucerne. These cantons were poor and found mercenary service abroad a considerable resource. Zurich and Berne, on the other hand, were rich cantons and Zurich's violent opposition to mercenary

The history of the Reformation is also the history of certain towns which played a crucial role. As places of refuge for exiles and as examples for believers throughout Europe, Luther's Wittenberg, Calvin's Geneva and Zwingli's Zurich were the capitals of nascent Protestantism.

Zurich Cathedral at the time of Zwingli, painting on wood by Hans Leu the Elder and Hans Leu the Younger. Musée National Suisse, Zurich.

145

The Reformation divided Switzerland in two: on one side, the cantons which were won over to Zwingli; on the other, those which remained faithful to Rome. Berthold Haller (1492–1536) helped the new ideas to triumph in Berne, while Johannes Oecolampadius (1482–1531), a humanist very close to Erasmus, became pastor of the cathedral at Basle. The most tragic episode of the confrontation between these two parties was the battle of Kappel in 1531, which cost Zwingli his life.

View of Basle, engraving by H. Schedel taken from the *Nuremberg Chronicle*, 1493. Bibliothèque Nationale, Paris.

Portrait of Berthold Haller, engraving taken from Reussner's *Icons*, 1587. Société de l'Histoire du Protestantisme Français, Paris.

Portrait of Johannes Oecolampadius, painting on wood by Hans Asper, 16th century. Oeffentliche Kunstsammlung, Basle.

The battle of Kappel, engraving taken from the *Chronicle* of Johannes Stumpf, Zurich, 1548. Zentralbibliothek, Zurich.

service is well known. The war of ideas between the two confessions was accompanied by acts of violence such as the burning of a charterhouse or the execution of a pastor travelling over Catholic territory. The primitive cantons wanted to exclude Zurich from the renewing of the federal pacts on the pretext that it had denied the true faith – the federal pact of 1291 began by invoking God. Zurich and Berne stood for the notion that on the confessional question, each canton should be able to choose which faith the citizens wished to hold.

St Gallen, Appenzell, Glarus, Schaffhausen and Basle were on the point of siding with the Reformation. Before this dangerous prospect, the cantons which remained attached to the old faith, a majority in the federal diet, asked for the convening of a disputation which took place at Basle in 1526 and in which the renowned doctor, Eck, took part. Zwingli did not attend, in view of the danger he considered this meeting had for him, but Oecolampadius took the lead in opposition to the Vicar-General, Faber. Zwingli was of course condemned, but the arrogance of the five forest cantons ended by alienating the moderate, mediating cantons, which now inclined towards the Reformation. Lucerne had threatened Berne over an area where the interests of the two cantons came into conflict, and so Berne took offence and permitted the free preaching of the Gospel, while placing all its monastic houses under the civil administration.

In an attempt to regularize everything, Berne convoked a disputation in January 1528 of which Zwingli was the leading light. Scripture alone had naturally to be the decisive authority for the discussions. The representatives of the five forest cantons refused to attend, as did the Bishops of Constance, Basle, Lausanne and Sion. But on the other side a number of Reformers were present: Haller, who introduced the Reformation to Berne; Vadian, the medical doctor and Reformer of St Gallen; Oecolampadius from Basle; Capito and Bucer from Strasburg (there were at the time very strong links between that city and Switzerland). It was therefore only fair that the victory went to the partisans of Reform. Zwingli had preached there on the Creed to make the point that the intention was to stay within the Catholic Church and that what was needed was to reform it according to Holy Scripture.

The expansion of the Reformation

The repercussions of this disputation were considerable, given the position of Berne. The power which this big canton represented, and the respect which it inspired, even with the King of France, played their part. Jean Viénot, the French historian of

the Reformation, goes so far as to write that without the disputation of Berne and its favourable outcome for the Reformers, Protestantism in French-speaking Switzerland and even in France would not have been possible.

On 7 February 1528 the Reformation was officially established in Berne. The following summer pensions from abroad and mercenary service were forbidden in that canton, and the Reformation established in the countryside too, even if there were a few incidents here and there. With Berne won over, Basle soon followed. The Reformer there was Oecolampadius, a Hellenist who had worked with Erasmus on the publication of the Greek New Testament, and who with Capito's support had been appointed to a post in Augsburg. He returned to Basle in 1522, worked for the reform of the Church there, and took an important part in the disputation of Baden. At Basle the Reformation was officially established at the beginning of 1529. In the spring, the cathedral chapter and certain burghers attached to the traditional faith left the city, and several members of the university, including Erasmus, went off to Freiburg-im-Breisgau. At Bremgarten, the young Heinrich Bullinger, Zwingli's future successor at Zurich, was already making a name for himself.

Of the thirteen cantons, therefore, three were won for the Reformation. But relations were tense because the Reformers had made alliances with foreign cities, while the forest cantons had made a treaty with Austria. Another antagonism, that between Luther and Zwingli from the political as well as the religious point of view, was coming to a head, and the Colloquy of Marburg in 1529 formalized the discord between the two main centres of the Reformation.

At Zurich, Zwingli was the undisputed master and a member of the privy council, the highest civic authority; he was also nothing less than 'the prophet'. More and more he was given the lead in both spiritual and temporal affairs; and although he had always distinguished the two spheres in his writings, in practice they were constantly mixed. While clouds gathered in the outer world with the second Diet of Speyer, war seemed inevitable between the proponents of the two confessions in Switzerland. It nearly broke out in 1529 and is actually known as the first war of Kappel. But Aebli, the landamman of Glarus, succeeded in preventing any fighting, and the adversaries met on the frontier round a cream soup to seal their reconciliation: the forest cantons acknowledged they had been worsted. But Zwingli was anxious. He composed the hymn beginning with the words, 'Lord, direct thou our chariot, or we drive to the abyss'. In fact, the forces of the forest cantons remained united but dissensions were appearing among the Reformers. Berne was developing political ties chiefly westwards, and had not the same immediate interests as Zurich, disliking the latter's tendencies towards hegemony.

In the common bailiwicks like Thurgau, religious houses were suppressed and ecclesiastical property disposed of. Roman Catholic minorities had a hard time of it. When Zwingli proposed to declare war on Austria, the cities of southern Germany

147

Antoine Froment (1509–81), together with his compatriots Farel and Calvin, was one of the leaders of the Reformation in Geneva. A preacher of great talent, he was also the historian of his adopted town.

Froment preaching at Le Mollard, 19th-century engraving. Bibliothèque Publique et Universitaire, Geneva.

At Geneva, the victory of the Reformation involved the departure of the prince-bishop, Pierre de la Baume, who had to yield power to Guillaume Farel and Antoine Froment.

Portrait of Bishop Pierre de la Baume, 19th-century painting on wood, inspired by the reredos of the cathedral at St Claude (Jura). Bibliothèque Publique et Universitaire, Geneva.

The Spaniard Michael Servetus (1511–53) denied both the Trinity and the doctrine of Original Sin, thus contradicting the teaching of both Catholics and Protestants. He took refuge in Geneva in order to escape from the Inquisition, but was condemned to death as a heretic. Many Reformed Christians subsequently regretted this intolerant act which put Calvin's friends on the same footing as their persecutors. An expiatory monument now stands at Champel, Geneva.

Portrait of Michael Servetus, burnt alive on 27 October 1553, 16th-century engraving.

one after another replied coldly to his overtures. With the height of misjudgement, the Reformed cantons which did not like the idea of war agreed to a food blockage of the forest cantons, which poisoned the situation. These cantons prepared for what they considered inevitable civil war, while at Zurich the military leaders who were disaffected were kept away from the army.

In the domestic life of the city, citizens disliked the powers the magistracy had been given to interfere with their private lives. Resentment focused on Zwingli, whose authority was at its height, but who had to face a growing discontent. In view of this situation, he offered his resignation as pastor and prophet, but this was not accepted because the situation was so serious. The second War of Kappel broke out in 1531, a bloody affair which was resolved by the death in battle of Zwingli and the defeat of the Zurichers. People there were carried away by pacifist sentiments. Berne prudently pulled its irons out of the fire, perhaps in the long run to the advantage of the evangelical cause, and the progress of the Reformation was halted in Switzerland.

Peace concluded, the two confessions remained entrenched in their positions and began a period of cold war. The Protestant cantons were allowed to hold to their own beliefs so long as they left the others 'incontestably to their true and undoubted Christian faith'. The Reformed communities in the common bailiwicks were authorized to keep their new faith, but whoever wished to return to the old faith was to be free to do so. Catholic preponderance was thus well established, and was to remain so for a long time. However, the Church of Zurich strengthened and

reorganized itself, under the influence of Bullinger who succeeded with the aid of a far-sighted magistracy in maintaining Zurich as capital of Reformed Switzerland.

Obviously both the Confederation and the Reformed Church came out of the crisis weakened by it. But thanks to the later activity of Calvin, who has good cause to be called Zwingli's true successor, the influence of the Zurich Reformation spread through the intermediate agency of Geneva to France, to Scotland, to Poland, to Hungary, to the Low Countries and finally to North America. Ernest Gagliardi, in his history of Switzerland, sums up the situation accurately when he writes that 'the judgement we make on the value of Zwingli's theocracy must depend on what was really lasting in what it created'.

The part played by Berne in the sixteenth century must also be judged by its long-term results. The 'gentlemen of Berne', different in character from the Zurichers, made up a powerful and assured body. Their political activity was decisive in the eventual entry into the Confederation of the regions which today make up the French-speaking part of Switzerland. Furthermore, they used their Reformed faith to expand westwards. The man who typifies this movement is Guillaume Farel, from Gap in the Dauphiné. In contact with Lefèvre d'Étaples, a member of the group at Meaux with Briçonnet, this great traveller was to be found at Strasburg with Capito and Bucer, at Basle and at Zurich with Oecolampadius and Zwingli, at the Disputation of Berne and at the Synod of Chanforans (1532) when the Waldenses of Piedmont joined the nascent Reformation. Whether at Aigle, Morat, Grandson, Moutier or Neuchâtel, Farel preached the Reformation under the protection of Berne; according to Jules Petremand, he was 'more or less in the position of being the agent of his principal [Zwingli]'. Under his influence the valleys of the Jura rallied to the new faith, and then, indefatigable, he turned his attention to Geneva.

The victory of the Reformation in Geneva was assisted by the Bernese who invaded the Pays de Vaud in January 1936 and in October organized a religious disputation in Lausanne.

The Bernese invade the Pays de Vaud, engraving taken from the *Chronicle* of Johannes Stumpf, Zurich, 1548. Bibliothèque Publique et Universitaire, Geneva.

Geneva, the 'Protestant Rome'

At that time, Geneva, an imperial city, was surrounded by the lands of the Duke of Savoy. Its sovereign was a prince-bishop who was devoted to the interests of the powerful duke. Under the influence of a few patriotic citizens Geneva began to shake off its yoke and depended for that purpose on a treaty of fellow citizenship with Fribourg and Berne which was finalized between 1520 and 1526. From 1530, Berne undertook a campaign in the direction of Geneva to keep the duke from dominating the end of the lake, with a thought to one day annexing the city. A treaty was concluded with the duke in 1530 at St Julien, by which he agreed to abstain from all acts of violence towards the Genevans and granted them freedom of trade. Where this peace was violated, the Bernese and Fribourgeois would have the right to take possession of the Vaud which had been Savoyard until then. The duke, who did not consider himself beaten, succeeded in profiting from the troubles brought about by the preaching of Ferel and his colleague Antoine Froment. He intervened and secured their departure from Geneva. But the two preachers were reinstated in Geneva by the city of Berne, and the prince-bishop left his city by night, never to return.

So, resisting Berne which wished to dominate them but open to Farel's preaching, the Genevans provisionally abolished the mass in 1535 and took an oath the next year to observe 'the holy evangelical law and word of God', thus adopting the Reform of the Church. That same year, as the Duke of Savoy was hardly holding to his promises, Berne invaded the Vaud with the evident desire to annexe it, and met with practically no resistance. Naturally that situation was endorsed by the

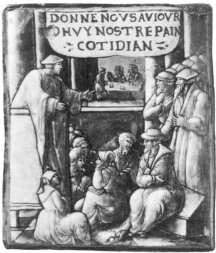

Another great Reformer, the Swiss Pierre Viret (1511–71) exercised his ministry at Orbe, Grandson, Payerne and Lausanne, before having to take refuge in Geneva. He died at Orthez, in Béarn, where the Queen of Navarre had summoned him to teach theology. On the plaque to the right he preaches before Calvin and Theodore de Beza.

Limoges enamels illustrating the Lord's Prayer, works by Colin II Noaihler, 16th century. Musée du Louvre, Paris.

Reformers. Not content with permitting preachers to exercise their ministry, the Bernese encouraged them, and to that end organized a religious disputation at Lausanne which took place in October 1536, despite the opposition of the cantons which remained loyal to the old faith. Farel and Viret, the latter the Reformer of the Vaud and eventually a close collaborator of Calvin, played a decisive part. Calvin, who had just arrive in Geneva, joined in, but in a discreet way. At the end of the disputation, images were removed from the churches, and the Bernese government published an edict of Reformation which among other things forbade games and dancing. Ecclesiastical property was confiscated and in the recognized Reformed tradition an academy was founded at Lausanne in 1537. Thus began a fundamental change, not only from the political but from the confessional point of view: French-speaking Switzerland would in future become a nursery of the Reformed faith.

In the same year that Berne, occupying the Vaud, established direct communication with Geneva, John Calvin, a lawyer from Picardy twenty years younger than Farel, arrived in the city and was kept there by Farel, after a dramatic discussion, to organize the Reform of the Church. On his deathbed in 1564 Calvin was to say of that time: 'When I first came to this church there was practically nothing; there was preaching but that was all . . . There was no Reformation, all was in an uproar'. In fact, a new stage was beginning in the history of the Reformed churches.

Calvin's beginnings in Geneva faced difficulties and issued in his and Farel's expulsion. The two men had wanted to make arrangements, among other things, about barring people from the Lord's Supper, but met the resistance of the councils, influenced as these were by those whom they called 'libertines', and who had no

intention of being delivered from subjection to the bishop only to find themselves under new masters worse than before. Calvin left for Strasburg where Bucer claimed him back; Farel for Neuchâtel where he remained, except for frequent visits to Geneva.

Calvin remained for three years in Strasburg, as head of the parish for French refugees. During that period Cardinal Sadoleto, the Bishop of Carpentras, wrote his well-known letter to the Genevans, to try to persuade them to return to the Roman communion. The Genevans were not won over by this appeal, and finding a suitable person among the pastors who had remained at Geneva to reply to the bishop, asked Calvin to do so from Strasburg. He agreed and in a celebrated letter clearly set out the position of the Reformed faith against the Roman one. At Strasburg Calvin was in touch with an organized church, many features of which resembled those of Zwingli at Zurich, although there was a clearer separation of the minister and the magistrate than in the earlier model.

Finally the Genevans came to realize that they badly needed Calvin back in his former place with them, and asked him to return. Farel begged Calvin to accept, which he did unenthusiastically and on two conditions — that they would accept an ecclesiastical discipline independent of the State, and that a catechism should be published. Ordinances which he wrote were promulgated, regularizing the existence of four ministries in the Church: teachers, pastors, elders and deacons; a catechism was published, whose teaching and even wording reflected the one Bucer had created for Strasburg. A consistory was formed, composed of the pastors of the city and former members of the town councils; its duty was to see that doctrine was adhered to, and to function as a court of morals. The pastors were formed into an association with Calvin as Moderator — it was a copy of the

Strasburg 'ecclesiastical convention' — and met in 'congregations' to study the Bible, in the manner of the *Prophezei* at Zurich.

Once the worst dangers had been averted and a calmer period in relations with Berne had begun, Calvin began to meet resistance in the ranks of those who had previously supported him. The consistory attacked not only abuses but also harmless pleasures. A councillor who had insulted Calvin during a meal was condemned to ask the Reformer's pardon clad in a shirt and with a taper in his hand. Worse came in 1547, when Jacques Gruet, a free thinker who had stuck an offensive placard about the ministry on the pulpit in St Peter's and had attacked the Christian religion, was arrested and executed. A year later, Ami Perrin, the former leader of Farel's party, put himself at the head of the opposition and had a measure of success. For some years his supporters were in a majority on the council and the hostility towards foreigners was exploited in order to make Calvin's position difficult. One of these foreigners, Jerome Bolsec from Paris, attacked the doctrine of predestination, an essential one for Calvin. He was arrested, brought to trial, and, despite the intervention of various Swiss churches, banished.

Calvin could well fear being expelled again himself, with the Perrinists holding power, xenophobia flourishing and feelings becoming more and more heated. During this period he and Bullinger led the proceedings which issued in 1549 in an agreement on the Lord's Supper known as the *Consensus Tigurinus*. This sealed the tradition which from the 1570s would be called 'Reformed', by which the Eucharistic doctrines of Zwingli and Calvin would be expressed in one single text.

In the midst of this tense situation there arrived in Geneva one day in 1553 Michael Servetus, the Spanish doctor who was the first to describe the double circulation of the blood in the human body. He was imprudent enough to go to hear

This 19th-century drawing illustrates how Calvin won respect for the moral order in Geneva. It is known that the Reformer did not hesitate to concern himself with the smallest details of daily life and that he insisted on great austerity in clothing, behaviour and attitudes.

Calvin refusing the sacrament to the 'libertines', watercolour and gouache drawing by Jean-Leonard Lugardon, 19th century. Musée Historique de la Réformation, Geneva.

Calvin preach and was recognized and arrested as an anti-trinitarian and an opponent of infant baptism, views which were considered at that time to be a great danger to both Church and city. It seems certain that Calvin had been indirectly involved in the searches that had been made for Servetus in Vienna. But in considering the latter's trial it is worth remarking that apart from certain people very much in advance of their times, notably Castellion who had moved from Geneva to Basle, everyone, including the Swiss churches who were consulted, thought that Servetus should be executed. He thus went to the stake at Champel, where this sad episode is commemorated today by an expiatory monument.

Servetus had been condemned by a magistrate who belonged to a party opposed to the Reformer, but who had been obliged to apply the law. The result was that notwithstanding the danger that had been avoided over the burning of Servetus, Calvin's partisans obtained a majority on the council in 1555. A fair number of French exiles were then welcomed into the ranks of the burghers. Perrin and his friends intrigued together against the 'tyranny' of these foreigners, but with no success; most of the opposing councillors were able to escape from Geneva, but four were arrested and executed. Calvin had triumphed.

All this made Geneva stronger in its independence, to the very great indignation of Berne, which still had to conduct its affairs in the light of the Duke of Savoy's desire to take it back and the King of France's political aims. Another complication was the fact that in the Vaud certain disciples of Calvin, notably Viret, were trying to establish an ecclesiastical discipline on the lines of that at Geneva, a discipline independent of the civil power and so disagreeable to Berne. The struggle became fierce, particularly concerning the academy – so much so that the Calvinist teachers there, including Theodore de Beza, Viret and Mathurin Cordier, left Lausanne.

These events happened in 1559, an important year for the Reformation, because it saw the Treaty of Cateau-Cambresis which ended the war between France and Spain and allowed them to fight more actively against heresy. An important year too, as the future was going to prove, because it was the accession of Elizabeth to the English throne. That then was the moment chosen by Calvin to create the academy which would constitute the crown of his work. He summoned to Geneva the professors who had been chased out of Lausanne and formed the teaching body of the 'college and academy', which had an immediate success. Thus were negated the pessimistic claims of Haller, the Bernese Reformer, that to create such a school at such a time was madness, because no one would come there. Quite to the contrary, students came from far afield. Florimond de Raemond, a Catholic author, described students from Guienne 'putting their bags together and making their way by day and night to Geneva' and compared their joy at the sight of the city to that of Godfrey de Bouillon 'seeing the long desired walls of Hiérusalem'. The classes at the college were soon doubled, and hundreds of listeners followed Calvin's courses.

'The academy thus acquired an international importance', wrote Gagliardi, 'as the seedbed of Protestantism, and to a great degree it was in the lessons there that the energy was absorbed which would victoriously resist Catholicism.' In that same year, 1559, appeared the definitive edition of the *Institutes of the Christian Religion*, Calvin's master work, the first edition of which had been published in Basle in 1536. The last of the four books, much more advanced than the previous editions, concerned the doctrine of the Church.

The Lausanne disputation was an important stage in the spread of the Reformation in Geneva and the Pays de Vaud. The principal participants were Farel and Viret, but the intervention of Calvin, who had recently come to the area at a time when the Reform movement was suffering a slight setback, was no less decisive.

Sketch of *The disputation of Lausanne*, wash on paper by François Bocion, 19th century. Musée Cantonal des Beaux-Arts, Lausanne.

Five years after founding the academy, Calvin died, respected by all. He had made of Geneva a city to be known as the 'Protestant Rome'. His career had been able to unfold at Geneva because peace reigned on its frontiers under the protection of Berne, while the Duke of Savoy was still making war. Things were no longer the same when his successor, Theodore de Beza, took in hand the destiny of the Church. While the latter was Moderator, the Church grew stronger, but in an atmosphere of war which kept the population on the alert. The Duke of Savoy's repeated incursions continued until the end of the century and culminated in the famous night of 12 December 1602 when Duke Charles Emmanuel was given a painful and decisive check. From then on, the Reformation of the Church was solidly planted in Geneva, from where it could radiate across all Europe.

After Calvin's death, the atmosphere of relative security in Geneva was transformed into dread of invasion. Cavoy's attempts to crush the Reformation in the lakeside city culminated in the assault of 12 December 1602, an abortive attack which allowed the Reformed religion finally to establish its sway.

The assault on Geneva, copper engraving by Hogenberg, 1602. Bibliothèque Publique et Universitaire, Geneva.

153

PART THREE

CHRISTENDOM SHATTERED

Italy and Spain: diffusion, failure and survival of Reforming convictions

In one way, the Reformation began in Italy before it reached Germany. Savonarola (1452–98) preceded Luther in his determination to change religious practice and return to the simplicity of the Gospel in open opposition to the papacy. Between 1494 and 1497, he established his leadership over the city of Florence, one of the richest and most industrious cities of the time, and introduced measures which ostensibly foreran those of Luther and Calvin: the banning of profane festivals and gambling, austerity of dress and the removal of images from places of worship. But the experiment did not last as the Dominican's career ended at the stake.

Portrait of Savonarola, 17th-century engraving. Bibliothèque Nationale, Paris.

Canon Manufacture in Florence, painting by Pocetti, 16th century. Galleria degli Uffizi, Florence.

The Martyrdom of Savonarola, anonymous late 15th-century painting. Museo di S. Marco, Florence.

The Reformation met with a similar fate in Italy and in Spain. In both countries it came up against opponents who were on their guard and determined to do their utmost to prevent it from gaining a hold. The Italian and Spanish Protestants adopted every form of disguise and took all sorts of precautions, but to no avail. They were mercilessy hounded by the Inquisition and were able to take part in the great Reform movement only outside their own countries.

The causes of the failure in Italy

The roots of the Italian Reformation go back to before Luther's time; they are a continuation of the humanist legacy of Savonarola, of the *Sola Fide* and of Marsilio Ficino. But it was the Lutheran revolution which gave it its real impetus. To the principle of justification by faith (*Sola Fide justificari*) was added that of reference to the authority of the Scriptures alone (*Sola Scriptura*) – thus moving from an evangelical Paulinist stance to Protestant convictions accompanied by a Protestant concept of the Church, of a Protestant sacramental doctrine, and in certain places, of Protestant rites. But, overall, Italian Protestantism remained a clandestine movement whose history comes down to us through the reports of interrogations conducted by the courts of the Inquisition which were hostile to it, rather than through the testimonies of the Protestants themselves.

The centres of this clandestine movement in Venice, Cremona, Modena and Lucca were declining when the movement surfaced in the mountainous regions of the Piedmont, united itself with Geneva and, in 1561, even gained a limited freedom of worship. The Protestant tendency in Piedmont and at Lucca can be described as Calvinist. In Venice, the Baptist partisans who were opposed to the dogma of the Trinity were dominant. As for numbers, it is only possible to estimate. Historians think that at the time when Protestantism was at its height, in the 1540s, Italy had a population of about 12 million. The supporters of evangelism, of justification by faith or of a Christianity based on the Sermon on the Mount, akin to that of Erasmus, numbered hundreds of thousands. Erasmus made a profound impact on Italy, the country of humanism *par excellence*, but the number of Protestants and crypto-Protestants could not have been more than a few thousand.

The failure of the Reformation in Italy was due primarily to its content, its geographical structure and its human adherents. The content did not represent a uniform doctrinal teaching, as it did in France, Saxony, Scandinavia and elsewhere. Calvinism undoubtedly prevailed, but the Baptists were so powerful in Venice that they were able to hold an international council and make decisions which clashed headlong with Protestant orthodoxies. There were also Lutherans and a number of people whom the Inquisition called *Luterani* because they departed from Catholic

The centres of the Italian Reformation were the University of Padua and the court of Ferrara where Renée of France (1510–75), a pupil of Lefèvre d'Étaples, gave hospitality to a number of Protestants, including John Calvin himself. But, after the establishment of the Society of Jesus in Rome in 1540, the Catholic reaction was vigorous and effective. Men like Fausto Sozzini (1539–1604), the anti-Trinitarian heresiarch, had to leave Italy – Sozzini continued to preach a caricature of the Reformation in Poland.

The University of Padua, 16th-century engraving. Bibliothèque Nationale, Paris.

Portrait of Fausto Sozzini, 17th-century engraving. Bibliothèque Nationale, Paris.

Portrait of Renée of France, Duchess of Ferrara, 19th-century copy of a lost original. Société de l'Histoire du Protestantisme Français, Paris.

Ignatius Loyola handing over the rules of the Society of Jesus to Pope Paul III, engraving by C. de Malloy, 16th century. Bibliothèque Nationale, Paris.

doctrine. It was still too early for the appearance of Protestant ecumenical trends striving for unification at the core of the doctrine.

Geographically, the whole of mainland Italy and its islands were effectively infiltrated, to varying degrees, by Protestantism. The Reformation generally found more supporters in the cities than in the countryside, in the north rather than the south. Protestantism was widespread in the universities, from Padua to Naples, and in the liberal professions – especially among doctors – in the middle classes and among craftsmen. Clergy were followers in such large numbers that when the persecutions began, they made up the majority of the refugees. The peasants on the other hand were absent. In the mainly rural regions, such as the Appennines, in the far north and in the far south, there were few Protestants. In fact, a large proportion of the population had remained at the stage of a Christianity based on myths and legends, so much so that the Jesuits of the Counter-Reformation sometimes had the impression they had been transported to India.

Italian Protestants of high intellectual standard had mostly frequented the lecture theatres of the University of Padua. Therefore, why didn't Padua become a centre of cultural influence and spiritual reform, like Wittenberg or Geneva? Disregarding for a moment the quarrels between the professors who taught there, it must be said that the religious convictions of Padua were often 'intellectualized', and that the relationship with the inner feelings, the heart, which was characteristic of the Lutheran and Calvinist centres, was cruelly lacking. From the human point of view, Italy had never had a personality strong enough to lead a Reform movement and organize it, backed by military and political strength, by moral and theological authority and by talent as a preacher. The town closest to the ideal represented by Geneva was Ferrara, where the Duchess Renée of France granted her protection and where the defrocked Capuchin Bernardino Ochino was the authority on matters of religion. But Renée of France's husband, Ercole II d'Este, did not put his political and military power at her disposal, and Ochino, an individualistic theologian and charismatic preacher, very soon had to leave Italy. Nobody else was equal to the task of uniting a heterogeneous movement, giving it direction and the means to expand through missionaries. Galeazzo Caracciolo, Giovanni Bernardino Bonifacio, the two

Sozzinis and Biandrata all had to content themselves with gathering their followers around them in exile.

Other reasons for the failure of the Italian Reformation were the influence of the Church on everyday life and the power exercized by the hierarchy, especially the papacy. The Church insisted that people observe the many festivals and went so far as to ask their saints to intervene to protect military campaigns. The Counter-Reformation restricted these superstitious attitudes, but allowed a number of others to continue. On to these traditional forms of devotion it grafted a renewed moral conscience, thus taking the credit for one the essential demands of the Italian Reformation. Delio Cantimori, the master of modern Italian research, emphasized the importance of the need for moral reform on the eve of the Reformation.

The power of the ecclesiastical hierarchy – to come to the second factor based on tradition – rested on the extent of the lands owned by the Church, on its control over the whole of Italy through its dioceses and the authority of the Pope. During the course of the Reformation, the papacy, which the Italians automatically accepted both geographically and politically, was strengthened in a number of respects. With the help of the Jesuits, it once more became a leading spiritual authority. Thanks to the integrity of Giampietro Carafa and his successors, it was once more – apart from its dogmatic intolerance – morally unassailable. Through its weapons against heresy, the Inquisition and the Index, it extended its authority over all the members of the Church. From the second half of the sixteenth century internal reforms were dictated by the supreme authority of the Church. Italy, which was closest to that authority, was therefore the first to be affected.

To win back believers, the Italian Church relied both on a renewed moral conscience and on the traditional forms of worship such as pilgrimages and praying for the saints' intervention; they counted action invaluable.

Pilgrims at the tomb of a saint, painting on wood by the master of St Sebastian, late 15th century. Galleria Nazionale, Rome.

In Spain even more than in Italy, the Catholic Church relied on the courts of the Inquisition and on the *auto-da-fés* to eradicate the roots of the Reformation. This apparatus, set up against the crypto-Judaism of the Marranos, the converted Jews, also proved effective against the 'Luteranos'.

Auto-da-fé presided over by St Dominic (13th century), painting by Pedro Berruguete, late 15th century. Museo del Prado, Madrid.

However, elements of the movement survived abroad, where Italians founded unitarian churches – in the Carpathians, in Poland, Holland and America. What is more, they expressed ideas which became universal in the Age of Enlightenment, such as the connection between reason and the revelation, and the first applications of the principle of tolerance. The Italian Reformation, which in Italy flourished only for a few decades, taught the world, from exile, a crucial and lasting lesson.

The triumph of the Spanish Inquisition

To discuss the history of Spanish Protestantism, we must first of all prove that it existed. In Marcel Bataillon's famous work *Erasmus and Spain*, where he gives a masterly account of the influence of Erasmus on Spanish spirituality in the sixteenth century, he denies the existence of the Reformation. He uses the word 'Lutheranism' in inverted commas from the first to the last page of his book. But he simplifies things rather too much when he makes Erasmianism the catalyst and common denominator of Spanish religiosity and does not attribute any importance to the Lutheran elements. Marcel Bataillon rejects the theory that certain so-called Erasmians could have used the famous master from Rotterdam to conceal their Lutheran convictions better. And yet such was the case with Juan de Valdès: the only book he published during his lifetime was for the most part a translation and adaptation of the works of Luther and Oecolampadius. The part of Valdès' *Dialogo de doctrina Christiana* which is authentically Erasmian comes from the colloquy *Inquisitio de fide*, where Erasmus lets Luther himself speak through the character of Barbatius.

Juan de Valdès' *Dialogo* is therefore an attempt to spread the fundamental ideas of the Reformation in the only way that was possible in Spain. The enthusiastic reception this little book received among the *Alumbrados* or 'enlightened', among the Erasmians and even among the supporters of de Cisneros' Reformation, must have convinced Valdès that he was not mistaken either in his choice of means or in the idea he had of his readers. Nevertheless, he was mistaken, as were many of his friends and protectors, in under-estimating the real power of the Spanish monks and in supposing that the inquisitors would make a distinction between Luther, Erasmus and the *Alumbrados*. One of the charges at the Inquisition trial of Juan de Vergara read: 'The errors of the so-called *Alumbrados* are almost identical to those of Luther . . . Erasmus was a second Luther who annotated his master and wrote terrible things.'

The connection between the doctrine of the *Alumbrados* and Luther's ideas is viewed in radically different ways by representatives of recent Spanish historiography. While A. Selke and A. Redondo speak of the direct influence of Luther on the *Alumbrados* Pedro Ruiz de Alcatraz and Isabelle de la Cruz, J.C. Nieto advance the unusual theory that the doctrine of justification by faith and other essential themes of Protestant theology were developed and formulated in Spain with no reference to Luther, and even before his time. In any case, the Spanish monks had no hesitation in linking Luther and Erasmus. The excessive confessions of some *Alumbrados* imprisoned by the Inquisition led to the conviction that there was a powerful Lutheran faction in Castille whose leaders were known Erasmians. It was only after countless interrogations, trials and torture sessions that the Inquisition finally had to admit the lack of proof. This did not prevent it from achieving its aim: after 1540, no one in Spain dared to utter the name of Erasmus.

It was also a great surprise when, in 1558, two large Protestant communities were discovered in Seville and Valladolid. Here too, Bataillon refrains from speaking of Protestantism, describing these two 'communities' as centres of evangelization using Erasmianism as a reference. But that is omitting the fact that the Seville Inquisition confiscated the works of seventy-two 'reformed' authors. What is more, the authentically 'Protestant' character of the Valladolid community has been proven with the help of a detailed memorandum from the Inquisition. In 1574, the Sevillian Corro wrote to Bullinger: 'I am one of those, a man of learning, who has attained a purer knowledge of the Christian doctrine thanks to your writings. This happened twenty years ago when divine providence afforded me the opportunity and I was able to look through your books which the Inquisition itself handed over to me.' And in his *Letter sent to his Majesty the King of Spain* (Antwerp 1567), the same Corro wrote: 'In addition, I made an effort to recover some books by Martin Luther and other Protestants from Germany, which those same officers of the Inquisition willingly gave me in exchange for some gift or service.'

This time, the Inquisition was not content with blaming everything on a few 'Erasmians', as in the 1530s. Anxious to satisfy an ageing Charles V, it reacted with such harshness that after the great *auto-da-fés* of Valladolid and Seville (1539–62), the 'reformed tendency' disappeared from Spain for several centuries. The later

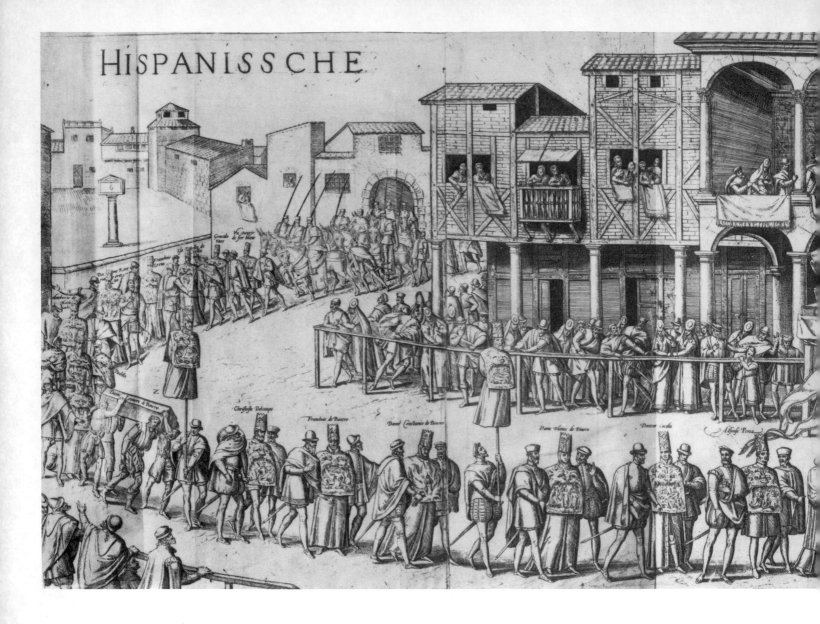

HISPANISSCHE

In 1558, the Inquisition was surprised to discover two large Protestant communities in Seville and Valladolid. It reacted efficiently and eradicated the Reformation from Spain once and for all.

Scenes of the Inquisition in Spain, engraving, 1560. Bibliothèque Nationale, Paris.

executions for Lutheranism affected mainly foreign traders or sailors who found themselves brought before the Inquisition courts by mistake. For example, among the 213 cases of Lutheranism which were tried in Galicia up until 1700, only two involved Spaniards.

The impossible Reformation

Any attempt at a statistical estimate of the Protestant movement in Spain is destined to fail from the outset. The charges of the Inquisition and reports of *auto-da-fés* provide dated information, it is true, which is fairly precise as to the number of people sentenced for Lutheranism. But, as well as the fact that the Inquisition was by no means aware of all the cases, more than three-quarters of the charges from the sixteenth century have disappeared. According to Henningsen and Contreras, out of the 49,000 trials conducted by the Spanish Inquisition between 1540 and 1700, by the fourteen provincial tribunals, only 3,140 concerned people who were accused of being Lutherans. In trying to assess the extent of Spanish Protestantism, if one takes into account the fact that not only the tribunals of the border areas but even those of Toledo judged many more foreigners than Spaniards, these figures lose much of their force of persuasion. In fact, the generic adjective 'Lutheran' was often used by the judges of the Inquisition without any real grounds.

Out of the 500 Spaniards accused of Protestantism according to the charges published by Schäfer, about 300 possessed an authentic Protestant spirit, even if the majority of them did not display an unshakeable faith before their judges. About ninety of the accused died at the stake, and seventy-seven of those came from the towns of Valladolid and Seville alone. They were all people of standing: clerics, monks, teachers, doctors, students, traders, craftsmen or nobles. There were many women among them, which in the Spain of

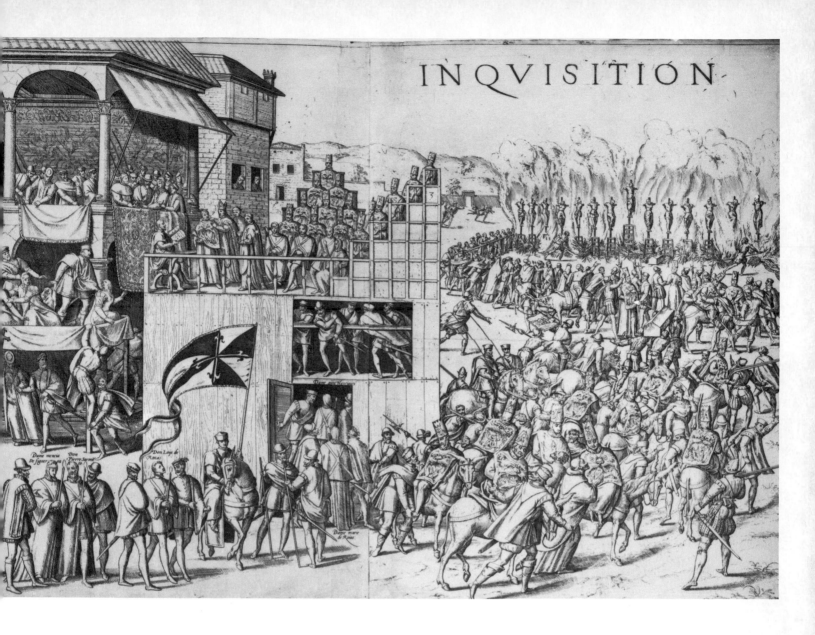

the *Alumbrados* was not surprising. That a large number of them were converted Jews, *Conversos*, does not require a lengthy explanation: because they belonged to a suspected but intellectually superior minority, they were vulnerable and ready to embrace any new religion as long as it promised an end to discrimination. Charles V was not mistaken when, shortly before his death, he demanded an exemplary punishment for the prisoners of Seville and Valladolid, '. . . especially for the *Conversos*, for they were nearly all the inventors of these heresies.'

The Protestant Reformation was never really accepted in Spain except by a small percentage of the population; in a country subject to a central power and to the omnipresent surveillance of the Inquisition, it could not represent a real threat. The only historical occasion which could have provoked profound changes was undoubtedly the revolt in 1521 of the *Communidades* who challenged the Inquisition and condemned the sale of Indulgences. One of its leaders, the Bishop of Zamora, Antonio de Acuna, was even called 'Luther the Second'. But this rebellion visibly lacked the profoundly religious element which was the strength of the German Peasants' Revolt. This major difference was clearly obvious to a Spanish Erasmian living in Avignon, the doctor Jerónimo López de Velasco: in a letter dated 1525 addressed to Bonifacius Amerbach, he equated the two revolts, disregarding the religious motivation. The revolt of the *Communidades* had broken out too early for it to be inspired by the spirit of the Reformation. When this spirit finally reached Spain, there was no longer an appropriate social ground for it to take hold, the radical repression of the bourgeoisie and the towns having been accomplished. The *homo oeconomicus* type, still rare in Spain, was slowly but surely replaced by the *hidalgo*, who completely identified his personal honour with that of the nation and with the aims of the monarchy. When, during the religious seminars held at

163

Although the role of the Inquisition was decisive, it is worth noting the work of the Cardinal de Cisneros (1436–1517), who paved the way for the Reformers by restoring discipline to the Spanish clergy and by fighting relentlessly against abuses. Inquisitor-General, a resolute and intelligent opponent of Islam, he was also a humanist open to Erasmus's piety.

Cardinal de Cisneros releases prisoners in Oran, painting by Jover Casanova, 19th century. Senate Palace, Madrid.

Cardinal de Cisneros in Oran, painting by Juan de Borgona, 16th century. Toledo Cathedral.

Ratisbon, Pedro di Malvenda saw his old friend Juan Diaz siding with the Protestants, he reproached him above all for betraying his country. And when, shortly afterwards, Alfonso Diaz had his own brother killed at Neuburg on the Danube, it was mainly to restore the honour of the family and of the nation.

Protestantism in Spain could only be the work of isolated individuals or small groups who, subject to the all-pervasive control of the hostile social environment and of the Inquisition, had to seek refuge in cleverly camouflaged propaganda. This was the context for the works of Juan de Valdès and the catechisms of Doctor Constantino, who was able to communicate the fundamental concepts of the Reformation with elegance despite the censorship of the Inquisition – regardless of the views of certain modern historians who interpret the writings of the Canon of Seville as the expression of a vague evangelism or Erasmianism.

Supporters of the Reformation were not prepared to risk prosecution by the Inquisition by referring openly to Luther or Calvin. The true professions of faith were uttered only in the gaols of the Inquisition, sometimes after the death sentence had been pronounced, or even at the stake. The accused very rarely took up specifically Protestant positions, which would have meant nothing to the judges anyway: the label 'Lutheran' was sufficient. The only Catholic theologian who was able to appreciate the different nuances of reform doctrine with extraordinary competence was the Franciscan Alfonso de Castro. He had read the 'books of Luther and of all his followers' at Trent, in the library of the imperial plenipotentiary, Diego Hurtado de Mendoza, as he recounts in his book *Adversus omnes haereses*. Among the zealous users of this library, there were also the theologians Bartolomé de

Reformed influences were found where they did not exist. The great Spanish theologian, the Archbishop of Toledo, Bartolomé de Carranza (1503–76), who was Mary Tudor's confessor and who fought against Protestantism in England, was accused of having let texts by Luther and Melanchthon slip into his catechism, for which he spent many years in the prisons of the Inquisition. The Catholic Church and science are both agreed today that this great Catholic prelate was wrongly blamed, the victim of a painful mistake.

Portrait of Bartolomé de Carranza, 16th-century painting. Escorial Monastery, Spain.

Carranza and Juan Morillo. But, while de Carranza introduced texts by Luther and Melanchthon into his catechism, interpreting them in accordance with Catholic doctrine, Morillo from Aragon moved away from the Council: he died as an Elder of the Reformed Church of Frankfurt.

The Spanish diaspora

Spanish Protestantism was only able to develop outside Spain and, like its Italian twin, it did so in directions which soon came into conflict with the churches born of the Reformation. Michael Servetus was greatly influenced by the Reformers, but it was from Erasmus's writings that he developed his theories against the dogma of the Trinity, defended free will and categorically rejected Luther's doctrine of imputed justification. Juan de Valdès was the first to have translated Luther's writings to include them in his own, but at the same time he had achieved a radical spiritualism which went further than Luther and condemned all dogmatism and all ecclesiastical organization as negligible affairs that it was not even worth combating. Francisco de Enzinas had been a close friend of Melanchthon, Bucer and Bullinger, and he too had translated Luther and Calvin. But he felt especially close to Castellion, whose Latin Bible he had translated into Spanish from the manuscript, without waiting for it to be printed. The same Castellion was a major influence on two other Spaniards, Antonio del Corro and Casiodoro de Reyna.

Since the essential monograph on the Sevillian Corro by Eduard Boehmer was published, it has been a well known fact that he aroused the suspicions of a number of people due to his admiration of Castellion, and because he frequently used the Savoyard's translation for his biblical quotations. On the other hand, people often forget that the *Letter Sent to the King of Spain* of 1567 was only a skilful adaptation of the *Conseil à la France désolée* and that the spirit of Castellion and his theological writings can be found in the *Épistre et amiable remonstrance aux Pasteurs d'Anvers*, in the *Tableau de l'oeuvre de Dieu* in the *Monas theologica* and, in particular, in the *Dialogus theologicus* or *Commentary on the Letter to the Romans* of 1574.

The same went for Casiodoro de Reyna, whom Corro always revered as his master, but whom the Spanish Calvinists held responsible for the decadence of the Spanish congregation in Geneva. On Calvin's suggestion the congregation was founded in the Church of St Germain and entrusted to the leadership of the very orthodox Juan Pérez de Pineda. And yet Reyna was of the opinion, 'that it was not good to have a Spanish church in Geneva because of the cruelty of the magistrature' and had apparently convinced a few refugee monks from Seville to emigrate with him to England, which had earned him the nickname of the 'Spanish Moses'. As soon as he arrived in England, he gathered all the members of the Spanish community together in a private house, and wrote, in its name, a courageous profession of faith which, despite a very orthodox tone, clearly shares many of Castellion's and even Servetus' ideas. When in 1563 Reyna was asked to justify himself before the Consistory of the French Church in exile in London, Spanish Calvinists did not omit to mention that he had, a few years earlier, addressed a letter to the *Doctus et pius vir Sebastian Castellio* and that, among his favourite books, as among those of his friends, there was 'a printed book which suggested that heretics should not be burned.' His detractors also claimed, with reference to Castellion's doctrine, that Reyna believed God's chosen could cause the failure of eternal predestination through evil deeds; that justification by God did not only imply faith, but also active contrition on the part of man; that instead of preaching about love and how to lead a Christian life, in Geneva they knew only how to give sermons against the Pope and the monks; that the Anabaptists too, despite their divergent opinions, should be considered as brothers; that, on condition the Gospel gained ground in France, Geneva could become a second Rome, and finally, that 'Servetus had been unjustly burned through lack of charity'.

Like his friend Corro, who always warned his readers against the temptation to consider the writings of Luther and Calvin as a fifth Gospel, Reyna never stopped condemning his co-religionists for wanting to monopolize Church censorship and to practise it with such fervour that any expression of a different opinion amounted to a death sentence. Reyna, who was born in Montemolin in the Sierra Morena, wrote his finest defence in favour of religious tolerance under the pseudonym of 'Reginaldus Gonsalvius Montanus'; it took the form of a long preface to his book *Sanctae Inquisitionis Hispanicae artes* of 1567. When the book was published a year later in Geneva under the title *Histoire de l'Inquisition d'Espagne*, the publisher had removed Reyna's pseudonym and reduced the preface to barely four pages. There was a good reason for this: the Genevans had noticed that many ideas and expressions had quite

166

simply been borrowed, almost word for word, from the works *De haereticis an sint persequendi* and *Conseil à la France désolée*.

The Spanish of the diaspora found it hard to fit into the established churches of the Reformation, but felt more at home with the radical dissidents of Italy and the Low Countries. There were also, of course, small orthodox groups in Geneva, Paris, Frankfurt and London; such well respected historians as Juan Pérez de Pineda and Cipriano de Valera document their existence. The Spanish exile was in fact characterized by a specific attitude; the former superior of the Calvinist consistory of Antwerp, Marcos Pérez de Segura, explains this in a letter addressed to Hubert Languet in 1570: 'It seems to me that an opinion which I see deeply embedded in the minds of all church ministers, be they Roman Catholic, Lutheran or Reformed, has always been and always will be the cause of the great ills of the Church of God. In other words, they believe that those who govern the Church cannot be mistaken. Hence their obstinacy: once they have received a doctrine, they will not concede the slightest point to others. As for myself, I don't think I sin badly in believing that as long as those who govern the Church are men, they will always err, and it will be all the more necessary to try always to learn and to correct oneself, aiming for perfection.' It is not surprising that from then on, certain Spaniards from Pérez's circle made constant attempts to achieve a union of all existing churches, or that they reached a total indifference to the various confessions, becoming simply members of the *Familia charitatis*.

In Spain, the whole society opposed Protestantism. The revolt of the *Comuneros* was contemporaneous, like the Peasant's Revolt, but it had no influence over the spiritual adventure of a Christianity which found its expression in another form of fidelity.

The Seat of the Inquisition in Seville, engraving from *Civitas Orbis Terrarum* by Braun, 16th century. Biblioteca Nacional, Madrid.

Execution of the leaders of the Comuneros' Revolt, painting by Gisbert, 19th century. Senate Palace, Madrid.

167

France: failure or spiritual heritage?

The French monarchy opposed the Reformation for political rather than religious reasons. Although it was not strongly opposed to the new ideas, it could not, on the other hand, accept the establishment of what was to be called 'the State within a State', or more simply the indiscipline of the country squires of southern France. Therefore Henry II accelerated the policy of persecution begun by his father Francis I towards the end of his reign, but had no scruples when necessity forced him to form an alliance with the German Protestant princes against Charles V. His widow, Catherine de Medici, was to move between unofficial tolerance and persecution as extreme as the terrible St Bartholomew's Day Massacre, depending on the demands of politics.

Portrait of Henry II, 16th-century painting. Musée Crozatier, Le Puy.

Portrait of Catherine de Medici, French painting of the mid-16th century. Galleria Palatina, Florence.

John Calvin saw his work in Geneva not only as a model but also a stage in the conversion of France to the Reformation movement. But in spite of the many advantages in their favour, French Protestants were unable to achieve their objectives as political interests soon overrode what were initially purely religious considerations. The threats, real or imagined, which challenged the authority of the State, led to terrible and violent confrontations which were to last until the end of the seventeenth century.

'Out of the depths. . .' (Psalm 130)
'Let God arise. . .' (Psalm 68)

France in 1559

During the sixteenth century, France was very nearly converted to Protestantism. But we are not here to discuss the consequences of a hypothetical situation, either on a national or a European scale. Nor do we intend to rewrite history but rather to analyse the motivations which made such a conversion a viable possibility, to shed some light on the reasons for its 'failure', and to reconstruct, within a given context and at a given point in time, the system of thought and the outlook of the different bodies involved: the Churches, the political parties and the powers which opposed them. A whole set of values was questioned, contradictions and abuses were denounced and a challenge was issued to authority. On the one hand and initially without support, was the 'message', the cohesion and relevance of which were based on the Word of God as interpreted and expressed by John Calvin in his *Institutes of the Christian Religion* and made accessible to the congregation through sermons, hymns and prayers. Opposing it was the power of the monarchy, the result of an alliance between royalty and the papacy, with its efficient administration, military and financial resources and political determination. The central drama, and fallacy, of the French Reformation lay in the attempt to win over the support of the monarchy.

The year 1559 was an important one. First, it was the year in which Henry II died. He had issued edicts banning Protestantism and signed the Peace of Cateau-Cambrésis which marked an agreement between France and Spain, uniting those two long-standing enemies against heresy and raising the question of whether the 'Spanish model' would be imposed on France. Second, the first national synod held in Paris in 1559 confirmed the strength of French Calvinism. A separate Confession of Faith, similar to that of Geneva, was drawn up and a religious code of conduct defining the institutions of the Church was developed. Liberal nineteenth-century historians such as Guizot, Mignet, Michelet and Martin assessed the situation accurately. They welcomed the sixteenth-century Reformation as the 'movement of freedom of thought' and saw the 1559 synod as 'the birth of the Protestant Republic'. But it was a republic which was united neither in essence nor in outlook. In 1559, the French Reformation could already be defined geographically and almost sociologically, but not as yet historically.

From the geographical point of view, according to the Venetian, Giovanni Michiel, in 1559 there was not a 'province which has not been contaminated by Protestantism, and in

169

some the contagion has spread even into the rural areas . . . which represent almost three-quarters of the Kingdom of France'. It was the 'established' churches which were important, places of worship with a minister, a consistory, elders and deacons. The map drawn up by the Protestant minister, Mours, shows France 'studded' with churches forming a circle between Sedan and Lyons, broken only by Lorraine and Franche-Comté. Altogether there were about 1,400, of which over half were in the south, with congregations totalling more than a million. Normandy was also well provided for, as were the Loire, Sedan, Metz and Paris.

Sociologically speaking, the Protestants came from very different walks of life depending on the region, the type of local authority, ease of communication, distribution of towns and living conditions. Although it tended to be centred around rivers and towns, the Reformation was based on the teachings of the Bible and the Word of God. Protestants were recruited from all sociological and professional groups, especially the more educated and the more innovative in the technical field. Court administrators and lawyers were well-represented from the outset, but in 1559 a new factor had to be taken into consideration. A certain number of noble families closely connected with the Court joined the ranks of the Protestants. The strength of these land-owning classes lay in controlling wealth and people, so they brought to the Cause their taste for fighting and their refusal of martyrdom, their ambitions, their supporters, their influence and their prestige in a society ruled by the sword. As a result of this complex network of feudal and family loyalties placed at the disposal of the Reformation, an aristocratic form of Calvinism developed which both rivalled and complemented the urban Calvinism of the bourgeoisie.

Historically speaking, the Protestant movement was neither history in the making nor a complete history in its own right. It formed part of an ongoing process at both the religious and the national level. In oppositon to the 'superstructures' erected by the Roman Church, the Reformation asserted the unique spirit of the original message of the Gospel. The concept of 'Salvation by Faith', which had

In the mid-16th century, following the lead of Paris, France came close to supporting the Reformation. Eighty per cent of Protestants, who numbered more than a million, were concentrated in the south-western part of the kingdom.

The Cemetery of Les Innocents during the Reign of Francis I, 16th-century painting. Musée Carnavalet, Paris.

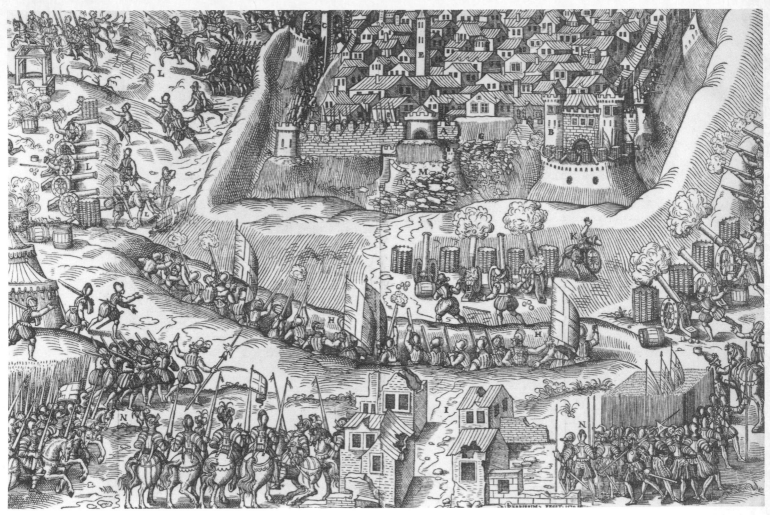

succeeded the humanist trend, was itself superceded between 1540 and *c*.1570 by the development of debate on the nature of the Christian Church, made more acute by the tension between the 'false' and the 'true' Church. The model with elders and synods was held to be exactly that given in the teachings of the Apostles as defined by the Holy Scriptures. In its newly discovered cohesion, the Reformation claimed to speak in the name of the true Church. National cohesion was also a major issue. In his *Institutes of the Christian Religion* Calvin appealed to the king as well as to the princes and the aristocracy, whose role was similar to that of the German princes and the Scottish lords. Finally Hotmann appealed in the *Franco-Gallia* (1575) to the General Assembly of the Three Estates, which could have provided the basis of a constitutional monarchy. Thus the development of national political thought went hand in hand with advances in the study of the Christian Church and the establishment of the 'Protestant party'.

This 'French model' was faced with a double challenge. The first came from Europe at a time when its geography was undergoing substantial changes because of the great discoveries which were being made and the movement of economies towards the West. New boundaries were being created and the national unities of France, Spain, England, Germany, Switzerland, the Low Countries and Italy were being integrated into the European context which was a source of requests, assistance, money, religious beliefs and armies. The challenge consisted in turning the crossroads into a melting pot, in an attempt to 'write history' incorporating the best of Bucer's Strasburg and Calvin's Geneva. These urban models had to be developed on a national scale in this Christian country which was in the process of trying to define itself, where the population was as ready to spill the blood of its children as to spend its wealth, and was generous with the blessings that God reserves for his chosen people. The 'miracle' was becoming a possibility and in 1559, hopes ran high. Although the parliaments were reluctant, the nobility appeared to have been won over to the Cause. Of the 12 per cent of the population which was Protestant, half belonged to the nobility, which was all the more surprising in a Europe dominated by Spain in the Mediterranean, and the Low Countries, and where the Council of Trent was trying to regain control by means of a crusade. The national interest appeared to coincide with the demands of conscience and France held the balance. This gave cause for concern in the camp

Religious opposition, exacerbated by political rivalry, led to a civil war involving many well-equipped armies. Saint Jean d'Angély, like La Rochelle, was one of the Protestant strongholds at the heart of the conflict. This important port was besieged by Charles IX in 1569 and razed by Louis XIII.

The seige of Saint Jean d'Angély in 1569, 16th-century engraving. Bibliothèque Nationale, Paris.

After his conversion to Calvinism in 1559, Gaspard de Coligny, Admiral of France, became leader of the French Protestant movement. The failure of Catherine de Medici's policy of conciliation provoked him to lead an armed resistance in 1562. Eight years later at the Peace of Saint Germain, he advocated an agreement between the two denominations, but in 1572 the St Bartholomew's Day Massacre marked the failure of the policy of intervention in the Netherlands.

Portrait of Gaspard de Coligny, 16th-century French painting. Société de l'Histoire du Protestantisme, Français, Paris.

of the Counter-Reformation which lasted until the fall of La Rochelle on 29 October 1628 and even until 1685, an important date in European history.

The second challenge was both political and social. It was superficially marked by 'significant' events from which 'noble' figures emerged and which gave rise to the 'historical mythology' of the warring factions. Underlying this was the desire to live according to the 'true religion' in the eyes of God and under the guidance of the consistories. But it is questionable whether it was in fact possible to change or rather 'reconstruct' the individual within the context of the community when France was suffering, over a period of half a century of unrest, from the problems arising from being an incomplete nation in the process of development. There was the problem of power linked to the crisis of the growth of institutions, the rise of the new nobility who sought positions sold by the State, economic problems and a 400 per cent increase in prices between 1550 and 1600. There were also social problems. Some people were ruined by the war while others made their fortune, despite the fact that the army formed an independent body. There was the increasing influence of money, a revival of the landowning and court nobility, the exaggerated division between town and country, between the various professions, cultures and regions, in short between northern, southern, eastern and western France.

Traditions were changing, authority was being challenged, but, as the register of grievances of the Estates General of 1561 shows, there was also an overwhelming desire to see an end to injustice and the threat of disorder and anarchy, in favour of the establishment of a new spiritual order. The future of the Reformation in Europe depended upon the attitude of France, and the success or failure of the French Reformation in turn depended upon the attitude of the monarchy. The problem had moved from the realm of the spiritual to that of the political and military.

The outbreak of violence

For half a century war was an everyday occurrence for the French people. Two aspects are particularly important: the traditional pattern of the eight Wars of Religion, and the violence which characterized them. Moreover, no clear line can be drawn

In the autumn of 1561, Catherine de Medici tried to reconcile the two sides by calling an assembly of Catholic and Protestant theologians at Poissy. But the colloquy failed over the question of transubstantiation and marked the beginning of the Wars of Religion.

The Colloquy of Poissy, painting by Joseph Nicolas Robert-Fleury, 19th century. Société de l'Histoire du Protestantisme Français, Paris.

between civil war and external conflict since the Protestants appealed to England and Germany for help, and the Catholics appealed to Spain. The psychological factor is also extremely important. The determination and initial enthusiasm of the Cause's supporters made up for their lack of military equipment. Military skill was not lacking on the Protestant side as they had the assistance of experienced leaders who had fought in the Italian wars or served their apprenticeship in the Low Countries. Coligny was defeated at Moncontour in 1569 but he re-formed his army in the south and marched back to the Loire and from there to the gates of Paris. The wars saw the establishment of regular armies in which firearms replaced the pike, halberd and the bow favoured by the English. Mercenaries were joined by supporters rallied by the local churches. The democratization of the army paralleled the secularization of prayer and lent dignity to the troops whose honour lay in the service of God.

However, what is most noticeable is the rhythm, the spasmodic nature of the conflicts in which war alternated with short-lived periods of peace and the intensity of the fighting varied. This is symptomatic of a complex political and religious situation and suggests that there were different levels of confrontation. On the one hand a strong Protestant minority wanted recognition for its right to exist and to this end sought to gain the personal support of the King and the influence of the Council, while on the other, the Catholics were divided into various parties until the formation of the Catholic League led by the Dukes of Guise. Between the two was the King who was bound to uphold traditional religion but who refused to ally himself totally with the aristocratic and feudal factions which used the established Church as their rallying point. This resulted in policies which for the most part avoided the issue but which did not preclude extreme measures. The most well-known of these was the 'great outbreak' of the St Bartholomew's Day Massacre on 24 August 1572.

The beginning of the rupture between the Reformation and the monarchy came in 1534. The initiative taken by Antoine de Marcourt to affix virulent placards to the door of the King's chamber on the one hand provoked a split between moderate and hard-line Protestants, and on the other angered Francis I. The 'expression–repression' cycle had been set in motion and the edicts banning Protestantism followed one another in quick succession. The warning issued on 10 June 1559 by Henry II to the Paris high court, and the execution of Anne du Bourg, provided

174

startling proof that as far as the King was concerned, unity of faith was essential for the State which was allied to the Catholic Church.

After 1559, when the balance of power of the different forces involved had been modified and the way seemed clear, there were three major developments involving the Huguenots. First of all there was a peaceful mass demonstration at Amboise with the intention of presenting the reformed Confession of Faith to the new king, but against the advice of Coligny and Calvin it was infiltrated by a few country gentlemen and ended in disaster. The result was the blood bath the Dukes of Guise had wanted. However, the edict of January 1562 provided the first official recognition of the Protestant faith. Secondly, the Calvinist bourgeoisie, turning their civil liberties to advantage, seized certain towns. Rouen, Lyon and the cities of the Loire were captured and lost again almost immediately while towns such as Nîmes, Montauban, La Rochelle, La Charité sur Loire, Sancerre, Nérac, Lectoure and Castres, names which became symbolic for the Protestants, were held until 1598. Thirdly, there were three wars followed by three treaties granting freedom of thought, relative freedom of worship and 'safe areas'.

But in 1572, the St Bartholomew's Day Massacre, apart from being remembered for the atrocities carried out, marked a double split. On a practical level, Protestantism moved southwards creating what might be called the 'United Provinces of the Midi'. There was an increase in conversions through terror as well as the number of emigrations. On a more abstract level the principle of the right of resistance was developed, which was directed at the King, 'who massacres his subjects'. But on becoming heir presumptive to the throne, Henry of Navarre renounced his Protestant faith, and this last military and political phase was marked by the abjuration of Henry IV on 25 July 1593, his consecration on 27 July, the entry into Paris on 22 March of the following year and the departure of the Spanish. Peace was restored, but with it ended the dream of French Protestantism; the Edict of Nantes in May 1598 introduced a new political and religious regime.

Open war was only the most spectacular aspect of the demonstrations of aggression. In fact it wasn't a simple matter of outbreaks of 'pure violence', but of creating an atmosphere of fear and suspicion in an attempt to oppose a distorted point of view which presented violence as enforced and legitimate. Massacres and sacrifices were carried out in the name of an avenging and jealous God, but beneath the surface lay the desire to defend the 'true and pure doctrine' and to protect the community from the impurity which provoked the anger of God. For the Protestants this atmosphere was created by the reassertion of the value of individual martyrdom and by the military response to the policy of repression. For the Catholics it was the scandal of broken images, the defiling of sacred vessels and places of worship, blasphemy and insults to the Virgin Mary and the saints. In addition there was, on both sides, the feeling that the political and religious authorities were either not doing their duty or that they were unable to carry it out without help. But inspiration came from on high and the Protestants drew sustenance from the epic of Israel as told in the Bible.

Violence would break out as a result of a particular point of view, a gathering, a religious service or celebration involving processions or the singing of hymns which in a blind, irreversible process aroused popular feeling which in turn led to riots and revolts. Whereas the Protestants vented their anger on objects rather than people, the Catholics attacked Protestant ministers and their congregations. Those actively involved in the riots were craftsmen, tradesmen, shop assistants, representatives of the law, clerks, pastors and monks. Doctors, professional people and former soldiers led the ordinary people, including women and impulsive adolescents. The riots affected all social groups. Against such a background, the St Bartholomew's Day Massacre was only exceptional in terms of the involvement of the authorities, the extent and violence of the massacre, the spread of violence across France, and the naivety of the Protestant nobility who had entered the lion's den. Assassinations were avenged by massacres, but these were above all symbolic gestures carried out within a climate of 'redress' and in an apocalyptic atmosphere where the deed was justified by the death of the 'Antichrist'.

In both their spontaneous and their calculated excesses, the people believed they were fulfilling a religious and judicial mission, by summarily executing those they considered to be guilty. In November 1567, the Vicar-General, five canons and two priests died in the Michelade of Nîmes. This was an attempt by the inhabitants of Nîmes to punish those by whom they felt they had been unjustly treated. In November 1561, the assassination of Baron Funel in the region controlled by Monluc appeared to be a spontaneous and bloody popular uprising. But one wonders whether the murder was in fact entirely the work of the Huguenots and whether the

Religious fervour, personal ambition and the desire to avenge his father made Henry, Duke of Guise (1549–88) the most intransigent leader of the Catholic party. During the night of 23 August 1572, acting without the authority of Catherine de Medici, he organized the massacre of Protestant leaders in Paris. This was the terrible St Bartholomew's Day Massacre which cost the lives of more than three thousand people.

Commemorative medal of the St Bartholomew's Day Massacre (top: *The Massacre of the Huguenots;* bottom: *Pope Gregory XIII*). Bibliothèque Nationale, Paris.

Massacre of the Huguenots, painting by Giorgio Vasari, 16th century. Vatican Museum.

Portrait of Henry, Duke of Guise, c.1580. Musée des Beaux-Arts, Rennes.

►
The St Bartholomew's Day Massacre, painting by François Dubois. Musée Cantonal des Beaux-Arts, Lausanne.

uprising was exclusively Protestant. By presenting it as such, it was possible to create 'the terrible image of the revolutionary Calvinist, destroying the basis of society and refusing to pay tithes and taxes' as described by J. Garisson Estèbe. The same problems occur when trying to analyse the rural unrest in Vivarais and the Dauphin during 1578–9, in the mountains to the south of the Massif Central between 1591 and 1596, and in the Périgord, Quercy and Limousin during 1594–5, where Catholic and Protestant peasants, known as the Croquants, revolted against State taxes, tithes and feudal rights. The Protestant revolt can in no way be seen as the beginning of a violent social revolution. It is at the very most a revolt involving the spread of the influence of the Gospel.

Gatherings, riots, revolts, massacres and regular fighting were the various forms of violence which are merely an introduction to a study of the preoccupations of a period in which suffering and death were commonplace, but so were faith and the joy of belief. Mental and physical suffering, fear and anguish, for oneself and for others, at the thought of what the next day might bring, were all part of the Protestant population's determination to resist and equally of the commitment of the popular forces which opposed them.

The organization of the Protestant Church in France

The ultimate test for the Reformation was that of organization. How were people to live out their faith according to their personal experience of the Bible? What were the limits and nature of authority and who represented it? How did it relate to the civil authorities? How could an authentic religious way of life be integrated into a society which was reluctant to accept it or even to understand it? The fact of the matter was that the institution must either be established or disappear.

The principles outlined by Calvin and the model offered by Geneva in the *Ecclesiastical Ordinances* of 1539 aimed to establish on Earth 'the political order' of the visible Church which tried, through discipline, restraint and faith, to regenerate and maintain in the Way of the Lord a society corrupted by original sin: 'because we are weak we must continue to study throughout our lifetime; only then can we leave school . . . Outside the shelter of the Church, we cannot hope for the forgiveness of sins or any form of salvation'. Hence the necessity for the disciple to contribute to his own religious instruction, as well as the need for a solid framework, permanent control and the flexible and practical organization recognized by the Edict of Nantes (1598) which allowed 'consistories, colloquies, provincial and national synods to be held by the permission of His Majesty'.

'The duty of the elders is to keep watch over the flock with the pastors, to see that the people attend gatherings and that everyone is present at the said congregations, to report any scandals and transgressions and in general to be jointly responsible with the pastors for matters concerning the order, maintenance and government of the church as an institution, as well as of each individual church.' Therefore, discipline was the main concern of the consistory, that essential body which combined the four orders established by the Lord: 'pastors, doctors, then elders . . . and fourthly deacons'. In Geneva the elders and deacons were entrusted with separate responsibilities, whereas within the organization of the French Protestant Church, they formed the 'Church Senate' whose reponsibilities were both spiritual, as in the choosing of ministers, and temporal, for example raising money and administering finances. They were re-elected by co-option which ensured the permanence, stability and the implementation of the renewed religion. Above the consistories were the regional and provincial ecclesiastical councils, the assemblies, which varied in size, and the synods. These completed 'the pyramid of ecclesiastical assemblies whose deliberations are carried out according to a very strict set of rules which ensures an effective co-ordination between local churches, in spite of there being no form of episcopacy'.

What was a great wave of enthusiasm in 1562 became, especially after 1572, a religious revival accompanied by renewed political and institutional awareness as the State declined. There were deep-seated reasons for the success of Calvinism in southern France between La Rochelle and Grenoble. It was a long way from the capital, it had the support of the lesser nobility and the gentry, the local authorities were powerful and there was a strong tradition of autonomy which meant that secular and sacred matters were gathered into a single responsibility. Added to this was the relative affluence of the western and southern regions which had been revived by river and sea-going traffic, and a degree of pride at finding their rightful place within the French monarchy of the sixteenth century. La Rochelle became a symbol of Protestantism, as much on account of the National Synod of Reformed Churches presided over by Theodore de Beza, who came from Geneva at the

In spite of war and persecution, the Protestant community organized itself on the basis of the institutions founded by John Calvin in the protected city of Geneva. Consistories, colloquies and synods provided a framework which ensured control of the day-to-day lives of the congregation and their religious education.

National Synod held in France in 1596, late 16th-century engraving. Bibliothèque Nationale, Paris.

request of the Queen of Navarre, as on account of the siege of 1573. Another siege was to follow in 1628.

More important and less tangible is the question of Protestant contribution to the field of political thought and practical politics within the system of the French monarchy. Not only can we recognize the structured thought of Calvin, which was the result of a logically developed consideration of the Holy Scriptures and of his experiences in Strasburg and Geneva, but also the 'explosive outbursts' of people who were actually in the process of experiencing events and considering the problem of authority within the Church and the State. The initial considerations were focussed on the principle of authority within the Calvinist system in which everything stemmed from the basic principle of a triple mechanism of election, representation and participation, even if it could result in a democracy of 'notables'. In Geneva, following the Ordinances of 1561, the elders were no longer appointed exclusively from among the members of the Councils but from among ordinary citizens regardless of status. Their election by the Little Council was supervised by the pastors and ratified by the General Assembly. In his *Treatise on Discipline and Christian Polity* (1561), Morelli claimed the right for questions of doctrine and morals to be judged in the final analysis by the entire assembly of the congregation. His opinions were condemned by the second Synod of Paris. Then came the problem of the actual idea of the State in terms of its structure. According to the monarchy the State should be united, whereas the assemblies of the Protestant Republic of Geneva had developed a federal system described by Thou in his *Histoire Universelle*. Ultimately the State remained united and gave its allegiance to Henry IV.

With regard to the right of the Christian to resist the State, Calvin had proposed a solution which reconciled respect for civil authority with the rights of conscience. In *Iure Magistratum* (1575), Theodore de Beza, who was responsible for the 'second generation' of the Reformation in France, laid the foundations of the theory of the contract: 'Kings exist for the people, the people do not exist for kings.' Duplessis-Mornay, in *Vindiciae contra Tyrannos* (1579), outlined the dual alliance which was to leave its mark for a long time in Protestant thought and expression: the alliance between God and the people and between the people and the King. The Catholic League was to repeat these ideas and take them to extremes in the idea of the popular State, and they reappeared in England and France in the seventeenth and eighteenth centuries.

The creation of a 'new man'

How far can the desire to create a 'new man', affirmed in the *Confession of Faith* and reiterated in *Ecclesiastical Discipline*, be considered to have been successful? It must be recognized that political and military events produced values which did not always coincide with the evangelical virtues and which therefore did not always contribute to this renewal. As a result, the role of the consistories and the bodies set up by Calvin became all the more important. Education, personal development, the use of example and the feeling of solidarity were much more effective than repressive measures and were achieved within the context of the community, which was a fundamental aspect of religious life.

Everything was based on the reading of the Bible and in particular of the Ten Commandments, the basic code of civil and religious conduct. The congregation studied the Gospel, and the sermon explained the theological truths and incorporated them into daily life by translating them into practical rules for an everyday code of behaviour. Calvin's catechism was taught by the deacons and ministers. Every Sunday, the faithful worshipped in church and after the sermon, the entire congregation sang a psalm. The texts chosen for services in French churches to accompany the preaching and the sacraments were the *Liturgy of Strasburg* and the *Genevan Psalter*. 'When we sing, we are certain that God puts the words into our mouths, as if he himself were singing his praises within us.'

Translations of the psalters by Marot and Theodore de Beza were printed in Lyons. Claude Goudimel, who died in the St Bartholomew's Day Massacre, adapted the simple melodies of the original psalter for four voices, and they were sung by Protestants on their way to church. In the seventeenth century, this 'open air' religion was to be considered an infringement of the Edict of Nantes. There was a significant development in the field of poetry. In Agrippa d'Aubigné's biblically inspired *Tragiques*, lyrical images are variously combined, for example 'Fire' represents the Cause, 'Blood' conjures up memories of the wars and 'Water' is the element of peace. For the most committed Protestants the inspiration of the Scriptures became the blood and the body of thought.

The written word played an important part in the spread of the Reformation. Calvin asked Christians 'not to give free rein to their curiosity, not to indulge in idle

La Rochelle became symbolic in the history of French Protestantism. On two separate occasions, in 1573 and 1627–8, this Atlantic port, converted to the Protestant cause, fiercely resisted the royal army, which represented both the Catholic party and central authority. And it was La Rochelle which adopted the Confession of Faith affirmed by all Reformed Churches in France.

The Seige of La Rochelle in 1573, 16th-century engraving. Bibliothèque Nationale, Paris.

speculation or trivial questions', as he considered that 'scriptural sobriety should be enough to satisfy God's children'. The rhetoric of Protestant speech was not composed of a series of techniques used in an attempt to be eloquent or persuasive but was rather 'the expression of all knowledge and all virtue' which echoed the Word of God. In the early stages of the Reformation preaching was peaceful, moving and linked to the idea of repentence and conversion, but in the apocalyptic atmosphere of anguish and oppression it became aggressive. The 'Beast', the modern Babylon, the 'Antichrist', as the Synod of Gap described the papacy in 1603, must be destroyed. In the Churches of the Refuge, where the idea of an international community was to be discovered for the first time, as well as in the national churches, 'practical concepts' emerged which were embodied in the key words: 'Scripture', 'Promise' and 'Gospel' – and given new significance in the minds of the people through poetry, hymns and recitation as well as the theatre, which was used as a vehicle for education in schools. This had the effect of strengthening the main, northern French language; there is no translation of the Bible in the 'langue d'oc', the language of southern France.

In response to secular problems, Calvin developed his own version of the *Ecclesia mater*, the main work on the Christian Church inherited by the Reformed Churches, in which he restated the necessity for God's chosen church to extend its works of salvation and to reform men in his image under the guidance and control of the consistory and the synods. It was also the basis of the importance of the four ministries in which pastors and congregation alike share the responsibility of the proclamation of the Word of God, the administering of the sacraments of the baptism and holy communion around which the life of the community revolved, and

180

in the establishment of the Church as a social and legal community according to the ideal envisaged in the early centuries of its existence.

This utopian society went against contemporary custom by being strict about festivities, yet it was to gain control in parts of Europe and America. Certain aspects of it were to be adopted by the legislation of the monarchy and also by the Catholic Counter-Reformation. The two aspects most worthy of note are its charitable works and its struggle against witchcraft. Charitable works were part of the vast movement which had been organizing help on a community basis since the end of the fifteenth century. Following Erasmus, Calvin made the distinction between the 'true poor' who needed the help of the Christian community, the 'false poor', 'all vagabonds, disreputable people and idlers' and the full-time beggars 'to whom God has given the strength and capacity for work' (implying 'but not the will'). From this, a policy was developed which was both strict in that it banned alms and flexible in its desire to integrate the poor into the body of society. The struggle against witchcraft formed part of a widespread intellectual movement of the period to oppose all forms of 'superstition', those 'abominable heresies' which might be political like those of du Rosier, Ramus, Morelli and their followers, or religious as in the case of Jean de Serres' *Apparatus ad fidem catholicam* for which he was condemned in 1598 by the Synod of Montpellier. But in particular, it was a fight against magic, the 'idolatry' of the Roman Church, and witchcraft which was to spread throughout the regions of the Rhine and certain areas of France, though not the Protestant south.

Success or failure?

The Edict of Nantes, which brought the advantages of civil peace and official recognition, marked a stage in the institutional rather than the religious development of French Protestantism. According to Léonard, the edict granted civil status to Protestantism while still not approving it as a religious body. Protestant worship was not generally accepted, but 'safe areas' were tolerated.

In terms of the institutions, the basic text of the edict was questioned by the monarchy in the seventeenth century. Firstly, the political and military system was destroyed by the war of 1620–21, the siege of La Rochelle in 1628 which raised the town to a symbolic level, and the Peace of Alais in 1629. Then came the destruction of the judicial and religious system as a result of the restrictive interpretation of the edict, the exclusion of Protestants from the professions, the abolition of the law courts provided for in the edict which were preparing a policy of conversion and, after 1661, the harrassment of billeting soldiers and the banning of the synods. The Synod of Loudun held in 1659 through the influence of Turenne was the last national synod to be held before the Revocation of the Edict of Nantes. The efforts of Ruvigny, the general representative of churches within royal influence, could not prevent the final blow. On 17 October 1685, all forms of public worship were banned and an order was issued to destroy the churches and expel the ministers. The only concession made was to allow private worship 'in the hope that God would enlighten the Protestants as he had done the rest of the population'. The declaration of 8 March 1715 was to put the finishing touches to these extremes of absolutism by banning freedom of thought!

A more delicate question was that of the intensity of religious life. After Claude Brousson, who wrote on the situation immediately after the Revocation of the Edict of Nantes, Alexandre Vinet, Mathieu Lelièvre and Emile Léonard violently condemned the 'feeble body' that Protestantism became during the seventeenth century. They paid particular and mordant attention to the polite and deferential forms of address used for the king, to arguments on points of doctrine, to sterile polemics and personal preoccupations. They repeatedly criticized the cold quality of preaching, the temptation to ecumenicalism expressed in over-zealous discussions leading only to future abjurations, and the conformist teaching in the academies.

Some of their accusations were accurate and were levelled at the 'excessive individualism' for which French Protestantism has been criticized at various periods during history. For a time it appears to have abandoned its role as the driving force in the history of religious and political thought. This noticeable lack of activity can be explained by new political and sociological conditions and, in the very midst of the ideological change of direction which took place between the 1620s and 1640s, by a double transfer brought about by the Catholic Church. The new political conditions were created by an increase in absolutism and yet, faced with a Catholic victory, the only hope for Protestantism, which was now very much on the fringe of society, was the monarch who at times appeared to distance himself from the Pope. The new sociological conditions were created by the constraints imposed on the exercise of the professions, but also by a revival of the nobility. This was due on the one hand to the attraction of the Court and royal favours, and on the other to the

The Catholic League, an extreme anti-Protestant movement led by the Duke of Guise until his death in 1588, was strongly sympathetic towards Spain and refused to recognize Henry IV because of his religious convictions. But after the King had made his abjuration, the leaders of the Catholic League pledged their support one after the other. This marked the end of the Wars of Religion, the French version of a confrontation which had affected the whole of established Christianity.

Procession of the Catholic League in 1590, from Bunel's studio, late 16th century. Musée des Beaux-Arts, Valenciennes.

Portrait of Henry IV by Frans Pourbus, late 16th century. Galleria Palatina, Florence.

The Abjuration of Henry IV, 25 July 1593, engraving, late 16th century. Bibliothèque Nationale, Paris.

effects of the policies of de-militarization of Louis XIII whose aim was to separate religious and military objectives and who presented the crusade against the Protestants as a struggle against enemies of the State. And finally, there was the double transfer. This was geographical, in terms of the shifting of the alliance with the countries of the Rhine and the Low Countries, to an alliance between Madrid and Paris, which gave additional strength to the 'Spanish model', and it was also spiritual as Calvinism no longer held the spiritual monopoly. This deep soul-searching opened the seventeenth century to a Catholic Church which had regained its self-confidence while the Protestants, who were still disillusioned and reeling from the blow of many individual and collective betrayals, reacted by closely observing the letter of the law in an attempt to protect what they had.

But 'political submission does not mean that faith has been abandoned or weakened'. On the one hand, the structures of the Church as a legal and social entity as represented by the provincial synods were seen to function successfully. These synods met regularly and maintained a small permanent assembly in Paris which presented observations concerning the restrictive measures adopted towards members of their faith to the ministers of Louis XIV. On the other hand, the exemplary attitude of the Protestants during the Fronde earned them the declaration of 1652, granted by Mazarin in spite of the observations of the Assembly of the Clergy, and which confirmed the Edict of Nantes, annulling all judgements passed by various royal courts. The lack of gratitude on the part of the monarchy, shown by the declaration of 18 July 1656, could not eradicate the loyalty of the 'little flock' which continued to seek spiritual life within the family, the community of the Church, the schools and the professions.

In towns such as Montauban, Issoudun, Lyons, Charenton and in the Academy of Geneva, the preservation of the libraries indicated the high level of culture of the Protestant bourgeoisie, among whom there was a shift from the administrative to the commercial sector, which was concerned less with political questions than with amassing individual and collective wealth. The modest archives studied by Philippe Joutard revealed the immutability and intensity of this spiritual life in the rural areas of strong resistance such as the Cevennes, Lower Languedoc, Vivarais, the Dauphiné and the Black Mountains which were almost entirely Protestant at the time of the Revocation of the Edict of Nantes. In 1683 this was to inspire the first open resistance and, a little later, to fuel the flame of the Camisards. A new form of awareness, in which prophesying had its place, emerged during the persecutions but its origins lay in the fund of mercy and faith built up during the seventeenth century.

So, was the Reformation in France a success or a failure? On the level of political reality, it was an obvious failure. Demands were presented to the Estates General of 1561 as a result of the increasing involvement of the Church in politics and military matters, the movement of the French monarchy towards absolutism, the absence of an undisputed leader in the early stages of the movement, decisions made by the noblity and the lack of cohesion between the egotistical rival social groups. But the demands were ignored by the nobility as well as by the Third Estate, which was making representation to the king that a national council be held, that all controversial points be decided only according to the Gospel, that the wealth of the clergy be sold for the benefit of the monarchy, nobility and the Three Estates, and their stipend decided by the public treasury, that magistrates be elected and the Estates General be convened every two years.

But in 1598 they were a long way from having these requests granted, and even further away in 1629, 1656 and 1685, since the monarchy remembered the opposition of critical and carefully considered free thought and was only too ready to consider the consistory as 'a dangerous government which produced Republicans'. From the spiritual point of view, however, the Reformation was a success, as much in terms of religious doctrine as in the spirit which inspired the Protestants and united the two essential concepts of tradition and modernism beyond the short-lived extremes of absolute monarchy. The tradition of the Scriptures and the new interpretation of the Word of God went hand in hand with the modernism of the changing world of humanism and the Renaissance. The Europe which had succeeded Christendom was taking stock of itself, putting its thoughts into order, taking control of its language, its vocabulary and its methods of analysis.

It was within this context with its critical points of view and its closely related theological and institutional developments that the debate started by the French Reformation continued, concerning the nature of Church and society. The term 'Christian Institution' (the literal translation of Calvin's title) was surely significant and relevant for all nations in one great European brotherhood, although for many the basic question still remained concerning which Church guaranteed eternal salvation. Rome condemned Galileo, Luther rejected Copernicus, Cartesianism was

In fact the Wars of Religion did not come to an end with the accession of Henry IV. The struggle between the monarchy and the Protestant community lasted throughout the 17th century. For the most part it lay hidden beneath the surface but sometimes open warfare was declared as, for example, during the second sieges of Saint Jean d'Angély and La Rochelle. It was Louis XIV who settled the question 'definitively' with the Revocation of the Edict of Nantes which forced the Huguenots to emigrate or openly to admit defeat.

Louis the Great, triumphing over the heretics, 17th-century engraving. Bibliothèque Nationale, Paris.

banned by the universities. During the great debates of the 'posthumanist' period, when an expectant and hopeful western Europe was eager to bite into the fruit of knowledge and ready to reject established ideas, the various Churches responded with the strictures of the Lutheran Ordinance of 1598, the Formula of Concord, Tridentine episcopal reorganization, and obedience to the State.

Faced with this resumption of control, it was left to French Calvinism, in a reduced but more forceful and traditional form adapted to the period, to raise the important questions of power and authority within the general atmosphere of anxiety. These included the question of Holy Scriptures, of the relationship between State and Church, of the organization of the Church and of the place of the layman within that organization. It was important to create a 'people of God', as illustrated by the Assembly of Montauban which demanded of the offended Catherine de Medici that the victims of the St Bartholomew's Day Massacre, that 'crime of the century', be rehabilitated. 'You are no longer dealing with princes, admirals and members of the nobility, but with the lower ranks and poor country squires, with cobblers, tailors, masons and locksmiths, blacksmiths and other people of low status, who are willing to bear arms and fight', united in the defence 'of the glory of God'.

The engraver Abraham Bosse (1602–76), remained faithful to his Calvinist convictions throughout his life, which often led to confrontations with officialdom and caused him many problems. His extensive works give us a very complete picture of Parisian society under Louis XIII and Louis XIV, and in particular of the seriousness and austerity of the life of the Protestant community.

Grace before the meal, engraving by Abraham Bosse, 17th century. Bibliothèque Nationale, Paris.

The spread of the Reformation in Germany and Scandinavia (1530–1620)

The Reformation movement in Germany and Scandinavia was directly affected by the struggle for political power. Religion, which was both the end and the means, was not so much a matter of individual conscience as an affair of state, since subjects had to adopt the faith of their prince. And yet this encroachment of temporal power into the spiritual domain did not hinder the development of an authentic Lutheran culture based on sincere piety under the guidance of skilled pastors.

The division of Germany

The failure of the Diet of Augsburg in 1530 had the effect of reinforcing the Lutheran doctrine, which was substantially different from Swiss Protestantism and which from then on made use of a standard text, the *Confessio Augustana* or Augsburg Confession. During the next twenty years, the Protestant princes were mainly concerned with strengthening the Reformation against the imperial threat. So in February 1531 the anti-imperial Schmalkaldic League came into being. It was formed by the princes and the free towns and led by the Elector of Saxony and the Landgrave of Hesse, the two most powerful leaders in the Lutheran territories. In the Truce of Nuremberg of 1532, Charles V granted Protestants the right to maintain their positions in matters of religion. For the first time a heresy, recognized and officially defined as such, was tolerated within the Empire by a judicial act. In 1534, Philip, Landgrave of Hesse, captured Württemberg from Ferdinand, King of the Romans and brother of Charles V, and restored it to its rightful prince, Ulrich, Duke of Württemberg. From then on, it became the Lutheran stronghold of southern Germany. Two years later, the theologians of the free towns of the south, who supported a course mid-way between those of Wittenberg and Zurich, reached an agreement with Luther on the controversial question of the Lord's Supper. This was the Wittenberg Concord, which created unity of doctrine between members of the Schmalkaldic League.

A final attempt at establishing agreement between Lutheran and Roman Catholic theologians took place in 1540 under pressure from the Emperor, who was anxious to re-establish religious unity. Three colloquies were held consecutively in Hagenau, Worms and Ratisbon. Bucer of Strasburg and John Gropper, Chancellor of Cologne, were strongly in favour of an agreement and were encouraged by Charles V and Philip, Landgrave of Hesse. An agreement based on the central theme of 'justification by faith' was rejected by several princes of both faiths and in particular by Luther and the Roman curia. The theological split was already too pronounced for a general agreement to be reached.

Charles V was extremely displeased by this failure and decided to settle the matter by force. After very careful preliminary negotiations, he had the two leaders of the League banished from the Empire. The fighting was short-lived. Between July 1546 and April 1547 the Emperor subjugated the imperial towns of the south and imposed heavy fines on them before going on to win the decisive victory at Mühlberg in Saxony on 24 April 1547. Turning his victory to advantage, he eliminated the two threats to his power by an institutional and religious reorganization of the Empire, achieving the return of the Protestants to a reformed Catholic Church and the subjection of the German princes, which was imposed by the 'armed' Diet of Augsburg (1547–8). The Diet also proclaimed the Augsburg Interim, a 'compromise'

In Germany, where Lutheranism was as strong in the towns as in the rural areas, the Protestant princes united against Charles V. Even the victory of the Emperor at Mühlberg in 1547, the capture of the Landgrave of Hesse and the compromise of the Augsberg Interim could not prevent the Reformation being permanently established in Germany.

1. *Philip, Landgrave of Hesse (1504–67)*, 16th-century wood engraving by Lucas Cranach the Elder.

2. *Lady of Nuremberg being escorted to the Temple by two senators*, 16th century engraving. Bibliothèque Nationale, Paris.

3. *Detail of Equestrian Portrait of Charles V at the Battle of Mühlberg*, painting by Titian, 1548. Museo del Prado, Madrid.

2

2

O FELIX AGRIPPINA NOBILIS ROMANORVM COLONIA

Ancilla Auguſtana.

SIc bis cinĉta forum peto proſpeĉtura culinæ,
    Sicq̃, foro redeo rurſum onerata domum.
Augusta Augustæ qua ſurgunt templa, puellis
    Gratus vbi hic noſtræ conditionis honos:

Pellito in nodum tortas cohibere galero
    Non flexu errantes libertore comas.
Et tunicæ extremas lumbis bicoloribus oras
    Signare, ac cupidum hac vrere veſte procum.

1   F 2   Sũcui-

The chronology of the German and French
Reformations are completely different. At the
time of the French Wars of Religion Germany was
enjoying a period of civil peace following the
Religious Peace of Augsburg. With the exception
of specific cases such as that of Cologne,
Germany enjoyed an untroubled period until
1618, which marked the beginning of the terrible
devastation of the Thirty Years War. France's
position lay mid-way between that of war-torn
Germany and the relative shelter of England.

1. *Ancilla Augustana*, engraving, 1586. Bibliothèque
Nationale, Paris.

2. *View of Cologne*, wood engraving by Anton von
Worms, 1531.

3. *The Priests*, engraving by Jost Amman, 1568.
Bibliothèque Nationale, Paris.

which was to be enforced by all German churches while awaiting the final decision of
the council. The Interim upheld Catholic doctrine in extremely vague terms and
enforced the re-establishment of Catholic rites, but made no reference to the
question of secularized Catholic possessions. The only concessions made to the
Lutherans were on communion in both kinds and the marriage of priests.

But the attempt came too late. The Interim had caused a great deal of unrest and
revived the religious feeling of the 1520s. Charles V encountered strong opposition
from many of the princes and towns led by his own ally Maurice, Elector of Saxony.
It was possible to enforce the Interim only in places where the Emperor had military
control, namely in the towns of southern Germany and in Württemberg. But in free
towns such as Augsburg, Biberach, Dinkelsbühl and Ulm, the re-introduction of
mass often marked the beginning of the co-existence of the two faiths. But the
religious storm also revealed a deep-rooted Lutheranism among a large proportion of
notables and local authorities, the nobility as well as the bourgeoisie, while the lower
classes often systematically boycotted mass. The ordinary people, *gemeine Mann*, were
the mainstay of the resistance. About four hundred pastors were exiled, including
such famous reformers as Osiander of Nuremberg and Brenz and Blaurer of
Constance. In central Germany, the Interim contributed to the deep and permanent
division of the theologians of Saxony into the supporters (Philippists) and opponents
of Melanchthon, whose influence had been weakened.

The resistance is all the more surprising since Lutheranism was deprived of its
political leaders, who had all been subjugated, as well as of its religious leaders.
Luther had died in 1546, Bucer had been exiled and Melanchthon lacked firmness in
matters of doctrine. For three years little changed. Then in 1552 Maurice, Duke of
Saxony, altered the course of German religious history when, within the space of a
few months, he became a key figure in the German Empire. In January 1552 he
signed the Treaty of Chambord with the King of France and several German princes.

His rebellion forced Charles V to flee to Italy and resulted in the Treaty of Passau, signed by all the German princes except the Emperor. The treaty abolished the Interim, guaranteed future religious peace and accepted the principle of Protestant states, recognizing their right to forfeited Catholic possessions.

After the religious Peace of Augsburg (1555) which legally recognized the members of the Augsburg Confession, the two religions, the Catholic Church and the Protestant *Augsburgischen confession verwandt*, co-existed. The Zwinglians and Calvinists were excluded as they were not officially recognized until 1648. Religious freedom was only granted to states within the German Empire, of which there were about 390 including the free towns. It was extended to the knights and nobility but forbidden to the princes of the church, thus ensuring that the Catholic Church would retain extensive territories in the south and west. But this religious freedom was limited to the 'direct' princes of the Empire and to the knights and nobility, in other words to 0.0025 per cent of the poulation. The German people had only one alternative: to submit or to emigrate with their wealth. The Peace enforced unity of faith in each territory on the basis of *cuius regio, eius religio*.

In the Protestant states, princes and urban magistrates were granted the same rights as bishops, a decision sanctioning a process which had been developing since the 1520s and which from then on extended the authority of political power into areas of religion, the Church, morals and culture. Lutheranism had been recognized and was now legally protected. This contributed to the creation of a Lutheran mentality, which was jealously possessive, rather than directed towards spreading the Word – and which was further encouraged by the division of territories.

The Peace created a pause in the history of the German Empire in the sixteenth century. It put an end to the unrest caused by the outbreak of the Reformation and ensured peace, which was to last for sixty years and allow the individual Protestant churches to establish themselves before the outbreak of the Thirty Years War.

Sacerdotes. Die Priester.

TEmpla Sacerdotes à uestro Praesule lecti,
  Incolumus ueterum more decente Patrum.
Lenimusq́ pijs offensi Numinis iram
Cantibus, ad caelos & referamus iter.

Vulgus & à factis rude deterremus iniqui,
  Solamur lapsos, erigimusq́ reos.
Et bona quae maneant indeficienti ò iustos
  Pandimus, ad Christum cum uocat ulla dies,
Suppliciuḿq mali crudele minamur, & igues
  Sulphureos quos non finiat hora sequens.

3   A 4   Caesar.

187

It was indeed a period of peace, but the life of the Empire came to be dominated by confessional conflicts over ecclesiastical principalities, particularly those of Cologne and Strasburg, which in both cases led to a localized war. The result of these tensions was a gradual paralysis of all institutional structures after 1600. This in turn resulted in the formation of two religious groups, the Evangelical Union and the Catholic League which dominated German history between 1608 and 1618 and contributed to the outbreak of the Thirty Years War.

The establishment of Lutheranism

The Peace of Augsburg marked the stabilization of the spread of the Lutheran Church within the German Empire, with the exception of three subsequent if somewhat limited advances — into the Rhineland between 1556 and 1560, into certain towns during the 1570s and from Ratisbon into the hereditary territories of the House of Habsburg.

There were two main areas and three distinct types of church involved in the spread of Lutheranism. The area of central and eastern Germany between the Weser, the Main, the border of Poland and the Baltic consisted of large principalities which represented a compact block. This was the centre of Lutheran culture and faith dominated by Saxony. In the Rhineland and the south, Lutherans were in a minority and, apart from at Württemberg, set up only urban churches or very small territorial ones. The two main types of church were the territorial churches of the princes, the *Landeskirche* whose name still survives, and the town churches which came under the jurisdiction of the magistrates. In fringe areas, Lutheranism penetrated the territories belonging to Catholic princes under the protection of the local nobility and the knights, but its position was precarious in Austria and in the Duchy of Cleves.

Apart from these, all Lutheran churches were politically controlled. This consequence of the Reformation was reinforced by the Peace of Augsburg (1555), which transferred the power of the bishops, *iura episcopalia*, to the princes and free towns. The role of the prince was defined by the concepts of *custodia utriusque tabulae* which stated his responsibility for the temporal and spiritual salvation of all his subjects, and of *praecipuum membrum ecclesia*, according to which he was the most distinguished member of the congregation.

The rights of the prince included the nominaton of pastors, the visitation of churches, the power of legislation, the administration of justice as well as the right to impose his confessional faith on his subjects. They were carried out by new institutions set up in the capital or the residence of the prince. Saxony provides us with the most developed model. The Elector, *summus episcopus* over all his subjects, was assisted by an upper consistory, composed of jurists and two theologians, which was entirely responsible for the life of the church and implemented the decisions of the two regional consistories of Leipzig and Wittenberg. This involved the nomination of qualified pastors and schoolmasters, the control of finances and the administration of various parish matters. At regular intervals, the upper consistory convened a synod, composed of an equal number of members of the laity and the church, which confirmed the nomination of pastors, ordered inspections of the churches and nominated superintendants who were also referred to as inspectors. A second model is provided by Württemberg where the consistory was a branch of the committee of inspection. In the small territories, the prince's council was responsible for ecclesiastical matters. It consisted of several jurists, who were sometimes assisted by a general superintendant responsible for all pastors. Finally, in the free towns, these matters were dealt with by a magistrate's committee.

The ecclesiastical inspectors formed an institution which was common to all Lutheran territories. Responsible for the pastors within a particular district, their role was to guarantee the orthodoxy and moral conformity of the clergy and to ensure that all ecclesiastical legislation was rigorously enforced. In fact, the majority did an enormous amount of work, as is proved by the vast number of visitation reports. In spite of the criticism levelled against them, their role as inspectors and advisors made a positive contribution to the spread of Protestant churches, although it is true to say that it did restrict the individual initiative of the clergy and parishes.

The power of the bishops was also exercised through edicts and inspections. During the sixteenth century a large number of *Kirchenordnungen* were issued which provided specifications and instructions on matters of doctrine, worship, the administration of the sacraments, education, the ordination and dismissal of pastors, and the assistance and control of church life.

Another important aspect was the 'visitation', which enjoyed considerable success in nearly all Protestant principalities, with the exception of the towns. Its status as a standard procedure was reinforced by its inclusion in the church ordinances. The

Philip Melanchthon (1497–1560), professor of Greek at the University of Wittenberg, was Luther's companion from the beginning. After fighting at his side for nearly thirty years, Melanchthon replaced Luther at the head of the Protestant community after his death. Both a conciliator and a moderate, he made many enemies as a result of his synergist doctrine and his attitude during the Interim, according to which he believed that man had a share in divine grace.

Man infested with lice, caricature of Melanchthon, 16th century. Musée de l'Histoire de la Médecine, Paris.

Double portrait of Luther and Melanchthon, painting by Lucas Cranach the Elder, 1543. Galleria degli Uffizi, Florence.

model of the visitation was provided by Saxony in 1528, where it was developed under the influence of Luther and Melanchthon and became a privileged weapon of government for princes who had been given the task of creating a Christian state, by submitting the population to the Ten Commandments and the absolute authority of a dictatorship. Between 1540 and 1570, visitations were directed towards controlling religious and moral behaviour in such matters as regular attendance at worship, family cohesion and social relationships, as well as overseeing the legal state of the parish (including problems with benefactors, patrons of church livings and tithe-owners), the material and financial state of places of worship, and the religious life of the clergy. After 1570, visitations reinforced orthodoxy by detecting heterodoxy and the inroads of princely power, which was the reason for the increased importance of administrative documents. In spite of its limitations, the Protestant visitation, which was both regular and extremely detailed, is one of the main sources of the religious, liturgic, demographic, cultural and social history of the life of the parish.

This legislative activity gave rise to a Lutheran system of ecclesiatical law. In fact the Protestant princes maintained the status quo within the legal context (with the right to confer livings), as well as the material (the maintenance of places of worship and presbyteries) and the financial (the preservation of tithes and the original method of payment of clerics). The main innovation was the introduction of a matrimonial court and a law allowing divorce in favour of the innocent party.

Lutheran orthodoxy and the progress of Calvinism

The organization of institutions and the standardization of the religious service were accompanied by the establishment of orthodoxy, but not until the deep divisions which had preoccupied theologians between 1546 and 1576 had been resolved. These disagreements were caused by Melanchthon's change of position towards a more spiritual conception of the physical presence in the Lord's Supper which was forbidden by the Swiss, and by the stressing of certain points of Luther's doctrine by his followers after his death. Theologians were well and truly divided and some, known as the *Streittheologen*, became quite fanatical in their arguments. The disputes were aggravated by a political conflict between the Elector of Saxony and his cousins from the Ernestine branch of the family whose support of Luther against Melanchthon had been well-received by the University of Jena.

In the face of these conflicts, the princes took action in order to reach an agreement which was proving difficult to conclude. The Formula of Concord of 1577 was mainly drawn up by the theologian Jacob Andreae of Tübingen and was signed by eighty-six princes and towns and by 8,500 pastors on pain of dismissal. It became the standard doctrine for two-thirds of German Protestants and formed the basis of Lutheran orthodoxy for more than a century and a half. In a reaction against the Reformed, it differed noticeably on two sensitive points: namely its view of Christ and the Lord's Supper. Orthodox belief stressed the two natures of Christ (human and divine) and his physical presence. This explains the importance attached by the faithful to the physical suffering of the Passion (which, like Good Friday, is an important date on the liturgical calendar), and later those Jesuolatrous deviations within mysticism and Pietism. From the 1560s onwards, the view of Christ was based on the concept of Ubiquity which became the touchstone of Lutheran orthodoxy. The Formula of Concord described it as follows: 'Christ is present everywhere, not only as God, but also as Man.'

Although Luther was unofficially canonized by subsequent generations, Lutheran orthodoxy was in fact a combination of the ideas of Luther and Melanchthon, the latter being responsible for the belief in justification by faith and predestination and for an increasing Aristotelian influence in theology.

In the years following 1577, each faculty of theology published an enormous treaty, a Compendium or *Loci communes*, each composed of several large volumes and giving prominence to the doctrine of Ubiquity. The most important of these were the works by Chemnitz, Hutter (whose Compendium was for a long time the catechism of Lutheran orthodoxy), Heerbrand and Johann Gerhard. Gerhard's *Loci theologici*, in nine volumes which continued to be published until the nineteenth century, is the most important example of Lutheran dogma, and in 1688 Bossuet described him as 'the third man of the Reformation after Luther and Chemnitz'.

Several universities, in particular those of Wittenberg, Jena, Tübingen, Strasburg and Giessen, became strongholds of orthodoxy, which played a dual historical role.

It offered generations of Lutherans a biblical and theological *Weltanschauung* and provided an intellectual framework which protected pastors and their parishes from external influences. Admittedly, its claim to being the one true Church and its absolute confidence in the revealed Truth encouraged an attitude similar to that of the Catholic Church. But the Christocentrism of orthodoxy gave it spiritual force, spread by many instructive treatises (*Gebetbücher*), and directed towards a *praxis pietatis* of which Johann Valentinus Andreae proved to be a brilliant exponent in Württemberg from as early as 1620.

The polemic tendencies of orthodoxy were encouraged by the appearance of rival doctrine. Although Calvinism was not legally recognized, it had the support of Zurich and Geneva and had spread into the Lutheran territories. The way had been paved by the doctrinal attitude of Melanchthon who, in 1540, had remodelled the articles in the Augsburg Confession relating to the Lord's Supper, to give them a more spiritual meaning. Moreover, the University of Wittenberg became increasingly close to Zurich and Geneva in doctrine up to 1574. After 1577, the doctrine of Ubiquity was rejected by certain academics who had been influenced by humanism. Thus an area of common ground was gradually established between the humanists, Philippists and Calvinists.

Their success continued unbroken between 1560 and 1613. The reasons for this were various. First of all there was the Palatinate. Following an exchange of polemics between his theologians, Prince Frederick III, after three years of indecision, was converted to the Protestant faith as expressed in the Heidelberg Catechism of 1563. A combination of the beliefs of Melanchthon and the theologians of Zurich and

Most of the great German painters supported the Reformation. Albrecht Dürer, Lucas Cranach, Hans Baldung-Grien and Hans Holbein contributed to the spread of the tenets of Lutheranism throughout Germany.

1. *Christ of compassion*, by Hans Baldung-Grien, early 16th century. Fribourg Museum.

2. *Christ dead*, painting on wood by Hans Holbein the Younger, 1521. Kunstmuseum, Basle.

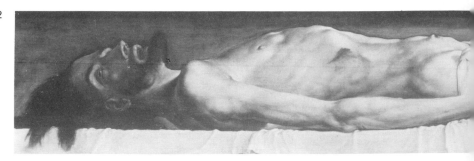

Geneva, it became the faith of all German Reformed and made great progress in all Presbyterian churches after receiving the support the Synod of Dordrecht in 1618. In 1573, the Duchy of Nassau-Dillenburg was converted to Calvinism. After 1580, most of the territories which refused the Formula of Concord followed suit and underwent a second Reformation, according to the wishes of the princes and their religious advisers. This mainly involved the Duchy of Zweibrken, a dozen small principalities situated between the Main and the North Sea, and the city of Bremen. In 1605 Maurice, Landgrave of Hesse-Cassel, was converted, and in 1613 John Sigismund, Elector of Brandenburg, followed suit and encountered opposition from the Estates. From then on, the rulers, supported by a Protestant minority of officials, acted much more openly, relying on a new concept of professional and state control. As well as being the Church of princes, Calvinism could also exist as a minority Presbyterian Church under the direction of Dutch refugees in the Duchies of Cleves and East Friesland, which held regular synods.

In terms of institutions, these churches in the principalities were not very different from the Lutheran churches. The role of the local consistories was one of detection supervision and reconciliation. In fact, a more extreme form of absolutism was allowed by Calvinism than in the Lutheran territories, which explains why it was more popular with certain princes. In terms of doctrine, the main differences lay in the interpretation of the Lord's Supper, the concepts of Christology and predestination, doctrines which were largely inspired by Melanchthon, Calvin and Bullinger. In addition, there was strong feeling against the use of sacred images and a desire for a faith which was purged of all traces of Catholicism, such as the host, the crucifix, and images. From this stemmed the desire to carry out a 'second Reformation which would cleanse the popish leaven [Lutheranism] of the last remaining vestiges of Catholicism'. Lastly, the Reformed wanted solidarity within Europe between those of the same faith.

The spread of Calvinism and the Catholic revival, which began to take place from the 1580s, gave rise to bitter polemics from the pulpit and a deluge of pamphlets and lampoons in an atmosphere of intense religious feeling which reached its peak with the anniversary of the Reformation in 1617. The polemics were directed against the Catholics, and particularly the Jesuits, but also against the Calvinists. It is true that the second Reformation was accompanied by a widespread and systematic dismissal of all pastors who had retained Lutheran tendencies, and by the abolition of the Lutheran communion rite. The main centre of Lutheran resistance was in Saxony where it was nearly twice defeated by the crypto-Calvinists, in 1574 and again in 1591. On both occasions there was a violent Lutheran reaction in the form of dismissals, banishments and prison sentences. These conflicts provoked two waves of polemics similar to those directed against the Catholics. The first occurred after 1563 between the theologians of Heidelberg and those of Tübingen and Strasburg, and the second after the Formula of Concord.

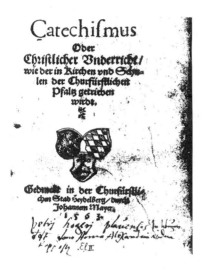

At the end of the 16th century, the Heidelberg Catechism became the religious text used by all German 'Reformed'.

Title page of the original edition of the *Heidelberg Catechism*, 1563. Bibliothèque Nationale et Universitaire, Strasburg.

The pastors

A specific culture developed during the period 1530 to 1620 which created a deep division between Lutherans and Catholics. Its main vehicle was the pastorate, a new social group which was educated, capable of indoctrinating populations which were often barely Christian, and strictly orthodox. After 1550, veritable dynasties emerged, in particular in Saxony and Württemberg, which lasted from the sixteenth to the eighteenth century. Apart from instances of marriage into other social groups, the pastorate came from the urban middle and lower-middle classes, that is from the ranks of artisans, teachers and minor civil servants. Almost everywhere there was an increasing tendency towards the granting of the right of citizenship to the local inhabitants. Between 1590 and 1620, there was a marked increase in the number of pastors who studied theology at university. After 1565, as the pastorate was oversubscribed, recruiting became more selective and there

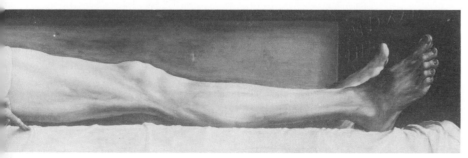

From the early stages, the Reformation enjoyed extremely close links with German culture. Sculpture was the first art to be used in its service, followed by music and architecture from the end of the 16th century. To some degree, the work of Heinrich Schütz was a forerunner to that of Johann Sebastian Bach. The new form of piety, which was mainly Lutheran but also Reformed, extended into all areas of daily life, starting with the education of children who learnt to use the German language through Luther's translation of the Bible.

Portrait of Heinrich Schütz (1585–1672), anonymous 16th-century painting. University Library, Leipzig.

The Schoolroom, wood engraving, 1592.

was a general raising of standards. For the civil authorities it was a matter of recruiting servants not only of the Church but also of the prince, a choice whose criteria were theological competence, standardized according to Melanchthon's *Examination of the Ordinands*, visible orthodoxy, political conformism and satisfactory moral behaviour.

The duties of the pastor were extremely demanding and were usually carried out with devotion, although occasionally in a somewhat half-hearted manner. They were defined by edicts issued by the Church which left little or no room for initiative. There was therefore a risk that the ministry was seen as a career for the unimaginative and uninspired civil servant rather than as a missionary engagement full of prophetic spirit. Although the catholicity of the Church was not endangered, spiritual paralysis was already a reality in the rich parishes of Württemberg and the north where, according to Johann Valentinus Andreae, the ambition of the young theologian was to become a *Dekan* (dean) as quickly as possible, to preach short sermons and eat long sausages.

The social situation of the pastors was varied. It was better in the larger territories than in some others, where many theologians were forced to run farms. Performing the marriage service enabled them to become more involved in their parish, as did the many christenings. In this way the minister occupied a central position both culturally and socially. The pastor's family took over from the monasteries their role of helping the poor. Their example favoured the development of family values and made a positive contribution to improving the religious and moral standards of the congregation. Because they valued education, pastors' families provided the best candidates for the political, intellectual, legal, scientific and medical professions within the Lutheran territories in the seventeenth and eighteenth centuries.

After 1560, and sometimes under pressure from the authorities, many pastors did not hesitate to invest a considerable part of their income in books. Generally speaking, there were four main categories of works, namely interpretations of the Bible, the study of religious doctrines, polemics and collections of sermons. But the pastors were also humanists, following the example of Melanchthon. He had been concerned with the purity of the Latin language, and was a literary scholar who appreciated the Greek and Roman authors, as well as being interested in history, science, geography, medicine and law. The churches therefore became small centres of culture which were able to provide the population, and particularly the rural population, not only with a simple and clear expression of faith, moral precepts and maxims but also with elementary medical and legal knowledge.

Naturally, these defenders of the Gospel, having adopted the doctrine of Luther with an absolute conviction which made them impervious to doubt, remain very much children of their time. They seem to us little more than public officials entrusted with the task of repressing certain religious and social customs, and appear mere agents of the absolutism of the princes – puppets who subordinated their religious function to the defence of institutional structures and who saw their

parishioners above all as an audience. Yet because they were responsible for their salvation, they considered themselves to be servants of Christ. To a large extent it was this personal devotion, put to the test particularly during periods of confessional changes and the Thirty Years War, which enabled Lutheranism to take deep root.

Interior of the church at Freudenstadt, in the Black Forest, constructed between 1601 and 1608 on an unusual L-shaped design.

Lutheran piety, worship and culture

The most visible expression of the new religion was through worship. Unlike the Reformed, Lutherans limited their changes to the suppression of the Latin language, distributing Communion in both kinds, a slight 'tidying up' of the content of the mass, and the abolition of the belief in purgatory, the worship of the Virgin Mary, the saints and the dead. Central and northern Germany were characterized by the importance attached to liturgical service, although this did not preclude certain regional variations. In many churches vespers were retained, as were prefaces and hymns translated into German, individual confession and exorcism at baptism. In southern Germany, worship was based mainly on preaching.

From the beginning, hymns were an important aspect of worship. They were written by Luther, by many German poets and by the Moravian Brethren. From the 1550s, the chorale became a musical form in its own right. The collections of hymns were widely circulated, particularly the collection by Bapst, published in Leipzig in 1545 and consisting of 124 hymns which for centuries formed the nucleus of Lutheran spirituality. The hymns composed during the second half of the century were deeply introspective. They were directed particularly towards the indvidual enlightenment of the congregation and emphasized the mystical aspect of the Faith.

Religious music enjoyed remarkable popularity and influence, with its sacred melodies sung by either soloists or choir. After 1600, it was dominated by Heinrich Schütz, 1585–1672, who succesfully combined Lutheran language and sacred

music. The organ played an increasingly important part in liturgy and chorale.

With the exception of the construction of the galleries, few changes were made to the religious buildings in rural areas. The new churches, built mainly in the principalities and the towns, were characterized by high galleries and a raised altar, pulpit and organ. Pulpits were being installed throughout Germany and were usually placed at the far end of the choir and the nave. In central and northern towns, a reredos was often set above the altar and in many places images were retained, for the excitement of iconoclasm had been felt only in the south.

The absence of schism within the church allowed a specifically Lutheran form of piety to emerge gradually through teaching based on the catechism. The concept of collective salvation, achieved through the performance of religious rites, developed into a sense of individual salvation achieved by a belief in simple doctrines which could only be assimilated by a personal intellectual effort. However, in the collective subconscious, the pastor remained the essential intermediary entrusted with pronouncing the correct formulae without which a ceremony was invalid.

Piety was first and foremost defined by the frequency of church attendance, which was compulsory, and by the singing of hymns which provided an emotional and sentimental reinforcement of belief. The best-known hymns were those written by Luther, their success due to their easily remembered tunes, the conviction of the faith they expressed, their confidence in divine succour and their assurance of salvation. These hymns developed religious feeling, encouraged values such as faithfulness and the desire for renewal, and enabled many hardships to be confronted. The other religious instrument was the Lutheran catechism, a simple, practical manual containing the basic principles of his theology such as faith, confidence and neighbourly love. Acquaintance with the catechism, although extremely varied in practice, led to a religion which provided a feeling of security and stressed the importance of confessional knowledge. The spread of literacy contributed to the increased popularity of religious books, two of which swamped Lutheran areas for several centuries. Habermann's *Gebetbüch*, influenced by Jesuit literature, had a moralizing aim but an undeniably biblical tone. On the other hand, the *Vier Bücher vom Wahren Christentum* by Johann Arndt endorsed a kind of mysticism.

Lutheranism had brought the fear of death under control by its recovered stress on the concept of resurrection, particularly in pastoral practice and hymns. It played on the opposition between the 'vale of tears' and eternal happiness, between the corruptible body and the soul.

Finally, through the Ten Commandments, the Reformation encouraged an ethic which valued work, the family, dignity and obedience to the authorities. It also championed literacy with a view to reading the Bible and other religious works. After 1555, schools were set up in nearly all Lutheran territories with encouragement from the princes, pastors and local communities. Even the idea of compulsory schooling was introduced, pioneered by the states of Saxony and Württemberg, which had 400 schools in 1600. They taught above all a culture based on the Bible and a practical wisdom which drew its inspiration from the books of Proverbs and Sirach (Ecclesiasticus).

For the education of administrative officials many secondary schools were set up, with curricula inspired by Melanchthon and John Sturm. These were either urban gymnasiums or schools sponsored by the princes, which aimed at teaching a *sapiens atque eloquens pietas*, combining humanism and religion and adapted to the demands of the period. This rapid development of schools had the effect of producing an increase in the total number of university students, particularly in the faculties of art and theology. In Saxony, the Universities of Wittenberg and Leipzig alone produced a quarter of all German graduates, which explains the political and cultural dominance of Saxony. During the lifetime of Luther and Melanchthon, Wittenberg enjoyed considerable influence throughout Europe. New arrivals were said to join their hands in prayer on catching sight of the city. Until 1600, an average of 853 students a year enrolled at the university. Of the five universities founded *after* the Reformation (Marburg, Königsberg, Giessen, Jena and Helmstedt), the last two had, respectively, the sixth and third largest number of enrolments in the country, while Tübingen emerged as the stronghold of orthodoxy in southern Germany. From then on, a true university education and intellectual life became the prerogative of the big Lutheran universities of the east and north, while the Catholic universities found themselves relegated to a sort of provincialism.

Lutheranism in Scandinavia

Whereas within the German Empire Lutheranism had to compete with two other faiths, in Scandinavia it took over completely. It established national churches which bore a strong resemblance to the medieval Church, in liturgy and buildings, and

The new ideas were spread in north Germany and Denmark by one of Luther's friends, Johannes Bugenhagen (1485–1558), a preacher and theologian at Wittenberg who played an extremely important part in the development of primary education.

Portrait of Johannes Bugenhagen, 1537, painting by Lucas Cranach the Elder. Wittenberg.

Ordinationsbuch from the church in Wittenberg, with corrections written by Bugenhagen, 1539. Wittenberg.

particularly the hierarchy of the episcopacy, maintained with bishops and even the Archbishop of Uppsala. After 1600, Lutheran orthodoxy made its presence felt in the form of a strongly centralized State Church and strict religious discipline. As in Germany, the Lutheran Church fostered the development of national languages. These common characteristics, however, did not preclude differences which were due to the political situation and the relationships between the Scandinavian countries.

In Sweden, the personality and popularity of King Gustavus I (Vasa) enabled him to place the Church under the royal aegis, along the lines of the German model. Laurent Petersen, Archbishop of Uppsala, was responsible for the translation of the Bible into Swedish. In 1593, the Synod of Uppsala introduced the Confession of Augsburg as the doctrinal standard. In spite of the royal aegis, the Church retained a degree of autonomy and managed to resist the attempts of two kings, John III (1569–92) who wanted the Church to move towards an Erasmian form of Catholicism, and then Charles IX (1598–1611) who was in favour of a more austere form of service closer to that of the Protestants. The Swedish Church expanded under Gustavus II (Adolphus) who became a hero of the Lutheran cause and was said to have been 'anointed by the Lord'. His church defended an orthodox theology inspired by Melanchthon, but was opposed to the Formula of Concord. As a result of teaching by catechism it was able to develop unhindered towards a specific form of Lutheranism adapted to the national character, of which the University of Uppsala became the centre after 1620. Sweden was the only Lutheran state where pastors and episcopate formed one of the estates of the legislative assembly.

In Finland, which was then part of Sweden, the Reformation was mainly the work of theologians educated at Wittenberg by Luther and Melanchthon. Their work was reinforced by two bishops, one of whom was Mikael Agricola, Bishop of Turku from 1554–7. He created the Finnish language through his translation of the Bible, and his publication of a catechism, a liturgy and a collection of prayers which respected most of the established traditions, including Mariology and purgatory. In this way he achieved the least obvious split of all the European countries. His colleague Juusten, the first Bishop of Viborg (1554–76), and known as the 'Finnish Melanchthon', worked for the education of pastors and the provision of schools. After 1580, a collection of hymns, a more developed catechism and a collection of sermons were published in Finnish which contributed to the establishment of a national Church. In Denmark, the Reformation was officially introduced in 1537 by King Christian III who issued an ecclesiastical ordinance and nominated seven superintendants who were later to be called bishops. The two most noteworthy were Tausen, author of a collection of sermons and one of hymns, and more importantly Palladius, an advisor to the king and lecturer at the university. Through his writings and numerous visitations, the latter was instrumental in converting to Lutheranism the clerics, who had all remained in office, and also the parishioners. King Christian III imposed a virtual dictatorship and a doctrinal uniformity which scarcely allowed the clergy any autonomy. The Danish language was fostered by a translation of the Bible in 1550, and numerous pastoral and pious writings as well as a collection of hymns. In the latter half of the century, the main theologian was Hemmingius whose works on the Bible, doctrine and pastoral practice had a circulation throughout the Lutheran territories of Europe. But the King refused the Formula of Concord on political grounds.

The Reformation was introduced into Norway by the Danes in 1537, and appears to have been a manifestation of their cultural imperialism. Danish replaced Latin as the language of the liturgy and continued to be used for centuries despite the fact that the population found it difficult to understand. The laity resisted until the early seventeenth century, maintaining their attachment to certain Catholic traditions. Legislation and orthodoxy followed a similar pattern of development to Denmark, but in 1607, the country received its own *Kirchenordnung*, although it was not substantially different from the Danish one. The episcopal system was maintained. In Iceland the Reformation was connected with the re-establishment of Danish authority, so it was resisted over a long period, from 1538–52. The episcopal system was maintained and the Church benefited from translations into Icelandic of the Bible in 1584 and a collection of sermons by the German, Corvinus. After the disintegration of Teutonic control in Livonia in 1561, Lutheranism, which had been carried there via the ports and by the nobility, became the official religion of Estonia, annexed by Sweden, and Courland, an independent duchy. In these two territories, religious works were translated into Latvian and Estonian. Lutheran parishes were formed in Lithuania on the Prussian model which led to translations into Lithuanian.

The 'noble' form of Protestantism resulting from orthodoxy and episcopalian structure was rooted in society, a source of spiritual wealth and cultural identity as well as a civilisation which was to survive in rural areas until 1914.

The King of Sweden, Gustavus I (Vasa) (1496–1560) founded both the national dynasty and the Lutheran Church. Placed under the royal aegis, and extremely moderate in its enforcement, the Reformation changed traditional Christianity imperceptibly and yet profoundly.

Portrait of Gustavus I (Vasa), 16th-century engraving.

The Rhineland success

After 1518 Luther's 95 theses were displayed in Strasburg. The Reformers soon gained the upper hand and made the city on the Rhine one of the capitals of European Protestantism, an example and a sanctuary. The success of the Reformation is largely the work of Martin Bucer, the former Dominican from Alsace (1491–1551), a conciliatory man and a great preacher who ended his days in England.

The Town of Strasburg, wood engraving from the Nuremberg Chronicle, 1493. Bibliothèque Mazarine, Paris.

The Rhine valley proved fertile ground first for humanism and then for the Reformation. The Reformation came down the river from the Swiss mountains to the shores of the North Sea, spreading among the myriad states, towns, city-states, principalities and bishoprics on either bank of the river. The Strasburg, Palatinate and Low Countries models are more than just individual cases: they are vivid examples of the causes and the manifestations of the Reformation's success.

Unity and diversity in Rhineland countries

Paradoxically, the Reformation met with its most spectacular success in the frontier region separating France and Germany, all along the Rhine, particularly at the two extremities, Alsace and the United Provinces. A frontier of sensibilities between two rival entities, this Rhineland region presented elements of unity which contrasted with the differences conditioned by history and politics. There was a common civilization founded on historical tradition, a system of economic and cultural ties and exchanges, and urban prosperity. This last was a decisive factor in the intellectual revival at the end of the fifteenth century, which wanted to destroy the old framework of scholasticism and thereby posed the fundamental problem of the reformation of the Church. In 1480 began the prodigious ground swell of humanism which brought tremendous hope and great enthusiasm to the cultured classes, in no way incompatible with the deep and fervent piety of the masses who were faithful to Mary and the patron saints.

At the beginning of the sixteenth century in the Rhineland countries, there were two possible avenues to follow: on the one hand was the humanist option, stressing man's development and his potentialities, which had to put up a tough fight in the universities before rallying cultured urban opinion to its cause; on the other, the monastic option stressed openness of the will to God and a thirst for the absolute, in response to the desire to return to the original sources of the Word of God. The answer was provided by Luther. *Sola fide*, the free gift of salvation and the reality of the Incarnation, became the keystone of the Protestant Reformation.

The first period was that of the 'explosive burst', the different aspects of which have been analysed by Marc Lienhard. The second, after 1529, that of 'ecclesiological construction' which, despite various obstacles, was to take on a certain originality in the Rhineland, a holy area with a strong religious tradition, but made up of a heterogeneous assortment of territories. This affected the 'institutional writings'. The territorial State tended to take over the hierarchical structure of the new churches. The political medley tended to be mirrored in the religious one in the towns, the princely territories and the episcopal principalities. The interplay of political mechanisms and interests fostered the explosion of ambitions and desires. Legitimacy was obtained either by strength of arms – the first half of the century was that of the Wars of Religion and of the Schmalkaldic League in alliance with the King of France against the Emperor – or by diplomacy: the Peace of Augsburg of 1555 organized the life of the Empire on the basis of the existing state of affairs, recognizing the equality of the Lutheran and Catholic Churches. Newcomers, such as Calvinists and Anabaptists, were exluded, feared and proscribed. The specific character of the territories which defined themselves by their religion was the result of a dual movement, firstly one of dissociation from the old law by the assertion of

identity, and then a movement of convergence in an attempt at coherence and alliance, which proved to be a necessity in the face of political and military threats. This led to the elaboration of formulae of concord, after attempts at compromise through (failed) policies of discussion.

The setting was a region compartmentalized by nature, developed in diverse ways by men whose unifying link was a river. A region that was pleasant to live in, with a more congenial climate than the rest of Germany, profoundly influenced by the Romans, where the landscape included vineyards and medieval walled cities. The Rhine was a major link between the Mediterranean and the North Sea, crossed by major east–west routes. It boasted an ancient rural civilization and a strong urban development with cities that were financial, religious and university centres. It was a 'Europe in transition', ready to respond to the call of new worlds, but in which the rise of princes and States was becoming more marked and a new geography was taking shape, determined by religious imperatives which would govern consciences and policies according to new models.

The Strasburg model

Strasburg, a free republic within the Holy Empire, was responsible for the spread of European, if not world Protestantism, both directly with Bucer and Sturm, through the constitution of the Church in its relations with the magistrature, and indirectly through the influence exercised over Calvin before his departure for Geneva.

During the period from 1523 to 1529, Strasburg was part of the evangelical movement. The assembly of 300 aldermen convened by the magistrature voted by a two-thirds majority for the immediate abolition of mass. The cultural changes took place, but the themes adopted by Luther – justification through the faith, authority of the Bible, Christian freedom, love of one's neighbour – took on an original slant with Bucer. He placed such importance on the Old Testament that the stories had to be transposed to sixteenth-century Alsace. He emphasized even more than Luther the specifically religious role incumbent on the magistrature according to what Francis Rapp called 'municipal patriotism': the care of the town and its religious life, aid to the poor and the organization of the Church.

The 'period of emergence' gave way to that of organization. Firstly, there was the problem of the dissidents: Strasburg, a city of refuge, had taken in the Anabaptists, who challenged baptism and the taking of oaths. The magistrature, faced with the doctrinal demands of the preachers, wished to maintain a certain tolerance, avoid executions, and advocated exile or prison. The confession of faith was a theological problem but also a political one through the interplay of alliances which it implied. One option open to them was agreement with the princes and German towns and adherence to the Augsburg Confession, presented to the Emperor. Alternatively, there was the Swiss option and contact with Zwingli. John Sturm was the first to sign the Augsburg Confession. At last, the Synod of 1533 adopted a position on the question of relations between the Church and the magistrature; the 'moral role' of the Church was maintained and the ambitions of the preachers who hoped to make Strasburg a 'holy city' curbed. On 29 January 1548, a disciplinary ruling was promulgated in the same spirit. The tension between the magistrature and the Church increased at the time of the Interim, a set of compromises imposed by Charles V: on the one side was *raison d'etat*, and on the other the confessionalist attitude of the preachers who were continually guarding against the re-establishment of the papistry in Strasburg. Bucer went into exile in England.

From 1525, French refugees had been flocking to the town where the 'Gymnasium' was created in 1538 in which Calvin taught, as well as being pastor to the refugees. He married Idelette de Bures, the widow of an Anabaptist he had converted. In Strasburg, Calvin published a considerably enhanced second edition of his *Institutes of the Christian Religion* (1541). Sensitive to what gave the Strasburg theologians their originality – putting faith into practice and exercising pastoral care – he was fully aware of the importance of the religious customs, prayers and confession of sins, and appreciated the presbyteral ministry which was to play a major role in the whole of Protestant Christianity. He collected the psalms which appeared in the Huguenot Psalter and nourished the spiritual life of the French Church during its growth and at the time of persecution.

In the realm of the faith, Bucer was a fierce partisan of unity and conciliation. From 1536, he had been reconciled with Luther and was a supporter of the Wittenberg Concord. In 1581, the *Book of Concord*, a compromise agreed between the Lutheran churches of Württemberg and Saxony, became the doctrinal foundation of the Strasburg Church. In 1598, the magistrature published a new ecclesiastic

Portrait of Martin Bucer at the age of fifty-three, an engraving by René Boyvin, 1544. Société de l'Histoire du Protestantisme Français, Paris.

The Interior of St Pierre le Jeune church in Strasburg.

Among the many French refugees in Strasburg, the most famous was John Calvin, summoned by Bucer, who was both minister of the little French church and teacher at the 'Gymnasium'.

The Strasburg Gymnasium, vignette from a 16th-century engraving. Bibliothèque Nationale et Universitaire, Strasburg.

Pierre Toussain was the Reformer of the Montbéliard region, where he received the support of the ducal family of Württemberg. Pastor from 1537 to 1571, he developed a confession of faith and enabled the establishment of a State Church.

Defence of clerical matrimony, handwritten letter by Pierre Toussain, Montbéliard, 1539. French National Archives, K2173, *d.II, p.1*.

ordinance which became the foundation of spiritual life in strict Lutheran parishes until the French Revolution. It maintained the confession of sins and absolution at the beginning of the service, but remained in the Bucerian tradition in that it was far removed from the sumptuous ritual of the churches of northern Germany.

This type of urban church, dominated by the magistrature, began to be established in other towns in Alsace with slight variations depending on the situation, the government and outside pressures. Haguenau, where there was a Protestant parish from 1564, had to give way at the time of the Thirty Years War to the dual offensive of the Jesuits and Wallenstein. In Colmar, the Reformation triumphed in 1575; attacked at the beginning of the Thirty Years War, it was restored by the Swedes and honours the Protestant hero Gustavus Adolphus to this day. Mulhouse, which was near Basle and had been linked to the Swiss cantons since 1515, took part in the Reformation in association with the work of Oecolampadius. In 1566, Mulhouse adopted the *Confessio Helvetica posterior* drawn up by Bullinger, forging the kind of man who in the eighteenth century would take up the challenge of the industrial revolution.

The influence of the Strasburg model spread into the lowland, mainly on account of Bucer, advisor to the princes in the seigneuries of lower Alsace and Hesse. Among the seigneuries, Hanau-Lichtenberg, Fleckstein and Oberbronn had a family atmosphere, both in their methods and in their very 'air'; they exemplified closed rural Protestant society, just as the patrician house of the Quai des Bateliers in Strasburg was typical of the Lutheran 'urban system'. Acts drawn up by notaries, inventories and parish registers are precious documents as are the registers of the Convention or the deliberations of the Prince's Council, his superintendent being in charge of ecclesiastical affairs.

In May 1545, pastors and advisors of the Count of Hanau-Lichtenberg gathered at a first synod in Bouxwiller; in 1573 an ordinance from the Count, inspired by that of Württemberg, paved the way for assimilation into the orthodoxy of the *Formula of Concord* which was formally recognized in 1577. It had been completed with the addition of educational rules in 1574 and the establishment of a Latin school, which in 1658 was transformed into a Gymnasium like the one at Strasburg.

This Lutheran rural block, built on a solid ideological and institutional framework, has survived until the present day. Firstly, there were the books: Luther's catechism, holy history and Sunday sermons on the texts of the pericopes of the liturgical year, heard from adolescence to old age. Farming needs and everyday preoccupations figured prominently in the important prayer of intercession read every Sunday to beseech favourable weather: not too much rain, or a drought which would crack the earth and dry up the plants, nor hail or the wrath of the heavens. The songs echo and illustrate this harmony which unites heaven and earth: *Geh aus mein Herz und suche Freud* is a hymn rejoicing in the beauty of nature in the spring, evoking with rustic poetry the flowers, the trees and the birds, and celebrating the growth of the corn in the blade. Everywhere, Nature sings the glory of the Creator. The song ends in thanksgiving, like a prayer; it expresses the thanks of the farmer and his family for the bounty of the heavens, good health, the house and the farm, the harvest, the plentiful, robust livestock – before the ordeal of the Thirty Years War.

That is the image, both rural and urban, of piety as it was practised in Strasburg, based on a 'model' which, fearing sterile or harmful theological speculation, gave thanks in family, in home and city to the Creator, bestower of joys and sorrows.

Another princely institution which is noteworthy for its uniqueness in France was the French language Lutheran Church in the Montbéliard region. The Lutheran Reformation was originally established by William Farel, then abandoned after the Peasants' Revolt. It was revived between 1535 and 1538, then in 1552 it gained a permanent hold after the Peace of Augsburg, establishing the uniqueness of the principality of Montbéliard, part of the Empire governed by the ducal family of Württemberg, a Protestant bastion between Spanish Franche-Comté, Habsburg Sundgau and the prince-bishop of Basle's Ajoie.

The process was classic: the preaching of Pierre Toussain, the elaboration of a confession of faith, the action of the prince who appointed Toussain superintendent of the new Church and lastly the confirmation by the institution of the State Church in 1555. Then came the struggle against doctrinal deviations and ecclesiological development by the great ecclesiastical ordinance of 1573 and the compulsory signing of the Formula of Concord of the Churches of the Augsburg Confession in 1577. Lastly, there was the final effort to reach an agreement between Lutherans and Calvinists. At the colloquy convened by the prince in March 1586, the matters under dispute were debated – the person of Christ, baptism, The Lord's Supper, predestination and forgiveness, the use of organs, the role of images and altars in churches. Finally, the ordinance of 1588 banned any service other than the one defined by the Augsburg Confession and the ecclesiastical ordinance,

while the theological training of pastors was provided by the Lutheran University of Tübingen.

The role of the prince was defined in the preamble to the ordinance of 1577: 'The law is the task of the prince and the prince is the torch, the image and the representation of the living God on earth.' From there it went on to the powers of the police, to warnings 'against oaths and blasphemies, drunkenness, festivals, dances with musical accompaniment and dissolute or immodest songs'.

A society was born. The Church had inherited financial resources as a result of the sale of ecclesiastical property ordered in 1584. There was the same concern as elsewhere for education which was made compulsory for both boys and girls, although they were segregated. A Gymnasium was set up where Latin, Greek and local languages were taught. It was through Luther and Melanchthon that children learnt to read, before the scourges of the seventeeth century – war and the plague – compromised the destinies of the small, isolated flock in the face of powerful neighbours and the ambition of the Sun King.

The Palatine model

The new – and revolutionary – event that marked the second half of the sixteenth century and the beginning of the seventeenth century in the Rhineland was the establishment of Calvinism with its proselytizing fervour, at a time when the great theological struggles seemed to have subsided. It was not the strict Genevan doctrine, but a revised, elaborated one, to suit better the aspirations of the princes if not those of their subjects.

The history of the Palatinate, an 'electoral' member of the Holy Empire, is a disjointed one. This collection of separate territories on either side of the Rhine, scattered over an area of about 5,000 km, had a population of about 3–400,000, grouped into 360 parishes. The interrupted successions created a lack of religious continuity leading to a complex ecclesiastical history, linked to the application of the 1555 principle: whoever rules decides the religion. Frederick III (1525–76) became a follower of Luther through his marriage to Marie de Brandenburg-Bayreuth and developed the Reformation brought into his state by his predecessor, the Elector Otto-Henry. But, troubled by the upholding of the dogma of the 'real presence', that 'bastion of papism', in Luther's doctrine, and despite his wife's fears and the opposition of the evangelical princes, he went on to a radical Reformation. In his electorate he forbade holidays dedicated to the Virgin and the saints, religious paintings, altars, baptismal fonts, organs and chanting. On his death, his son Louis VI restored Lutheranism for a short time (1576–83), then Calvinism once again triumphed with his successor John Casimir (1583–92), guardian of the young Frederick IV, raised in the same faith despite the wishes of the deceased. Only the upper Palatinate remained Lutheran. Frederick IV, who married one of William the Silent's daughters, died in 1610. His son, Frederick V, married Elizabeth Stuart, daughter of James I of England, in February 1616, before claiming the crown of Bohemia in 1618.

These few facts give an idea of the Palatinate's impact on the European stage, particularly through the alliances of the royal families. They underline one of the key ideas of Palatine Calvinism, that of international solidarity, with French Calvinism, with the Low Countries and with the Swedish king. In fact, John Casimir twice led an army to the help of the Protestants, in 1567 and in 1576. The influence of the Palatinate also came from the doctrine expressed in the *Heidelberg Catechism* (1563), a synthesis of the doctrines of Melanchthon and the theologians of Zurich and Geneva, a diluted Zwinglianism, and a living testimony to the evangelical faith to which the Synod of Dordrecht (1619) added its support. The text of the compromise, set out by the *Formula of Concord* (1581) led to a 'reaction of rejection' in different territories along the Rhine as far as the North Sea. The influence of Dutch refugees was as decisive for the economy as it was for the Church. The Rhineland extension developed first in Nassau-Dillenburg favoured by the connections between the ruling family and William of Orange. Next it spread to the Duchy of Zweibrugge, on the left bank of the Rhine, with a population of 60,000 grouped in 70 parishes where the Lutheran Church accepted Calvinism in 1588 from the hands of John I (1569–1604).

This 'Palatine model', a tangible expression of episcopal power, fell into two main types: the princely type and the presbytero-synodal system. The former prevailed in the Palatinate, Hanau-Dillenburg and Hesse-Cassel which remained close to the institutional Lutheran system, with the general consistory, the synods and pastoral visitations, while the latter was widespread in the Rhineland, Friesland, and few parishes of refugees in Strasburg, in Frankfurt and Cologne remained in the pure Calvinist tradition. In both branches, there was the same conception of the Lord's

Supper, the same concern to rid a renewed faith of every trace of popery, the same crusading ardour and the same international solidarity.

There remains the thorny problem of religious life and the behaviour of the faithful in the face of the legal and sociological pressure of the new ecclesiastical structures of government imposed from above. Let us say that there was an almost general respect for the Sunday service at which attendance was compulsory, worshippers generally listened attentively to the sermon and participated moderately in hymn singing, while the splendour of the major festivals was maintained and given a new significance by Lutheran Christocentrism. The Lord's Supper became the bone of contention between the denominations: although the theologians' debates on the subject were beyond the understanding of the average worshipper, the latter felt the effects which were contrary to the very essence of thanksgiving and fraternal communion. Between 1555 and 1618, there was a profound transformation of popular thinking and the new religious convictions became solidly rooted in the family and the parish, thanks to the efforts of a married, determined and educated clergy.

Protestant offensive and new Catholic triumph

At the beginning of the sixteenth century, the Rhenish bishoprics and arch-bishoprics of Speyer, Worms, Trier, Mainz and Cologne were remarkable for the fervour of popular faith tinged with anti-clericalism, the humanism given prominence by the printing press, the turbulent unrest of the knights and the activeness of both the universities and the priests. The Lutheran tornado came down initially on this closely woven episcopal fabric, a tempting prey for secularization. The surprise effect was total, hidden tensions exploded: the whole area nearly swung to the new faith. It was only towards the second half of the century that, in opposition to Protestantism, Roman Catholicism regained the upper hand slowly, taking on an original character depending on the place, the personalities and the time.

In Mainz, Albert of Brandenburg, the archbishop who was also Archbishop of Magdeburg and Arch-Chancellor of the Empire, played an important role in the development of humanism and the beginnings of the Reformation. Luther and Melanchthon placed their hope in him. But, having remained faithful to the Roman Catholic Church, he took part in the Jesuits' early offensive and worked on reforming the clergy, a huge, thankless task which his successors Sebastian von Heusenstamm (1545–55) and Daniel Brendel von Homburg (1555–82) also took on. 'Mainz has a Catholic prince,' wrote an eye witness in 1581, 'but the government is conducted by his Protestant subjects.' There was a shortage of able priests with pure morals but the chapter was opposed to all reforms. A few young people were sent to the colleges of Cologne or Mainz, but the support of the nuncios was vital, as and when they were able to reappear in those parts. The slow recapture continued gradually with Wolfgang von Dalberg but it was not effective until 1648. Likewise for the bishoprics of Speyer and Worms, enclaves in Palatine territories: anti-Roman Catholic hostility was the most notable feature.

It was the same scenario in Trier, but in a more emphatic way. Opposing the Archbishop Richard von Greiffenklau (1511–31) was Franz von Sickingen, the elected leader of the 'Fraternal League of the Nobility'. He led an army of mercenaries 'to make a breach for the Word of God', defying Richard, 'Archbishop of Trier, guilty of high treason towards God, towards His Imperial Majesty and the laws of the Empire.' Sickingen failed in his attempt to transform the Archbishopric of Trier into a temporal principality. But the Protestant Reformation took hold: 'The latent Protestantism of a number of bishops who have remained outwardly Catholic,' wrote Archbishop Jean de Leyen, 'did a lot more harm to the Church and to Catholics than a downright apostasy.' In 1559, there was a serious riot in the town; it failed, but 'the heresy divides and poisons people's minds', wrote Commendone, the Pope's envoy. The Counter-Reformation did not make any real progress until the advent of Jacob III von Elz (1569–81).

The Archbishopric of Cologne seemed even more tempting. On two occasions, it nearly swung to the Protestant side. Firstly with Hermann de Wied, elected in 1559, who reformed his clergy with Bucer's help, but failed; then with Gerhard Truchsess, elected in 1577, who wanted to transform his diocese into a temporal principality. His aim was to crush all the partisans of the 'Roman Antichrist' in the Empire of Germany. The Pope excommunicated him and appointed in his place Ernest of Bavaria, who was already Bishop of Freisingen, Hildesheim and Liège. The Cologne war ravaged the lowlands; in the absence of any real Protestant solidarity, it

View of Mainz, engraving from the *Chronicle of Nuremberg*, 1493. Bibliothèque Nationale, Paris.

ended in January 1584 with Ernest of Bavaria's taking Bonn. There had been considerable alarm among the Catholics.

The town of Aachen was particularly coveted by both sides because of its position. After 1567, thousands of Calvinist refugees from the Low Countries flooded into western Germany and Aachen, Wesen and Cologne, became key towns in the vast net stretching from Emden to Heidelberg which linked the scattered Calvinist communities – centres of implacable hatred of Catholicism. After 1592, The question of Aachen became a subject of dispute in the diets; twice the town came under the ban; in 1614, Spinola captured it and exiled the Protestant preachers.

The War of the Bishops also raised the problem of the Bishopric of Strasburg. A Jesuit college opened in 1580 in Molsheim. On the death of the bishop in 1592, the Protestant part of the great chapter elected John George of Brandenburg as administrator of the bishopric while the Catholic group elected Charles of Lorraine, already Bishop of Metz and a cardinal. In the devastating war, the town sided with the Protestants. In 1604, the Treaty of Haguenau recognized Charles of Lorraine as Bishop of Strasburg. The Catholic offensive was renewed from the beginning of the Thirty Years War with varying fortunes, not least the intervention of the Emperor in 1629 and the King of Sweden in 1632.

That then was the spectacle offered by the Rhenish bishoprics. They were a prime target for the extension of the Protestant Reformation due to the aggravation of grievances against the economically and legally privileged, the higher clergy's taste for luxury, their grasping mentality and egoism, and the lower clergy's pastoral inability, lack of culture and corruption. As the likelihood of conflict increased, the bishoprics were like highly sensitive nerve centres in that vital holy area which had been weakened by the election system, the durability of an administration won over

In the first half of the 16th century, the Reformation made continuous progress, but after a few decades of constant defeats, the revived Catholic Church launched into a counter-offensive. In spite of the hostility of a vast number of their subjects the Archbishops of Magdeburg held out, preparing the Counter-Reformation, while the archbishopric of Cologne narrowly escaped falling into the hands of Protestants. The Catholic Prince Ernest of Bavaria captured Bonn, the residence of the Elector princes, in January 1584.

The Surrender of Bonn, 16th-century engraving. Bibliothèque Nationale, Paris.

to the new ideas, the difficulty of recruiting priests, the attraction of the secularization of property and clerical marriage. Both the Reformation and the Catholic Counter-Reformation found this difficult ground for reshaping Christian society, a long and difficult task supported by Rome, the nuncios and their visits, the action of the Jesuits, men of the land, and of their colleges. At the same time, catechism for children and books abounded. The collective memory was the converters' main tool.

From religious reform to national independence in the United Provinces

On coming under the authority of Charles V, the seventeen provinces which today make up Belgium and the Netherlands already had their own tradition of provincial states and of the Estates General, whose rights were respected by the Emperor. After the Edict of Worms of 8 May 1521, the Emperor led an attack against the Lutherans, who were numerous – especially in Antwerp, the economic capital of the West dedicated to humanism. In 1532, the first Protestants were burned at the stake; in 1536, the Emperor turned against the Anabaptists, a much more formidable sect. Calvinism spread into the Low Countries after 1544. Pierre de Brully, a former pastor of the Protestant parish of Strasburg, sent to Tournai and Valenciennes, died at the stake on 19 February 1545. Calvinism then became a crusade: in 1560, there were 16,000 Protestants in Antwerp. Guy de Brès, a friend of de Beza, Viret and Calvin, was born in Mons and settled first in Antwerp, then in Tournai. He published the *Confessio belgica* in Walloons in 1561 recommending the institution of the consistory composed of pastors, elders and deacons, 'chosen by legitimate election of the Church'. Translated into Flemish in 1562, into German in 1564, revised in 1566 by François de Jong, a pastor from the Berry, the *Confessio belgica* was made compulsory by the first synod of Walloon and Flemish Churches, held in Emden in October 1571.

As in France, this was the beginning of a second period which, due to the political situation – in 1555, Philip II succeeded Charles V and his policies regarding the autonomy of the country were much less cautious – saw the Church go into action, and the arrival on the scene of nationalist elements, together with the nobility. The chief of these was William of Orange, a prince of the Empire, who, in 1573, professed Calvinism. At his side were the two Marnix brothers from St Aldegonde, fierce adversaries of the Roman Catholic Church. Guy de Brès sought sanctuary in Sedan, with Robert de La Marck, Duke of Bouillon. His Reformation work there was closely akin to Calvin's in Geneva. In his desire for union, he received and approved the *Wittenberg Concord* drawn up by Bucer. In 1566 a religious peace seemed to be setting in. Just as in France at the time of the 'placards' incident, the rupture occurred, between 11 August and 16 September, when a wave of rioters 'left a vast trail of devastation and fires across the Low Countries, from Armentières

Philip II was attached to the Spanish way of reconquering and, with far more powerful means than Charles V, showed less flexibility than Charles towards the Low Countries. A strong sense of regional identity and Calvinist convictions were at the root of the Beggars' Uprising, the nickname given to the rebels as a result of the beggar's disguise worn during the banquet of 5 April 1566. With grating humour, Bruegel dressed his famous cripples in these symbolic rags.

1. *The Beggars*, painting by Pieter Bruegel the Elder, 1568. Musée du Louvre, Paris.

2. *Barbarian Cruelty of the Beggars*, Catholic propaganda engraving, 16th century. Bibliothèque Nationale, Paris.

3. *Portrait of Philip II*, painting by Pantoja de la Cruz, late 16th century. Bibliothèque Nationale, Paris.

1

2

to Leeuwarden'. Groups of rebels terrorized Valenciennes, Antwerp and Rotterdam, creating divisions in the party of the 'Beggars' and facilitating repressive action by the Spanish government.

The following period was marked by an attempt at unity which was both religious and political. In the face of savage repression by the Duke of Alba, who arrived in Brussels in 1567 and set up the Council of Blood followed by the sacking of Antwerp, the Prince of Orange demanded the departure of foreign troops and the right of the two religions to co-exist, by means of a religious truce. But circumstances decided otherwise: the Huguenot pamphlets precipitated by the St Bartholomew's Day Massacre, the *Réveille-Matin*, the *Franco-Gallia*, the *Vindiciae contre tyrannos* and *De iure magistratum in subditos* were translated. At the Cologne councils, the right to rebel was deemed to be a natural right for the first time. The Walloon Catholics preferred peace with the King of Spain to the Protestant revolution. At the Confederation of Arras (1579) followed by the Treaty of Arras, about ten Catholic provinces in the south sought reconciliation with Philip II. Farnese's victory added Ghent, Brussels and Antwerp, which capitulated after a long siege. On 25 January 1579, the Union of Utrecht united the seven northern provinces which had remained Calvinist. It was the end of William of Orange's great political and religious dream. These two divergent developments were accompanied by a spate of writings of all sorts, on controversies over dogma and faith, on tolerance and freedom of conscience. The strong personalities of eminent thinkers were backed by the action of political and social forces, influences from the outside and from provincial synods, pastors and universities. Thus a 'new world' was engendered, a world characterized by the variety of opinion among the Protestants and by its tolerance for freedom of thought.

One question arises from this great epic marked by the steady but difficult progress of a community towards national sovereignty: to what extent was this the fruition of the ethical and legal thought of the Reformer aiming to assert the rights of the community of believers? In fact, this policy did not imply any of the great freedoms of opinion, of conscience, of the press or of worship. The government remained aristocratic, although on a popular ticket. It was marked by the special character of Dutch Calvinism which came from three sources: local franchise, tradition – embodied not in individuals but in institutions – and above all, the principle, dear to Calvin and to de Beza, of government not by a brutal majority, but by the *senior pars*, that is the religious, fervent and enlightened élite, whom Pierre Chaunu calls 'the yeast in the dough'.

The elements of success

After this brief outline which covers a century and an area stretching from Basle to the sea, is it possible to try to sum it up? The basis is the confession of faith. A book, the Bible; a sovereign, the omnipotent God; an inspiration, that of the Holy Ghost; an example, Christ. Some have laughed at the 'varieties of Protestant Churches'; in

3

To combat the beggars, Philip II depended on the Italian Legion and the Duke of Alva, appointed governor of the Low Countries in 1567. But despite his ruthless repression, Alva was not able to put down the rebellion, which became widespread. Leading the uprising was William of Nassau, Prince of Orange (1533–84), who became *stathouder* of the seventeen provinces. Although the southern regions were soon recaptured by the loyalists with the help of the Spanish, in the north, the Republic of the United Provinces was consolidated.

1. *Portrait of William the First of Nassau, known as The Silent*, engraving by Hogenberg, early 17th century. Bibliothèque Nationale, Paris.

2. *The Tyranny of the Duke of Alva*, 16th-century Flemish painting. Byloke Abbey, Ghent.

3. *The Tomb of William of Orange in the New Church at Delft*, painting by Emmanuel de Witte, 17th century. Musée des Beaux-Arts, Lille.

fact, these variations express a concern, a constant searching. *Ecclesia reformata semper reformanda* said Liebniz, contrasting man's infidelity to God's fidelity. Without a doubt, the great writings are from the first half of the century. But, after 1555, 'ecclesiological construction' developed in the Rhineland, precisely because the land was parcelled into small, fragmented units, so that a desire for unification in this land of frontiers took on the appearance of 'national defence'. It was also due to the 'Palatine betrayal' and to the Calvinist breakthrough which created that theological advance linking Geneva to the sea. Through the Palatinate, Hesse-Anhalt, the Duchy of Cleves and Juliers, the county of Nassau, eastern Friesland and Bremen, Calvinist doctrine and, to a certain extent, Calvinist discipline reached the sea and the ocean which opened up much broader horizons. Even Cologne, the capital of Rhenish Catholicism, numbered no fewer than four Calvinist communities, one French, one Dutch and two German. *Sole Scripturae*. The decisive texts made their mark: the Heidelberg catechism (1563), the Formula of Concord (1580), the ordinances of the magistrature (Strasbourg 1598). After 1563, however, the Catholic countercurrent insinuated itself everywhere in that trench warfare where every bishopric, every abbey, every little fief counted, and had at its disposal, thanks to the Council of Trent, the ideological arsenal which had hitherto been lacking.

The ecclesiological construction was the result of a close alliance between the new churches and the royal administration, an alliance which was legitimized after the Peace of Augsburg for both Lutherans and Catholics, and which again emphasized the fragmentation of territories. A legislative arsenal had been gathered which was both offensive, to combat ignorance, indifference and superstition, and defensive, to protect the faithful from the traps of papist Babylon and the kingdom of Satan, from which the Calvinists or the Anabaptists, these enemies of the social order, could not be excluded since they were so near. This alliance with the temporal power did not go unchallenged and led to significant spiritual sacrifices, even though both powers invoked to the Bible. Only external dangers, internal threats, financial advantages and the affirmation of the benefits of religious and social unity can explain the durability of a solution which reinforced the 'confessional gulf' between two closed worlds, thus creating two forms of civilization which were almost incompatible, if not actually inimical.

In this 'spiritual cathedral', the construction of a new Protestant society, the true dialogue was established between the worshippers and the pastors, interpreters of The Word of God. Doubtless, among the worshippers, only a small minority possessed a true religious sensibility, and similarly, in spite of unsettled times, dismissal and exile, the pastors were not saints or heroes. But, in town and countryside alike, a new

notion was born concerning individual responsibility in the family, the Church and the community, through participation in collective effort, in religious and sacramental practice and in the education of the children. The role of the school was inherent in the idea of universal priesthood, especially among Calvinists, who were instinctively more egalitarian and more open to the world. Although the princes' monopoly of the Church led to a strange marriage between absolutism and morality, that could only have taken place throuh hypothesis of the 'godly prince', and in a common submission to divine laws in reciprocal and mutual fidelity. Owing to their location, to the overlapping of confessions and territories, to the importance of commercial movements and of the main towns as places of sanctuary, the Rhineland countries remained a centre of reflection and of cultural influence exemplified by universities such as Marburg, Tübingen, Heidelberg and Herborn.

This spiritual communion was expressed in music, that 'splendid gift from God' as Luther called it. The role of Strasburg in the elaboration of the new liturgy was crucial both for the Lutheran choral and for the Reformed psalm. The works of Wolfgang Dachstein, the famous *Argentinensis organista*, and of Wolfgang Musculus, supported by the choirs of Walliser, *cantor* and music teacher at the gymnasium, enhanced by three generations of German musicians, were to lead to the works of the greatest *cantor* of all times, Johann Sebastian Bach.

3

England: the 'via media'

Nowhere was the connection between religious change and political power more apparent than in England. Nowhere, it must be added, was it more paradoxical: it was Henry VIII, a fervent Catholic, who introduced the Reformation to his kingdom; it was an inflamed adversary of Protestantism, Mary Tudor, who reinforced it by the vehemence of her persecutions; it was Elizabeth I, whose inner convictions remained a mystery, who definitively instituted Anglicanism as the State religion. The result of this political to-ing and fro-ing conforms to the English nature, for it signifies a compromise, a middle way between two opposing camps.

The origins of the English Reformation

1

In 1584, William Allen, leader of the English Catholic refugees on the continent and later to become Cardinal of England, included his own brief summary of the history of the Reformation in England in a book titled *A True, Sincere, and Modest Defence of English Catholics*. Allen labelled the settlement established by Henry VIII, most explicitly by the Act of Supremacy of 1534, as still Catholic but schismatic; that established for the boy-king Edward VI (1547 to 1553) as Zwinglian; and the one established by Mary Tudor, who reigned from 1553 to 1558, as again Catholic. The settlement established by Elizabeth I soon after her accession in 1558 he termed Calvinist. This is a hostile view from a man opposed to the introduction of Protestantism into his home country. It is also a highly schematic view. But it does contain some important kernels of truth. The nature of the religious establishment created in England during the sixteenth century did change significantly with each of Henry VIII and his three Tudor successors, and its form was deeply influenced in its Protestant phases by theologians on the continent, most prominently by Huldrych Zwingli during the Edwardian period and by John Calvin during the Elizabethan period.

The way to Reformation in England had been prepared by the spread in the fourteenth and fifteenth centuries of Lollardy, a popular heretical movement originally inspired by the ideas of John Wyclif (1330–84), an Oxford teacher of theology who also became a political activist. By the sixteenth century, however, formal knowledge of Wyclif's theology had effectively been eliminated by more than a century of savage repression. All that remained were small groups of disaffected peasants and artisans, still called Lollards, who had lost respect for the Roman Catholic clergy and sacraments, but who had not formulated any sophisticated or coherent alternatives and thus cannot truly be called Protestant.

The real Reformation in England was initiated by Henry VIII, the second of the Tudor kings, who started his reign as a young and immensely popular figure, a splendid athlete and a skillful showman. It is ironic that it was Henry who prompted this religious change, since he was well informed on the theological issues involved at the beginning of the Protestant revolt and was thoroughly committed to the Catholic side. Indeed he had personally written a defence of the Catholic sacramental system in direct response to Luther, entitled the *Assertio septem sacramentorum*, or *Defence of the seven sacraments*, and for this slashing polemic he gloried in the award to him by a grateful Pope of a new title: *Defensor Fidei*, Defender of the Faith. There were few rulers in all of Europe with the intellectual equipment required for a theological treatise of this sophistication.

It was Henry's desire for a new marriage that led to England's initial break with Rome. Henry was married to his brother's widow, Catherine of Aragon – an

arrangement by the ruling houses of England and Spain to preserve an alliance of importance to both countries. Marriage to a brother's widow was prohibited by the law of the Catholic Church, but a compliant Pope had granted a special dispensation in this case. So when Henry succeeded his father, Henry VII, as King of England in 1509, Catherine became his queen. That marriage, however, did not produce the male heir that the King wanted so badly. Indeed the only surviving child of Henry and Catherine, Mary, was in precarious health. And Henry had fallen in love with Anne Boleyn, a younger woman from a prominent English aristocratic family. Henry thus sought from the Pope an annulment of his marriage to Catherine, so that he might be free to marry Anne. In effect he was asking the Pope to rule that an earlier Pope had erred in supplying the dispensation that had made his marriage possible, that such an exception to Church law violated Biblical injunctions against marriage of a brother's widow, and that Henry was therefore now free to marry as he wished. This request put the Pope in a delicate position, however, for Catherine's nephew, Charles V, the Holy Roman Emperor and King of Spain, was in possession of much of Italy and his troops had recently sacked the city of Rome. And Catherine and Charles were both fiercely opposed to this annulment which would have the effect of declaring Catherine to have been living in sin for more than twenty years. Faced with pressure from both sides, the Pope for years did nothing. This resistance to his wishes infuriated Henry. He submitted the case to a court of English ecclesiastics presided over by Thomas Cranmer, Henry's new Archbishop of Canterbury, and this court dutifully granted the King his annulment. Rome, alarmed at the evasion of usual canonical procedure, finally ruled that Henry's first marriage to Catherine was indeed valid and levied ecclesiastical censures on the kingdom. England thus discovered that it had been ejected from the Roman Catholic Church.

The breach had meanwhile been hardened by a number of laws enacted by the English Parliament. In turning to Parliament, Henry and his ministers were seeking to gain the support of the English people, particularly the more influential segments of that population among the aristocracy who sat in the first chamber of Parliament, the House of Lords, and the gentry and townspeople who were represented in the second chamber of Parliament, the House of Commons. Henry used his Parliament so extensively to win support for his religious policy, indeed, that he made of it a more important part of his government than did most contemporary continental monarchs. The ecclesiastical laws adopted by Parliament had the effect of systematically cutting all institutional ties between the Church of England and the Roman curia. It was made illegal to appeal legal cases to Rome, like the case granting Henry's annulment; to send money to Rome; and to accept nominations to clerical positions from Rome. Finally the Act of Supremacy provided a climax in 1534 to this campaign for legal separation by declaring the King to be 'the only supreme head on earth of the Church of England', by tendering to all officials of Church and State a loyalty oath to the King as head of the Church, and by prescribing draconian penalties for all who failed to subscribe to this oath. It was for refusing to take this oath that Thomas More, the great humanist and formerly the King's Lord Chancellor, was put to death. These laws made the Henrician schism complete.

The religious politics of Henry VIII

Although England was now no longer a part of the Roman Catholic communion, she had still not joined the Protestant movement. A growing number of Englishmen were informing themselves about Protestant ideas and several of them banded together to spread these ideas, notably a group in the university town of Cambridge, who first met in the White Horse Inn. But those of them who were not very circumspect were attacked and treated harshly, even put to death, by the Henrician government. There was an early penetration of Protestant practice, to be sure, in the growing use of Bibles translated into English. The first of these translations, of a New Testament by William Tyndale, was of obviously Lutheran inspiration. It was published on the continent and smuggled into England. But the government actively sought to prevent its use and Tyndale, then in residence in the Spanish Netherlands, was betrayed by an English agent into Spanish hands, tried as a heretic, and executed in 1536. Only a year later, however, the English government permitted the publication of a complete English Bible, including the Tyndale translations and some fresh translations by Miles Coverdale. In 1539 the first edition of Great Bible was published, translated entirely by Coverdale and printed with assistance from the government. Henry by proclamation required that a copy of the Great Bible be placed in every parish church in England, each chained to a lectern so that it would be always available. The availability of this Bible, with its text in

2

The Reformation was introduced into England from on high: royal passions and the struggle for political influence were the catalyst; the driving force was the current of humanism flowing through all the European States. After the failure of Cardinal Wolsey, the Lord-Chancellor, to obtain papal annulment of the King's marriage to Catherine of Aragon, Henry VIII broke with Rome and married Anne Boleyn. This decision was criticized by the great humanist, Thomas More, who was imprisoned and then, in 1535, executed.

1. *Cardinal Wolsey* (1475–1530), engraving by Fourdrinier, 16th century. Bibliothèque Nationale, Paris.

2. *Portrait of Anne Boleyn* (1507–36), drawing by Hans Holbein the Younger, first half of the 16th century. National Portrait Gallery, London.

3. *Portrait of Thomas More*, extract from a 16th-century engraving. Bibliothèque Nationale, Paris.

3

A tragic event which inspired artists and dramatists, the beheading of Thomas More on the orders of his old friend, King Henry VIII, rendered the split irreversible. In effect, the celebrated author of *Utopia*, through his attachment to the Catholic Church and his desire for reform, was the only person capable of reconciling the different sides. The pretext for his execution was even more frivolous when Henry VIII freed himself of Anne Boleyn in 1536 in order to marry Jane Seymour (1509–37).

Detail from *Arrest and Supplication of Thomas More*, painting by Antoine Caron, first half of the 16th century. Musée de Blois.

Portrait of Henry VIII (1491–1547), painting by Hans Holbein the Younger, first half of the 16th century. Thyssen-Bornemisza collection, Lugano.

Portrait of Jane Seymour, painting by Hans Holbein the Younger, first half of the 16th century. Vienna.

English and its dependence upon Luther's German Bible for many of its key readings, helped to spread Protestant ideas in indirect and subtle ways.

Henry VIII moved England further towards a Protestant position by dissolving the monastic communities and chantries. These institutions held substantial property, perhaps as much as 10 per cent of all the landed wealth in the kingdom; most of them, however, had long since ceased to be vital centres of religious activity. They were thus very vulnerable to seizure, and Thomas Cromwell, Henry's chief minister in these years, decided to close them. Teams of royal visitors were sent throughout England to investigate the conditions of all the convents and monasteries in the country, on the model of traditional episcopal visitations. They brought back reports full of lurid tales of misgovernment and lax living in these establishments. While there is no doubt that the royal visitors knew that they were expected to return with damaging information, there is also little doubt that many of the monastic communities were in fact riddled with scandal. This evidence was then turned over the Parliament, which in 1536 dutifully ordered the closing of all the lesser monasteries, those with less than £200 of income per year. It was argued that only the wealthier monasteries had the resources to meet their social obligations.

The closing of the lesser monasteries may well have provoked the first violence of the English Reformation – the Pilgrimage of Grace, an armed revolt against royal authority in the northern counties of Lincoln and York, led by local nobles and gentry but probably goaded to action by a number of abbots and priests. That revolt was quickly crushed by a royal army, and armed with this evidence that monastic communities encouraged treason, Cromwell turned to a campaign against the larger monasteries. He bullied them into voting their own dissolution, and Parliament ratified their action by a law adopted in 1539.

There is continuing debate as to what happened to the members of religious orders and their property following the dissolutions, and continuing research is necessary to answer these questions fully. A certain number of monks and friars became parish priests or found other positions in the secular clergy; some of the older ones and the members of female orders were awarded small pensions and returned to secular life with their families. Some monastic buildings were converted to other religious uses, and one can still find abbeys that became parish churches and monastic properties that were assigned to the support of university colleges. But most of the property seems to have been seized by the royal Treasury, and then auctioned off over the following decades to members of the nobility and gentry. In many areas the aristocratic families that had originally created a monastic community in the Middle Ages by their pious bequests now simply bought the land back for their own use.

The closing of the monastic communities obviously created a certain amount of social distress. But it stimulated remarkably little formal protest after the collapse of the Pilgrimage of Grace. The only order whose members protested the dissolution in

significant number was the Carthusians. Many of them were treated very harshly, being put to death on charges of treason. The sale of the monastic lands, furthermore, created a considerable vested interest in the preservation of the Reformation regime in England. All over England there were members of powerful local families who had benefited from the acquisition of monastic lands. Fully converted to Protestant doctrine or not, they were unwilling to lose this new property. Those English Catholics who were shrewd observers accepted this social fact. When Mary Tudor returned England to obedience to Rome in 1553, she did not dare rebuild the monastic communities. Her failure to do so upset the Pope, but she appreciated the dynamics of English society in a way that Rome did not.

Even though Henry VIII had broken with Rome in all these ways, he still regarded himself as committed to Catholic theology. And he demonstrated this commitment most emphatically by persuading Parliament to adopt a doctrinal statement in 1539 called the Six Articles. It was the first of a series of doctrinal definitions adopted by Protestant churches on the continent. It provides yet more compelling evidence of the role of Parliament in the English Reformation. The Six Articles made no attempt to be comprehensive in defining the Christian faith; they simply required all Englishmen to accept six doctrines commonly rejected by Protestants. Every English subject was required to believe in transubstantiation, the received Catholic description of what happens to the elements of bread and wine in the Eucharist, and was expected to receive communion in one kind only, with the cup reserved to the priest. The importance of vows of celibacy for the clergy was affirmed, and monastic vows were declared inviolable. Private masses were permitted, and the importance of oral confession to a priest re-affirmed. Draconian penalties could be levied against any who dared to reject these Catholic doctrines.

By the end of Henry's reign, therefore, Catholics were being put to death on charges of treason and Protestants were being put to death on charges of heresy. Henry VIII had created a Church independent of Rome and without monastic communities, but it was a Church still very much committed to fundamental Catholic doctrine. Those who remain loyal to Rome certainly feel justified in calling the Henrican Church schismatic; many others prefer to call it Anglo-Catholic.

Shortly before Henry VIII died, he set down his wishes on the succession. After his death, he expected to be succeeded by Edward, his young son by his third queen, Jane Seymour. If his son died before maturity, the next in succession should be Mary, his daughter by Catherine of Aragon. If Mary died without issue, the throne should go to Elizabeth, his daughter by Anne Boleyn. In the view of his contemporaries there was little logic in this line of succession and few expected that it would in fact be followed. Any yet that is precisely what happened after Henry died in 1547, as each of these three children of his became in turn ruler of England.

Continental influence

When Edward VI acceded to the throne, he was only nine years old. Obviously this situation demanded a regency, and a council of great aristocrats was created to exercise supreme power. That council was dominated in turn by two men. From 1547 to 1550, Edward Seymour, Duke of Somerset, the King's uncle on his mother's side, was in charge; from 1550 to 1553, John Dudley, Duke of Northumberland. The shape of the religious settlement, however, was controlled in much greater degree than before by the Archbishop of Canterbury, Thomas Cranmer, and certain other ecclesiastical leaders of the Church of England. They now revealed themselves to be much more sympathetic to Protestantism than they had appeared to be under Henry VIII. Cranmer went so far as to make public his marriage, contracted several years before on a diplomatic mission to Germany, with the niece of a Lutheran minister of some eminence, Andreas Osiander.

Cranmer and the Edwardian government threw England open to Protestant influence in the most decisive possible way by inviting scores of prominent continental Protestant leaders to the country. Entire congregations of continental Protestant refugees were encouraged to establish themselves in London and in other cities. The largest of these was a group of Dutch-speaking refugees from the Low Countries who were awarded use of an Augustinian cloister, still known as the Austin Friars' Church. There were also large groups of refugees who spoke French and smaller groups who spoke Italian or Spanish. A Polish nobleman of Zwinglian tendency, Jan Laski, served in London as superintendent of these foreign congregations.

Of even greater influence on the Edwardian regime, however, were foreign theologians invited to England to teach. Cranmer first attempted to persuade Philip Melanchthon, Luther's most prominent successor and the most influential single

The Archbishop of Canterbury Thomas Cranmer (1489–1556) was one of the principal artisans of the establishment of Protestantism in England. After having annulled the marriages of Henry VIII with Catherine of Aragon and Anne Boleyn, he started a lengthy correspondence with Melanchthon and Calvin, and brought over continental preachers such as the Italian Peter Martyr Vermigli, who taught at Oxford and participated in the development of a new liturgy.

Portrait of Peter Martyr Vermigli, engraving from the *Icônes* . . . of Reussner, 1590. Société de l'Histoire du Protestantisme Français, Paris.

Portrait of Thomas Cranmer, painting by Gerlach Flicke, 1546. National Portrait Gallery, London.

creator of Protestant educational curricula and institutions, to come to England. When that failed, he instead persuaded Martin Bucer of Strasburg and his colleague, Peter Martyr Vermigli, to accept English academic appointment. Bucer, a former Dominican friar and Reformer of Strasburg, became a royal professor at Cambridge University. Vermigli, a former Augustinian friar who had fled from Italy and accepted a teaching position in Strasburg, became a royal professor at Oxford University. Bucer had an easier time of it, since Cambridge already contained more sympathizers with Protestant doctrine. But both fought strenuously for the adoption of a fully Protestant theology, within their universities and within the circle of Cranmer's advisers. Their efforts bore fruit.

Several concrete developments reflect the continental influences mediated through Bucer and Vermigli and others. Perhaps the most important is to be found in a new liturgy. For some time, Cranmer had been working on a liturgy in the English language, a liturgy that would translate into the vernacular the guides to service found in the traditional Roman missal. In 1549, soon after the accession of Edward, Cranmer finally promulgated a service book, the first *Book of Common Prayer*. It reflects careful study of received Catholic liturgies, including ones suggested by reforming humanists like the Spanish Cardinal Quiñomez and ones adopted in parts of England like the diocese of Salisbury. It also reflects some examination of the vernacular liturgies Luther developed for the Germans. Finally, it incorporates Cranmer's very real genius in handling the English language: his stately prose continues to be of abiding influence in all parts of the English-speaking world. Nevertheless, this first *Book of Common Prayer* was not fully Protestant.

That flaw was soon remedied by Bucer when Cranmer asked his opinion of the new service book. Bucer prepared a close critique, a *Censura*, of the new liturgy, in which he criticized it for retaining too many remnants of Roman Catholic belief and practice, for not being truly Reformed. Cranmer then completely rewrote his liturgy and issued a second *Book of Common Prayer* in 1551. This second version was clearly Protestant in doctrine, even if its form remained in part Catholic, and it was this version that survived, to be treasured by Protestant exiles under Mary Tudor and revived in the Elizabethan period. It constitutes, without doubt, the most important inheritance from the sixteenth century for English-speaking Protestants world-wide.

In consultation with Bucer and Vermigli and others, Cranmer then went a step further and drafted a confessional statement defining the theological position of the Church of England in a far different and far more comprehensive way than the Six Articles of Henry VIII. This became the Forty-two Articles, and went well beyond the Lutheran position on many issues and reflects the influence of the Zwinglian doctrine. Bucer and Vermigli did not hide their sympathy with this, and it was an influence supported with even more enthusiasm by Laski – and there were numerous other exponents of a Zwinglian position then active in England. By this time, however, the health of the young King was failing and Cranmer obtained endorsement of the Forty-two Articles by the Royal Council. But before it could be ratified by Parliament the King died, and the religious establishment of the kingdom was subject to yet another change.

The failure of Mary Tudor

The next ruler of England, Mary Tudor, had been raised a committed Catholic by her mother, Catherine of Aragon, and she quickly used her powers under the Act of Supremacy to return England to obedience to Rome. To support this policy of return to Catholicism, she married her Habsburg cousin Philip, soon to become king of Spain. She deposed Cranmer and several of the Edwardian bishops and, after spectacular show trials, had them burned to death for heresy. She encouraged so many heresy trials and permitted so many executions, indeed, that she became known to Protestants as 'Bloody Mary'. And she called back from Rome her kinsman, the liberal Cardinal Reginald Pole, to become Archbishop of Canterbury and primate of England. Her reign was too short to permit a thorough-going re-establishment of Catholicism; moreover, the Pope, Paul IV, was so deeply suspicious of the liberal tendencies of Pole and his associates that he offered little help to the English monarch.

It can be argued that the most enduring contribution made during this period to religious reform in England was the driving into exile of several hundred prominent English Protestant leaders. These leaders took up residence in communities in Switzerland and the German Rhineland, and in towns such as Frankfurt, Strasburg, Zurich and Geneva. In these communities Englishmen forged the alliances to

Reformed leaders like Calvin and Bullinger (Zwingli's successor), which were to play such an important role in the further development of the Reformation in England.

Elizabeth and the middle way

When Elizabeth I came to the throne in 1558, many were uncertain of her religious commitments. In contrast to her brother and sister, she was to become an enormously popular monarch, like her father during the early years of his reign. Under her rule England was to experience a tremendous outburst of advances in economic prosperity, in the arts, and in national pride. This is the period aptly called the Age of Shakespeare, after the great dramatist who so eloquently heralded its accomplishments. But on many issues Elizabeth kept her opinions to herself. She clearly understood the issues involved in the Protestant Reformation, for she was superbly educated, easily handled several languages, and had read extensively in theology – studying closely, for example, the *Loci communes* of Philip Melanchthon, perhaps the most influential summary of Protestant theology produced in the sixteenth century. Her own reactions to these issues, however, were never clear, and scholars still argue whether she was at heart a Catholic or a Protestant.

Whatever the case, her political position required Elizabeth I to become Protestant. Only Protestants accepted fully her right to become queen and many, including some of Catholic sympathy, had been angered by the type of Catholicism Mary had attempted to introduce with Spanish support. So soon after her accession, Elizabeth persuaded Parliament again to sever ties with Rome, by passing a new Act of Supremacy, this time declaring the monarch to be 'supreme governor' rather than 'supreme head' of the Church of England, and also by passing an Act of Uniformity, decreeing that only the one type of worship described by a slightly revised version of the Edwardian *Book of Common Prayer* was to be permitted in the realm. She had the good fortune to come to power at a time when there were many episcopal seats vacant. Mary's primate, Pole, for one, had died at about the same time as his patron. Elizabeth filled these vacancies with committed Protestants. She appointed as her primate Matthew Parker, a historical scholar and good Protestant who had been close to the family of her mother, the Boleyns. She appointed to the key diocese of Salisbury John Jewel, a student and close friend of Vermigli, who had gone with him to the continent during Mary's reign. These new bishops drafted a revised Confession of Faith and secured its support, after unusually extended negotiation, by Parliament in 1571. The Thirty-nine Articles remain to this day the most definitive statement of Anglican faith.

The restoration of catholicism attempted by Mary Tudor (1516–58) failed. The daughter of Catherine of Aragon acquired the nickname 'Bloody Mary' as a result of her persecutions, in which many protestants lost their lives – among them Cranmer. After a brief interlude (1553–8), the *via media* was even more strongly Reformed and took up its stand once again, consolidating its influence on Elizabethan England.

Entrance into London of Queen Mary and Princess Elizabeth in 1553, painting by John Byam-Shaw, 19th century. House of Lords, London.

Portrait of Mary Tudor, painting by Antonio Moro, 1554. Museo del Prado, Madrid.

The doctrine defined by the Thirty-nine Articles can fairly be labelled Calvinist. This is most obvious in the articles on the Eucharist. They formally condemn Catholic interpretations, most notably the doctrine of transubstantiation. They also reject some Lutheran interpretations – rejections more obvious in preliminary drafts prepared by Parker than in the final version endorsed by Parliament, but the end result is clearly more acceptable to Calvinists than Lutherans. Furthermore, writings by Calvin and his leading continental disciples were reprinted in London, both translated into English and in the original Latin. Bishops of the Church of England frequently cited Calvin as a leading authority, even in their debates with his more uncompromising followers within the realm. In 1595, in the Lambeth Articles, came formal acceptance of the Calvinist theory of predestination, without doubt the most controversial issue of Calvinist doctrine. Even Richard Hooker, the celebrated apologist of the Church of England, in the late sixteenth and early seventeenth centuries, acknowledged that Calvin was the greatest theologian produced by the French Church, and that his *Christian Institutes* and biblical commentaries deserved the respect they received in England.

But if Elizabethan England followed Calvin in theology, her leaders would not follow him in liturgy and in ecclesiology. The Queen and her bishops clearly

preferred a Church that remained more Catholic in its modes of worship and in its church organization. They encouraged parish priests to wear the traditional vestments, rather than the simple academic robes favoured by Calvin and his associates. They maintained without significant change the *Book of Common Prayer* as drafted by Cranmer, resisting all attempts to simplify it and make it more nearly like the austere liturgies of Geneva and Zurich. They also kept all temporal control of the Church within the hands of bishops appointed by the Crown, rather than developing the mechanisms of representatives and congregational control favoured by continental Calvinists. Only bishops were allowed to ordain parish priests; they controlled most church property; they continued to collect the substantial incomes allocated to them in the Middle Ages and maintained large staffs of canons and other agents to assist them in church administration; they also remained peers of the realm and sat in the House of Lords, the senior of the two chambers of Parliament.

In this Elizabeth may well have been reflecting the wishes of the majority of her subjects. There is substantial evidence that many of the ordinary people in England, particularly the peasants in rural areas, did not really understand the theological changes adopted by their leaders and and preferred the rituals to which they had become accustomed over the centuries. In areas in which fully educated Protestant ministers were appointed to village parishes, local people often shrank from accepting their leadership and turned instead to 'village wise men' or to witches. Many ordinary people wanted the semi-magical rites which they had received from the medieval Church to cope with their daily problems and allay their continuing fears. If they were unobtainable within a Christian context, they could be found elsewhere. It has been estimated that in some areas there were as many sorcerers as clergymen. Often the former were seen by clergymen as deadly competitors.

The leaders of English society wanted a Church governed by bishops. The Crown and most aristocrats preferred an ecclesiastical government parallel in structure to the secular government, with an orderly hierarchy and clear lines of responsibility, and with supreme power vested in one man, a primate of England, who reported only to the Queen. A structure of this type made it easier for the leaders of society to manipulate the general population and maintain its docility. One-man rule seemed more 'natural' to them than the shared types of church governance developed among Reformed Protestants on the continent.

In the end, the government of Elizabeth I developed for England a special type of Protestant Church, a Church of the *via media* or middle way. In its formal theological commitments it was clearly Protestant, close to Calvinism, thus providing a platform for co-operation between the English and the continental Protestants in France, in the Netherlands, in the German Rhineland, and in Switzerland. In its liturgy, however, it remained largely Catholic, moving to a Protestant position only on a few highly visible details – as in translating the liturgy into vernacular English and in offering the elements of both bread and wine to all the faithful in the sacrament of communion. In its organization it retained most Catholic institutions, including the bench of bishops – but was cut off from all connection to Rome and the rest of the universal Church. The final ingredient of this uniquely English form of Protestantism was a high degree of control by the secular government, over the nomination of bishops and the details of permitted practices of worship.

Civilian peace was restored by Elizabeth I (1533–1603), who pursued the remaining Catholics and opted for the middle way: adoption of Calvinist doctrine in main issues, but maintaining a hierarchy along Roman lines. The reign of this new queen, who enjoyed immense popularity, coincided with the accession of England to maritime strength and with an artistic and intellectual renaissance.

Portrait of Elizabeth I (with the 'Invincible Armada' in the background), anonymous painting of the 16th century. Private collection.

The Arrest of Catholics (under Elizabeth I), 16th-century engraving. Bibliothèque Nationale, Paris.

The Armour of Lord Compton, engraving from *Album of an Elizabethan Armourer* by J. Halder. Victoria and Albert Museum, London.

Puritan dissent

The nature of compromise is to have malcontents on both sides. If the majority of the English were happy with the Anglican *via media*, if the Catholics who remained faithful to Rome had the choice between exile and secretiveness, an important minority can be reckoned to have been left in mid-stream. These partisans of Calvin and the other main continental Reformers took their tenets to Scotland, where John Knox established the Presbyterian Church, but they came up against the royal and episcopal power of England. Thus may be explained the departure of certain communities for the new American colonies and, in a more general way, the expansion of Puritanism into Australia and Korea.

The 'vestiges' of Catholicism

On 6 August 1629, a company of English immigrants to the new North American colony of Massachusetts created a church in the new town of Salem by subscribing to a 'covenant'. In this they were breaking with the recent past by creating a church of a new type, a type soon to be labelled 'Congregational'. These settlers were not appealing to a centuries-long set of traditions conserved by a linear series of bishops as would the more Catholic of their contemporaries. Nor were they appealing to a fully articulated 'confession' of the main points of the Christian faith as would the more Protestant of their contemporaries. They were rather binding themselves to a mutual contract that would tie them all together in a tightly integrated local community both secular and ecclesiastical. The content of that Salem covenant was very simple, extending for only one sentence: 'We covenant with the Lord and one with another; and do bind ourselves in the presence of God, to walk together in his ways, according as he is pleased to reveal himself unto us in his blessed word of truth.'

The settlers who created Salem were Puritans. They were part of a large group of English Protestants who were not satisfied with the shape of the Church of England as given form by the government of Queen Elizabeth I. They were more radical, to be sure, than the majority of Puritans. But they serve as a striking example of a large and influential by-product of the English Reformation.

For if the Anglican *via media* proved acceptable to the Queen, the leaders of English society, and many of the common people, it did not satisfy a large and vocal minority. These people were often called Puritans because they wished to 'purify' the Church of England of all its Roman Catholic remnants and make it truly Reformed, on the model of the newly Reformed churches of the continent. These people were also sometimes called Precisians because they wanted their church to follow Scriptural mandates precisely, without any compromise or deviation. They included many of the most highly educated people in England, within both the clergy and laity. They were protected by the nobility and gentlemen in many parts of the country, including much of the city of London, eastern counties around Cambridge, and sections of the south, west and middle parts of England. Only the north tended to resist their penetration. They were led most prominently by men who had been exiles under the reign of Mary Tudor, who had lived with a different form of Protestantism in the continental cities of the Rhineland and Switzerland, and were

eager to introduce it to their native country. They were encouraged from abroad by such Reformed leaders as de Beza of Geneva and Gualter of Zurich.

The first fault of the Church of England seized upon by these Puritans as justifying their attacks was its maintenance of traditional vestments for the clergy, in particular the white surplice and the square cap worn by every priest for divine services. These vestments to the Puritans were clear and visible remnants of the Catholic past, reminders obvious to even the humblest and least educated that the customs of Rome had not been rooted out completely. Puritans did not want their own preachers to wear these vestments and they wanted their use proscribed throughout England. This was a demand which had first been voiced by Bishop Hooper and others in the more radical branch of the Edwardian Church. In the place of these vestments, the Puritans wanted their ministers to wear simple black academic robes, of the sort that any student or professor in a university community would wear. They wanted their ministers in this respect to follow the practice of Geneva and Zurich.

The Puritans appealed to the theologians of the continent for support in this debate. They did not, however, receive much sympathy. Bullinger of Zurich in particular could not believe the issue was of enough importance to risk schism. While he preferred the black academic robes he himself used, he did not think the difference was of enough consequence to justify the polemics then issuing from England. The Puritans, however, continued to voice their complaints. Some bishops of the Church of England retorted by requiring use of the traditional vestments by all clergymen within their jurisdictions. A few Puritan ministers actually accepted dismissal from their parishes rather than obey these injunctions.

The question of education

The second justification offered by the Puritans for their attack on the Church of England was its failure to provide proper education in Reformed Protestant ideas. They were particularly critical of the low intellectual standards set for the clergy, of the fact that so many priests were barely literate, could do nothing in service but read the assigned passages of the *Book of Common Prayer* and sometimes an assigned homily from a collection such as Bullinger's *Decades*, and were completely incapable of informed and lively preaching of their own.

To remedy this situation, Puritans created new educational institutions. In the cities, and particularly in London, they endowed dozens of lectureships. The

2

The middle way, satisfying for the great majority of the English, nevertheless attracted the opposition of a very active minority of 'Puritans' who were anxious to be rid of the last vestiges of traditionalism and of Catholic custom, particularly the traditional clerical vestments. The intransigence of these 'radicals', who were numerous in London and in several other parts of the country, did not receive the support of Heinrich Bullinger (1504–75), the successor of Zwingli in Zurich, and was fought by the Archbishop of Canterbury, John Whitgift.

1. *Portrait of John Whitgift*, 16th-century engraving.

2. *Portrait of Heinrich Bullinger*, engraving from Theodore de Beza's *The True Portraits of illustrious men*, 1580. Bibliothèque Nationale, Paris.

3. Map of London from *All the towns of the world* by Bauer and Hogenberg, Cologne, *c.* 1550. Biblioteca Victor-Emmanuel-II, Rome.

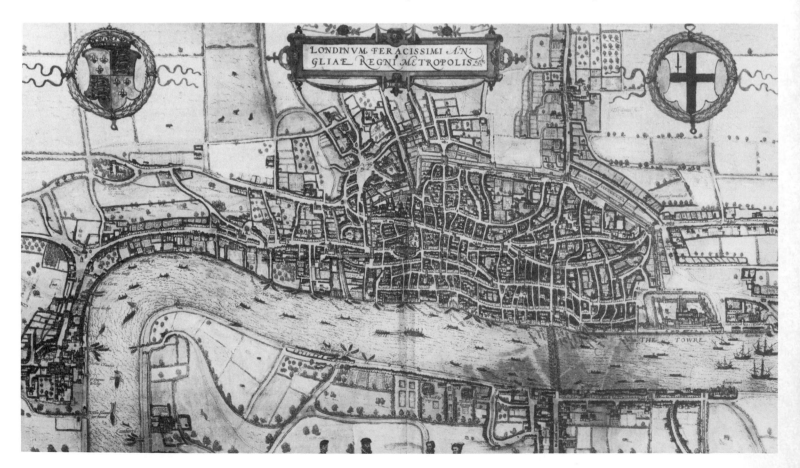

LONDINVM FERACISSIMI AN:
GLIAE REGNI METROPOLIS

THE TOWRE

lecturers hired to fill these positions were generally students of theology, often from the universities. They presented several times a week formal lectures on theology, often in the shape of expert commentary on a selected book of the Bible. In this they were installing in England a practice initiated in a number of continental cities, most notably in Geneva by Calvin. For Calvin, it must be remembered, had originally been hired by the Genevans not as a minister but as a public teacher, charged with instructing the citizens on the nature of the new faith to which they had committed themselves. The Puritan lecturers were often better paid, from private endowments, than parish priests. And they were in evident competition with the parochial clergy, to the confusion of some of the laity, and to the distress of the established clergy and their episcopal leaders.

In the towns, particularly the market towns of East Anglia, the Puritans established another educational institution – the 'prophesying'. This institution was a kind of informal class in Biblical studies, involving several ministers of a region. A panel of minsters would gather on an assigned day and discuss an agreed-upon passage of Scripture or a theological problem, with each in turn expressing his formal opinion. Sometimes educated laymen would be invited to attend the 'exercise' and were allowed to volunteer their opinions or ask questions. This institution was also based upon a continental model, called a 'prophesying' in Zurich, a 'congregation' in Geneva. Meetings of these groups had been responsible for hammering out some of the most controversial theological positions with which the Reformed were identified. It was at a Genevan 'congregation', for example, that Calvin and his colleagues had developed their most extreme early statement of their doctrine of predestination, in reaction to the criticisms of Jerome Bolsec. The government of Elizabeth I took a dim view of these 'prophesyings'. They saw in them institutions beyond control of the bench of bishops and of the royal government, potential seedbeds of conspiracy and sedition against the established institutions of society, and made periodic attempts to stop them.

For or against consistories

The Puritans criticized the Church of England thirdly for its failure to maintain true discipline. In company with many of their fellow Reformed on the continent, these Puritans had become convinced that there were really three 'marks' or signs that a given community were truly Christians. To the two criteria specified by the Lutheran confessions and acknowledged by all Protestants – the true preaching of the Gospel and the right administration of sacraments – they added the presence of a disciplinary system, a means of ensuring that Christians lived their faith.

The type of disciplinary mechanism favoured by these Puritans was the type developed in Geneva. There a consistory made up of lay elders nominated by the ministers but elected by the city government, assisted *ex officio* by the ordained ministers, kept tight control over the ideas and behaviour of the entire community, calling numbers of the residents in for examination every week, using the dreaded weapon of formal excommunication for those who were found unrepentant or whose offences were deemed flagrant, referring to the secular courts for further punishment those found guilty of crimes. This type of tight control over community behaviour was not acceptable to all the continental Reformed, for many found it too reminiscent of the controls exercised by Catholic episcopal courts. Difference of opinion over this issue, indeed, threatened to separate Geneva and Zurich. When the government of the Rhenish Palatinate decided to turn from Lutheran to Reformed worship, there was a sharp debate over how to maintain discipline. One party, led by Olevianus, a preacher trained in Geneva, urged creation of a consistory on the Genevan model. Another party led by Erastus, a physician with close connection to Zurich, urged that control of discipline be left to the secular government. There were sharp written exchanges between Erastus in opposition to the consistorial system, and Theodore de Beza of Geneva in support of it. These treatises were not published in the 1560s when they were written. The government of the Palatinate decided to follow Genevan practice, but leaders there and in Geneva and Zurich decided to keep the fact of disagreement private, to avoid 'washing dirty linen in public' to the probable dismay of their supporters and delight of their enemies.

There were Englishmen in Heidelberg at the time of this Erastian quarrel, who were involved in these debates. In the years that followed they saw increasing relevance in this exchange to problems in their home country. As a result the Erastian arguments were later published in England. Erastus' treatise attacking consistorial discipline and defending the role of secular government in the maintenance of order was sent to England after his death and there printed, with the explicit approval of

With the exception of the Catholics, who were in hiding, and the Puritans, all classes of society maintained the moderate religious politics of Elizabeth I, as proved by the understanding established with the Commons.

The House of Commons under Elizabeth I, 16th-century engraving. Bibliothèque Nationale, Paris.

a Confectioner   a Smith   a Sho=maker   a Taylor

a Sadler   a Porter   a Box=maker   a Sope-boyler

a Glover   a Meal-man   a Chick en-man   a Button-maker

Tailors, shoemakers, saddlers, smiths and millers: Puritans recruited a large number of their followers from the ranks of artisans and businessmen, in so far as the ruling classes and the peasants were attached to tradition and to the hierarchy of the Anglican Church.

Puritans, 16th-century engraving.

John Whitgift, the resolutely anti-Puritan Archbishop of Canterbury and primate of England in the later years of Elizabeth's reign. And de Beza's treatise defending consistorial discipline, in retort to Erastus, was similarly printed at that time, in both Geneva and London, to support the position of English Puritans.

The use of these arguments from the continent became so pervasive that the episcopalian party within England came to be called 'Erastian', and that term itself came to be broadened somewhat, to apply to all who would reserve to the State the ultimate power to superintend the structure of the Church rather than allowing the Church any institutional autonomy. The Puritans of England thus came to stand for the maintenance of strict discipline within their local communities by the creation of new disciplinary institutions in part created and controlled by the local church. Their opponents, while conceding a need for discipline, wished it to be controlled by existing institutions – the ecclesiastical courts of bishops and the secular courts of the royal government. In practice these surviving courts were less demanding in England than the newer institutions of the Puritans. This is the reason Puritans came to be identified widely in the popular mind with very strict control of behaviour, with demands that the morality recommended by the ten commandments and other parts of the Bible be enforced with rigour in all Christian society. This in turn created the surviving stereotype of the Puritan as a thin-lipped kill-joy, determined to force his vision of Biblical morality upon all his neighbours. The Elizabethan government, in addition, saw Puritan disciplinary institutions as subversive, as competing with and undermining the authority of existing courts. This provided Elizabeth and her bishops with yet another reason for attempting to stamp out Puritanism.

The Presbyterian model

The fourth and final fault of the Church of England seized upon by Puritans as justifying their attacks was its government by bishops. For the bishops of the Elizabethan Church came to be seen as tyrants who frustrated the Puritan demands for reform in every field. And their office was also seen as un-Scriptural, since they were selected neither by their fellow clergymen nor by the members of the flocks which they were called to lead, but were rather imposed upon the country by its royal government. Many Puritans turned, therefore, to the search for a new and more satisfactory form of church government, a form that should prove more sympathetic to their general campaign for religious reform, a form that should be more consonant to the government that God himself had established for the earliest Church as described in the new Testament, primarily in the Acts of the Apostles.

217

Early Puritans could not agree among themselves, however, on the actual shape of proper church government dictated by Scripture and demonstrated by Reformed experience. Some of them preferred a government by a hierarchy of representative councils. They came to be called Presbyterians. Others preferred a government in which each local church was autonomous. They came to be called Congregationalists.

The Presbyterians were considerably influenced in their model of church government by continental Calvinists, particularly the Calvinists of France and the Low Countries. The Reformed movement in both these countries had created a hierarchy of representative bodies: consistories or 'classes' on the local level, colloquies on the regional level and synods on the provincial and national levels. Each of these bodies normally included concerned clergymen and lay Elders, and ruled as a collective, constantly rotating its presiding officer or moderator, so that there would be no semblance of monarchic one-man rule of the episcopal type. In both France and the Low Countries appeal was possible from local representative bodies to ones of wider geographic coverage, and ultimate power rested in national synods, which typically drafted a Confession of Faith to define and publicize their beliefs and a Book of Discipline to serve as a constitution for their national Reformed Church.

This Presbyterian model of church government was first imported into Britain by the Scots, who created in the 1560s a Reformed Church governed by a General Assembly, with power mediated to the general population by regional presbyteries and local kirk sessions. The Scottish adoption of Presbyterian institutions did not, to be sure, mean the immediate abandonment of episcopacy. For the better part of a century Reformed bishops or superintendents survived in Scotland as the executive supervisors of groups of churches, often in alliance with the royal government but often also in uneasy and occasionally stormy competition with the hierarchy of sessions, presbyteries and General Assembly. By the mid-seventeenth century, however, Presbyterianism had triumphed and episcopalianism had been rooted out. The Reformed Church of Scotland had become thoroughly Presbyterian in its structure, and in this resembled the Reformed churches of France and the Low Countries far more closely than the Church of England.

The Presbyterian model of church government was also introduced into England in the Elizabethan period. Spokesmen for it, led by Thomas Cartwright at the University of Cambridge, persuaded many of its superiority. And devoted Puritan clergymen began creating local 'classes' in parts of England, particularly in the eastern areas around Cambridge. These classes were designed to serve as English equivalents to Scottish presbyteries and French colloquies. The one about which we are most fully informed was the *classis* of Dedham. Petitions to support the further spread of institutions of this type, furthermore, were introduced into Parliament by sympathetic gentlemen.

This development greatly angered the Queen and most of her bishops. These local classes were seen as direct threats both to control within the Church by bishops and control over the Church by the Crown. The royal and episcopal authorities were particularly upset by the assertion by some local classes of the right to ordain clergymen. So they went to strenuous lengths to identify all such local representative institutions, and then either to abolish them entirely or strip them of all real powers.

Congregationalism

The Congregationalists were also considerably influenced in their model of church government by continental Calvinists, especially those in the Reformed churches created for refugees of Dutch or French origin in Strasburg by Calvin himself, in Frankfurt and in other German cities. They also followed Reformed churches created for English refugees under Mary Tudor in the same cities and in Geneva itself. Each of these churches was autonomous, to the degree allowed by the host government. Each selected and ordained its own ministers and felt free to dismiss them. In each the congregation selected an appropriate liturgy – an adaptation of the Edwardian *Book of Common Prayer* by the English in Frankfurt, for one example, and a translation of Calvin's liturgy by those in Geneva, for another. In each the congregation selected its own elders and through them exercised discipline over the entire membership. The scattered refugee congregations did, to be sure, keep in touch with each other. And they also turned for advice to church leaders of general eminence, most obviously to Calvin himself. But they conceded to no person or institution the right to legislate for them, to define their doctrine or control their behaviour. Each claimed for itself autonomy.

This congregational model of church government was first introduced into England by Puritan radicals. Those returning from exile under Mary Tudor tended

either to accept episcopalian government or call for Presbyterian government. But as the Puritan campaign for reform became increasingly frustrated by royal opposition, some of the younger and more radical members of the movement created separatist congregations, congregations that would accept no external authority. The first church of this new type was created by a former Cambridge divinity student named Robert Browne, who refused to accept ordination from either bishops or fellow ministers, but instead gathered a 'company' of loyal followers in the city of Norwich, in about the year 1581. Similar congregations were reformed by other radical Puritans in following years, often attracting bitter persecution from the authorities. Some of their leaders were even put to death by the Elizabethan government, and this persecution drove a number to seek refuge in the Low Countries and yet others on the American continent.

Each of these early congregational churches bound its members together with a covenant, a classic example of which is the Salem covenant we have already examined. As Congregationalism developed in New England, it also laid great and increasing emphasis on religious experience. Each member of a local congregation was expected to provide a 'relation' of a conversion experience, in which God acted upon him or her directly and persuaded her or him to be a loyal follower. These relations were to be presented orally at a meeting of the entire congregation before an individual could become a full voting member. The body of converted members who subscribed to the local covenant then controlled the local congregation. They chose and could dismiss its ministers, its teachers, and its elders. They could and did communicate with other churches and seek their advice. But they were in no way bound to accept the rule of any external authority.

Defeat in England, victory in Scotland

The roots of English Puritanism go back to the Edwardian period. It was considerably developed by the experience of continental exiles during Mary's reign. But it took its most enduring shape during the Elizabethan period. It was during this reign that the Puritans formulated their most developed demands for vestiarian, educational, and disciplinary reforms. It was in this period that many of them turned to Presbyterian or Congregational models of government, and that the negative attitude of the Crown and actual persecution drove some Puritans to exile or violence. Some of the leaders of Elizabethan society, to be sure, favoured the Puritans. Robert Dudley, the Earl of Leicester, Elizabeth's favourite during the early stages of her reign, sympathized with and protected Puritans. And even some of the bishops of the Elizabethan Church sympathized with at least a part of the Puritan programme. Edmund Grindal, for example, Elizabeth's second Archbishop of Canterbury and primate, who had himself been an exile on the continent under Mary, favoured many Puritan reforms, most notably the practice of 'prophesying'. For this he earned the dislike and distrust of the Queen, and ended his career after only a few short years with many of his powers stripped away and in virtual disgrace. His successor as primate, John Whitgift, while a thoroughgoing Calvinist in his theology, was also resolutely anti-Puritan and drove them into an increasingly bitter opposition. That opposition became ever more intense in the seventeenth century,

In spite of the support of some important figures, such as Edmund Grindal, Archbishop of Canterbury and Primate of England, the Puritans were held in suspicion throughout Elizabeth I's reign. In the 17th century, tension rose to such a level that emigration appeared the best solution to many.

Portrait of Edmund Grindal (1519–83), 16th-century engraving.

Disembarkation of Puritans in North America, 19th-century engraving. Bibliothèque Nationale, Paris.

Between 1643 and 1660, the Puritans triumphed and inspired loathing under Oliver Cromwell (1599–1658), but this victory was short-lived: the restoration of the monarchy was accompanied by a return to the *via media*.

Portrait of Oliver Cromwell, painting by Sir Peter Lely, 17th century. Galleria Palatina, Florence.

and thousands of Puritans left England for the American colonies after the founding of the first New England colony in 1620. But the pressures became even greater with the accession of William Laud as Archbishop of Canterbury in 1633. Laud's commitment to relentless repression of all forms of Puritanism, coupled with his preference for the modified Calvinist theology of the Arminians, helped provoke the Puritan revolution of 1640.

That revolution led to the establishment of Puritanism as the official religion of England, but only for a twenty-year period. When the revolution began, an invading Scottish army co-operating closely with the Parliament that had driven the King from his throne, helped impose upon England a Presbyterian settlement. The Westminster Assembly of divines called by Parliament in 1643 drafted a confession which still defines much of the belief of the modern Presbyterians in England, Scotland, the United States of America and elsewhere. But that Presbyterian regime was soon replaced in its turn by an Independent or Congregational system preferred by the New Model Army and its commander, Oliver Cromwell, when they seized control of the English government. Neither parliamentary presbyterianism nor military congregationalism, however, won the support of the general population in England. When the monarchy was restored to power in 1660, England reverted to an episcopalian establishment of the type developed by Elizabeth. From that time on, Puritans remained a dissenting minority within England.

If Puritanism became a permanent minority within England itself, however, it grew into the prevailing form of Protestantism in other English-speaking countries. Scotland remained a Presbyterian country, with its established church retaining the structure developed in the seventeenth century. A significant Catholic minority, to be sure, held on in certain parts of the Scottish highlands and on some of the islands of the Hebrides, and it was mightily reinforced in the nineteenth century by large groups of Irish immigrants moving to Glasgow and other major Scottish industrial centres. And there are significant minorities of episcopalians and Congregationalists. But Presbyterians set the tone.

America and the rest of the world

Puritanism also flourished in the English colonies of North America. Episcopalian churches on the Anglican model, to be sure, were established in some of these settlements, most notably in Virginia, the very first of those colonies. But even these churches contained a visible Puritan influence. There were no bishops in the American colonies, only commissaries acting at the direction of the Bishop of London, so there was no attempt to establish a fully episcopalian type of church polity. And the early settlements of Virginia were so isolated that it was hard for their churches to be governed from any central point. Local vestries tended to take over real control, giving these churches a polity in fact, if not in law, much like the

The 'Society of Friends', founded by George Fox (1624–91) in the middle of the 17th century, rejected Anglican conformism and the Calvinist doctrine of absolute predestination alike. Moreover its members, known by the nickname of 'Quakers', attracted numerous enemies and often had to seek safety in emigration to America.

Reunion of Quakers, 17th-century engraving of the school of E. Heemskerk. British Museum, London.

The minority in England, the Puritans could live according to their convictions in America. Even Virginia, where the churches modeled themselves on the Anglican tradition, was profoundly influenced by them.

Map of Virginia drawn by John Smith and published in 1624. British Library, London.

polity of congregationalism, even if they did remain faithful in liturgy to the English *Book of Common Prayer*.

Congregationalism became the established form of Christianity in the next group of colonies created in America, the northern colonies of Massachusetts and Connecticut. The Pilgrim Fathers, a group of Separatist Congregationalists including a number who had first taken refuge in the Low Countries supplemented with others leaving England for the first time, created the first settlement in this area, at Plymouth on Cape Cod. They were soon overwhelmed numerically, however, by much larger groups of Puritans who settled in and around Boston. These Puritans came directly from England and had been members of regular Anglican parishes, although with all the resentment of episcopal refusal to push reformation further that pervaded the entire Puritan movement. They came with their ordained ministers to establish new churches. These preachers provided the real social and intellectual leaders of the Massachusetts colony, men of the stature of John Cotton and three generations of Mathers – Richard, Increase and Cotton. But these Puritans abandoned the episcopal church polity in which they had been raised and adopted the Congregational polity that had already been brought to the colony by the Plymouth Pilgrims, tying their churches together in loose associations, creating a general structure for the entire colony with the Cambridge Platform of 1647.

If this structure resembled in some ways that advocated by Presbyterians, however, the congregationalist associations never gained the legal authority and clout of Presbyterian synods and assemblies. Their organizational weakness was demonstrated by the ways in which other more radical systems of belief proliferated

in the American colonies. When Anne Hutchinson and Roger Williams were disciplined by the established churches in Massachusetts, for example, they simply moved to the new colony of Rhode Island and established churches which became Baptist. When the Quaker followers of George Fox were rebuffed with savagery in Boston, they simply won a royal patent permitting them to settle in Pennsylvania. And even within the Congregational establishment of Massachusetts, minor variations in belief led to the creation of new churches gathered on ideological lines. The traditional parish system of Europe, which had been accepted and developed in every Protestant country including Britain, thus collapsed in America. From that time to the present, American churches have been organized along ideological lines or ethnic lines, not along the geographical lines of traditional parishes as in Europe. About the only exceptions are to be found in certain large cities which became primarily Roman Catholic because of fresh immigration in the nineteenth century.

Presbyterianism became the established form of church government in a third set of American colonies, those in the middle, between Virginia to the south and Massachusetts to the north. New York was originally settled by immigrants from the Low Countries and they brought with them the Presbyterian polity of the Dutch Reformed Church. In later waves of immigration, large groups of Scots arrived in the American colonies, moving to the frontiers of New York and Pennsylvania, then fanning out into the western parts of other colonies. They brought the Presbyterian polity of Scotland with them. So did some of the many German immigrants to the middle colonies, those from such Reformed states as the Palatinate. Other German immigrants, of course, brought versions of Lutheranism with them, with its relative indifference to forms of church government. There were small groups of Roman Catholic settlers in the American colonies, most noticeably in the colony of Maryland, established by the Catholic Lord Baltimore. But the big immigration of Catholics to America was to come only in the nineteenth century, with first the Irish and then continental Europeans from such Mediterranean countries as Italy and from such eastern Slavic countries as Poland arriving in tremendous numbers. There was a small group of Jews established in colonial America, primarily in New York, but it was also not of great numerical importance.

When the English colonies on the North American continent revolted from Britain in 1776, therefore, and created for themselves the new United States of America, they created a country that was primarily Puritan in its religious orientation. But they also created a country that was already religiously pluralistic, permitting many forms of Puritanism, other types of Christianity and even non-Christian religions to live together in relative peace.

Puritanism also spread to other parts of the English-speaking world. It became strong in Canada, particularly following large-scale immigration of Scottish Presbyterians to Canada. It spread to South Africa, Australia and New Zealand. It even began spreading to parts of the world not dominated by either the English or other Europeans. During the twentieth century, for example, there has been a particularly impressive growth of Calvinist Presbyterianism in the Republic of Korea. It was first introduced there late in the nineteenth century by Presbyterian missionaries primarily from America. It became a rallying point for resistance to foreign oppression in the early twentieth century, as native Koreans sought alternatives to the Shinto worship of Japan being imposed upon them by the military government of occupation. And it has blossomed since the Second World War into a major Presbyterian church, rivalling in numbers many of the European churches which claim descent from those established by Calvin and his associates back in the sixteenth century.

So Puritanism, even if ridiculed in many twentieth-century circles for its rigidity and moral austerity, still survives in many parts of the world down to the present. The attempts of early modern English governments to suppress Puritan dissent ultimately failed and that failure has had lasting consequences. Some of them are still visible on the international religious scene.

The spread of the Reformation in eastern and northern Europe

The Reformation moved eastwards from the German
Rhineland and Switzerland into Poland and Hungary
where Lutherans, Unitarians and Calvinists challenged
the traditional beliefs of the established Churches. But the
successful resistance of Roman Catholicism in the rural
areas of Poland and the continued dominance of the
Orthodox Church in Romania and Ruthenia meant that
these multinational states were forced, often reluctantly,
to accept religious pluralism and the attendant toleration.

The spread of the Reformation in Poland and Hungary

It is all too easy to forget that, during the sixteenth century, the area between
the eastern borders of the Germanic Holy Roman Empire, the birthplace of
the Lutheran Reformation, and the Slavonic countries controlled by the
eastern Orthodox churches, was an important area for the development of the
Protestant Reformation. In 1567, Hungary adopted the *Confessio Helvetica
secunda* written by Bullinger. Poland, today a stronghold of Roman Catholicism, was
also extremely receptive to the different European Protestant movements. This vast
region included present-day Poland, Lithuania, Slovakia, Hungary, part of Romania
and the principality of Transylvania. Christians familiar with the persecution which
went on in western Europe may well be surprised at the lack of opposition to the
spread of the new doctrines into northern and eastern Europe and at the ease with
which they won, albeit short-lived, victories.

From 1520, the doctrines of Luther and Zwingli spread discreetly through Poland
where the court of Cracow and the upper echelons of the clergy were followers of
Erasmus. This meant that the edicts condemning heresy were not enforced and the
Reformation was able to take advantage of this, making its way unobtrusively
through the country until the accession of Sigismund II Augustus in 1548. The
German bourgeoisie living in the towns had already been converted to Lutheranism.
In Danzig (Gdansk), the Dominican friar, Knach, preached the ideas of the
Reformation, while since 1519, the Germans of Cracow had been disseminating the
Lutheran doctrine and the Franciscans had been spreading the new faith in Eastern
Prussia, the territory of the Teutonic Knights.

The King of Poland, Sigismund I Jagiello, and his Archbishop, John Laski, gave
their full support to the principles of toleration advocated by Erasmus who, in a
letter of 15 May 1527, praised the policies of the King and addressed the educated
élite of the country who were familiar with the *Enchiridion militis Christiani*. The
Archbishop, who was hostile to the Germans and opposed an alliance with the House
of Habsburg, favoured reform within the Church and used his position to encourage
the Erasmian policies of Sigismund. Although he was responsible for the issue of
seven edicts against the Lutherans between 1520 and 1527, they were never enforced
and there were no victims. In reply to John Eck, he said that the struggle against
heresy was the concern of the Pope and the bishops and not a matter for the secular
authorities. He did, however, introduce censure and asked Pope Clement VII to
convene a general council with the aim of reforming the Christian Church. He sent
his nephew to Basle to study with Erasmus who was encouraged by the Poles to
publish his *De libero arbitrio*.

During the reigns of Sigismund I Jagiello
(1506–48) and his son, Sigismund II Augustus
(1548–72), the Reformation gradually became
established in Poland. Although the rulers
themselves remained faithful to the Catholic
Church, they were also extremely tolerant. This
was, in all probability, the result of their Erasmian
beliefs and the contemporary political situation.

*Portrait of the King of Poland, Sigismund II Augustus
(1520–72), 16th-century engraving by Custos
(Dominicus de Coster). Bibliothèque Nationale, Paris.*

Until 1596, Cracow was the capital of Poland. During the 16th century, the Jagellonian University, founded in the 14th century, became an important humanist centre where Lutheran texts were studied, commented on and often endorsed.

View of Cracow, 17th-century painting. Bibliothèque Polonaise, Paris.

In 1525, Sigismund preferred to negotiate with Albert of Brandenburg, Grand Master of the Teutonic Order, when the latter secularized the wealth of the order to his own advantage and in so doing formed Eastern Pussia. The Polish senate, against the advice of the Archbishop, decided that the Grand Master, who had become the Duke of Prussia, would be a loyal servant of the Polish State, and Sigismund agreed to a compromise which resulted in the creation of a German Protestant principality on Polish territory.

Although the University of Cracow continued to favour traditional scholasticism based on the ideas of Aristotle, Bishop Tornicki encouraged the teaching of Greek and Hebrew, while Canon James of Ilga developed Lutheran ideas which gradually detached the young theologians from their Catholic beliefs. The Jagellonian University eventually became the most important humanist centre in eastern Europe and made a significant contribution to the development of the vernacular languages. The first Hungarian grammar was compiled in Cracow in 1527 by John Sylvester.

The Reformation progressed much more rapidly in Hungary than in Poland. By 1521 it had spread from Wittenberg to Buda where the teachings of several of the college professors were inspired by Luther, and where Queen Maria, sister of Charles V, gave her protection to refugees. By 1552, young people were leaving Buda to study at the University of Saxony. The new ideas were taught by preachers in many towns where the bourgeois population was of German origin and culture and where they had the support of the local magistrates.

The action taken by Szatmári, Archbishop of Hungary, had little or no effect. He published papal bulls condemning Luther and in 1523 he and the diet, which was controlled by the nobility, renewed the strict legislation issued in the fifteenth century against the Hussites. The edicts issued by the diet of 1525 were even more severe. According to Article IV, Lutheranism had to be stamped out and the ecclesiastical and secular nobility were invested with the power to arrest Lutherans and have them burnt alive.

The general anarchy which followed the collapse of the Hungarian State a year later

1

224

3

By an ironic twist of fate, the Protestants of Hungary were saved by the Turks. It was the victory of the sultan, Suleiman the Magnificent, at the Battle of Mohács on 29 August 1526, which cost the life of Ludvik II and resulted in the collapse of the Hungarian monarchy. The intended persecutions were never carried out against the Protestants who were able to gain much support, particularly in the capital, Buda.

1. *The Fortress of Buda in 1541*, late 16th-century German watercolour.

2. *Single combat beween Hungarians and Turks before the Battle of Mohács*, miniature from a manuscript preserved in the Topkapi Palace Museum, Istanbul, from a Hungarian facsimile edition.

3. *Hungarian nobles at the Court of the Turkish Sultan at the end of the 16th century*, early 17th-century German watercolour. Private collection.

2

prevented this rigorous legislation from being enforced. In fact, at the battle of Mohács on 29 August 1526, the Hungarian feudal army was defeated by Suleiman the Magnificent. The young King, Louis II Jagiello, and six bishops were killed on the battlefield and the country was laid waste by the Turks. The kingdom was quickly divided into three: the great plain, including Buda, became part of the Ottoman Empire; the north and west came under the rule of Archduke Ferdinand Habsburg who had himself elected King by a small section of the nobility, while Eastern Hungary and Transylvania remained under the control of a national king elected by another section of the nobility who were opposed to the House of Habsburg.

Although the battle of Mohács was a disaster from the point of view of the State it did, however, favour the development of the Reformation. Despite the fact that both sovereigns were themselves practising Catholics, neither Ferdinand I nor John Zapolya was in a position to defend the interests of the Roman Church as they were dependent upon the support of their respective subjects. Therefore they did not prevent the magnates who had been converted to the Reformed faith from appointing preachers educated at Wittenberg, and allowed the municipal magistrates to practise the evangelical faith. In order to finance

After the Battle of Mohács, Hungary was divided
between the Turks, Ferdinand I of Habsburg,
brother of Charles V, and John Zapolya, King of
Hungary. Both Ferdinand and John Zapolya were
strongly opposed to Protestantism but were too
busy fighting and, in the case of Ferdinand, too
busy fighting the Turks, to oppose the progress
of the Reformation.

Portrait of Ferdinand I of Habsburg (1503–64),
painting by Hans Maler, 1524. Galleria degli Uffizi,
Florence.

King John Zapolya (1487–1540), 18th-century
engraving.

the war against Turkey and to gain support, they either secularized Church property or
transferred it to members of the aristocracy. In this way, the huge estates of the Bishops of
Oradea and Alba Iulia (Karlsburg) were confiscated by John Zapolya. The parish clergy,
deprived of guidance, resources, and who were often of very average moral standards and
intellectual ability, proved incapable of resisting the spread of Lutheranism. The German
mercenaries recruited by Ferdinand Habsburg to fight the Turks were mainly Lutherans
and their commanders sometimes imposed their beliefs by force. As for the Turks, they
were totally indifferent to the religious disputes of the infidels. However, they did prefer
that the Christians did not come under the jurisdiction of the Pope who often supported
their enemies, the Habsburgs, and that their Hungarian subjects were organized in small,
autonomous communities which were easier to control. The churches of the Reformation
were the perfect answer to their concept of the State.

Finally, the attitude of Pope Clement VII shocked those members of the
Hungarian nobility and peasantry who had remained loyal to the traditional
religion. By supporting the League of Cognac in 1527, the Pope was effectively
allying himself with Francis I and Suleiman the Magnificent. As he did not hesitate
to excommunicate John Zapolya, the national party had a complete change of heart
and the laws of 1525 became obsolete. Although by 1550 the Catholic Church had
virtually ceased to exist in Hungary, the old structure was not abolished and the
Habsburg king continued to appoint canons, bishops and archbishops who had
neither congregations nor income and lived on small pensions in Vienna or at the
imperial court in Prague. The Emperor also encouraged the foundation of Jesuit
colleges. In 1585, the papal nuncio, (Aloysius) Lippomano, considered that with a
population which was 85 per cent Protestant, Hungary was a lost cause for Rome.
There were only 300 priests and monks, mainly concentrated in the Catholic
Kingdom of Croatia, who represented perhaps 5 per cent of the population, while
the remaining 10 per cent were Orthodox.

The collapse of the Roman Catholic Church was accompanied by a concerted effort
on the part of priests and monks who had been converted to the evangelical faith.
Preachers were established with the help of the local authorities, the nobility in rural
areas and magistrates in the towns. On the great plain, the indifference of the
Turkish authorities proves that the peasants who had remained there welcomed the
new faith. The moderate ideas of Melanchthon, taught by students who had returned
from Wittenberg, were extremely popular. They stressed the moral aspect of
Christian freedom, which could under no circumstances lead to social reform. The
Confession of Augsburg inspired Johannes Honterus, born in Brasov in Tran-
sylvania, to organize the autonomous Saxon Church of Transylvania. In 1546, a
Confession of Faith was adopted by five towns in Upper Hungary. In 1544, Matthew
Biro, a Franciscan preacher from Transylvania, converted the population of Szatmár.
In 1545, he converted the inhabitants of Oradea and convened the first Synod of
Eastern Hungary, during which the *Confessio Augustana variata* was adopted.

But the Augsburg Confession was soon replaced by the sacramentarian ideas
inspired by Zwingli and disseminated by Bullinger. Theologian, pacifist and an
advocate of reconciliation, Bullinger came into contact with the Hungarians in the
1540s and played a decisive role in discussions on the exact nature of the Lord's
Supper. He was impressed by the moderation demonstrated by the Hungarians in
such delicate matters, which had been the cause of implacable hatred among
Christians. Bucer, a moderate theologian from Strasburg, also had a considerable
influence on the Protestant communities which set themselves apart from the
severity of Lutheran orthodoxy. The development of the Hungarian churches was
virtually unique within the European context. Having given their full support to the
Confession of Augsburg, between 1550 and 1565 they abandoned it in favour of
Calvinism and became one of the strongholds of the Reformed faith.

The 'faith of the nobility' in Poland

The accession of Sigismund II Augustus in 1548 greatly advanced the progress of the
Reformation in Poland. Although the new ruler was a Catholic, he was nevertheless
influenced by his crypto-Lutheran chaplains. He did not suppress theological controversies and was hostile to the Council of Trent which he considered far too biased.

In 1552, in the Orzechowski affair, the diet ruled in favour of Stanislaus Orzechowski, a
canon who was also a member of the nobility and who wanted to marry. Thus toleration
was granted to the nobility, or in other words to 10 per cent of the population. The State
also refused the support of the secular authorities to bishops who persecuted Protestants.
The three names which dominated the religious life of Poland were Stanislaus Hosius,
Andrew Modrevius and John Laski. If Hosius, a bishop of German origin, was considered

the leader of the supporters of the Roman Catholic Church, the Polish moderates were represented by Andrew Modrevius, a member of the nobility and a student at Cracow. He was secretary to John Laski and then left for Wittenberg where he became friendly with Melanchthon and was later chosen to accompany the Polish bishops at the Council of Trent. His open-mindedness is demonstrated in his *De republica emendanda*, a work in five volumes published in 1551, in which he stated that all Christians were equal, that Polish feudal society should be drastically Reformed, but above all that the ultimate authority in matters of faith was the Word of God and possibly an ecumenical council on which both priests and congregation would be represented. In fact, Modrevius was skillfully defending Protestant ideas and Pope Paul IV had the work included on the Index.

The most important Polish Reformer was John Laski, better known as John Lasco, nephew of the Archbishop. He studied at Bologna, Padua and then at the Sorbonne and Basle where he was the pupil of Oecolampadius. He was appointed Bishop of Veszprém in Hungary by King John Zapolya but was never invested. As he was unpopular with Sigismund, he left for the Low Countries, was married at Louvain in 1540 and became superintendant of the Frisian Church where he banned the Catholic form of worship. He maintained a regular correspondence with Bucer, Bullinger and Calvin. In 1547, Laski was invited to England by Archbishop Cranmer and settled in London in 1550 where he was responsible for the Church of the Strangers attended by Walloon, German and French refugees. In 1552, he collaborated on the *Book of Common Prayer* adopted during the reign of Edward VI, but the following year was forced to flee the persecutions of 'Bloody' Mary Tudor. He resumed his wandering life, finally returning to Poland in 1556 – the year in which he published his treatise *On the form and content of the ecclesiastical ministry*, which was inspired by the Genevan ordinances of 1541.

On his return from Germany, Laski founded the Church of Little Poland. He went to Vilnius (Wilno) where he obtained the protection of Radziwill, the Lutheran Chancellor of Lithuania who had been responsible for the organization of the Evangelical Church in the grand duchy. He then drew up the Pinczow Confession of Faith which was common to both Lutherans and the Bohemian Brethren. Although it was never published and the original text has been lost, it formed the basis of the doctrine of the Church of Little Poland. It also provoked the Calvinist *Consensus of Sandomir* of 1570 which was obviously inspired by the *Second Helvetic Confession* adopted by the Hungarian Reformed Church in 1567.

Protestantism in Poland probably reached its peak with the Confederation of Warsaw which had the authority to make the bishops and Catholic majority accept a legal ordinance guaranteeing freedom of thought for the nobility. It also marked the success of the policy of religious toleration of Sigismund II Augustus, who in 1557 dismissed the nuncio of Pope Paul IV and appointed Bishop James Uchanski, a moderate like Andrew Modrevius, as Archbishop of Poland.

The death of Sigismund II Augustus raised the question of whether the diet should elect a foreign Catholic prince. The Protestants dreaded the election of Henry of Valois only a few months after the St Bartholomew's Day Massacre and wanted positive guarantees in advance by way of protection. An agreement was quickly reached which sanctioned regional agreements developed by the provincial diets. The personal safety and protection of property of non-Catholics was guaranteed on condition that they undertook to observe the peace. The Polish nobility agreed to settle religious disagreements by non-violent means. Only the bishops were reticent as they were afraid that a permanent law of toleration might encourage the spread of heresy. However, the absolute authority of each lord within his own territory was recognized and he was given the power to introduce the Reformation and to abolish Catholicism. The nobles who had been converted to the Reformed faith expelled the priests and replaced them with pastors, but the peasantry remained unswervingly loyal to their traditional religion. According to a Dominican friar writing in 1620, 'the lower classes were initially unable to adapt to the new religion and remained loyal to the Catholic faith with the result that Lutheranism was commonly referred to as the faith of the nobility and Catholicism as the faith of the people.'

Conflict and toleration

Religious pluralism was also established in Transylvania and Hungary, although it was not officially recognized by the Habsburg king until 1606. Calvinism quickly gained ground during the 1550s amongst the rural population of Eastern Hungary. They welcomed the preachers of the Reformed Church who confronted the false dogmas of the Antichrist with the truth of the Gospel, as well as developing the idea of personal salvation. Their message of forgiveness, that God would pardon the unjust and grasping

The great Polish Reformer John Laski (1499–1560) spent the greater part of his life travelling in Europe and developing his ideas as a result of contact with other Reformers such as Calvin, Zwingli, Melanchthon and Bucer. He returned to Poland a few years before his death and founded the Church of Little Poland.

Portrait of John Laski, engraving from *Icones* (Images), a gallery of portraits of learned and pious men, by Theodore de Beza, 1580. Bibliothèque Nationale, Paris.

The first Hungarian grammar, compiled by John Sylvester in 1527, was published at Cracow University. Due to the combined influence of humanism and the Reformation, which favoured the vernacular languages, the idioms of many European languages were written down in the first half of the 16th century.

Title page of the 1539 edition of the *Grammatica Hungaro-Latina* by John Sylvester.

227

The Pole, engraving from the collection of costumes by John Sluper, Antwerp, 1572. Bibliothèque des Arts Décoratifs, Paris.

The Hungarian, engraving from the collection of costumes by John Sluper, Antwerp, 1572. Bibliothèque des Arts Décoratifs, Paris.

nobles if they showed genuine repentence, won them the support of the nobility. From 1560, Peter Melius Juhász, pastor of the Protestant community of Debreczen, was extremely successful and in 1562 published a collection of sermons. In the same year, the Synod of Tarcal decided to recognize the *Confessio Christiana Fidei* of Theodore de Beza, while his *Brief and Pious Institutes of the Christian Religion* had been in circulation since 1559. The year 1567 marked an important point in the history of Hungary. It was the year in which the Synod of Debreczen convened the pastors of the eastern feudal territories and adopted the *Second Helvetic Confession*. From this point on it is possible to refer to the Hungarian Reformed Church.

A major concession was made to the religious orders in matters of control by retaining the old hierarchical structures. In parish assemblies, authority was placed entirely in the hands of the pastors who were themselves appointed by the local lord. The episcopal system, so foreign to the Genevan ideal, was retained and, as a result, the Transylvanian Church was subjected to very close control by the prince. In this way, the nobility was able to maintain its right of inspection over the Church. The influence of Bucer can be recognized in this subordination of the spiritual to the temporal authorities. Bucer had become known through his writings, his disciple, the pastor Bellenyesi, and his correspondance with Caspar Heltai. The *Second Helvetic Confession* was to remain the basis for the doctrine of the Hungarian Reformed Church until 1881.

The successful development of the Reformed Church in Hungary was due, paradoxically, to the short-lived success of Unitarianism in eastern Europe. The movement was started by the theologian Thomas Müntzer, an opponent of Luther who had led the rebellious peasants during the Peasants' Revolt. Although Müntzer was killed in Thuringia in 1525, his millenarian theories spread across central Europe and reached Hungary in 1530. The Hungarian Anabaptists (known later as Mennonites), whose members were recruited from among the lower classes, were pacifists, but they nevertheless opposed the Unitarian movement: it was considered subversive on a temporal level and scandalous on a religious level by the noblity, aristocracy and pastorate. It was condemned without appeal by the diet of 1548, but continued to develop illegally and managed to survive. Tolerated in Poland and accepted in Transylvania by the end of the 1560s, it then regained ground in Eastern Hungary where the Unitarians were responsible for an outbreak of millenarian violence in 1569. A serf, George Karacsony, declared the 'holy war', initially against the Turks, and then against all forms of oppression. It was a repetition of the Jacquerie, the great peasant uprising of 1514. Soldiers and poor alike rose against the Turks and soon after turned against the landowners. The magistrate of Debreczen ordered the arrest and execution of Karacsony in 1570, and the rebellion was crushed by royal troops. From then on, the Unitarian movement was discredited in Hungary.

However, the theories of Faustus Socinius were more favourably received elsewhere. The Italian doctor, known for his rejection of the doctrine of the Holy Trinity, was a member of a discreet and extremely cautious group of intellectuals. Fearing for his safety, he fled to Transylvania where the way had been paved by other Unitarians: his colleague and compatriot Blandrata, the Greek, Jacob Palaeologus, and the German, Johann Sommer. They received the protection of the prince, John Sigismund, son of John Zapolya, and were soon granted official recognition. Through the medium of the preacher Francis David, the Unitarians of Transylvania attacked not only the divinity of Christ, the sacraments and feasts, but all forms of religious ceremony. They rejected the doctrines of predestination and the immortality of the soul and disputed the notion that the Scriptures were inspired by God. On the other hand, the Unitarians stressed the importance of religious toleration and maintained that the 'religions of the Book' – Judaism, Christianity and Islam – were all inspired by the Bible, and all had the same value.

They won an important victory in 1568 when the diet of Transylvania granted freedom to preach all beliefs on the basis that 'faith is a gift from God which is brought to men through the Word'. Although this decision was revoked by the diet of 1571, it did recognize the Unitarian faith, in the same way that the Augsburg Confession had been recognized in 1546 and the Reformed faith in 1564 on the conversion of John Sigismund to Calvinism. Traditional religion also maintained its position which meant that there were four legally recognized faiths in Transylvania. Thus the example of religious toleration was being set by a small principality in eastern Europe where the Romanians, although not officially recognized for socio-political reasons, were not persecuted for their beliefs as members of the Greek Orthodox Church. Attempts to convert them to the Reformed faith were as unsuccessful as they had been among the orthodox Ruthenians in Poland. Evangelicalism was in reality only successful in the West: the eastern Church remained faithful to its traditional beliefs.

The Unitarians were also accepted in Poland and the dogma of the Holy Trinity was challenged for the first time at the Synod of Little Poland in 1556. After the death of

John Laski, a Piedmontese doctor, Blandrata, who was closely associated with the Socinians, influenced Chancellor Radziwill and provoked a split within the Church of Little Poland. The Unitarians founded the *Ecclesia Minor* or Church of the Polish Brethren, who were referred to as Arians by their opponents. Soon after, Blandrata was summoned to Transylvania and left Poland to become royal physician to John Sigismund. The preacher David was influenced by his ideas and he was involved in the founding of the Unitarian Church of Transylvania, which went through a difficult period after the death of its protector John Sigismund in 1571: the diet appointed a Catholic, the Hungarian magnate Stephen Bathory, as his successor. The new prince, concerned by the radical nature of the Unitarian Church, had David brought before a tribunal of pastors which condemned him. David was arrested and imprisoned in 1581 and later died there, as did Johann Sommer. Many Unitarians fled to Poland where they were given asylum on the estates of the Leszczynski family. Faustus Socinius settled in Cracow, and most of the remaining congregation joined the Reformed Church.

The Reformed Churches were still not legally recognized in Hungary by the end of the sixteenth century in spite of having a total congregation of some three million. From 1590, Rudolph II carried out violent attacks against the rural communities and even against Calvinist magnates such as Illesházy, whereas the Jesuits tended to favour individual conversions to Catholicism. In 1604, the support given by the troops of the Holy Roman Emperor, the Habsburg King of Hungary, against the town of Koszyce provoked a rebellion led by Stephen Bocskay, a powerful lord from Eastern Hungary. He rallied the religious orders as well as the ordinary people in an armed struggle against the Habsburgs in which the latter were defeated and forced to accept a compromise, the Peace of Vienna of 1606. This remained the legal basis of Hungarian Protestantism and continued to be referred to by the diet during the course of subsequent struggles. The churches of the Augsburg Confession and the Reformed Churches were recognized on the same basis as the Roman Catholic Church and formed the evangelical orders in the diet. This compromise was comparable to the Edict of Nantes, but the power of the nobility which controlled the State apparatus guaranteed its observance. It is not without reason that Bocskay appears on the monument to the Reformation in Geneva. The only way in which the Habsburgs were subsequently able to reconvert a section of the population to Catholicism was by violence.

Reasons for success

The Reformation's success along the eastern borders of Europe was due to the fact that Poland and Hungary were developing states, and to the effects of the Turkish invasion. The first factor to consider is the range of linguistic and national variations within the countries. Of Poland's population of five million, only 2.5 million were Polish. The majority of the population of the south-eastern territories were Orthodox Ukrainians, and in the towns and Eastern Prussia were predominantly German settlers. The Grand Duchy of Lithuania, which stretched from the Baltic to the Black Sea, had a population of two million: Lithuanians recently converted to Christianity, a rural population which remained deeply pagan, and a high proportion of Ukrainians and Orthodox White Russians. The delicate balance established in 1386 could only be maintained by respecting the cultural and religious differences of Lithuania, and by taking account of the Orthodox Church. In 1562, Hungary had a population of four million but the Hungarians, mainly concentrated on the central plain, never assimilated the Slovaks from Upper Hungary, the Orthodox Romanians of Transylvania, the Croats or the Ruthenians. German ethnic minorities lived in the towns and in Transylvania.

monarchies of France, England and even Spain. Power was divided between the rulers, the religious orders, the aristocracy, the lesser nobility, the clergy and the towns. The Crown was elective and authority was generally decentralized. In Hungary, the feudal territories which formed the administrative divisions of the State were administered by the local nobility and officials had no power of decision. In Poland, the provincial diets controlled local administration and palatines and chatelains chose whether or not to obey. A general increase in the power of the landed nobility during the sixteenth century gave the landowner economic as well as administrative and judicial control over the peasantry. Finally, the State had very limited financial resources of its own and these were confined to royal privileges, since taxes were fixed and collected by the religious orders. The army was restricted to a feudal basis. Only the Habsburgs used German mercenaries, recruited and maintained to fight the Turks, financed from their hereditary territories. A Catholic ruler therefore had no means of imposing his will on the religious orders and politics were a matter of negotiation and consensus. If a ruler used violent methods, as in the case of Rudolph II, he would immediately come up against a nobility which could exercise

During the reign of John Sigismund, the town of Debreczen became known as the 'Hungarian Geneva'. In 1567, it was the seat of an important council of the Reformed Church.

The Calvinist church in Debreczen, Eastern Hungary.

The son of John Zapolya, John Sigismund (1540–71), was officially King of Hungary, but in reality only ruled over Transylvania. Unlike his father, he recognized freedom of Protestant worship in 1557.

John Sigismund, King of Hungary.

CATECHISMVS
mellybe a men‑
NYEI TVDOMANNAC
Sommáia, à deréc ßent ırásból,
es ſoc kereſıtyén Tanıtók‑
nac ıráſokból röuideden
egybe ſıerzetettöt es
befoglaltattot:

HELTAI GASPARTOL
à Coloſuarı Plebanoſtól.

Az egyůgyů kereſıtyének ·
nec epıtéséıe:

COLOSVARBA.
1 5 5 3.

It was Calvinism rather than Lutheranism which spread through Hungary. In fact, the introduction of the Reformation coincided with the desire to be free from the cultural dominance of Germany. It was a period of substantial development for the Hungarian language due to the works of Caspar Heltai who published short stories, a *Chronicle of the History of Hungary* and a translation of the Bible.

Title page of the *Catechism* of Caspar Heltai, published in Kolozsvar in 1553.

The Temple of Meszko, from a postcard of period 1920–30.

military strength and was prepared to defend its independence and religious freedom.

Thirdly, there was a right inherent in the feudal system which is all too often ignored because historians only consider the power of the bishops within the Church. This right, known as the Right of Patronage, was established by the Church during the Middle Ages and gave the founder of a parish and his descendants the right to appoint the parish priest. It was also accompanied by a revenue, as well as tithes which were collected by the feudal lord and not the priest. The lord could be a member of the laity, as in 92 per cent of cases in Poland, a monk, a bishop or the King. When a lord adopted the Reformed faith, it was very easy to replace the priest by a Protestant minister as there was no need to consult either the bishop or the congregation. Hence it was of paramount importance to convert the nobility, as it was much more effective in the short term to convert a rich magnate who controlled a large number of subjects than to preach 'the word' to the peasantry. The nobility were jealous of their personal freedom and the absolute authority they had over their lands, and refused to be dictated to either by the king or the bishops. They fought not for universal toleration, but for their own freedom to worship as they chose. Their subjects, who represented 90 per cent of the population, had no alternative but to follow the teachings of the pastors. This was a two-way process which worked in reverse if a noble was converted to Catholicism: mass was re-established and the minister of the Holy Word was expelled from the parish and replaced by a priest. This makes it easier to understand why young people of all religions and from every walk of life were attracted into the Jesuit colleges, where instruction was at first limited to humanist teaching of high quality so that later, gentle persuasion could be used to re-convert the sons of the nobility to the Catholic faith, while the poor students were recruited into the priesthood.

The exercise of the right of patronage enabled the religious question to be settled on a territorial rather than a national level, and the Protestant Reformation to be established with relatively little opposition. The fact that it was received differently in Poland, Lithuania and Hungary is ultimately explained by the situation within the traditional Church around 1530. In Lithuania, which had been converted to Catholicism after 1386, the peasantry made no attempt to resist Calvinism as they were indifferent to the actual form of the Christian religion. In Hungary, the Christian population was becoming rapidly disillusioned with traditional religion due to the preaching of the Hussites and the non-conformist Fransiscans, which had sown the seeds of opposition. The Calvinist preachers in particular had convinced the Hungarians that they were the new people chosen by God to drive out the Turkish infidel if only they repented and lived according to 'the word'. But there has never been any satisfactory explanation as to why the Hungarians were so easily persuaded to abandon the ideas of Melanchthon for those of Calvin. The fact that the Germans and Slovaks remained faithful to the *Confessio Augustana* while the Poles were won over to Calvinism might justify an interpretation based on nationality. Neither the Hungarians nor the Poles wanted to remain culturally dependent on Germany, and a non-German, western Protestant doctrine had every chance of appealing to people who were also in the process of developing their national culture as a result of the Reformation. The Hungarian translation of the Bible by the pastor Caspar Heltai did as much for his mother tongue as Luther had done for the German language. Calvinist theology also provided the Hungarian religious orders with a doctrine of legitimate resistance to the Habsburgs and enabled the medieval *ius resistendi* to be re-introduced, as demonstrated by Kalman Benda. The Calvinists deemed that, according to the Golden Bull of King Andrew II, an old text dating from 1222, they had the right to rebel against all unjust measures implemented by the royal power.

The failure of the Reformation among the lower classes in Poland can be explained by the fact that during the sixteenth century, the attitude of the traditional Church was reasonably acceptable. In 96 per cent of situations the priest lived in the parish, which also had a school. There was, on average, one priest for every 550 members of the congregation and the profession was highly enough considered for one in three of the clergy to be a member of the nobility. The members of the clergy were honourable and educated men and many Dominican and Franciscan missionaries travelled throughout the country. If their priests were expelled by those members of the nobility who had adopted the Reformed faith, the peasants would refuse to attend church and went out of their way to hear mass in another parish.

The characteristics of the Reformation on the eastern borders of Latin Christianity were various. It provided sanctuary for those on the religious 'fringe', promoted religious pluralism, a spirit of toleration and a taste for adaptability and moderation in matters of religious controversy, as well as encouraging restraint in the exercise of authority, a spirit of resistance to oppression and faithfulness to the Word of God. Although they were to a large extent based on the Swiss and Rhenish Reformations, these characteristics demonstrated time and again that the pupils were equal to their masters.

Protestant orthodoxy

The era of the pioneers and innovators gave way to that of disciples and organizers. Luther, Zwingli and Calvin paved the way, conquered hearts and minds and answered the essential questions. To their followers now fell the task of giving the Protestant doctrine a systematic and global character.

A necessary task

Protestant orthodoxy is not very well thought of: it is seen as a period during which the inspired and generous intuitions of the Reformers became rigid in an arid scolastic system. The lively faith of the early days was transformed into a dry legalism, and the theology of revelation into a rationalizing ontology. This is a grave error of perspective which does not take into account the developments of history and, what is more, gives a false picture of the beginnings of the Reformation. The period of orthodoxy certainly witnessed the flourishing of vast theological surveys, which are fairly inaccessible to the twentieth-century reader, and saw a return to metaphysics and the generalized institutionalization of the Reformation. Surely these phenomena were inevitable as the Churches which arose from the Reformers' preachings established themselves in time as well as in space. The direction taken may be regrettable, but it cannot be denied that it had to happen.

The mid-sixteenth-century generation of pastors and theologians who assumed responsibility for the young Churches, both Lutheran (Germany) and Calvinist (Switzerland, the Low Countries, France, Scotland), found themselves facing insurmountable difficulties. They had to consolidate the organization of the Churches in all the states which had decided to adopt Protestantism either through the authorities or by popular consent. For this purpose, they needed symbolic documents enabling them to establish, teach and live out the new faith, as well as ecclesiastical ordinances, hence the plethora of confessions of faith, catechisms and liturgies. They had to provide for the training of a competent clergy, and set up academies which were to become the cradles of the great theological summe of Protestant scholasticism. They had to defend themselves theologically, spiritually, and sometimes physically, against the threats of the Catholic counter-offensive which, although late, was vigorous, deriving a considerable revitalizing strength from the canons of the Council of Trent. They also had to contend with an interdenominational controversy of increasing subtlety, using the sophistication of formal logic, and theology acquired an increasingly marked polemical and rationalizing character. Lastly, they had to answer new questions, ethical, political and cosmological – which the Reformers had barely touched on – using the resources of profane philosophy but enlightened by the Word of God.

All this had to be carried out within the narrow confines of fidelity to the message of the founding fathers – fidelity natural in an age unfamiliar with the idea of progress, in which conformity to the original seemed to be the best guarantee of Reform truths and authenticity. Was not the Reformation itself a return to the source? These men kept repeating this, for they saw innovation as the gateway to deviant opinions and even heresy, as was shown by the constant spectacle of the Anabaptist problems and the Socinian and Arminian disturbances.

This outline makes it possible to grasp the process of orthodoxy and to understand the major role played by the academy teachers. Servants and interpreters of the Protestant heritage, very often carrying out important responsibilities towards their

This painting, depicting Moses and the Ten Commandments according to Exodus, Deuteronomy and the Gospel according to St Matthew, was meant to be hung in a church. As well as being decorative, it contained texts appropriate for preaching and prayer.

Moses and the Tablets of the Law, a late 16th- or early 17th-century painting on wood. Musée Bargoin, Clermont-Ferrand.

churches – take for example Johann Gerhard in Jena, Abraham Calov in Wittenberg or François Turrettini in Geneva: it was they who had responsibility for defining the faith and training a clergy who would in turn transmit the new beliefs to the faithful. They played a role similar to that of a Catholic bishop in his diocese within the framework of the territorial churches. It has been said, quite rightly, that the history of Protestant orthodoxy is the history of its academies.

The period of orthodoxy

The period of orthodoxy lasted from the mid-sixteenth century to the end of the seventeenth century. Between 1545 and 1565, a certain number of events marked a turning point in the field of political and religious forces in Europe. Politically, the Peace of Augsburg of 1555 legitimized the division of the Empire between the old Church and the new territorial churches, and guaranteed the principle of co-existence for the old and the new faiths. It marked the failure of Charles V's universal religious policy. He abdicated the following year and justified his son Philip II's hegemonic, Catholic and Spanish policies. As for religion, the death of Luther in 1546 marked the beginning of the quarrels over the correct interpretation of his works. From 1560, Calvinism quickly became a third denominational force: it spread in France, the Low Countries, some German principalities, Hungary and Poland and, for the price of a few concessions concerning the Lord's Supper, recorded in the *Consensus Tigurinus*, became widely accepted in the Swiss cantons and Geneva.

Anglicanism broke definitively with Rome at the beginning of Elizabeth I's reign (1558). The Council of Trent set itself to reform the Roman Catholic Church from 1545 to 1563, and the Society of Jesus had a promising beginning. At this time boundaries were established, even though denominational frontiers shifted until the end of the seventeenth century. From now on, opposition between Protestant and Catholic forces was one of the fundamental elements of European politics.

The Treaties of Westphalia (1648) marked a stage in the development of orthodoxy. They put an end to the Thirty Years' War, during which diplomatic stakes came to be reinforced by religious stakes: had it not been for the intervention of King Gustavus Adolphus of Sweden, Protestantism might have been stamped out. After that, people no longer died on the battlefields as Lutherans, Calvinists or Catholics; denominational interests were reabsorbed into national politics; the Pope lost his political clout and religious quarrels were no longer automatically matters of State. The *raison d'état* became absolute and progressively broke away from religious considerations. However, the latter did not disappear overnight: Cromwell's Puritan revolution (1649) and the Revocation of the Edict of Nantes (1685) showed the durability of religion at the heart of the State, and Jansenism, Gallicanism, the Jesuits and pietism created further upheavals in society.

From the start of the Reformation, the condemnation of images was mitigated by their use for pedagogical purposes. Much of Dürer's work must be considered in this light, likewise that of Baldung and Cranach. The semi-circle running through the ten scenes below is a rainbow symbolizing the alliance between God and man.

The Ten Commandments, painting by Lucas Cranach the Elder, early 16th century. Lutherhalle, Wittenberg.

While civil and ecclesiastical jurisdiction remained closely linked, it is also true that the middle of the seventeenth century saw the beginnings of a transformation in thinking that was to have profound repercussions on theology, piety and the conception of the world, sounding the death knell for orthodoxy. This critical change came about as the other sciences prevailed over orthodoxy – sciences which, independent of the Bible, Ptolemy or Aristotle, discovered the laws of nature, from Galileo to Newton, through Descartes and Gassendi. The traditional tenets of the faith were rocked by the criticism of a Biblical exegesis according to the norms of profane philology, influenced by a Cartesian logic that was growing increasingly confident. These tenets rapidly lost their normative authority on questions of piety and ethics and gave way to a natural theology which was more in line with recent scientific enlightenment and better adapted to the new utilitarian or eudaemonist morality. From now on, orthodoxy appeared at best old-fashioned, at worst repressive.

Although it survived into the eighteenth century among the Lutherans with theologians such as Valentinus Löscher (1673–1749) or J.B. Carpzov (1720–1803), it ended with the last generation of the seventeenth century in Reformed areas. And then it was the beginning of the religion of enlightenment, where revelation no longer contradicted reason and where religious practice became individualized. Powerful thinkers flourished and moved from theism to deism, often to conclude with the coldest and most secularized kind of atheism.

One of the reasons which prompted Charles V to abdicate in 1555 was his inability to restore the monopoly of the Catholic Church: a few months earlier, through the Peace of Augsburg, he had been forced to grant Lutheran princes freedom to worship and ownership of the lands of the secularized clergy.

Abdication of Charles V, painting by Frans II Francken, early 17th century. Rijksmuseum, Amsterdam.

Two German theologians close to Melanchthon's position were challenged by the supporters of Lutheran orthodoxy: Georg Major, who maintained that good works played a part in salvation, and John Pfeffinger, who emphasized the collaboration between God and man in the process of salvation.

Portrait of Georg Major, 16th-century engraving. Société de l'Histoire du Protestantisme Français, Paris.

Portrait of John Pfeffinger, 16th-century engraving. Société de l'Histoire du Protestantisme Français, Paris.

Controversies over Luther's legacy

Even while Luther was still alive, theological controversies broke out in the churches which had grown out of his preaching. Although the subject of these controversies might appear technical, the repercussions for Protestant piety and doctrine were very serious. For example, in 1527, and again between 1537 and 1540, John Agricola, a schoolmaster from Eisleben, reacted against Melanchthon's teaching on penitence, by pushing the Lutheran distinction between Law and Gospel so far as to state that the law of Moses played no part in the economy of grace or in Christian life: true repentence came not from the impossible observance of the commandments, but only from the discovery of the love of God through the preaching of the Gospel. Sin was not violation of the law, but violation of the Son. This 'antinomianism' was unacceptable to Luther, for it attacked justification by faith. In his *Wider der Antinomer* (1538), he demonstrated that although the Law might not justify, it still forced the sinner to receive the Gospel. If there was no distinction between the Law and the Gospel, the specificity of Jesus Christ as redeemer could no longer be perceived.

Shortly after Luther's death, in addition to the antinomian controversy came a series of conflicts over the Reformer's legacy which set supporters of a Lutheran interpretation in opposition to supporters of a Melanchthonian interpretation. After the defeat of the Protestants by the Schmalkaldic League in 1547, Charles V imposed texts – the *Interims* – aimed at bringing the evangelical territories back on to the path of re-Catholicization while waiting (*interim*) for the Church to complete the long-awaited Reforms. The *Leipzig Interim* (1548), in the drafting of which disciples of Melanchthon shared, considered liturgical ceremonies and ecclesiastical structures as 'things indifferent' (*adiaphora*). It imposed on Saxon Protestants a liturgy and an organization very close to Catholicism. Philip Melanchthon and his disciples – the Philippists – were fiercely attacked by Matthias Flaccius Illyricus (1520–75) from a Magdeburg besieged by the imperial troops. He emerged as the head of the authentic, strict Lutherans. He maintained that in a time of persecution for the faith (*in statu confesseonis*) it was illegitimate to yield on the *adiaphora*. Thus the Lutheran camp was divided between Philippists, gathered around the University of Wittenberg, and 'gnesio-Lutherans' who made the University of Jena their centre.

The quarrel over the *adiaphora* had more of a strategic than a theological impact. The argument which broke out in 1552 at the instigation of Georg Major (1502–76), a teacher at Wittenberg who was close to Melanchthon, touched on a central point of Lutheran doctrine: the role of charitable works in salvation. For Major, although men were justified without charitable works, they were necessary – out of a necessity of consequence – for salvation. Without wanting to reintroduce the notion of merit, he implied that justification depended on subsequent sanctification, while in the *Sola Fide*, Luther had stated that salvation was given fully in justification. Major was challenged by Flaccius Illyricus and Nicolas Amsdorf, an old companion of Luther. The former stated that God was not interested in charitable works and the latter, more extreme, claimed that charitable works could even jeopardize salvation.

Then, from 1555 onwards, Lutheranism was subject to another, even more serious, debate concerning the collaboration between God and man in the salvation process, the synergism quarrel. Once again, the roots of the quarrel went back to the position taken by Melanchthon, who believed that God did not act without the concurrence of man, in particular of his own free will, defined as the 'capacity to appropriate grace for himself'. This was taken up again by John Pfeffinger, superintendent and teacher at Leipzig, who thought that 'there is something within us that makes some of us consent to salvation and others not consent'. These Erasmian ideas were fiercely disputed by Amsdorf, and especially by Flaccius Illyricus. The latter maintained in 1558 that on his conversion, man is not only passive as a rock or a block of wood, but that he is recalcitrant because of sin. In 1560, he went so far as to defend against Victorinus Stregel the idea that after the fall of Adam, sin was not just an accident but became the very substance of man. Thus the guardian of orthodoxy went much further than the doctrines of his master.

These theologians' quarrels had political ramifications, first in Saxony, when Duke John Frederick sided with the strict Lutherans against the Philippists – also accused of crypto-Calvinism because of their position on the Lord's Supper – while the Philippists had the support of the Duke's rival, the Elector Augustus of Saxony. The rift developed dramatically at the Colloquy of Worms (1557) when, in the presence of the Emperor Ferdinand, who was anxious to reconcile Catholics and Protestants, the gnesio-Lutherans refused the Philippists the right to refer to the Augsburg Confession. For twenty years, one failed attempt at reconciliation followed another, while abuse, imprisonment and banishment of theologians and pastors continued.

At the centre of the debate between Lutherans and Calvinists was the manner of expressing Christ's presence and the resulting different positions on the way of celebrating the Lord's Supper.

Communion under both kinds, engraving by Lucas Cranach the Elder, early 16th century.

Two factors at least helped put an end to this ill-feeling and restore a united front. The first, just after the end of the Council of Trent, was the publication of two documents giving a doctrinal unity to Catholicism and a clear basis for Roman Catholic orthodoxy: the *Professio Fidei Tridentina* by Pope Pius IV in 1564, and the *Roman Catholic Catechism* by Pius V in 1565. The reality of the Catholic threat in Bavaria was evident, for the priest Canisius and his Jesuit brothers had reinstated Catholicism by eliminating all traces of Lutheranism. Secondly, Calvinism was making rapid progress across imperial territories; it had been adopted in Frederick III's Palatinate, and in 1563, on the request of the Elector, the Heidelburg theologians wrote a document which was to become one of the most famous texts of the Calvinist Reformation: the *Heidelburg Catechism*. Furthermore, Bremen and the principalities of Anhalt, Hesse-Cassel and Lippe had given in to Reformed influences.

Ubiquity

The need for a united front against the Calvinists deserves an explanation. Historians know little of the reasons for the confrontation between Lutherans and Calvinists which was so extreme that Lutherans proclaimed: 'rather Catholic than Calvinist'. Calvinists responded with insults of which the least — but by no means the least significant — was, 'Eaters of Christ's flesh'. The root of the lack of understanding between the two main families of the Reformation, even though they shared the central beliefs concerning justification, can be found in their differences on the subject of the Lord's Supper. The conflict, which had already set Luther and Zwingli in opposition at Marburg in 1529, reached a new peak after the conclusion of the *Consensus Tigurinus* in 1549, which drew together Calvin and Bullinger's points of view regarding the Eucharist. The Lutheran theologians likened Calvin's postion to that of the symbolists so abhorred by the Zwinglian sacramentarians and began to attack the Calvinists. Then, from 1552, Joachim Westphal, the hot-headed pastor of Hamburg, challenged Calvin. The main grounds for the quarrel were concerning Christ's presence in the Lord's Supper: could Christ's body, after the Ascension, be present in the bread and the wine of the Eucharistic meal? In other words, did it have the property of ubiquity? Calvin and his successors, who believed that Christ's presence in the Supper was spiritual, did not think so. Anxious to safeguard the integrity of the two natures of Christ, they stated that the body of Christ, which after the Ascension sat on God's right, could not be simultaneously in the bread and wine. If this were the case, not only would this jeopardize the principle of identity which forbade 'that a body be both body and non-body at the same time', according to the Aristotelian physical concepts which were shared by all at that time, it would also be a perversion of 'the order of the wisdom of God'. Since Christ was given a

The leader of the authentic Lutherans, Matthias Flaccius Illyricus (1520–75), defended orthodoxy against the Philippists, disciples of Melanchthon, most prominent of whom were Georg Major and John Pfeffinger. According to him, God was not concerned with good works, and man was unable to contribute to his salvation in any way whatsoever. The violence of the arguments sometimes pushed him into adopting extreme positions, far removed from Luther's doctrine.

Portrait of Matthias Flaccius Illyricus, 16th-century engraving. Société de l'Histoire du Protestantisme Français, Paris.

body like ours, this body had to have the same properties as ours. The glorification of Christ's body did not change its nature which remained the same as others, and did not change it spiritually. 'It is not Aristotle,' said Calvin, 'but the Holy Spirit who teaches that the body of Jesus Christ, after being brought back from the dead, remains as it is and is received in heaven until the last day.'

As believers in consubstantiation (that is, in the real presence of the body and blood of Christ united with the substance of the bread and wine at the moment of celebration of the Lord's Supper), Lutherans considered that the body of Christ was ubiquitous, so that after rising to heaven, Christ has the ability to be present everywhere, not only as God, but also as man. This major difference stemmed from the different ways of understanding Christ, in particular the relationship between his divine nature and his human nature. For the Lutheran theologians, in particular John Brenz (1499–1570), a Reformer from Swabia and a great theoretician of ubiquity, there was an authentic communication of 'idioms'– that is, properties between the two natures. This communication took place by the substitution of accidents of the divine substance for accidents of the human substance. Thus the glorified body of Christ, sitting at God's right hand, continues to benefit from this substitution and is able to be everywhere at once, including within the elements of the Eucharist, by reason of the divine nature of ubiquity.

Brenz's Calvinist adversaries, foremost of whom was Theodore de Beza, had every reason for reproaching him for minimizing Christ's humanity and accusing him of monophysitism or even docetism. It is true that, faithful to Calvin, they tended to over-emphasize the distinction between the two natures and to judge therefore that the Lutheran communication of the idioms made the unity of the person of Christ into a confused mixture whose divine nature was the first to suffer. In the person of the Son, divinity and humanity retained their respective characters. Thus divine nature preserved its properties, and Calvin refused to allow human nature to share the quality of ubiquity. Christ surely lowered himself to our level in taking on human nature, but he 'gave up nothing of his Majesty, nor did he lessen or diminish his eternal glory'. At the risk of endangering the fundamental unity of the person of Christ, Calvin stated in a number of famous formulae, later qualified as extra-Calvinisticum: 'The Son of man was in heaven and on earth, because Jesus Christ, according to the flesh, lived here below during his mortal life, and yet did not cease to live in heaven, as God. Therefore . . . it is said that he came down from heaven, not because his divinity left heaven to be enclosed in the flesh as in a lodging, but because he who fulfils all has nevertheless lived bodily and in an inexpressible way in his humanity.'

With their doctrines of the Lord's Supper, Lutherans and Calvinists wanted to reinforce the basis of their faith and show the importance of the communion with Christ for the life of the Christian. While the Lutherans emphasized the value of physical elements in the transmission of the divine graces, the Calvinists preferred to avoid all confusion between the divine and the human, seeing in these same elements only the opportunity to perceive Christ's spiritual presence and his mercies. Lutherans allowed the *manducatio impiorum* (receiving of Christ's body by the impious) and the adoration of the sacrament during the celebration of the Lord's Supper, while the Calvinists only tolerated a *manducatio spiritualis* (receiving of Christ's body through the faith, thanks to the Holy Spirit).

These conflicting opinions gave rise to a long and bitter argument which reached its climax in the second half of the sixteenth century. On the Lutheran side, the protagonists were John Brenz, Tileman, Heshuss, Jacob Andreae, Lucas Osiander and Nicolas Selneccer. The principle Reformed supporters included de Beza, Lambert Daneau, Henry Bullinger, Girolamo Zanchi and Zacharias Ursinus. The conflict went on into the seventeenth century and, together with Lutheran measures against Calvinist predestination, explains the long rupture between the two branches of Protestantism. Only at the beginning of the eighteenth century, when the orthodox problematics began to waver under the blows of criticism, tolerance and even indifference to dogma, were the two branches able to envisage a tentative peaceful co-existence.

The 'Formula of Concord'

In the 1560s, no such pacifism was appropriate: it was essential to put an end to the divisions among Lutherans and establish the basis for an orthodox interpretation of Luther's legacy, in order to withstand the Reformed and Roman Catholic offensives. This elusive union was the work of Jacob Andreae (1528–90), Chancellor of the University of Tübingen.

At the request of Duke Christopher of Württemberg, whose territory had become

the hub of German Lutheranism, and who was concerned about the spread of Calvinism in the neighbouring palatinate, Andreae wrote in 1567 a *Short declaration* which satisfied neither the Philippists nor the strict Lutherans. Undaunted by a number of failures, in 1573 he succeeded in publishing *Six Christian sermons* dealing with the subjects under dispute among Lutherans. These texts found a large readership among theologians. Consensus was made easier by the fall of the Philippists of electoral Saxony, accused of crypto-Calvinism regarding the Eucharist, and by the banishment of strict Lutherans from ducal Saxony. Andreae published the content of his sermons in the form of articles in the *Swabian Concord* which, revised and corrected, led to the *Book of Torgau* in 1576. This long process towards peace came to its conclusion at the Convention of Bergen in 1577 where the *Book of Torgau* became the *Solida declaratio*, in other words, the most important part of the famous Lutheran *Formula of Concord*.

Andreae did not want to make it an independent confession: he presented it as a commentary on the Augsburg Confession, settling the points that had been under dispute for forty years regarding the pure doctrine, true to the Word of God. So, for example, sin is described as a fatal illness, which, against the advice of Flaccius, does not belong to the essence of fallen man; it is a corruption that has to be distinguished from the nature of man as he was created. In opposition to Melanchthon and Major, the powers of free-will in the process of conversion and regeneration are disputed. Natural man, before conversion, faces salvation like 'trunk and stone'; the initiative returns to the Word of God and, even after conversion, it is still under the guidance of the Spirit that the regenerated will toils daily to repent and to do good works. The *Formula of Concord* upheld, among other things, the *Manducatio indignorum et impiorum*: 'The body and the blood of Christ are received with the elements, not only spiritually through faith, but also by mouth . . .in a supernatural and celestial way, in accordance with the sacramental union. In addition, it is not only those who have true faith and who are worthy, but also the unworthy and the unbelievers who receive them; the latter do not receive them for life, but for their condemnation.'

The *Formula of Concord* also condemns the extra-Calvinisticum and approves ubiquity: 'It is not only as God, but also as man that Christ is all-knowing and all-powerful, and is present for all creatures. That is why he can, very easily, be present when he distributes his real body and his real blood in the Lord's Supper.' Contrary to Agricola, it recalls the necessity for the constant preaching of the law: because of the old Adam who still resides in the reason, in the will and in all the human faculties, men must be guided and enlightened by the Law of God. Like Flaccius, it admits that in times of persecution, one must not yield where the *adiaphora* are concerned. And lastly, it fiercely rejects the Calvinist doctrine of double predestination, likely to cause believers to despair and to comfort the unrepentent in their dissolute life.

Through this harsh condemnation, through its Christological and Eucharistic statements, the *Formula of Concord* read more like a text to combat Calvinism than a text aimed at uniting Lutheranism. Thus conceived, it took its place, in 1580, in the *Book of Concord*, beside the three ecumenical symbols, the Augsburg Confession and its Apology, the *Schmalkaldic Articles*, Melanchthon's treaty *De potestate et primatu papae* and Luther's *Great* and *Little Catechisms*. The canon of Lutheranism was thus definitively constituted: fifty-one princes and thirty-eight towns — the major part of the German evangelical states — accepted it and more than 8,000 theologians signed it. The *Formula* appeased the quarrels within Lutheranism, but at the same time it sanctioned the rift with the Reformed theologians.

When Calvin died in 1564, his succession was assured by Theodore de Beza (1519–1605), the theologian and brilliant organizer who had actively participated in the Colloquy of Poissy three years earlier. De Beza devoted his talents as writer and polemicist to the cause of defending Calvinist orthodoxy.

Portrait of Theodore de Beza, anonymous painting, 1597. Société de l' Histoire du Protestantisme Français, Paris.

Lutheran 'high orthodoxy'

Signed by all new Lutheran pastors, the *Formula of Concord* served as the doctrinal framework and parameter for reflections on orthodoxy which developed in the theology faculties. The faculty most laden with history was that of Wittenberg, the *cathedra Lutheri*; the most illustrious were Jena, Tübingen, Strasburg, Leipzig, Giessen, Rostock and Königsberg. There were no particularly marked tendencies or serious conflicts between these establishments, but, for example, an argument arose in 1616 between Tübingen and Giessen on the subject of the activity of the divine nature of Jesus Christ during his incarnation. The theologians of Giessen, led by Balthazar Mentzer (1565–1627), considered that the humbling (*kenosis*) mentioned in the *Letter of Paul to the Philippians* (2.8) means the suspension of all activity of the divine nature during the incarnation, while the theologians of Tübingen, led by the Chancellor of the University, Matthias Hafenreffer (1561–1619), Brenz's son-in-law, thought that in accordance with the substantial union of the two natures, it

meant that Christ, during his stay on earth, did not forgo his divine nature, but merely concealed it (*krupsis*).

The Giessen kenoticists won the argument with the krypticists of Tübingen, for they managed to convince the community of theologians that they were the more faithful to the foundations of the Lutheran Reformation. The episode is revealing in that it demonstrates the subtlety of the problems dealt with by orthodoxy. Those who cannot see that such questions are not gratuitous would be quick to call such questions inane, but in fact they were the outcome of profound reflection on the biblical revelation. The monumental surveys of orthodoxy – Lutheran and Reformed – are a testimony to this effort to embrace all the problems posed by revelation, from creation to redemption. With a biblical and patristic erudition that was astonishing, thanks to a genuine mastery of Aristotelian logic, the orthodox theologians wanted to present clearly and methodically everything that creatures could hope to know about God and his work. The certainty of their pronouncements reflects their boundless confidence in the possibilities of an absolute knowledge of truth. This confidence is mirrored by that expressed in the return to Aristotelian metaphysics of theologians like Jacob Martini (1570–1649). This return to a natural fundamental ontology and theology rests on the certainty that there exists a perfect equivalence between means of knowledge (*intellectus*) and things perceived (*res*).

The size and the precision of this theology is illustrated by the work of the three principle masters of Lutheran high orthodoxy. Johann Gerhard (1582–1637), who taught at Jena and was superintendent of the Duchy of Coburg, was the author of *Loci theologici* (1610–21) which filled nine volumes. Meanwhile, Abraham Calov (1612–85), who taught at Rostock, Königsburg in Danzig and, from 1660, at Wittenberg where he was also superintendent, wrote a survey of 'fundamentalist' Lutheranism in twelve volumes, the *Systema locorum theologicorum*, (1655–77). Johann Andreas Quenstedt (1617–88), his father-in-law (although younger than him) and himself Gerhard's nephew (note the dynastic character of orthodox Protestant theology), who taught at Wittenberg, published in 1685 his *Theologica didactico-polemica sive Systema theologicum*. Although less voluminous than the other two, the work was still greatly valued and served as a compendium of Lutheran orthodoxy.

Without going into an analysis of these great surveys, it is worth mentioning that one of the authors' main preoccupations – and on this point they were in sympathy with the Reformed theologians – was Holy Scripture. For a confession which made *Sola Scriptura* the basis of its faith and its preaching, it was necessary to question the way in which God reveals himself in and through the Scriptures. The result was a strengthened affirmation of the divine authority of the Scriptures as a norm for salvation and arbiter of religious differences of opinion. Its perfections are described thus: sufficiency for salvation – to the exclusion of the Catholics' tradition and of the individual revelations of the spiritualists –, intelligibility in the passage necessary for salvation (*facultas se ipsam interpretandi*), and efficaciousness.

This vision of Holy Scripture rests on the doctrine of literal inspiration. The orthodox theologians departed from the position of Luther, who favoured certain books of the Bible and concluded that the prophets and the Apostles were 'the hand and the pen' of the Holy Ghost. Quenstedt shared the opinion of the Calvinist Voet and the authors of the *Consensus Helveticus* that the vowel-points of the Hebrew text had a revealed character and, in particular, he believed in the formal infallibility of the Bible. Johannes Musäeus (1613–81), the theologian, thought that literal inspiration also allowed non-Christians to interpret the biblical texts, so long as they formally recognized the fact of revelation. Theology was thus practised like any other science. But this theology of non-regenerates (*theologia irregenitorum*) encouraged the factors which brought the period of orthodoxy to an end: on the one hand the development of natural theology during the Enlightenment remotely linked to the Christian revelation and, on the other, the rejection through pietism of a theology without faith.

In his task as Calvin's successor, Theodore de Beza was supported by Lambert Daneau, pastor of Gien who sought refuge in Geneva after the St Bartholomew's Day Massacre, and ended up teaching theology at Castres.

Entry by Lambert Daneau (no. 1731) in the *Livre des habitants de Genève*, 1572. Archives d'État, Geneva.

Reformed orthodoxy

At the moment when the conflicts which preceded the drafting of the *Formula of Concord* were in full swing, Calvin had barely finished the definitive version of the work which was to serve as a reference for future reformed orthodoxy: the *Institutes of the Christian Religion* (1559–60). In other words, the beginnings of Reformed orthodoxy came later than those of Lutheran orthodoxy and they did not come from the same need to settle quarrels over interpretation.

In this respect, the *Harmonia confessionum* compiled by Jean-François Salvard in 1581 did not have the same aim as the *Formula of Concord*. Instead it continued the noble intentions formulated in 1566 by de Beza in his *De pace ecclesiarum*, of unifying

'tLicht is op den kandelaer gestelt

Lutheran and Calvinist Protestantism with a view to supporting the French Huguenots. The *Harmonia confessionum* claimed not only to harmonize the Reformed confessions of faith – Gallican, Scottish, Bohemian, Swiss, etc. (an easy task since their shared doctrine was so evident apart from different wording and emphases) – but it also wanted to harmonize these confessions with the Augsburg Confession and other symbolic Lutheran texts to achieve the unity of the Reformation. Despite its failure, the incident is worth mentioning as it shows that for men like de Beza, the quarrels about ubiquity should not have stopped the theologians on both sides from remembering that the issues that united them were more important than those that divided them. Obviously, the Lutherans did not see things that way, and Calvinist orthodoxy developed independently from Lutheran orthodoxy.

The beginnings of Reformed orthodoxy are attributed, quite rightly, to Theodore de Beza (1519–1605), Calvin's colleague and successor as head of the Church and of the Geneva academy. Through his teaching, often based on the *Institutes of the Christian Religion*, and his work editing and annotating the Bible, through his tireless activity as an anti-ubiquity and anti-Roman Catholic polemicist, and his formulation of the doctrine of double predestination in his famous *Tabula praedestinationis* with the significant title of *Summa totius christianismi*, through his role as consultant to the Reformed Churches in Europe for nearly half a century, de Beza was the embodiment of the great Calvinian despot.

At his side, men like Lambert Daneau (1535–95) adapted the Calvinian doctrine to the needs of school teaching. Under the influence of Melanchthon and Andreas Hyperius, they used the resources of dialectic and rhetoric to structure theology. They cautiously resorted to some metaphysical elements to deal with theological areas only touched on by the Reformers, such as the essence of God, and they endeavoured to approach important subjects like physics, politics and ethics in the Calvinian way. Imbued with classical and patristic culture, with a smattering of knowledge of medieval scolastics, their still clumsy attempts preceded the better balanced and more profound syntheses of the seventeenth-century Reformed theologians, such as the philosopher and theologian Bartholomaeus Kerckermann (*Systema S.S. theologiae*, 1611), or the Basle theologians A. Polanus de Polansdorf (*Syntagma theologiae Christianae*, 1624) and Johannes Wolleb (*Christianae theologiae compendium*, 1624).

The mention of these three names emphasizes the fact that, from the last quarter of the sixteenth century, Geneva ceased to be the only centre of Reformed orthodoxy. Other academies were established or developed: in Switzerland, Basle, as is illustrated by Polanus, Wolleb, Zwinger, Gernler, the Wettsteins, the Buxtorfs and the Werenfels; in Germany, Bremen and Heidelberg with Zanchi, Ursinus, Olevianus,

The 'Candlestick' Is in a way the Dutch equivalent of the Genevan Wall of Reformers. In this 'Protestant Pantheon', seated from left to right are: Bucer, Hus, Melanchthon, Van Praag, Luther, Calvin, de Beza, Wyclif and Flaccius Illyricus; standing, from left to right: Bullinger, Vermigli, Knox, Zwingli, Zanchius, Perkins and Oecolampadius.

The Candlestick, engraving by Jan Houwens, 17th century. Bibliothèque Nationale, Paris.

The Dordrecht synod (November 1618–May 1619) sided with Gomar who professed a strict interpretation of the double predestination theory, against Arminius (*d.*1609) and his disciples according to whom grace and its benefits were available to everybody. God's will was reaffirmed by the Dutch theologians, who were direct followers of Calvin and de Beza.

Portrait of Francis Gomar (1563–1641), 17th-century engraving. Bibliothèque Nationale, Paris.

The Dordrecht Synod, vignette from an engraving, 1621. Bibliothèque Nationale, Paris.

Herborn, Pezel, J. Piscator and Alsted. But it was especially in Holland that Reformed orthodoxy took a hold. Lambert Daneau himself, de Beza's right hand man in Geneva, settled there in 1581, in Leiden where there had been a university for six years. Other academies opened in Franeker in 1585, in Groningen in 1616, in Utrecht in 1634 and in Harderwijck in 1648. It was at Leiden that the crisis erupted which shook the Reformed Churches and faculties for the whole of the seventeenth century and characterized the period of Calvinist orthodoxy: the Arminian Affair.

The Dordrecht Synod and the Arminian Affair

In 1589, the pastor Jacob Arminius (1560–1609) was given the task of refuting the latitudinarian and anti-predestinarian opinions of the famous moralist Dirk Coornhert. He disappointed the orthodox theologians by questioning double predestination: he thought, like Melanchthon, that Christ died for all men and that free grace was accepted or received by virtue of a decision of each person's will. Appointed Professor at Leiden, Arminius clashed with his colleague Francis Gomar (1563–1641) who defended supralapsarianism, the doctrine according to which God decreed that some people would be destined for salvation and others for damnation even before (*supra*) having decided to create the universe to allow the fall. In Gomar's opinion, Arminius and his theories were Pelagian. The controversy continued after the death of Arminius in 1609, further complicated by political interests.

In 1610, in a *Remonstrance* in five articles to the States of Holland and of West Friesland – which earned them the name of 'remonstrants' – the Arminians refined their doctrine and drew closer to orthodox positions: before the creation of the world, God decided to save those who, through the grace of the Holy Spirit, believed in the Son and persevered in this faith right to the end, and to condemn by abandoning them to their sins those who in their unbelief rejected Christ. And yet they rejected points which, since de Beza, seemed crucial to orthodox theologians: they refused to consider grace as irresistible; they based their predestination on God's prescience and not exclusively on his wishes expressed in the will of his decree. They repeated that Christ died not only for the elect, but for all men, while recognizing that salvation was only granted to the believers. After numerous political and religious incidents, the matter was dealt with by the Synod which met at Dordrecht during the winter of 1618–19. In addition to the sixty-five Dutch pastors, twenty-eight delegates from England, the Palatinate, Hesse, Bremen, Geneva and the Swiss cantons – the Huguenot delegates having been kept away by Louis XIII – made this assembly a true Reformed council.

The synod preferred the more moderate position of infralapsarism to supralapsarism: God made the decree of predestination after (*infra*) the decree of creation and that of the fall. The synod still condemned the Arminians, who were forced into clandestine existence. It decided that God chose not in consideration of the faith he anticipated or of a particular quality in man, but purely according to his wishes. What is more, the Canons of Dordrecht rejected outright the idea that the effectiveness of God's appeal to all men depended on the reply of each individual. They stubbornly affirmed the primacy of the initiative and the glory of God, a central aspect of the thought of Calvin and de Beza. Accepted by the Reformed Churches of the United Provinces, by France, Geneva and the Swiss cantons, the decisions of the Dordrecht synod governed the teaching and debates of Calvinist orthodoxy. They influenced the great surveys by Dutch theologians, such as Gisbert Voet (1589–1676), a teacher at Utrecht and an opponent of Descartes, and Samuel Desmarets (1599–1673), Gomar's successor at Groningen.

The main discussion of the synod's decisions took place in France, at the Saumur Academy. Founded in 1599–1600, under the aegis of Philippe du Plessis-Mornay, statesman and friend of Henry IV, the academy gathered a series of distinguished professors who gave it great prestige in France and Reformed Europe. They tried, among other things, to bring the Dordrecht doctrine more into line with the words of the Bible. John Cameron (1580–1625), of Scottish origin, and his successor Moses Amyraut (1596–1664), thought up the theory of hypothetical or conditional universalism which aimed to tone down the particularism of orthodox predestination, reserving salvation for the elect alone. God, they said, wants to save all men, on condition that they believe. Despite these universalist aims, Amyraut did not avoid particularism and his doctrine was a modification – almost a rhetorical one – of the Dordrecht orthodoxy rather than a step towards the Arminians. He considered that faith was created in man only as a result of grace. This grace was not granted equally to

everybody: God chose to give faith, the condition for salvation, to some people, to the exclusion of others. In fact, God's general wish for salvation postulated by Amyraut was reduced to a special decree of election and to a particular exercise of will.

The Saumur theories gave rise to considerable debate in France. Pierre du Moulin (1568–1658), professor at the rival academy of Sedan, and his brother-in-law André Rivet (1572–1651), professor at Leiden from 1632, led the fight for orthodoxy. At Geneva and in Switzerland, Saumur became synonymous with 'innovation' and with attacks on orthodoxy. Amyraut's colleagues included the Hebrew scholar Louis Cappel (1585–1658), who refused the idea of the divine inspiration of the vowel-points of the Old Testament, and Joshua de la Place (1596–1656), who disputed the immediate and automatic imputation of the guilt of Adam's sin to all his descendents. To curb the progress of these innovations which were widespread in Geneva and Switzerland, Jean-Henri Heidegger (1633–98) from Zurich, François Turrettini (1623–97) from Geneva and Lucas Gernler (1625–75) from Basle drew up the *Formula consensus ecclesiarum Helveticarum reformatarum* (*Consensus Helveticus*), which was adopted in 1675 by most of the Reformed Churches in Switzerland. This document defended the literal inspiration and the absolute integrity of the Hebrew text, including the vowel-points. It restated the Dordrecht doctrine of predestination (the restriction of salvation to the elect alone) and the immediate imputation of the guilt of Adam's sin to all his descendents.

In 1679, one of the authors, François Turrettini, published the three volumes of his *Institutio theologiae elencticae*, a survey of Calvinist orthodoxy, which was admirable for its clarity and its construction. Shortly after this the period of Reformed orthodoxy, which had begun with Calvin's *Institutes*, came to an end. The manner in which orthodoxy officially ended in Geneva, the capital of Calvinism, is significant: in 1706, under the influence of François Turrettini's son, Jean-Alphonse, who adapted the legacy of the Reformers to the Age of Enlightenment, theologians ceased to demand subscription to the *Consensus Helveticus* and, in 1725, to the Dordrecht Canons, and required adherence only to, 'the doctrine of the Holy prophets and Apostles as it is understood in the books of the Old and the New Testament, which doctrine is summarized in our catechism'. Orthodoxy was a thing of the past.

Contrasts of orthodoxy

In the same year as the *Consensus Helveticus*, a text was published which served as a programme for the movement which was partially to replace orthodoxy. This work, the

The 16th century in Holland marked the height of Calvinism and of artistic creation, especially painting. The two phenomena were united in the work of Rembrandt, who liked to depict scenes of family worship in addition to paintings inspired by the Scriptures.

Pastor Anslo and his wife, painting by Rembrandt, 1641. Gemäldegalerie, Berlin.

Pia desideria (1675) by J. Spener, a veritable charter of pietism, made the *Consensus* look like a hopeless struggle and orthodoxy look out-of-date. Through his proposals and criticisms, Spener revealed the weaknesses of ageing orthodoxy, both Lutheran and Calvinist – that the essence of faith was obscured by polemics and rigid doctrines, and that burgeoning pietism showed that despite close links with the political powers, orthodoxy had not succeeded in accomplishing the moral reforms that society needed: only individual conversion could lead to a real moral change, and for that it was not necessary for the Church to be bound up with civil jurisdiction.

The demand for a living faith and the criticism of a theology that was too far removed from the life of the faithful should not however cause the importance of the period of orthodoxy for Protestant piety to be forgotten. It was the era when the practice of worship in the home developed, when reading the Bible, the singing of hymns or chorales, prayers and providentialist explanations of events punctuated the rhythm of domestic life, where the father played a major, patriarchal role in the spreading and consolidation of the Protestant faith. It was the era of such famous works as Johann Arndt's (1555–1621) *Vier Bücher vom wahren Christentum* (1595–1669), or the *Consolations de l'âme fidèle contre les frayeurs de la mort* (1651) by Charles Drelincourt (1595–1669); it was also the era when, in a context of suffering and sadness, remarkable hymns of hope and joy were composed by Pastor Gerhardt, otherwise a champion of orthodoxy. And lastly, there was the parallel development of artistic, cultural and economic life in what is known as the Dutch 'Golden Age' and the development of Reformed orthodoxy in the United Provinces.

This flattering picture of the spirituality of orthodoxy has its limits in the persistence of superstitious practices throughout the whole of this period. The prevailing providentialist mentality saw the hand of God in every event. The result was not only to encourage the faithful to have an increasing confidence in the Word of God. On the contrary, there were many who fell back on age-old practices akin to magic, watched the comets, believed in sorcerers and evil spririts and took part in the traditional festivals whose function, in the purest pagan vein, was to ward off the perils of nature and of man throughout the seasons. The period which produced such rich expressions of the faith as the works of Schütz or, later, of Bach, who was a contemporary of the waning fires of Lutheran orthodoxy, was also the period which believed it was necessary to burn witches and sorcerers at the stake to safeguard its faith.

Protestant orthodoxy did not leave baroque monuments as evidence of its piety; it made up for this in music, the preferred means of expression for Protestant sentiment and its inner nature. However, in the vast theological surveys one can discern an audacious architecture of thought and there were just as many cathedrals built from the writing desk, pen and paper, constructed with devotion, art and most probably with too great a confidence in the powers of the intellect, to the glory of the divine revelation.

Abraham Bosse, who in his numerous engravings depicted the daily life of his fellow Protestants, sometimes departed from his customary seriousness. In this painting, he echoes the theme of an engraving from the famous series of *The Five Senses*, and shows his musicians singing Protestant hymns.

Hearing, painting by Abraham Bosse, 17th century. Musée des Beaux Arts, Tours.

PART FOUR

ANOTHER PATH

Daily life and the Reformed Church

The work of Calvin and his companions did not only upturn the formalities of Christian culture, the organization of the clergy and the spiritual life of believers: it also led to profound transformations in the daily life of entire communities. Austerity, numerous and varied restrictions, vigilant surveillance by consistories, the greatest importance accorded education and family culture: characteristics found in Geneva, the true model to emulate, and no less in the French Midi, in Scotland and in the Low Countries.

The Genevan model

When one thinks about a truly 'Reformed' lifestyle, the first thing that comes to mind is Geneva during Calvin's lifetime. There are good reasons for this opinion. Both in zealous Calvinist propaganda and in sixteenth-century reality, Geneva provided the basic model for a genuinely 'Reformed' life. John Knox, the most influential and enthusiastic of these propagandists, wrote that 'in other places I confess the Gospel to be truly preached, but manners and morals so sincerely reformed I have seen nowhere else'. At Geneva, where Knox had served as pastor to a community of English refugees, historical research has revealed remarkably low levels of illegitimate births and pre-nuptial conceptions; in both cases, the figures are ten times lower than in the rural parishes surrounding Geneva. Calvin's city acquired a durable reputation for austerity and extreme piety, a reputation which was tarnished but not destroyed by the combination of Voltaire, Rousseau and economic prosperity in the eighteenth century. The reputation was well-deserved.

Calvin did not succeed in imposing his Reformation on Geneva without difficulties. He first appears in Genevan records as an unnamed Frenchman, *ille Gallus*; expelled from the city in 1538, he returned only three years later. Afterwards, even though his authority had been confirmed by the Ecclesiastical Ordinances of 1541, he experienced considerable difficulties in overcoming the enemies of his godly discipline. On his death-bed in 1564, he shook his head sadly, recalling the 'perverse and unhappy nation' who had caused him so much trouble. The Genevans had ridiculed and opposed him in numerous ways, giving his name to their dogs or composing obscene versions of his French psalms.

His partisans gained political control of Geneva only in 1555; afterwards, the consistory could excommunicate sinners as it pleased while the magistrates awarded Genevan citizenship to the most qualified among the thousands of refugees from France, Italy or (like Knox) from more distant regions. Knox's enthusiastic letter dates from 1556. From this point onwards, during the final eight years of Calvin's life and the long career of Theodore de Beza, Geneva took pride in its reputation as an exceptionally pious city and made use of it for propaganda purposes. Thanks to its reputation, the city was able to obtain the money necessary for its political survival from other Reformed communities during the most critical moments of the Wars of Religion. Catholic texts used the expression 'heresy of Geneva' interchangeably with 'Calvinism'. Rarely in European history has a city been so closely linked with a doctrine, or with a reputation for extreme public morality.

Before examining how this pious Genevan society actually functioned, we should

study the reasons which prevented Knox, and the other men whose portraits adorn Geneva's Wall of the Reformation, from exporting this model to their own countries. In effect, 'nowhere else were manners and morals so sincerely reformed'. It was possible to copy confessions of faith, ecclesiology, educational regulations, and to create consistories like that of Geneva; but the political and social conditions of sixteenth-century Geneva were unique in Europe. Nowhere else could Reformed theologians imposed their priorities against a civil power as fragile as the Republic of Geneva, which had been founded only a few months before Calvin first went there; other governments were much older, far richer and more powerful, and far surer of themselves. Nowhere else did religious refugees have such importance; around 1560, Geneva's refugees were almost as numerous as its native population, and far superior in wealth and education. Calvin possessed the authority necessary to create such an austere society partly because of the remarkable weakness of the local state and partly because of the support of many people who had come precisely in order to create such a society. The only other instance where such conditions obtained in sixteenth-century Europe had produced the ill-fated New Jerusalem of the Münster Anabaptists.

The consistory and the enforcement of austerity

What were the principal characteristics of this 'sincerely Reformed' religion, both at Geneva and elsewhere in Europe? Ancient and modern commentators have usually insisted on its austerity and sobriety; through his clever formula of 'this-worldly asceticism', Max Weber captured a large pat of the social life of Reformed communities. It is evident that these qualities depended on both internal and external constraints, on self-discipline complemented by ecclesiastical discipline. Calvin admitted the importance of the latter on his death-bed, explaining that he would never have accepted his ministry unless the Genevans assured him control over the catechism and church discipline.

Maintaining this discipline was the responsibility of Elders sitting in a consistory. Many authors (mostly hostile ones) have described how the consistory of Geneva and its numerous imitations functioned. The Elders were the instruments through which Calvinism imposed its particularly radical version of the 'Triumph of Lent' on the laity and fought its wars against the pleasures of the flesh.

A careful examination of the work of Geneva's consistory during the 1560s, at the apogee of the Reformation, shows that a notable proportion of the Republic's adult population appeared before it every year: it excommunicated about 500 adults per year from a population barely exceeding 25,000. In a Protestant world which had abolished the sacrament of penance, the Elders resorted to sterner methods in order to compel sinners to repent. At Geneva during the 1560s, they seem to have succeeded.

Of course, Geneva's consistory did not always have the privilege of working among a population saturated with Calvin's sermons and taught by his catechism. In its earliest, heroic period, it had been justifiably worried by frequent challenges to its authority. During its first fifteen years of operations, Calvin's consistory struggled primarily against 'idolatry' and traditional superstitious practices, which were especially common among the peasantry living outside the city's walls.

Catholicism had not been eliminated at one blow in 1536; dozens of ex-clerics (including the famous 'prisoner of Chillon', François Bonivard) continued to live in Geneva; many residents had an imperfect grasp of Reformed doctrines and only accepted them reluctantly. Geneva's pastors visited every household annually in order to test their Christian knowledge. After the older generation vanished, ignorance of Reformed doctrine became relatively rare at Geneva, accounting for barely fifty of the 2,000 excommunications pronounced between 1564 and 1569. 'Rebellion' to the consistory's commands was somewhat more frequent (150 cases), but usually meant taking communion illegally rather than the more overt forms of opposition which had predominated before 1555.

At Geneva, most people summoned before their consistory had been accused of quarrelling with their spouses, their neighbours, or their kin. Between 1564 and 1569 the Elders excommunicated 700 people for such reasons; but they reconciled an even greater number, obliging them to shake hands, acknowledge each other as *gens de bien* ('honourable people') and promise to coexist henceforth in harmony. Only repeated offenders, the obstinate and the violent risked excommunication – but every year, no fewer than 140 incorrigibly quarrelsome people were found in this

The wall of the Reformers is dedicated to all those who made of Geneva the 'Rome of Protestantism'. It is a paradoxical monument, for the majority of these men came originally from other parts of Europe, but they were never able to reproduce in their own homelands the ideal model which they contributed to erecting on the banks of Lake Leman.

The monument of the Reformation in Geneva.

Under the governorship of Calvin, all details of daily life were regimented by the Elders. Calvin and his friends supervised the behaviour of their citizens and punished sinners, all the while presenting an exemplary attitude of sobriety, honesty and piety.

1. *Discord*, engraving after R. Boissart, end of 16th century or beginning of 17th century. Bibliothèque des Arts Decoratifs, Paris.

2. *Genevan Honesty*, wood engraving from the *Habitus praecipuorum . . .* of H. Weigel, Nuremberg, 1577. Bibliothèque Publique et Universitaire, Geneva.

FOEMINA HONESTA GENEVENSIS.

model community! At Calvin's death, the consistory was busily excommunicating such irascible Christians, as well as other people accused of loosely-defined 'scandals' and 'excesses'. Reformed discipline supplemented lapses of self-discipline.

Less numerous were the sinners guilty of such standard faults as fornication or adultery (160 cases), drunkenness (102 cases, barely 5 per cent of the total), blasphemy (66), gambling (35), dancing, or singing 'profane' songs (35), and usury (27). Another group of twenty-three people were deprived of Communion because they either ate too much or worked too little. Together, such victims of the 'Triumph of Lent' accounted for less than one-fourth of Genevan excommunications after Calvin's death.

Such sobriety was harder to impose on Geneva's rural subjects, who were frequently excommunicated for dancing and for singing 'profane' songs. Similarly, 'superstition' was a more serious problem in the countryside than in the city; it often involved consulting magicians who lived outside Genevan territory. On the other hand, quarrels among peasant couples or kin rarely came to the consistory's notice.

Protestants who had frequent dealings with Catholics were often charged with 'idolatry' by the Elders. If an adult Genevan had attended mass or heard a sermon by a Jesuit, he or she was excommunicated for a longer term than that given to ordinary sinners. Moreover, such offenders had to undergo a public penance in church before being re-admitted.

Overall, the Calvinist consistory carried on a tireless and generally successful struggle to preserve domestic tranquillity among its faithful. Contrary to a tenacious legend, the Elders spent more time reconciling neighbours, kin and spouses than they did punishing various kinds of sinners. Thanks to frequent sermons preached to large audiences, to catechism courses, and to annual doctrinal inspections of every household, the Reformed Church had virtually eliminated religious ignorance by 1560, and weakened the tacit opposition to the Elders' authority. However, given the doctrine of original sin, it is not surprising that the consistory still had so much work to do in its endless struggle against frivolity, luxury and superstition, or that it sometimes failed to control them.

Holy times, holy places

One essential dimension of Reformed austerity was its radical shrinking of holy times, its drastic reduction in the number of holidays. Of course, Sunday remained sacred and honouring it implied rest and sobriety. But the Reformed calendar truly promoted only four Sundays per year: the four annual Communions, where the faithful received the Eucharist. This stress on Communion, which became so

important because other religious celebrations had been eliminated, explains the special fascination of sixteenth-century Protestant theologians with Eucharistic doctrines; among the laity, the social primacy of Communion explains the extreme importance of excommunication, the ultimate weapon of the consistory.

Reformed Churches reduced holy space as well as holy times. The Eucharist, of course, could only be given in a 'temple', either an old church totally stripped of its 'idolatrous' ornaments or a new plain rectangular building as at Lyons or later at Charenton outside Paris. For the Reformed laity, the rituals of passage either took place inside the temple or else were de-sacralized; the former were incorporated into the holy time of the public sermon or *presche*. The structure of the three great rituals of passage – birth, marriage, death – became as different from Catholic practice as the discipline of the Elders was from confession.

Baptism, the only sacrament which Catholic doctrine allowed any adult to administer, became severely restricted, at least in theory. In order to be valid, it had to be administered by a Reformed pastor within a church. The consequences have become familiar to demographers: by the seventeenth century, Reformed babies were several days older than Catholic babies when baptized. This doctrine evidently produced anguish among parents of fragile newborns, and it seems possible that rural pastors sometimes baptized in private homes. Nevertheless, doctrinal logic remained unchanged: baptism was the only valid sacrament except Communion, so it had to be performed within the sacred space of the temple.

Reformed Christians also supervised baptism through the famous method of censoring baptismal names. Calvin persuaded Geneva's magistrates to allow pastors to refuse baptism if godparents or parents proposed an 'improper' name, one not found in Scripture. The effects of this decision were spectacular. Names drawn from the Old Testament – Abraham, David, Isaac, Samuel, or Sarah, Judith, Suzannah, Rachel – rose from 2 per cent to over 30 per cent between the 1550s and the 1560s in Geneva. Saints' names disappeared almost completely. Claude, one of the three most popular names for both sexes before the Reformation, was rigorously forbidden because the tomb and miraculous relics of St Claude were located only a few miles from Geneva. As with many other Genevan reforms, the pastors' veto over baptismal names was never replicated elsewhere in the Reformed world; no other government published a list of forbidden names. Nevertheless, Reformed congregations throughout Europe often tended to give their children Old Testament names, thus distinguishing themselves from Catholics.

Although stripped of its rank as a sacrament, marriage was also brought into the Reformed temple. Three important departures from Catholic traditions affected engagement, marriage and divorce. Although it was not necessary to celebrate pre-nuptial engagements before a pastor or in a church, they had to be spoken before witnesses and publicized in church through three successive bans, in order to avoid possible legal complications. The ceremony itself had to take place within a temple in order to be valid. Like baptism, marriage was incorporated into a regular church service; perhaps for this reason, around 1,600 Genevan peasants answered 'yes indeed' when asked whether marriage was a sacrament. The Elders had to decide whether or not 'clandestine' engagements (those made without parental approval) should be broken. The Reformed Church probably exercised stricter surveillance over marriage than its Catholic counterpart, even if they no longer considered it a sacrament.

The most remarkable consequence of this loss of sacramental status was obviously permission to divorce. In practice, however, Reformed theologians remained closely attached to Catholic rules governing legal separations. Adultery was the standard reason for husbands seeking divorce, and 'malignant desertion' the principal reason for wives. Although Geneva's consistory complained in 1610 that they had a 'reputation for breaking marriages easily', they actually granted few divorces with permission to remarry until the eighteenth century.

Removing a ritual of passage from the Church meant its total de-sacralization. Death, the final passage, had such a fate among the Reformed. It seems symbolic that Calvin wished to be buried in an unmarked grave – and remarkable that Geneva's government honoured his request. Although it proved impossible to suppress all traces of traditional funeral ceremonies, the habit of anonymous burial in unconsecrated ground, without the rhetorical exercises of funeral sermons or ritual distributions of alms, was necessary 'in order to avoid all traces of superstition', as a French synod put it. We must remember Protestant litanies against purgatory and the doctrine of works in order to understand this radical simplification of funeral practices, so radical that few customs more clearly separated Reformed Protestants from Catholics.

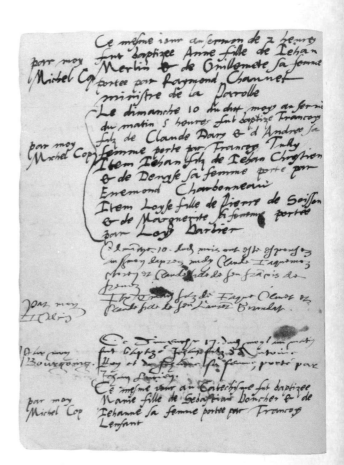

Marriage registered by John Calvin in February 1555. Archives d'État, Geneva.

247

In formulating the wish to be buried in an unmarked tomb, Calvin wanted to put into practice his rejection of funerary rites and Catholic 'superstitions' connected with death. The town of Geneva complied with his last wishes and agreed to de-sanctify the funeral of its Reformer.

Calvin's farewell to the four syndicates and the lords of Geneva on 27 April 1564, painting by Joseph Hornung, 1829. Bibliothèque Publique et Universitaire, Geneva.

The Temple of Paradise was constructed in 1564 on land near the town hall and paid for by the Protestant community of Lyons. This picture was probably brought to Geneva by a refugee, for the temple disappeared after the revocation of the Edict of Nantes.

The Temple of Lyons, painting attributed to Jean Perrissin, *c.* 1565. Bibliothèque Publique et Universitaire, Geneva.

Family worship

The reduction in holy times, the absence of holidays or holy bells ('it's an ugly habit to baptize bells', noted a Huguenot artisan in his diary in 1599) did not mean that the Reformed faith required less time from Christians than had the medieval Church. Rather the reverse, since so much of Calvinist religious time occurred not in church but at home. Calvin was extremely clear on this point. 'Every individual family must be a small separate church,' he once wrote to a French synod. Since historians have labelled the sixteenth century as the zenith of the patriarchal nuclear family, such doctrine implied a strongly patriarchal family worship. Many Reformed households experienced not the 'priesthood of all believers' proclaimed by Luther, but the 'priesthood of the *paterfamilias*'.

Reading the Bible at home was probably less common than pious tradition believes, since owning a complete Bible was relatively rare in the sixteenth century. Religious instruction remained the job of the minister. The most important aspects of domestic religious practice (about which we possess little direct evidence) were probably family prayers at mealtimes and family singing of psalms.

The role of music in the daily lives of sixteenth-century Calvinists seems paradoxical. Calvin's hatred of polyphony and his followers' general distrust of church organs removed the Reformed Church from the history of western music. In typically reductionist style, it concentrated its efforts on putting the Old Testament into music; and within such narrow limits, its success was considerable. The best French poets with Protestant sympathies, beginning with Marot, participated in the task, and the largest publishing project in Calvin's Geneva was neither the Bible nor the catechism, but a huge edition of 25,000 psalters. Equally significant, the only religious works printed by Huguenots in the spoken dialects of southern France were poetical translations of the Psalms into Gascon (1565) and Bearnais (1568). Catholics soon learned to recognize Huguenots by their habit of singing psalms in public. The Spanish Inquisition arrested Frenchmen overheard singing them, while Catholic captains in the French Wars of Religion learned that their enemies prepared for battle by singing psalms. Singing at home, an equally devout pastime, was far less dangerous.

The family nucleus was so important for Reformed piety that the Genevan authorities regarded bachelors with suspicion and the Elders sometimes reprimanded them. Calvin, a natural bachelor who found no higher praise for his dead wife than to claim that 'she never interfered with my work', never mentions unmarried men or women in his Scriptural commentaries. Reformed leaders took a severe view of

women who led an 'irregular' life: Geneva expelled its nuns, and we know of
Huguenot soldiers who cropped the ears of prostitutes (to the horror of a priest who
witnessed it) after capturing a town. Protestant scorn for celibacy embraced both
sexes, but for Reformed women, who had lost the prestigious refuge of a convent,
there could be no satisfactory religious life outside the home.

The Reformation in southern France

Treating the daily life of Reformed Protestants as a homogenous whole is valid only
up to a point. Although all Reformed communities during the sixteenth century
modelled themselves on Calvin's doctrine and Genevan discipline, it is obvious that
none of them, from the fiefs of Polish or Hungarian Calvinist noblemen to the small
farms of Scotland, replicated Geneva's conditions. Many significant differences
separated the Reformed communities scattered across Europe, and this survey will
merely try to sketch the principal nuances of its major components.

In Calvin's mind, establishing a Reformed discipline at Geneva served primarily
as an example to hasten the conversion of his native France – a goal which, with his
reluctant consent, ultimately led to civil war in 1562. The characteristics of the
French Reformed Church were strongly conditioned by the state of endemic war
throughout the rest of the century, and its minority status was in large part a
military consequence of those wars.

The new military code adopted by Huguenot armies in 1562 is interesting both
for its content and for its fate. If the King's soldiers were forbidden to play cards,
Reformed soldiers were forbidden to play any kind of games. If royal edicts regulated
duels, Huguenot edicts forbade them. The King ordered his men not to pillage
churches; the Protestants extended this prohibition to private houses. Of course,
Huguenot soldiers were forbidden to blaspheme and were required to attend prayers
twice a day. As one of their commanders reported in his memoirs, his troops
maintained this superhuman discipline for more than two months, before behaving
like ordinary sixteenth-century mercenaries.

Endemic warfare was not the only obstacle inhibiting the progress of the
Reformed faith in France. For political and military reasons, it flourished mainly in
the southern part of the kingdom; Jeanne d'Albret's principality of Béarn became the
first (and only) French region to adopt the Reformation by government edict in
1561. But in so far as the Reformation was a lay movement resting on knowledge of
the Bible in the vernacular, it was poorly suited to southern France, where only a
small minority could read the Gospel in French. Although the Huguenots made

The edicts and ordinances of the city of Geneva
prescribed in 1566: 'A pimp or procuress who
arranges one single lewd act will be ostracized
and publicly flogged and banished in perpetuity
on pain of death.'

Ostracism of women of the street and pimp in the 16th
century. Musée d'Art et d'Histoire, Geneva.

considerable efforts to expand the use of French, it remained (except for the Psalms, as we have seen) exclusively a liturgical language.

Janine Garrisson-Estèbe has demonstrated how the Reformed Church made a marriage of convenience with southern French civilization. The archives of Languedoc consistories show a much higher level of physical violence than those from the German Palatinate. Similarly, the paternalism of Roman law explains why southern French consistories intervened more often than those of the Palatinate to enforce filial obligations towards parents, but almost never worried about parental duties towards children. The Reformed Church gave fathers both extensive powers and considerable responsibilities. The father's authority over his children's marriage, already great in civil law, was reinforced by the consistories. But in exchange, the latter tended, at least in France, to make husbands responsible for misbehaviour by their wives – outlandish clothes, gossiping, dancing – while threatening them with excommunication for beating their wives. The traditional anticlericalism of southern France made them appreciate many points of Reformed doctrine, while the Calvinist accent on predestination joined with regional paternalism to reinforce paternal authority at the head of these 'small separate churches'.

Scottish success

Although Calvin and the Genevans believed that their most important goals lay in France, their greatest sixteenth-century success occurred in John Knox's Scotland. The reasons are as difficult to determine as those for the concentration of French Protestantism in the south rather than in French-speaking regions. After all, Shakespeare's *Macbeth* portrayed Scotland as a perfect example of barbarism. A low degree of literacy, primitive feudalism oppressing an unproductive agriculture, the small number of commercial centres constituted obstacles for the Reformed Church. Moreover, unlike southern France, Scotland had no tradition of medieval heresy. Knox and his followers had some advantages to exploit: a corrupt Church, easy to attack, and a weak monarchy, whose sovereigns in the 1560s were a young woman educated in France and a child. The Reformed Church converted many lairds, just as it won many French noblemen in the 1560s; but in Scotland the lairds ruled without obstacles for a full generation, long enough to implant a Calvinist Church permanently.

In some ways, Scottish Reformed life reads like an exaggerated version of Genevan discipline. While Calvin's Elders were content to exclude fornicators from Communion and let the magistrates imprison them for six days on bread and water, their Scottish colleagues condemned such people to appear, dressed in sackcloth, barefoot and bareheaded, at the church door and then on a 'stool of repentance' before the entire congregation for several consecutive Sundays. Excommunicated persons suffered severe disabilities; in 1572 the Scottish parliament decreed that they could hold no public office nor testify in court.

Scotland also pushed Genevan norms about observing Sundays to unheard-of extremes. In 1579, the Scottish parliament prohibited all work, all games and all alcoholic beverages on the Sabbath, and the Church added a prohibition against travelling anywhere except to church and back home. Elders obliged parishioners who had *not* worked on Christmas Day to perform a public penance. Although the Scottish episcopate restored the observance of the five major holidays in 1618, and the Archbishop of St Andrews ostentatiously played golf after Sunday sermon, Scotland remained famous into the twentieth century for the special rigour with which its good Presbyterians observed their Sabbath.

One of the least glorious characteristics of the Scottish Reformed community was the tight bond between the Church and the witch-hunters. In France, the practices of illicit magic rarely concerned Reformed consistories or synods; in the Low Countries or the Palatinate, witch-hunting virtually disappeared after the Reformed Church was established; at Geneva, the phenomenon long preceded the Reformation and persisted long afterwards. Scotland is therefore the only instance where the wave of witch-hunting coincided with the consolidation of the Reformed faith, and where it declined at the same time as religious fundamentalism. The number of witches executed in Scotland has been estimated at 1,350 in a total of 2,300 trials between 1560 and 1700; a specialist on the subject, Christina Larner, recently repeated the judgement of William Lecky in 1841 that 'Scottish witchcraft was but the consequence of Scottish puritanism'.

Here the Reformed Church successfully promoted sobriety and literacy among an under-developed population; the greatest historian of Scottish society, T.C. Smout, estimated that the towns were reformed by 1580 and the countryside during the following half-century: 'It seems that the average Lowlander began to attend church

Mary Stuart, who returned to Scotland after the death of her husband Francis I (1560), led an open political repression of Presbyterians, but her incompetences and lovers scandalized the Scots, who compelled her to abdicate. From 1568, the way was clear for the friends of John Knox.

Portrait of Mary Stuart, French painting of the 16th century. Musée Condé, Chantilly.

regularly, to pay reasonably attention to the sermons and to give a reasonable amount of respect to "the Elders".' But the price of such success was high.

Pluralism in the Netherlands

The United Provinces of the Netherlands became the final and most important European region officially to adopt the Reformed faith during the sixteenth century. Their social context was utterly different from that in Scotland, Béarn, the Palatinate, or French Switzerland; the territories comprising the seventeen provinces of the Low Countries had the highest level of urbanization and the most active commerce in northern Europe. The seven northern provinces, which united in 1579 to defend the first constitutional revolution of modern Europe (the legal deposition of a legitimate sovereign), were as prosperous and as advanced as the southern provinces when they established the Dutch Reformed Church. The northern Netherlands, moreover, had already produced the Brethren of the Common Life, Erasmus, and numerous Anabaptist groups well before the rise of Calvinism.

It is remarkable that the Reformed Church, despite its official status, never became a majority religion in the Netherlands. In no other part of Europe, except perhaps Ireland, was the established Church a minority faith. The contrast with Scotland is striking: in one case a rapid conquest, in the other an ineradicable religious pluralism. After 1553 there were no more executions for heresy in the province of Holland (an important centre of Anabaptism); even Sephardic Jews, originally mistaken for Catholics because they spoke Spanish, were welcome in the north. Rotterdam, a medium-sized town where Erasmus had been born, counted no fewer than ten different religious congregations in the early seventeenth century. Everywhere, Catholics formed the largest single bloc; when it was claimed in 1587 that only one-tenth of the population belonged to the Reformed Church, the *predikants* did not challenge the assertion. About 1650 the United Provinces were still nearly half Catholic, and this proportion declined only gradually thereafter.

Because of the necessity for religious toleration, it is sometimes difficult to appreciate the work of the Reformed Church in the United Provinces. The *predikants* may have succeeded in persuading the rural peasants to observe Sundays diligently and to shun 'papist' holidays like Christmas or St Sylvester's Day, but even at the peak of their authority around 1620 they were never able to close the theatres and dance-halls in the towns.

The best example of the practical limits of Dutch Calvinism is probably the evolution of the *kermis*, a traditional local holiday strongly ingrained in the Dutch character: they spoke of 'St Kermis' in the same way as one would St Nicholas at Christmas. No matter how much the ministers denounced this remnant of 'papism', this 'pagan superstition', the *kermis* continued to flourish. Even the pious House of Orange, pillar of the Reformed Church, cheerfully organized the annual *kermis* at the Hague in exchange for a share of the profits. Unable to destroy it, the synods could only legislate against the fighting and bloodshed which were customary during these week-long festivals. Bruegel's famous *Combat of Lent and Carnival* did not always end with the triumph of the former.

The Reformed laity

Like all other major religions, the Reformed faith had more success in changing external appearances than in persuading sinners to behave like the elect. Throughout Europe, sinners continued to sin, despite the risks of public humiliation if they were discovered by the Elders. However, one should not forget that at Geneva and elsewhere in Reformed Europe, these consistories were less preoccupied with threats of excommunication than with a patient task of reconciliation, arbitration, and polite but firm remonstrances.

Reformed Christians were distinguishable from other Protestants, as well as Catholics, by their Old Testament names, by the care with which they observed Sundays, by their refusal to hold elaborate funerals, and by their failure to observe traditional (to them, 'pagan') holidays such as Christmas. By 1600, outside observers seem most impressed with the austerity of the Reformed, whose sobriety of clothing and attitudes matched the austerity of their churches. 'I cannot help observing, to the shame of Catholics,' noted a Jansenist priest, 'that dancing is more rigorously forbidden by the discipline of the so-called Reformed Church in France.'

The daily piety of the Reformed laity remains largely invisible, having left relatively few traces on the historical record. Although they brought baptisms and weddings into church, much of their piety was expressed within their families

Newes from Scotland,
Declaring the Damna=
ble life and death of Doctor Fian, *a*
notable Sorcerer, who was burned at
Edenbrough in Ianuary laft.
1591.

Which Doctor was regefter to the Diuell
that fundry times preached at North Bar-
rick Kirke, to a number of noto-
nous Witches.

With the true examinations of the faide Doctor
and Witches, as they vttered them in the pre-
fence of the Scottish King.

Difcouering how they pretended
to bewitch and drowne his Maieftie in the Sea
comming from Denmarke, with fuch
other wonderfull matters as the like
hath not been heard of at
any time.

Publifhed according to the Scottifh Coppie.

AT LONDON
Printed for William
Wright.

In the course of the Scottish Reformation, witch hunts provoked an atmosphere of suspicion and caused the deaths of hundreds of unfortunate victims. These excesses surfaced also on the other side of the Atlantic, in Puritan New England.

Title page of *Daemonologie*, a treatise on sorcery published in London in 1597 following the publication of the original in Scotland.

In spite of undeniable success, the clergy could not reform entirely the customs of their citizens: in Holland, the *predikants* had to come to terms with the village fair, a festival of great importance to the population. One can even wonder who took the side of Lent or carnival, austerity or festival, in the painting by Bruegel.

Conflict between Lent and carnival, painting on wood by Pieter Bruegel the Elder, 1559. Kunsthistorisches Museum, Vienna.

through such private rituals as Bible reading, mealtime prayers and hymn-singing. Feminine piety, almost exclusively domestic, is particularly hard to grasp within a tradition which produced many women martyrs but few women authors. Despite the poverty of our sources, we know that their faith survived, transmitted from generation to generation thanks to a culture which was both oral and written. The Word, of course, but also songs and gestures, enabled it to survive both religious persecutions and the more insidious temptations of worldliness.

'Austerity' is the keyword in describing the attitudes, the vestments, the customs, and even the religious architecture, of the Reformed.

Interior view of the church of Saint-Bavon of Haarlem, painting by Pieter Jansz Saenredam, 1630. Musée du Louvre, Paris.

Men and ideas on the margin of history

1

Protestants and Catholics held many opposing views but they were united in the pitiless measures taken against witchcraft, heresy, paganism and all the deviations inspired by the devil. The practices of the Inquisition had their counterpart on the side of the Reformation such as witchhunts in Scotland and, some decades earlier, the bloodthirsty repression of the Anabaptists, the radical movement centred on Münster.

1. *Young witch and dragon*, drawing by Hans Baldung Grien, 1515. Staatliche Kunsthalle, Karlsruhe.

2. *Execution of the Anabaptists of Münster in 1536*, 16th-century German engraving. Bibliothèque Nationale, Paris.

3. *Execution of Jean de Leyde, leader of the Münster Anabaptists, in 1536*, 16th-century German engraving. Bibliothèque Nationale, Paris.

While Catholics and Protestants disagreed on practically every subject throughout the sixteenth century, there was one point on which they were agreed: the need to hunt down witches, heretics, sceptics, defenders of religious tolerance and the free spirits who bravely engaged in the great adventure of modern science.

The hunt for witches and heretics

The age of the Reformation was not only an age of religious and intellectual renewal; it was also an age of insecurity and fear. Many people lived not only in dread of natural catastrophies – war, plague and famine – but also of evil spirits and, above all, the devil. Agents of Satan appeared in the forms of heathens, Jews, Turks and women. Belief in the powers of magicians and occult sciences was widespread in every country in Europe. The Reformation did little to dispel such fears let alone change the situation.

Fear led to defensive reactions. The age of the Reformation was also an age of persecution and ruthless suppression of minorities, opposition fringe groups and outsiders. Any criticism of authority or tradition could sooner or later be dangerous for those who uttered it. Any original urge to master the confusions of the time was proscribed and regarded with suspicion; suspicion led to denunciation, painful investigations, judgement and expulsion from society, or in extreme cases, death. Such dangers were everywhere in Protestant as well as Catholic territories. There is a Reformation boast that in spite of everything, critics of authority and tradition could not be silenced. Yet one must add that the practical consequences of these criticisms did not appear until well after the Reformation.

The age of the Reformation was also an age of burning at the stake: thousands of people were condemned to die as witches or heretics. Such persecution was based on widely different forms of accusation and must be taken separately: witchcraft implied seduction of people in league with the devil, while heresy was deviation from true and officially declared Church doctrine, whether Catholic or Protestant. The persecution of witches and wizards (in the majority of cases it was women who were involved) started early in the fourteenth century, and the number of cases increased steadily throughout the fifteenth century. Papal bulls and numerous theological tracts, including the most famous, Jacob Sprenger's *Malleus maleficarum* in 1486, intensified the persecutions. Fear of witchcraft reached its climax in the frenzied years between 1560 and 1630, precisely at the moment when many European countries were shaken by wars and internal upheavals.

All in all, the persecution of witches was more fanatical in Protestant than Catholic areas. Luther supported it unreservedly, and other Reformers such as Melanchthon, Bullinger, Calvin and Vermigli thought as he did. The greatest number of executions took place in south-west Germany, Scotland and in Geneva, Canton Vaud and the Jura. In the United Republic of the Netherlands witchcraft trials ceased in 1610, while in Switzerland witches were still being executed up to 1782.

The official Catholic Church was relatively restrained in the matter of witchhunts: In the first instance neither the Roman nor the Spanish Inquisition was concerned with witchcraft trials. Not until the end of the sixteenth century did the Roman Inquisition start to turn its attention to black magic and sorcery. For the most part sentences handed out by the Inquisition against men and women accused of

witchcraft were much less severe than those of the civil courts north of the Alps and the Pyrenees.

The primary objective of the Inquisition in the sixteenth century was the campaign against heresy. As early as the end of the fifteenth century, the Inquisition was set up in Spain at the King's command to track down and punish converted Jews who were still practising their former religion in secret. But as time passed the Spanish Inquisition concerned itself increasingly with other opponents of Catholic unity, in particular Christian critics of Church traditions, such as 'enlightened ones' (*Alumbrados*), mystics, followers of Erasmus and the 'Lutherans', those supposedly or actually influenced by Luther's religious heterodoxy. The Roman, or papal, Inquisition re-established in 1542 was directed from the start against evangelical opponents and resulted in the large exodus of Italian 'heretics' to the Protestant centres in Switzerland, Germany, England and Poland, which was to have important consequences. Even if the courts set up by the Inquisition did not, in total, condemn to death as many heretics as is often maintained in contemporary writings, it acted as a very effective brake at the time on anyone who might have felt inclined towards dissension, criticism of tradition or too individualistic a way of thinking. The Inquisition is undoubtedly responsible for the failure of Reformation movements in both Spain and Italy. Anyone who allowed himself to be seduced by the Reformation's call for renewal, but did not wish to be in mortal danger, had no choice but to emigrate.

Persecution and execution of heretics was clearly not absent from northern Europe. The spread of Protestantism provoked repressive measures until the outbreak of open religious wars in Switzerland, the German Empire and in France. But Protestantism was not cowed by persecution or the execution of heretics. All the Reformers and every Protestant authority had to wage war on two fronts: on the one hand against the Catholic Church and on the other against the 'radicals' in their own ranks who stood well to the left of the new Christian movement, rejecting it as a feeble compromise with the wordly powers and claiming authentically evangelical completion of the Reformation when its mission was only half-accomplished. Among these radicals were the Anabaptist followers of Thomas Müntzer, many other pietistic groups and in England the early Puritans. All were persecuted by malicious Catholics, and especially by insecure Protestant authorities. At a time when there was a generally held belief that only *one* religion was possible in a state, religious dissension was automatically equated with political subversion and so attempts were made to suppress it.

2

The tolerance debate

Heretics were put to death in northern Europe, particularly in the Protestant countries, but not always by burning; many other methods of execution were used, almost always accompanied by symbolic forms of purification which appear cynical to us today, such as the drowning of the Anabaptists in Zurich. The most infamous and most significant execution took place on 27 October 1553 in Geneva when a Protestant authority, following the model of the Inquisition, ordered the burning of the Spanish anti-Trinitarian Michael Servetus. This execution inaugurated a considerable degree of disquiet and led to strong criticism among the French, Italian and Spanish refugees who had fled from religious persecution. This criticism prompted what could be called the great tolerance debate of the sixteenth century.

The arraignment of Calvin and all other leaders of the Reformation who supported him was taken up by Sebastian Castellio, a humanist born in Savoy but resident in Basle, who became the first systematic defender of religious tolerance. His most important, though by no means only, contribution to the debate was his compilation which appeared in March 1554, *De haereticis an sint persequendi* in which he expressed not only his own opinions but also those of a large number of other authors from early Christian times to his own. Castellio's argument for tolerance was based entirely on the Bible. His aim was still the restoration of Christian consensus, in other words the return of heretics to the 'true' Gospel by teaching and patient exhortation. In this context Castellio appears as a successor to Erasmus of Rotterdam. But while to the Dutch humanist, biblical revelation and Church tradition were always the basis of theological reflections, the Savoyard's idea of *liberum arbitrium* was much more clearly based on human reasoning. Unlike Calvin, Castellio did not regard the reasonable nature of man as being corrupted by sin but as something possessed by all individuals; as a light which aided the understanding of the essential and universally valid meaning of the Scriptures. This was his basis for affirming on the one hand, the value and necessity of critical philological

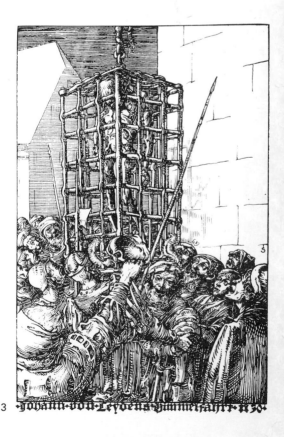

3 ·Johann·von·Leyden·himmelfart·1530·

Departure for the Sabbath, drawing by Albrecht Altdorfer, first half of the 16th century. Musée du Louvre, Paris.

Erasmus based his great religious tolerance on the parable of the wheat and the tares. Only God is competent to separate the good from the wicked at the Last Judgement. Men cannot take his place and make decisions to condemn anybody on account of their beliefs.

Separating the wheat from the tares, illustration from *Paraphrase of the Gospel of St Matthew* by Erasmus, translated by Renée de France, 1539. Bibliothèque Nationale, Paris.

examination of biblical text as taught by humanism, and on the other, the complete inadequacy of the whole Christian tradition in which every dogmatic requirement and all theological speculation rested on uncertain tradition. The central points of his argument remain constant: the appeal to God-given human reason comes again and again as the key to understanding essential Biblical teaching and it appears repeatedly, usually with reference to the parable of the wheat and the tares, with the thought that in condemning heretics mankind should never anticipate the Last Judgement — only God knows who is a heretic and no individual should be condemned to death on account of his religious convictions.

Some prominent Italian refugees of conscience among the spiritual heirs of Castellio continued to demand tolerance and religious freedom; among them were the former Capuchin General Bernardino Ochino and Giacopo Aconcio (Acontius) in England in the time of Elizabeth I. In the same tradition, towards the end of the sixteenth century, the Flemish lay theologian Dirck Volckertszoon Coornhert translated and published a large number of Castellio's writings.

The tolerance debate continued with great passion: Calvin, de Beza and their adherents defended themselves vigorously against Castellio. In common with all sixteenth-century Reformers the Genevans saw themselves as the executors of the divine will in cleansing the Church of wordliness and corruption. They were therefore unable to regard humanist demands for tolerance as anything other than a betrayal of their religious aims. It was indeed true that at least up to the second half of the sixteenth century, the call for tolerance came mainly from individuals who, while theologically and philosophically educated, were at the fringes of social and political life, and did not have any direct responsibility for the maintenance of existing order.

The debate on tolerance and the possibility of religious pluralism automatically involved political ideas and institutions. Wherever religious minorities came up against churches which depended on secular power, the question arose, 'Can a follower of a religion different from that of the government still be a loyal subject?' If this question is answered in the negative, as already stated, persecution and intolerance are the result. A decisive turning point was however always reached, when a prince or councillor saw that maintenance of political order was more important than Church unity and that religious pluralism did not constitute a danger to the State, but under certain circumstances could even be advantageous. So already before 1600 a relatively wide spectrum of different practical arrangements and degrees of tolerance of religious minorities had developed. The principle of *cuius regio eius religio* as exercised in Switzerland and, since 1555, in the German Empire, was basically a compromise solution which avoided pluralism. Different levels of practical tolerance of other beliefs in one and the same state were possible; these ranged from the merest recognition of a right to exist, to officially permitted public worship. The highest level of tolerance was reached when a ruler allowed unrestricted practice of all Christian cults throughout the territories under his control. In the sixteenth century, however, such a level of freedom was attained only in Poland and the principality of Transylvania. A high degree of religious freedom had been permitted already prior to 1600 in the United Republic of the Netherlands, but this had never been established by statute.

In the second half of the sixteenth century more people came to the defence of tolerance — people who were able to accomplish the transition from humanistic to purely political ideals of reconciliation, based on the arguments and practical requirements of the time. This phenomenon was particularly marked in France, as in the speeches of the chancellor Michel de L'Hôpital and the writings of many 'politicians'. This shows us that for many critical observers, maintenance of the French monarchy was ultimately more important than restoration of religious unity. Michel de Montaigne was also of the opinion that reconciliation of the confessional parties was no longer possible. With increasing persistence he demanded that freedom of conscience should be granted and renounced all forms of coercion in religious matters. Finally, Jean Bodin, author of the *Colloquium heptaplomeres*, which appeared in 1588, was also among the most radical advocates of tolerance.

While these authors wrangled and worried about the existence of the French nation, the same motives and principles of pluralism could also be seen behind the royal religious edicts passed between the January edict of 1562 and the Edict of Nantes in 1598, although always within clearly defined limits. The conviction that freedom of religion could also have advantages for the economic prosperity of a country was often affirmed in the seventeenth century, especially by English authors. The same belief had been held before 1600 and was especially marked in the Low Countries where William of Orange was one of its advocates. Here on the one hand

we see the integration of Catholics into the anti-papist resistance front and on the other, the protection of commercially very active Mennonite and Jewish minorities.

Demands for universal tolerance were not yet evident in the sixteenth century. Most protagonists of religious freedom favoured a confession of Christian (Trinitarian) faith, but authors such as Castellio, Aconcio, Coornhert, L'Hôpital and Montaigne – with their opposition to the execution of heretics and their reflections on the dignity of human conscience – were far ahead of their time. But the situation should not be idealized: if religious freedom did succeed in achieving a limited breakthrough here and there in sixteenth-century Europe, this was never due to the exhortations of perspicacious critics of the times they lived in, but came rather as a result of practical interests dictating the renunciation of discrimination.

Religious scepticism

The beginning of the tolerance debate in the sixteenth century can clearly be seen to be linked with the history of religious scepticism. Although in a historical perspective the two developments should not be confused, it is evident that they were at least partially upheld by the same people. Many sixteenth-century sceptical thinkers described themselves as true adherents of Christianity but repudiated all Church authority based on speculation, because they did not believe that there was sufficient evidence for any doctrinal system to pose as the one and only true version. Being a sceptic did not mean being an 'unbeliever', it merely meant being an 'undogmatic believer'. The opposite point of view from scepticism was not fideism but dogmatism.

We must therefore regard both Erasmus of Rotterdam and Sebastian Castellio as sceptics: the Dutchman on account of his *Diatribe de libero arbitrio* (1524), directed against Luther, in particular, and the Savoyard above all for his authorship of the comprehensive work *De arte dubitandi* (1563). It would appear obvious that tolerance must follow on the heels of religious scepticism.

In addition to Erasmus's humanist traditions, there was another route in the sixteenth century by which scepticism could be affirmed. This arose from the rediscovery and revival of the sceptical tradition of late antiquity – in other words,

This elephant ridden by Turks is an allusion to Protestant infidels; the attack is by masked Catholics dressed in green, the colour chosen by Gabrielle d'Estrées, Henri IV's favourite courtier. The elephant symbolizes Geneva, the Protestant fortress.

The elephant carousel, painting on wood by Antoine Caron, *c.* 1598. Private collection, Paris.

The rediscovery of the sceptical classical tradition led certain 16th-century authors such as Agrippa von Nettesheim (1486–1533), and especially Montaigne (1533–92), to conclude that there was nothing to choose between the parties. This attitude is well illustrated by *The cuisine of opinions*, a satirical engraving directed at Catholics, Lutherans, Calvinists and Mennonites (Anabaptists) all together; the Pope is seen taking his soup while Luther plays the guitar, Calvin is squeezing an orange (an allusion to the house of Orange), the Anabaptist is cleaning a fish while a woman, symbolizing reason, urges the sects to support each other.

Portrait of Michel de Montaigne, 16th-century painting. Bibliothèque Nationale, Paris.

Portrait of Heinrich Cornelius Agrippa von Nettesheim, 16th-century engraving. Société de l'Histoire du Protestantisme Français, Paris.

The cuisine of opinions, late 16th-century engraving. Société de l'Histoire du Protestantisme Français, Paris.

the Pyrrhonism of Sextus Empiricus (Pyrrho of Elis, *c.* 360–270 BC) and the ideas expressed by Cicero in the *Academica*. In this context many authors can be mentioned who took up and advanced Pyrrhonic or Ciceronian scepticism during the Reformation and the religious wars, among them the Italian philosopher Pico della Mirandola and the learned German Heinrich Cornelius Agrippa von Nettesheim, who was interested in the occult sciences. But without doubt the most important sixteenth-century sceptic, in thought and influence, was Michel de Montaigne. On reading the writings of Sextus Empricus (published by Henri Estienne in 1562) he adopted the motto 'Que sais-je?' for the whole of his philosophy. As leader of the 'new Pyrrhonists' he achieved lasting influence even outside France. This influence was based not only on the *Essais* but above all on the *Apologie de Raimond Sebond* (1575–6), regarded as the classic compilation of the sixteenth-century philosophy of scepticism.

Religious scepticism often forced its adherents to live on the margins of society. An impressive example of this was provided by the life of the learned 'wanderer' Sebastian Franck von Donauwörth who, disappointed with all current schools of thought, no longer wished to be identified with any party. He posed radical questions regarding the traditional definition of heresy and finally achieved a relativity and universality unique for his time. Another result of the sceptical stance was the surrender of certain central elements of Christian belief such as the Trinity. The anti-trinitarian position could not be expounded since those who – like Servetus – either confessed or could not allay suspicions on this point, were persecuted equally mercilessly by Catholics and Protestants alike. Similarly dangerous was a display of too open a general indifference to theological questions.

Several well-known figures on the fringe of religious scepticism have not yet been satisfactorily understood in their individualistic endeavours and critical attitudes towards Church traditions and the hierarchy. This applies in particular to certain French humanists from the circle of Marguerite de Navarre, such as Bonaventure des Périers, author of *Cymbalum mundi* (1537), Etienne Dolet, who was burned to death in Paris in 1546 and François Rabelais – despite the enormous quantity of literature which has been written about him.

At the time of the Reformation individualism, non-conformism and indifference were much more widespread than historians have wished to admit. Rejection of dogmatic faith and hostility to the Church occured not only in the ranks of the educated, but also among many simple people in both town and country, as has been established from Church instruments, legal statements, registers of alms and so on. Clearly many questions remain unanswered. The degree of complete atheism is hard to assess because even those with serious doubts were unable to express their views clearly in this matter, in addition to which there is the difficulty of defining with any accuracy what unbelief was in the sixteenth century. The great French historian Lucien Febvre made a start in this direction with his famous book on Rabelais (1942) but his results still need to be confirmed and expanded. It is easier to establish that certain radical thinkers with a tendency towards rationalism were *not* atheists. That is certainly true for Servetus and the Polish and Transylvanian anti-trinitarians who followed Faustus Soccinus and other Italian 'heretics'. A satisfactory, comprehensive history of non-belief in the sixteenth century has not so far been written.

The natural sciences

Criticism of tradition was not only to be found in the field of religion; it also arose from philosophy and observation of natural phenomena. The growth and stimulus of opinions, attitudes and new views was often brushed aside or regarded as trivial and contested at the time but later become generally recognized and accepted as extremely important.

Until early in the sixteenth century the interests of the educated humanist élite lay almost exclusively with mankind and his works, but in time they came increasingly to extend outwards from the human microcosm to the macrocosm of nature. These new interests became embodied in leading political thinkers such as Jean Bodin (the six books of *La République*, 1576; *Colloquium heptaplomeres*) and Tommaso Campanella (*Citté del sole*, written between 1602 and 1623). Other critical contemporaries dedicated themselves to the problems of understanding nature. Their efforts could be regarded as being of two different but interrelated types: the speculative and the empirical, in other words quantifiable methods of research.

What are known as the occult sciences – alchemy and astrology in particular – played a very important role throughout the whole of the sixteenth century and on into the seventeenth in the struggles relating to natural phenomena. The field of the occult sciences was the first to regard experiment as essential to modern natural sciences. The questions posed by experiments and the resultant findings contributed decisively to the success of quantifiable methods of research which characterize natural science to this day.

The University of Padua was an important centre of natural philosophical speculation and observation of natural phenomena and medical studies. The works of Aristotle had been interpreted here for centuries without the cloak of Christianity which was later hung around the Greek philosopher. After the death of Pietro Pomponazzi in Bologna in 1525, the college lacked any outstanding representatives but it continued to influence all Italian natural philosophers of note and students of physics and medicine throughout the second half of the sixteenth century.

The mathematician Girolamo Cardano, together with Aristotle's critics from Padua, attempted to unify a wide range of occult hypotheses. He was convinced of the value of practical experience but believed that experience always remained at a very superficial level without allowing the researcher to reach the heart of the matter. A more empirical researcher than Cardano was the physicist Bernardino Telesio, a few years his junior, who also greatly influenced Campanella and others. He is known for his principle of understanding *non ratione, sed sensu* – not by reason, but by the senses. Although in his case also metaphysical speculation finally got the upper hand over empirical knowledge born of experience, his reflections (amongst others *De natura rerum iuxta propria principia*, 1515) can be considered as an important milestone in the history of empiricism.

Giordano Bruno, the most important Italian natural philosopher in the second half of the sixteenth century, was also inspired by Telesio. He joined the Dominican order in his youth but soon came into conflict with the ideals of monastic life. In 1576 he fled from his monastery in Naples and, like so many other heterodox thinkers of his time, he led the life of a vagrant for some fifteen years. On his journeys he lingered in Paris, Geneva, Oxford, Wittenberg and Frankfurt-on-Main. His return to Italy in 1591 led to denunciation and brought him into the clutches of the Inquisition. On 16 February 1600 he died at the stake in Rome, all attempts to persuade him to recant his unflinching sense of mission having failed.

Bruno's kind of world picture was made up of many elements. Several ideas came from Lucretius and the late ancient mystic Dionysius Areopagita, from medieval philosophers and, above all, from Nicholas of Cusa. His own intuition and speculation combined the whole into a closed system of great and astonishing originality which was committed to print for the first time in England in *De l'infinito universo e mondi* and later frequently reprinted. Bruno postulated the existence of an infinite number of finite worlds in an infinite universe equated with God, since God was not accessible in any human sense. Men only have access to God through his works and especially when contemplating the infinite number of heavenly bodies. Bruno was not an opponent of empirical search for knowledge but his message regarding the infinity of the universe was the result of pure speculation. It was clearly obvious to Bruno's contemporaries that this was very far from the Christian view of the world and the image of God and he made no attempt to hide his alienation from Christianity. This theory of the plurality of the worlds threw up a number of disquieting questions on God's relationship to mankind, which had never been asked before, and none of the various branches of Christian theology could offer

As religion flourished, so did thought. Copernicus (1473–1543), and above all Galileo (1564–1642), put forward a vision which broke with the Aristotelian tradition adhered to by many theologians through force of habit – for reasons which had nothing to do with theology.

Frontispiece to the *Dialogus de systemate mundi* by Galileo Galilei, 1635 edition, representing Ptolemy, Aristotle and Copernicus. Bibliothèque Nationale, Paris.

Harmonia macrocosmica, engraving showing the Copernican system, 1661. Bibliothèque Nationale, Paris.

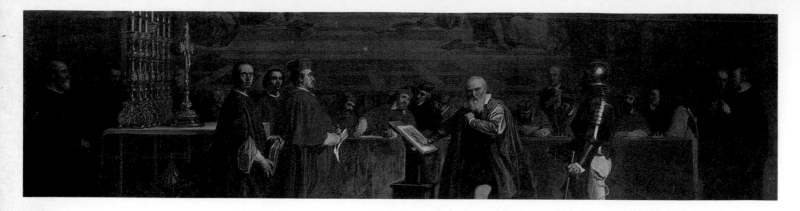

Despite the condemnation of the Church, the Copernican system, defended by Galileo, appealed to educated people. After the efforts of the Dane Tycho Brahe (1546–1601) to support the geocentric view, advocates of the heliocentric view of the universe did not have any further opponents of note.

Galileo before the Holy-Office in 1633, painted by Robert Fleury. Musée du Louvre, Paris.

Tycho Brahe in 1587, engraving from the *Atlas Blaue*, 1667. Bibliothèque Nationale, Paris.

any answers. Bruno's pantheism could no longer be reconciled with Christian fundamentals and he constituted such a danger to the Church that they silenced him.

Galileo

It is generally accepted that Italy, as well as France, played an important part in the history of intellectual criticism, religious scepticism and conscious retreat from Christianity. We should remember not only the evangelical 'heretics' before and after Faustus Soccinus, the Aristotelian critics from Padua or the appearance of popular unbelief as seen in Frioul, but also the individual critics in the Neapolitan south, such as Giordano Bruno and the Utopian Tommaso Campanella, whom we have already mentioned. They appear as the last spirits of the Renaissance and late humanism; the reading of their works and study of their fate were signposts to the seventeenth century. Together with Galileo Galilei they exemplify the leading role played by Italy in the formation of modern thought.

The decisive milestones for natural scientists along this path were, without a doubt, the observations of Galileo. The astounding achievements of this mathematician, astononomer and physicist from Pisa could be described in a nutshell as research into the movement of projectiles and falling objects, anticipating kinetic theory. Galileo was the first man to observe the stars through a telescope which led, among other things, to the discovery of the phases of Venus, the unevenness of the moon's surface and the moons of Jupiter. Above all, however, he proved the accuracy of Nicolaus Copernicus' recently established theory that the sun is the centre of the universe. Galileo confirmed that the Earth revolved around the sun and was not the centre of the universe.

The search which had been going on since the late Middle Ages for laws governing natural phenomena came to an end with Galileo's physical and astronomical research. He demonstrated that the true cause of things was not in other things or substances but in laws, and that these laws could be mathematically formulated and calculated. He assisted mathematical rationality to win its ultimate battle over the speculative Aristotelian natural philosophy.

It was clear that Galileo would not escape conflict with the Church, for as early as 1616 the Copernican system was ruled by papal decree to be heretical. Galileo's paper *Dialogo sopra i due massimi sistemi del mondo* brought him before the infamous court of the Inquisition in 1633 where he was forced to forswear the Copernican concept of the world. His last years were spent in house arrest on his country property near Florence.

Galileo was the first scientist to recognize that mathematics and physics supplement each other as scientific disciplines. He succeeded in uniting earthly and heavenly phenomena in a single theory, thus repudiating the traditional division of the world. His method combined experiment and calculations, abstracting from the concrete and tirelessly checking the results of these operations. The significance of this method exceeded by far even his most important physical and astronomical discoveries. His achievement in freeing physics from speculation is but partial manifestation of an event of universal significance: the victory of experience over authority. This scholar was closely linked with the tradition of intellectual criticism which asserted itself in so many areas of man's search for knowledge in the sixteenth century, the progress of which advanced the 'modernization' of European culture which could not be restrained despite all the suppressive measures of the established spiritual and temporal powers.

The rise of the schoolmaster

It is scarcely surprising that the emphasis of the Protestants on personal reading of the Bible should have led them to accord particular attention to teaching. Luther and Calvin, who both concerned themselves with educational matters, were naturally followed in this regard by their disciples, but were equally influential among their Catholic opponents. From that time on every church was aware of the power which teachers wielded.

> *'The transitory power of the schoolmasters*
> *founded the enduring empire of knowledge.'*
> Madame Necker de Saussure

The preacher and the schoolmaster

In the sixteenth century preachers were very willing to become schoolmasters. Guillaume Farel, for example, who was often beaten for his adherence to the Gospel, like his great predecessor the Apostle Paul, began his ministry teaching in the wine-producing town of Aigle. He arrived there in the autumn of 1526 on the advice of Berthold Haller, with no official post or salary, from Reformed Berne. He judged it advisable, therefore, to begin his work (under the pseudonym of Ursinus) by offering to teach the youth of the town – as much for the good of the population as to swell his purse a little. But soon some of the townspeople invited him to preach the Word of God to them, even though he was not ordained.

Since he had been expelled from Geneva in October 1532 for his views, Farel adopted the disguise of a teacher in order to introduce Reformed thought there too.

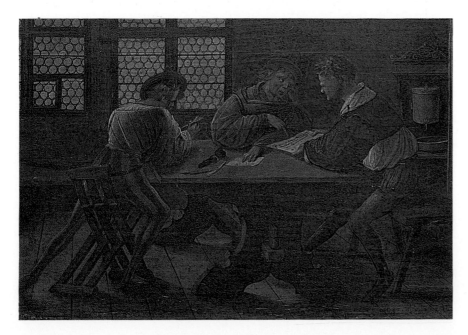

The line between pastor and schoolteacher was often blurred, for the Bible was both the unique foundation of the Reformed faith and the special text for teaching reading.

A schoolmaster teaching, drawn by Hans Holbein the Younger, 1516. Kunstmuseum, Basle.

Antoine Froment, the young minister of Yvonand, was sent by him to post all over the city small handwritten notices: 'A man has come to this town who will teach reading and writing in French in one month to all who would like to come, young or old, male or female, even those who have never been to school. If they cannot read and write within the said month no payment is asked . . .'

This enticing statement expressed exactly the belief of the teacher in what he promised. He knew himself to be a pedagogue and pupils of all ages flooded in. The Word of life made its way into their hearts as they learned to read it. For their primer, of course, was the Bible. But when the classroom became too small and they dragged the preacher out into the Place du Molard to hear him preach on 1 January 1533, Farel realized the imprudence of the action and was constrained to leave.

These two examples illustrate the role a school could play in a movement which sought the centrality of Scripture in the Church, the family and the individual. Its importance was recognized in the writing of Martin Luther and in the deliberations of the General Council at Geneva.

The beginning of compulsory education

On 21 May 1536, before the arrival of Calvin, Geneva declared itself Reformed by the sovereign decision of its assembled citizens. They had embarked on a course from which there was no turning back, for their prince-bishop would not return. Then, for the first time in history, a civil authority offered the right to education to the whole population. The council records state: 'At this point the article concerning schools was proposed and it was unanimously resolved to have a learned man undertake this who would be paid enough to feed and teach the poor without asking any money from them . . . and also that everyone should be responsible for sending their children to school and having them learn.'

The proposal was unambiguous. Everyone, including the poor, must have instruction and be received by the masters. This was in line with Luther's exhortation *To the magistrates of all the German towns, to invite them to set up Christian schools*, which had been published more than ten years earlier (1524). There the Reformer argued that parents could not be left with sole responsibility for the education of their children. Most of them had neither the competence, the time, nor always the concern for education. It was therefore necessary that the authorities, whenever they wished 'to do something for their people', should engage teachers. For who would undertake this if they did not? Not the princes, as Luther observed ironically, for they were too absorbed in their 'lofty and remarkable functions in the cellar, the kitchen and the bedchamber'. So let the towns open classes, for girls as well as for boys! Let them have no constraint with regard to the subjects taught! – as Luther again said in 1530 in his *Addresses on the right to send children to school*. And let Holy Scripture be the prime object of study!

Certainly the teaching was not to be exclusively biblical. Languages, arts, history, singing and arithmetic were to be included in the Reformer's large programme. He wanted a balance to be struck between intellectual culture, useful domestic arts and apprenticeship to a trade. But as early as 1520 in his manifesto *To the Christian nobility of the German nation*, he had already affirmed that the most important thing was that children should be brought into contact with the Gospel. 'Oh!' he exclaimed, 'How badly we treat that unhappy band of young people entrusted to us for guidance and education. We can hardly justify ourselves for not having set the Word of God before their eyes.' As he wrote elsewhere, was it not right 'that Christians should read Scripture with zeal as their own unique book'?

An active pedagogy

There was nothing dreary in education according to Luther: 'Given that the young must jump about and do something they enjoy, and that there is nothing bad in that – besides forbidding everything does no good – why should one not establish schools on that principle? Especially as now, thank God, children may learn with pleasure and in play . . . Our school today is no longer a hell . . . where we have to submit to torture.' He emphasized the supreme importance of a good teacher: there 'is no other occupation I would more willingly undertake'. He perceived that a teacher's influence is so great that no money could amply repay his work. Yet the *métier* had been shamefully underestimated by people who would call themselves Christian.

The same opinions were already being expressed in French-speaking countries by Mathurin Cordier, a man of whom too little is known today. He was a master at the Collège de la Marche in Paris, where he inspired Calvin with a love of fine Latin, and

The Schoolmaster, wood engraving by Albrecht Dürer, 16th century. Bibliothèque Nationale, Paris.

German school, wood engraving by Jacob Kobel, 1524. Musée des Arts Decoratifs, Paris.

the Reformer always remembered him with gratitude. Cordier was as severe as Luther on the faults of the traditional schooling of his time. In the Preface to his work on pedagogy *De corrupti sermonis emendatione* (1530), he distinguished and denounced two causes of the decline of the teaching of Latin in France. The first concerned the language itself, which was used infrequently and badly; the second had to do with religion and the person of Christ, to whom little respect was given. In both cases mechanical repetition was thought to be sufficient instruction. And since such a method totally excluded any pleasure in the subject it had to be whipped into the students. In such establishments pupils 'felt as if they were turning a grindstone or stagnating in prison'. They went in 'like little angels' but they came out 'like demons' because the master was quite indifferent to their progress, being concerned only to fill his purse. Eloquence and upright living left him cold!

Mathurin Cordier was an unshakeable opponent of corporal punishment, but went beyond criticism to make constructive proposals: 'Do you wish teaching to be easy? Begin with good habits. Begin with God and his heavenly benefits . . . Teach them, I say, to love Christ, to breathe Christ, to have the name of Christ on their lips, to do everything to the praise of God, for his glory . . . Put away the bundle of rods and take up the torch of piety.' The author of this fine text was not simply playing with words. His writing is given weight by the experience of teaching which he continued to his dying day. He was born in 1479 in Normandy and he taught almost everywhere: in Bordeaux at the Collège de Guyenne, under André de Gouvea; in Geneva in 1537–8, called to the post by Antoine Saulnier; in Neuchâtel at the invitation of Farel from 1539–45; then at Lausanne as the college Principal until 1558; and finally at Geneva where in his eighties he served as master of the fifth class until his death, just after Calvin's, on 8 September 1564. He was not a theoretician, even though the Reformer listened to his wisdom in teaching. He was a teacher. He knew pupils at first hand, talked with them and wrote for them *Les colloques*, a marvellous manual of Latin conversation, sparkling with real life.

School life had the flavour of a theatre in which the college student learned the accustomed vocabulary in relation to the principal actors in his familiar world: the Regent, who brought words to life and clarified them, going from the perceptible to the invisible, from the superficial to the profound; the more distant Principal, whom he learned to listen to attentively; the General Assistant, who was soon to be crushed under too heavy a burden; and the famous *observatores*, trusted senior scholars without whose supervision, in enormous classes of one or two hundred students, the school could not have been run.

This extended education was built on the most solid foundation. It recognized no divorce between the pedagogical content of a gradual mastery of fine Latin and the spiritual objective. Mankind is the creation of God. Men and women have received in trust the garden of Earth, which they have filled with children and for whose cultivation and preservation they are responsible. They must keep it intact, cherish it, develop its multiple potentialities, including their own. So they are by definition educators. They have to be teachers.

Mathurin Cordier was conscious of all that. Although he discerned brilliantly the particular psychology of education, and at the same time developed freely yet skilfully a sense of nuance in language, he was not confined by the syllabus. He opened windows on to the world for the students, introducing family relationships, civic affairs, the experiences of a merchant or a doctor, of an artisan or a wine-grower, a member of the Council among his peers, a traveller returned from Italy or a Protestant émigré about to leave for England where religious peace had at last been established. Thus the school learnt of current affairs. Nor was spiritual life neglected, for he taught the good news of salvation in Christ, and prayer, which together with love is the best means of combating ignorance (*Colloque* 66). Pupils were also welcome at their teacher's house. They shared his table and his conversation; they boasted of the quality of both, which made trustworthy publicity for the boarding establishment Cordier himself ran. Moreover, there one could see the man in his family setting, no longer as a schoolmaster but as a father in the midst of his children.

Erasmus (1469–1536) may be considered the great inspiration of the pedagogues of the 16th century because of his criticism of medieval scholasticism and his own erudite writings. Precursor, guide and model, he dominated the cultural life of his own time and succeeding generations.

Portrait of Erasmus of Rotterdam, copper engraving by Albrecht Dürer, 1526. Musée du Petit Palais, Avignon.

A more functional structure for schools

That masterpiece of Calvinist pedagogy was re-edited hundreds of times well into the nineteenth century in many languages – even, with some modifications, by the Catholics. It shows that Cordier was simultaneously a humanist, a grammarian and a Christian. He took part in the dynamism of Reform – indeed he incarnated it – but he associated himself, in Geneva and elsewhere, with a new system which gave education its modern shape.

The Middle Ages had had no such organization. At that time pupils of all ages used to gather round a master so that they might absorb his knowledge as best they

could. The first development came from the Brethren of the Common Life, founded in 1381 by the Dutch mystic Geert Groot, called Gerard the Great, to come together in a life of spiritual renewal – the *devotio moderna*. Their establishments were at first proponents of traditional scholasticism, but gradually they were influenced by humanism and became more effective. They divided their pupils into classes according to the level of their knowledge so that each might have his appropriate place and all might progress to their goal. The system was adopted one after the other by Liège and Sélestat, by Louvain in its trilingual college of Latin, Greek and Hebrew, by Bordeaux where Mathurin Cordier taught and by Strasburg where Calvin appeared in due course.

Johannes Sturm became Rector of the Strasburg school on 24 June 1538 and presided over the change. He had been a scholar at Liège since 1521 and had seen the new model flourish there. He made eight classes with two hundred boys in each: the first taught reading, writing and Latin declension, the second and third perfected grammar, the fourth added Greek, the fifth rhetoric and dialectic, the sixth the imitation of classical texts, the seventh, which had special masters, studied Aristotle, Plato and Euclidean mathematics while the eighth grappled with theology. The passage from one class to the next depended on examinations while promotions were celebrated by the award of prizes to the two best pupils in each grade.

Calvin helped to get this system under way during his stay in Rhenish Strasburg. One might even say that he collaborated in it. For at the same time as he was Pastor of the French church, he was also the teacher of exegesis at the Academy *(schola publica)* whose five-year course was conducted under the same roof as the nine-year education of the College *(schola privata)*. On the advice of Mathurin Cordier he inspired in the organization and spirit of the teaching at Geneva the *pietas litterata* of Erasmus – to live well, think well and speak well – which he had seen practised at Strasburg and which Lausanne commended in its *Leges scholae Lausanniensis* of 23 August 1547 and then put into intensive practice.

The Reformer could rely on scholarly knowledge in the Genevan community for that had greatly increased before the middle of the fifteenth century after the foundation in 1428 of a municipal Latin school, the Collège de Versonay, as a result of a decision by the General Council. This conception of public instruction may owe something to business relations with Italy, for in some Italian cities there was concern for public education. Echoes of the pedagogical innovations of Pier Paolo Vergerio or Guarino of Verona were heard north of the Alps. Vittorino de Filtre taught in his Mantuan *Casa giacose* through play, and made no differentiation between rich and poor, lord and vassal, boy and girl. Luther, as we have seen, held almost the same liberal views. But members of the fair sex were to be banished from colleges for a long time yet. They were to have their own little day schools and boarding schools, but in general had to content themselves with domestic education fit for the home, not for public life.

Calvin's humanism and methods were subject to the Gospel and thus kept at arm's length everything that concerned the ancient pagan cults. But in the republic of Geneva he found an attitude favourable to his concerns, for the city had long recognized its need and gave his pedagogical vision a clear field with none of the obstructions he had experienced hitherto. He reorganized the Strasburg model and limited it to a college with seven classes. Yet when the seventh class for the youngest pupils had an enrolment of 280 boys, he had to establish an eighth. A further ninth class, called 'reading', was begun in 1579. The establishment of the school in a new building on the airy heights of St Antoine began a new era. Up until then the Academy at Lausanne had been 'the unique and brilliant locus of reformed study for central Europe', but when it lost Viret, Cordier and de Beza (Rector of the institution Calvin founded), it began to decline. Geneva on the other hand was now the Protestant Rome with 2,000 pupils. The fame of the city spread so that students came to it from all over Europe.

The studies were arduous. Calvin desired neither diffuse study nor the overburdening of the student, but a balance based on the essential of Holy Scripture 'written in our hearts by the finger of the living God'. The students, who were equally afire with faith, submitted to the disciplined life drawn up for them: fifty-four hours a week attendance at lessons, sermons and catechetical studies beginning at 6 a.m. in the summer, 7 a.m. in the winter; only three weeks' holiday a year, at the wine harvest; a comfortless plank to sit on and another to write on; braziers for heating and no windows to begin with (they made some with paper as a stop-gap).

Yet all this conformed *grosso modo* to what was customary at the time. The most important consideration was the conviction with which it all functioned. The Reformer wished the master to be beloved by his pupils as he directed them to the joyful accomplishment of each daily task. Moreover, students of the *schola publica*

Under the direction of Sebastian Castellion, appointed by Calvin in 1541, the Collège de Genève became one of the great university centres in Europe on account of its adoption of humanist principles. It trained original Reformers from every country and served as a model for Heidelberg, Scotland and Holland.

The Collège de Genève, copper engraving by Pierre Escuyer, 1822. Bibliothèque Publique et Universitaire, Geneva.

were treated as citizens and so had no hesitation in taking up spades to work at the city's fortifications. They felt themselves to be part of the community.

Education for all

After the Reformation the development of educational institutions varied in different regions. In the French Protestant academies as in Geneva, which in turn inspired Scotland, Holland and Heidelberg, the study of Greek and Hebrew biblical texts flourished. But the important place given to logic encouraged the dominance of scholasticism, and during the seventeenth century a rigid dogmatism paralysed development. In the eighteenth century, therefore, the schools had great difficulty in adapting, even when *aggiornamento* was visibly necessary since inductive scientific thought had come on the scene and the glory of an academy rested on its galaxy of savants. Projects for the reform of the colleges frequently miscarried.

Catholic institutions, principally under the aegis of the Jesuits, were bent on rapidly equalling the Protestant foundations which had preceded and inspired them. With strictly supervised educational discipline, they succeeded wonderfully in serving the absolutism of the great monarchies. But with a mystical piety overflowing with images, and a glory contemplated by means of the beauties of ancient literature, their world for the most part remained unchanged, even though they welcomed mathematical study more readily than many Protestant colleges.

Some advances were made. In the German regions where Luther had already encouraged public schools to include the study of nature and arithmetic Wolfgang Radtke (1571–1635) proposed a twenty-five point programme with wisdom reminiscent of Cordier. Above all Jan Amos Comenius (1592–1670), having experienced the agony of Bohemia ravaged by the Thirty Years War, proposed the ideal of peace through education, recommended it as a roving ambassador for the Bohemian Brethren and adhered to the idea to his dying day. In his *Orbis pictus* pictures were used for the first time as a means of teaching, for he insisted that the word and the thing must be connected. Moreover his school was on an open site surrounded by a garden, and his programme reserved the morning for the study of difficult subjects and allotted singing, drawing and physical exercise to the afternoon. This was a foretaste, just as the eighteenth century dawned, of August Hermann Francke at Halle, of the Brothers of Jean-Baptiste de la Salle with their Christian schools in France, and of the nonconformists with their dissenting academies in England. All of these later establishments directed the student's attention to things, to experiences, to the observation of life and to economics. To a certain extent they included the largely-forgotten Czech pedagogy in their ambitious programme for a 'universal system teaching everything to everyone' in 'workshops of humanity' which schools had to become. Already the educational totality of Pestalozzi was on the horizon.

In every country the Reformation had pushed the educator into the limelight in its desire for literacy and instruction for all. Therefore by the end of the seventeenth century the north of Europe was better educated than the south, quite the reverse of the Middle Ages. Even in thinly populated areas like Lutheran Scandinavia or Presbyterian Scotland, the desire to give everyone the chance to read the Bible led to a significant increase in the number of readers and often of writers. Equally illuminating in that regard was the cultural, and hence economic, advance in the Protestant Swiss cantons.

The more dynamic evolution of Protestant countries was of course sometimes restrained by war, the decline of trade or the refusal to spend too much on the schools. Fortunately there were also factors which accelerated its progress. Life-expectancy increased by ten years in the eighteenth century and this made literacy much more economically attractive. Since Catholic education became less élitist it was caught up into this change as well. So a victory over mortality played its part, aided by Reformed preaching on the subjection of nature by regenerate man under God. The Reformation upheld the dignity of created men and women, affirmed their potential and respected their particular identity. Hence there was a desire to give every language group, however small, the Word of God in its own tongue. A humble but significant example is Jachiam Bifrun, a notary of Samedan and a disciple of Zwingli, who translated the New Testament into Engadine Romansh (thereby fixing its idiom) and published it at his own expense in 1560.

The Czech humanist Jan Amos Comenius (1592–1670) was a pioneer in modern pedagogical methods. He encouraged the use of pictures in teaching and a good distribution of subjects during the day's work. He recommended the teaching of economics, history, the arts and manual disciplines, and put into practice a new method of learning languages.

Title page of *Orbis sensualium pictus* by Jan Amos Comenius, 1658. Bibliothèque Nationale, Paris.

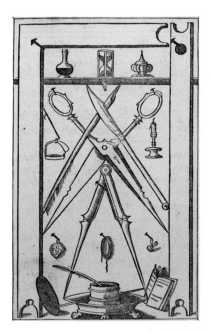

This engraving shows all the different tools needed for the task of writing: an ink bottle, a knife, a sander, a candle, pens, compasses and scissors.

Frontispiece from *Vera arte de lo excellente scrivere . . .* by G. Tagliente, 1524. Bibliothèque Nationale, Paris.

The Council of Trent and Catholic Reformation

Contrary to what has often been said, the Council of Trent did not simply represent a definitive reaction against the Protestant Reformation. In the first place the reforming movement had appeared within the Church long before Luther's revolt. Moreover the Council was not concerned merely with repressive legislation for it attacked the root causes of the religious crisis by combatting abuses, developing instruction for the faithful and seeking to find again an authentic faith.

The origins of Catholic Reform

Catholic Reform did not come into being with a sharp polemical intention at the Council of Trent. It already had a long history whose roots lie in the changing times of the fourteenth century among the Brethren of the Common Life, and the great mystics like Catherine of Siena, Meister Eckhart, Suso, Tauler and Ruysbroek, and among the first adherents of the *devotio moderna*. The spiritual restlessness tinged with subjectivism which characterized these pioneers developed by the next century into more ambitious projects of Reform which aimed at strict knowledge of the sacred text, ecclesiology, pastoral education and proselytizing mission.

Not surprisingly, the movement began in Spain, for after five hundred years of crusade the *Reconquista* of Spain from the Moors came to an end. Opposite Granada, the last Muslim bastion, Queen Isabella built the city of Santa Fé to show to the world that the issue was not only territorial gain but the faith itself. When Granada fell in 1492 Cardinal Mendoza, the Primate of Spain, went in person to occupy the Alhambra. He planted on the walls of the citadel a standard recently presented by Pope Sixtus V, the very standard which had flown in front of the victorious troops, as a way of showing the whole world that the Cross had triumphed over the crescent.

Although defeated, Islam remained a menacing presence for Christians in Africa, Asia and even in Europe because of the Danube and Balkan territories. This aspect of the end of the Middle Ages led to a desire for Christian ecumenicity. A Messianic restlessness ran through eastern European society and showed in the preaching of Savonarola. What modern historians call rather vaguely the 'Pre-Reformation' included the aspiration to Christian universalism, the removal of barriers between people and a response to the gospel desire for reunion 'into one flock'. This mystical dream flourished in Spanish universities influenced by Franciscan ideals. But how was the dream to be realized? Islam remained the enemy to be defeated by the spiritual forces of the crusades, for the Middle Ages readily saw religious geography in the form of a diptych (an inheritance from the thought of St Augustine but translated into geographical terms): on one side was Christ's Kingdom, spiritually unified by the Church; on the other the kingdom of the Antichrist, the Mussulman, the eternal enemy.

In this great duel Spain seemed called to a providential mission on account of her geographical position and long historical tradition. A simple and effective way to give Islam the *coup de grâce* was to take it from behind by making an alliance with the 'Empire of the Indies', reputedly Christian or at least favourable to Christianity. On these ambitious but vague foundations the project of 'the last crusade' was built, an Atlantic crusade which would defeat the infidel and establish Christian universalism. The dream was realized in the voyages of Columbus — not, certainly, in joining

In the first half of the 16th century European political history was not concerned only with the rivalry between Francis I and Charles V, just as religious history is not exhausted by the confrontation between Catholics and Protestants. Islam was a third contender for land and belief. The Ottoman Sultan Suleiman the Magnificent (1494–1566) was its most powerful representative; he allowed the Reformation to expand in Hungary.

Portrait of Suleiman the Magnificent, drawing by Albrecht Dürer, early 16th century. Musée Bonnat, Bayonne.

forces with the 'Empire of the Indies', but in reaching a new continent. The importance of this discovery was not only spatial: it was a turning-point for religion and philosophy as well. The principles of knowledge, established centuries earlier on the rules of Aristotle and expressed in scholastic philosophy, were shaken to their foundation. More positively, an unlimited field opened up for mission. The precept 'teach all nations' took on a new resonance, and led at the same time to a number of new tasks, for missionaries had to be prepared, traditional pastoral care had to be adapted and books had to be written.

Spain undertook this programme and was able to find the man to put it into practice – Ximenes de Cisneros, a priest of exceptional intellectual and spiritual quality. He was born in 1436, became first a secular priest and then joined the Franciscans when he was fifty. He came late to public life in 1492, becoming, in succession, confessor to Isabella, Archbishop of Toledo, Cardinal, and twice Regent of Castille – on the death of Isabella in 1504, then on the death of Ferdinand in 1516. Combining his administrative and political career with the achievement of a profound transformation of the spiritual life of his country, de Cisneros reformed the secular priests and monastic orders, and devoted himself especially to the dissemination of culture and teaching. He realized that the triumph of a Church whose mission was taking on global dimensions would occur not through local proselytizing, but through the development and transmission of knowledge brought by the formation and enrichment of the spirit. Out of that understanding came the foundation of the University of Alcalá, eight leagues from Madrid, a university completely new in its conception and completion. It was given over entirely to theological disciplines, drawing together Thomism, Scotism and Occamism in its teaching. Even humanism was not absent, for in 1516, de Cisneros invited Erasmus to share in the work towards an authentic text of the sacred books. A strong mystical

Six hundred copies of the *Complutensian Polyglot Bible* were published (1515–17) at the expense of Cardinal Francisco Ximenez de Cisneros, founder of the University of Alcalá. The last of its six volumes contains a Hebrew and Chaldean dictionary. This admirable work marks the zenith of humanism in Spain.

A page from the *Polyglot Bible* with the text in Hebrew, Latin and Greek; Henarès, Alcalá. Bibliothèque Nationale, Paris.

current flowed in this Christian humanism. There was interest too in authors of antiquity such as Plato, Aristotle, Cicero or Seneca, but their writings were held to be stages on the way to Christ and stimuli for the inner life.

Rigorous and avant-garde techniques supported this spiritual *élan*. Alcalá possessed a printing press where between 1515 and 1517 the celebrated *Polyglot Bible* was put together in six volumes with Hebrew, Latin and Greek texts accompanied by an imposing critical apparatus. It was published again at Antwerp at the end of the century under the title *Biblia Regia*. These learned preoccupations did not keep de Cisneros from his characteristically Franciscan concern to create a strong Christian culture for his people. In 1512 he had the gospels, the epistles and several books of the Fathers translated into Castillian; he also published one of the first catechisms in the east. He wished pastoral provision to be methodical, and so made enquiries and compiled statistics on sacramental practice. Thus he takes his place among the pioneers of religious sociology.

In this way the beginnings of Catholic Reformation were marked by a revolution in scientific study. More modest initiatives on the Spanish model appeared in several eastern dioceses such as Meaux, Toul and Verona, and so it became possible to envisage the progress of this kind of reform by stages throughout Christendom. But in 1517, the very year of de Cisneros' death, Martin Luther's summons challenged the world. Thereafter it appeared that the given contents of the faith, Christian relationship with the world, the authority of the *magisterium* and catachetical instruction all had to be redefined. Urgency was imparted to these tasks by the development of printing, which led to the exact and rigorous expression of all thought, religious or profane. Only an ecumenical council could succeed in such an immense task. The idea was attractive and won the approval of all ecclesiastical and political authorities.

This being so, why did the Papacy hesitate before so welcome a solution? The reason was that although the idea of a council was approved by everyone, it was not understood in the same way by all. Luther had been appealing for a 'legitimate and free' council since 1518, after his interrogation at Wittenberg. But he wished to include not only bishops but also priests and simple lay folk in the deliberative process. The Emperor Charles V saw in the ecumenical assembly the means of bringing the German world back into spiritual unity. And again some princes, and the King of France in particular, wished to grasp this unhoped-for opportunity ·to insinuate themselves into ultramontane politics. The Holy See itself, haunted by the memory of theses propounded in Constance and Basle in the preceding century, feared the return of past follies. Every precipitate solution had to be avoided so that this should be a 'council of reform' and not a 'council of crisis'. Therefore, after

During the pontificate of Paul III (Alessandro Farnese, Pope from 1534 to 1549), the Council of Trent was prepared and convened. It met from 1545 to 1549, in 1551–2 and in 1552–3. It represented an essential stage in the organization of the Roman Catholic Church into a counter-offensive to the striking success of the Reformation in the three preceding decades.

The Council of Trent, painting from the school of Titian, 16th century. Musée du Louvre, Paris.

Pope Paul and his nephews, painting by Titian, 16th century. Museo e Gallerie Nazionali di Capodimonte, Naples.

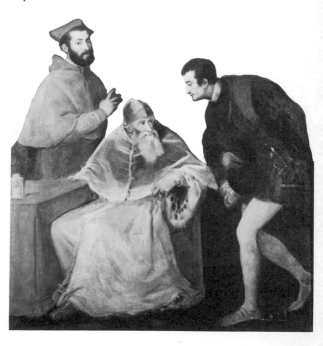

twenty years of calculated delay, a bull of Pope Paul III on 22 May 1542 proclaimed the convocation of the ecumenical council at Trent.

The work of the Council

The choice of the town of Trent seemed at first surprising, but it fulfilled geographical considerations and political imperatives. Trent occupied a favourable position in the Adige valley on the way to the Brenner Pass – at that time the most frequented route through the Alps for north–south traffic. It was therefore well placed to create easy relations between the Italian peninsula and the German world. Moreover the population was Italian and it was governed by its bishop, but it was at the same time part of the Empire and so served both the wish of the Pope to hold the Council in an Italian town, and the desire of the Emperor to hold it 'on German territory'.

The first session opened in 1545 and the last closed in 1563. But between these dates interruptions multiplied. A ten-year intermission from 1552–62 paralysed its work almost totally. Its chaotic state reflected the political divisions within Germany, and indeed in all Christendom. There was always equivocation about the aim of the Council's labours since Rome expected from them the definition of dogma and Charles V wanted Reform which could bring together Catholics and Protestants into a unified Church. The composition of the assembly also had a critical effect on the direction its debates took. In principle it was ecumenical, open without reserve to all Catholic bishops. But in fact it was a limited gathering, beginning with about sixty Church Fathers and culminating with 235 in the twenty-third session. Most were from countries bordering the Mediterranean – Italy, Spain, the Greek islands, France. Moreover the Council was dominated by the regular clergy since the Jesuits and the mendicant orders, particularly the Dominicans, took a pre-eminent part from the very beginning. Although these sociological and psychological features did not determine the nature of the Tridentine programme they did affect its 'style'. The national origins of the bishops explains the weight given to 'Mediterranean continuity' and the prominence of the regular clergy fostered the primacy of scholastic theology. The debates were full of tension and conflict. One of the most serious was between the 'Erasmians' on one side, represented by the legate Seripando, General of the Augustinians, who wanted to compromise with humanism and even with Lutheranism, and the 'rigorists' on the other, led by the Jesuits Lainez and Salmeron, who were anxious to maintain dogma in all its integrity. The latter were often victorious but the 'middle way' was never deliberately excluded. Since all

religious values were at issue the Fathers of Trent took on the crushing task of defining in its entirety the message of salvation and of making precise the mission of the Church in all its aspects.

Truth, the Council taught, comes from two sources: Scripture and 'tradition', by which they meant the orally transmitted teaching of Christ, the writings of the Fathers, the conciliary and pontifical magisterium and also the consensus of the universal Church inspired by the Holy Spirit. The existence of original sin and its transmission to Adam's descendants was reaffirmed, while baptism was held to cancel sin through the merit of Jesus Christ. This did not remove concupiscence, that natural appetite which must be strictly distinguished from sin and which, when victoriously mastered, offers a being the means of transcending itself to live a spiritual life. Since free will was not destroyed the Christian could progress on the way of justification by the constant co-operation of his own will with divine grace. The Council particularized the stages of this progress: first the birth of faith, then adherence to the message of the Church, consciousness of sin and the desire 'to put off the old man and put on the new'. This progression to an ideal of sanctity implied not only faith, but also the constant practice of good works and participation in the seven sacraments. Sacraments themselves were neither external rites inherited from ancient law nor simple spiritual stimuli. Rather they were 'efficacious signs' conferring grace on whomever received them with the right disposition.

A pre-eminent place among the sacraments was given to the Eucharist and in 1551, in the course of the thirteenth session, the Council proclaimed the reality of transubstantiation. The mass was also a mystical feast which re-presented, really though bloodlessly, the sacrifice of the Cross (twenty-second session, September 1562). The most serious difficulties with the Reformed Churches were to rise from that point of doctrine. The theology of the mass as sacrifice justified the sacrament of Holy Orders, for beyond 'universal priesthood' there was 'ministerial priesthood' consequent upon divine ordination for bishops, priests and lower ranks of clergy, and that gave the Church its strictly hierarchical structure. On 15 December 1563, its closing meeting, the assembly solemnly reaffirmed the existence of purgatory and the value of intercessory prayer addressed to the Virgin and the saints.

These were the main areas of Tridentine concern. Never in the history of the Church had a council promulgated so complete a collection of doctrinal definitions, together with disciplinary and pastoral canons. Yet Trent marked neither novelty nor rupture in the strict sense of these words. Many of its propositions on the priesthood, the sacraments, the relationship between spiritual and temporal authorities and on ecclesiology had been formulated earlier explicitly or implicitly by other provincial or general councils. But since its decrees were often arrived at in a polemical atmosphere they were expressed in strict formulae, with negative wording expressing an austere and almost abrupt legalism more apt for condemnation than dialogue. They offer little ecumenicity, at least not an ecumenicity of give and take.

The Council of Trent accorded a pre-eminent place to the Eucharist, affirming against Reformed doctrine that the Mass is not only a mystical meal, but a real repetition of the sacrifice of the Cross.

The Mass of the League, 16th-century painting. Musée des Beaux-Arts, Rouen.

Moreover the development of printing led to the definition of dogma in precise canons. The Tridentine assembly was contemporaneous with the development of the book and adapted itself to the imperatives of this new means of knowledge, expression and the dissemination of thought.

The Council can be seen as both within and outside the movement of history. Its origin, composition and entire programme were devoted to permanence rather than evolution, which gave it an air of timelessness. But it was also truly historical, sharing in the drama lived through by its contemporaries and having to give a positive answer to the anguish over individual salvation so vividly felt by Luther, and exacerbated by the loss of medieval cosmogonies. The Tridentine assembly ruled out all condemnation of the impulses of the heart by affirming the autonomy of the inner will, free in spite of original sin, and proclaiming that ideas, sentiments, indeed passions, could and indeed should be put to use for the common good and for progress. That principle is the origin of the dynamism which created the modern world and explains the apostolic and missionary zeal which multiplied the Church's works.

The Council of Trent did not give birth to Catholic Reform, but it co-ordinated its elements and gave direction to its vital energies. It produced both institutional structures and precise doctrinal rules, and purified pastoral practice by endeavouring to disengage the spiritual from the stranglehold of the temporal.

The struggle to reform abuses

The most urgent task, in the eyes of the faithful, was to remedy the situation in respect of abuses which tarnished the Church, and in fact nothing was excluded from the renewal. The most radical reforms were in Rome, the work of the pontiffs contemporary with or immediately succeeding the Council – Paul III, Paul IV, Pius IV, Pius V, Gregory XIII, Sixtus V. The sacred college was reorganized and in 1586 Sixtus V fixed the complement of cardinals at sixty-six, a number full of biblical symbolism, which remained unchanged until the pontificate of John XXIII. Intellectual life flourished since numerous colleges or universities disseminated high Catholic teaching. The most important of these was the Roman college which, through Gregory XIII, became the Gregorian University, a seminary open to all nations. Even the city changed its appearance. Renaissance Rome, with its permissive morality and its superfluity of *joie de vivre*, gave way to an austere city – almost a cloister, as a Venetian ambassador remarked – where public immorality and even simple lapses of language were banned with severity.

The reforming work of the Popes aroused admiration and gratitude among the faithful of every nation. That 'devotion' to the Holy See contributed to the strengthening of pontifical rule. In the following decades, at the end of the sixteenth and beginning of the seventeenth centuries Rome saw transformations in its monumental scenery and in its very soul. Absolute mistress of Tridentine orthodoxy, sure of its truth, capital of the world and a magnet for artists from every country, Rome saw rise up in a few decades a serried forest of domes for pontifical, parish, monastic or conventual churches, draping the slopes of the celebrated hills with sumptuous baroque ornament.

By degrees the spirit of reform spread from Rome throughout Catholic Christendom. The Council had defined clearly the bishops' role and the nature of their power. In the course of the debates two conceptions had been put forward. Were bishops, as most of the Italians believed, mere 'lieutenants' of the Pope with delegated authority? Or as successors of the Apostles, could they apply the power of their order directly? The latter conception was successfully defended, in particular by the Cardinal of Lorraine, the Archbishop of Rheims and Nicholas Psaume, Bishop of Verdun. The decision, taken during the twenty-third and twenty-fourth sessions, was one of the most important of the Council, for not only did it confirm bishops in their role of doctors of the faith, it also removed the danger of excessive pontifical centralization, creating a welcome balance between the Holy See and the local churches.

Nevertheless the Reform of the body of bishops was slow and incomplete, making real progress only after 1640. It encountered grave obstacles inherent in the very nature of a bishop's function, which was not only spiritual but also political, social and economic. A bishop administered Church property, set up charitable works, concerned himself with schools, hospitals and courts of justice. Collaboration with temporal power was sometimes extensive: in Germany the prince-bishops governed extensive territories like great lords. In many countries the papacy had yielded to kings the nomination of bishops through a series of concordats, the most famous being the

The selling of 'Indulgences', which played a part in the Reformation's origin, served, among other purposes, to finance the building of St Peter's in Rome. Far from returning to the simplicity of the Gospel, the Counter-Reformation employed all the splendours of baroque architecture to win people back. All kinds of artistic talents were expected to make a contribution after Michelangelo's example.

The original model of the Cupola of St Peter's made by Michelangelo. Vatican City.

1

Concordat of Bologna concluded in 1516 between Pope Leo X and Francis I of France. Monarchies also came to regard high ecclesiastical benefices as so many 'pension funds' at their disposal, and such a regime tended to perpetuate abuses. In 1596, thirty years after the end of the Council, about forty French bishoprics were still in the hands of the laity. One of the most scandalous cases concerned Henri de Bourbon-Verneuil, bastard son of Henry IV, who became Bishop of Metz at six years old and retained his diocese for forty years (1612–52) before being laicized and taking a wife.

The remedy for such evils came from the work of great prelates like Charles Borromeo, Secretary of State to his uncle Pius IV, then Archbishop of Milan for twenty years (1564–84). It has justly been said of him that he 'refashioned the episcopate in Europe' and that his Milanese curia was a veritable 'seminary for bishops'. Such examples, together with a spirit of reform, led to stricter requirements. The choice of bishops was not to be made on political grounds alone, but was to include churchmen of unassailable spiritual integrity – men like Cardinal Perron under Henry V, Bérulle and Père de Condren under Louis XIII, St Vincent de Paul in the regency of Anne of Austria. In every country bishops appeared who were notable for their learning or their sanctity, such as the Cardinals Bellarmine and Seripando in Italy, Stanislaus Hosius in Poland, Alain de Solminihac, François de Sales and Nicholas de Pavillon in France. A deepening of theological learning in the episcopate became evident as the new methods of choosing men took hold. Thus the Archbishop of Braga, Barthélemy des Martyrs, published his *Stimulus Pastorum* just after the Council of Trent. In it he taught the art of attaining pastoral wisdom through harmonious balance in contemplation, prayer and action. More immediately practical were the letters addressed by St Vincent de Paul to bishops and candidates for the episcopate, which constitute an inexhaustibly rich anthology of concrete directives on the setting up of charitable works, the organization of missions and the teaching of catachesis. In spite of slow progress, the seventeenth century marked the transition from the prelate as *grand seigneur* to the bishop as spiritual head.

Evils were to be found among parish clergy, but it was much easier to remedy them there. Some of the disorders were moral or disciplinary, like drunkenness, concubinage and usury, which had been allowed to flourish in the lengthy state of war. But intellectual bankruptcy was also common, for many priests were unable to read the missal with ease, knew no Latin and dispensed the sacraments with absolute whim. Rare indeed were priests who possessed a library. A few owned three or four books such as manuals of ethics, the catechism, a collection of sermons – that is, works which were of immediate use. A few had benefited from a university education, but most had no intellectual discipline at all. They were initiated into ecclesiastical knowledge by a parish priest who agreed to lodge them in return for small services.

Such abuses were ameliorated, and sometimes disappeared totally, with the institution of seminaries which had been decided on by the Fathers of Trent in the twenty-third session, July 1563. In countries like Italy, which had clearly remained faithful to Catholicism, seminaries appeared almost immediately after the Council. Elsewhere the movement was held up by religious wars, or by the reluctance of governments to put into practice the Tridentine decrees. France made a slow start and the great wave of seminary foundation did not develop until after 1620. The education they offered was at first very brief – only a few weeks in the *Maison de St Lazare* created by St Vincent de Paul – but it was steadily lengthened to anything from three to five years at the diocese's discretion.

The seminaries were establishments of advanced theological learning where sometimes contradictory systems ('Jansenist' and 'Molinist') clashed. But they were also – often especially – centres of spiritual formation. Every effort was made to inspire them with 'ecclesiastical spirit', a moral attitude which brings a Christian point of view to bear on everything. Several disciplines were involved in bringing this about, particularly a thorough examination of vocation. The idea of vocation was one of the most original religious contributions of the seventeenth century. In medieval Christendom it was not expected of future clerics to distinguish themselves through any particular sign. St Thomas Aquinas, for example, expected only a true dignity of life and the knowledge necessary for their function. Everything was geared to the needs of a church rather than to an individual's future course. That aspect of the clerical state did not entirely disappear, for entry into holy orders was still tied to the acquisition of a benefice. But from that time on more consideration was given to the positive nature of vocation. Four characteristics were generally agreed: purity of life, detachment from the world, steady inclination towards the 'ecclesiastical state', and capability for fulfilling sacerdotal functions. The state of the parish clergy was radically transformed by the application of these criteria which were described and

2

analysed in several treatises, such as Antoine Godeau's *Discourse on ecclesiastical vocation* published in 1651.

In this way the social and spiritual type of 'good priest' came into being. A 'mediator' *par excellence*, his mission was to spread grace through word and sacrament and to help each Christian to attain holiness. The 'good priest' was not merely a theoretical ideal, but was incarnate in every detail of a priest's life. The pastor was distinguished from the laity by external marks such as the cassock, abstinence from all unsuitable activity (business, hunting, gaming or drinking, for example), being moderate in speech and quietly virtuous. His piety showed in the slow, solemn, edifying way in which he celebrated the offices and in his faithfulness with daily mass. His flock was the object of his constant care. He dispensed the sacraments regularly, visited the sick night and day, taught doctrine ceaselessly through preaching and the catechism – but with no subjective interpretation, for everything conformed to the strict orthodoxy defined at the Council of Trent. The 'good priest' embodied the spiritual definition given by Bérulle: 'In the order established by God, there are two kinds of people: those who receive and those who communicate the spirit, light and grace of Jesus. The first are the faithful and the second are priests.'

Pastoral education

The Church's plan for Reform highlighted the importance of teaching. In the Middle Ages faith had been imparted through word, ritual and image. Stained glass windows had an important place in the formation of a corporate religious spirit. These avenues did not disappear but other, more didactic means tended to take their place from then on. First the Protestant Reformation, and then the Council of Trent, gave the Bible, the repository of sacred texts, an essential place in catechesis.

The most thorough knowledge of the Bible was attained and diffused by great intellectual centres like the universities and Benedictine abbeys, especially the famous abbey of *St-Germain-des-Prés*. There the bases of historical criticism were laid down and a positive theology was established, which sought the content of revelation through the scientific investigation of sacred texts rather than through deductive reasoning. But these techniques were confined to a small circle of *savants*, for the most part members of religious orders. The message of salvation came to the Christian masses by more accessible routes such as the catechism, school or mission.

From the beginning of the Reformation, Catholics and Protestants alike had made a point of teaching young children definite and sound doctrine. The first catechisms in the form of handbooks appeared almost simultaneously in Spain and in the German states. Luther's catechism, remarkable for its pedagogical rigour, had some influence in the Catholic world. Erasmus, Ignatius de Loyola and some bishops followed his example. But the great movement began when the Council of Trent enjoined the teaching of the faithful in their own languages. To that end a commission, directed by Charles Borromeo, composed a *Roman catechism*, published

The most effective instrument of the Counter-Reformation was the Society of Jesus. Founded in 1540 by Ignatius de Loyola, its members were as ready to preach in Protestant regions as in distant pagan lands. But men like François de Sales (1567–1622) were also involved in winning back lost ground, for this future saint and Doctor of the Church devoted himself as Bishop of Geneva to the struggle against Calvinism by proposing a different way of faith.

1. *Jesuits celebrating the centenary of their congregation in the church of Gesú*, painting by Andrea Sacchi, *c.* 1640. Palazzo Barberini, Rome.

2. *St François de Sales*, 17th-century painting. Church of St Louis-en-l'Ile, Paris.

3. *The Jesuit Father Thomas Conjer evangelizing in France*, late 17th-century engraving.

3

for the first time in 1566, which gave an exposition of Catholic faith as defined by the Council in analytic form, for the use of priests.

Catechisms multiplied towards the end of the sixteenth and especially in the seventeenth century. Although all were derived from the Tridentine model, they showed great variety in expression. Some were adapted to liturgical cycles, like the *Catechism for the schools in the diocese of Lyons* published in 1666 and divided into fifty-two lessons corresponding to the mystery celebrated each week, with iconographic illustration supplementing the text. Others, such as the *Catechism or digest of the Faith and Christian truths* (1687) by François de Harlay, Bishop of Paris, were almost entirely composed of the words of Scripture, the Fathers and the councils, and were thus part of the return to positive study. The catechism known as 'The Three Henries', published in 1676 by the bishops of Angers, Laval and La Rochelle, centred its whole programme on the question of salvation. It was conceived as a dialogue between God and the sinner, so that 'Christianity was presented not as a code of morals but as way to Christ's school' (L. Pérouas). The catechism represented the school of Christian life, conceived as the means of achieving holiness, and was the most effective instrument of Catholic Reform which acted simultaneously on works, doctrine and individual disposition. Because a printed text was involved rather than oral tradition, belief became consistently standardized and that led to 'Tridentine orthodoxy' as its popular dimension. Moreover, in making the priest a 'professor of religion' and a 'director of conscience', it gave religious approval to the spiritual dignity and social authority of the clergy.

The same aims were involved in the development of schools, which were not simply for practical purposes but rather reflected a new consciousness of the value of instruction in the regeneration of Christianity. This development also echoed the general spirit of the theology of St Augustine, Bishop of Hippo, which was congenial to the spirit of the seventeenth century. The bishop had envisioned the life of the world and of each individual as a constant conflict between concupiscence and grace. That dramatic tension was seen to affect every human being, but particularly the child, a feeble creature, a stranger to the laws of reason, particularly vulnerable to the attacks of evil, but who at the same time incarnated the transparent purity received through the grace of baptism. The child was an ambivalent being, powerless but innocent, who could realize the paradoxical mystery of Christian destiny in its fulness. Children, like the poor, were almost outside the social circle but at the same time they were the image of Jesus Christ. Thus the deep intentions of schooling were justified in a spiritual vision. The education of children became a vocation worthy of the concentration of all one's energy and life in its service.

For all these reasons there was a great growth in learning during the classical epoch of the seventeenth century. Parish priests, members of religious orders and special congregations made teaching their whole apostolate. Two churchmen played a decisive role in all this. Firstly Pierre Fourier (1565–1640) introduced the 'simultaneous method', which substituted for individual teaching the grouping of pupils at the same level, thus creating the 'class'. Secondly, Jean-Baptiste de la Salle (1651–1719) made this class principle systematic, drew up a progressive programme of learning and gave priority to the pupils' mother tongue.

As for the colleges, founded and inspired for the most part by Jesuits, they were distinguished by the quality of their teaching and the efficiency of their pedagogical methods. But their social function was even more important. They may not have *created* the bourgeoisie, but they certainly *developed* it, affirming its structures, shaping its culture and lifestyle. The colleges were, moreover, at the confluence of two cultural streams, Graeco-Latin thought and the message of the Gospel. That coexistence presented the Society of Jesus with a difficult problem. Should they welcome the pagan heritage so exalted by the Renaissance, or should they exclude it in the name of the purity of the faith? The Jesuits opted for the first solution. They presented classical wisdom as a stage in religious development and made room for what was called 'Christian humanism'. Such openness to the world, based on their belief in human nature, was to engage the Society in bitter, sometimes even violent confrontations with those who, like the Jansenists, systematically rejected pagan thought, believing that nature without grace must be corrupt. The function of the colleges, therefore, was less that of original intellectual creativity than the preparation of a sociological terrain, a place of confluence and confrontation for future ideological currents.

Catechesis entered Christian consciousness in other ways, particularly through preaching, mission and, above all, art. At all times art, which surpassed evasion or mere reverie, was understood as communication with the supernatural. Windows, tympani and frescos in churches were simultaneously homage to God and, for the

Just as education played a leading role in the Reformation, so it was given priority in the Counter-Reformation. One of the greatest Reformers of Catholic educational methods was Jean Baptiste de la Salle, founder of an institution of Brothers of Christian Schools, whose writing and practice encouraged teaching in French and by classes, rather than in Latin individually.

Portrait of St Jean Baptiste de la Salle, 17th-century painting. Chapel of the Brothers of Christian Schools, Paris.

faithful, a disclosure of Christ's message. Catholic Reform consecrated this tradition but also renewed its rules and its spirit, for in a time of controversy art had an apologetic aim, since it could express through iconography the work of the Council of Trent. Thus religious art became theology taught through pictures. In 1563, during the last session of the assembly, the following rule was formulated: 'The holy council forbids the placing in churches of any images inspired by erroneous dogma or which could mislead the simple. It desires that all impurity be avoided and that no provocative character be given to images.'

That principle was imposed in Rome where the Popes, at the end of the sixteenth and beginning of the seventeenth centuries, undertook a systematic purge of the liberties and excesses of sensuality enjoyed in the Renaissance. Excessive devotion was tempered by an attack on naked portraits and on all clumsy, vulgar representations which were objects of derision. In 1654, in the church of Bailleau-sous-Gallardon in the diocese of Chartres, the Dean of Épernon had an equestrian statue of St Martin removed: he thought it indecent that at the moment of elevation the priest had to present the host for the adoration of the faithful between the legs and under the croup of the horse! Rearrangements of this kind were not exceptional. They arose not merely from intellectual refinement but from the implementation of the fundamental principle of Catholic Reform, formulated by Le Brun, that pious iconography cannot elevate the soul except by banishing distraction and sensuality.

Thereafter new or renewed beauty radiated out through the Church, all of it with a didactc intention manifest in every motif and ornament, particularly and most fully in the reredos, which could be constructed like a vast reliquary or sometimes like a triumphal arch, but the function of which was always to reinforce the solemnity of the rites. Its aim however, like that of church windows, was to instruct. Its iconography conformed scrupulously to the Tridentine canons, bringing to mind the content of dogmatic treatises and catechisms. Thus the reredos was the instrument of the apostolate and a guide for moral life which connected the faithful with the glory of heaven without neglecting earthly conditions, especially through the place given to the patron saints of the trades, in particular to St Joseph, the protector of the infant Jesus and the model of a perfect artisan. Moreover, *all* families were honoured through the images of the Holy Family.

Through its didactic content, the art of the Catholic Reformation was often polemical in the spirit of the 'Counter Reformation' and a response to Protestant affirmations. In opposition to the austerity of the Protestant temple, the Roman Church developed splendid colours and majestic forms, themes of which exalted the very doctrines the Protestants contested. Many works were therefore devoted to the Marian cult, such as *The Virgin Triumphing over Protestantism* by Dominiquin in the chapel of St Januarius in Naples, or *The Immaculate Conception* as painted by Ribera,

The Counter-Reformation used a language of images which was accessible to all. On the left of this picture, the port of salvation, guarded by a tower crowned with angel-musicians, is ready to receive a large vessel whose sails are filled by the breath of the Holy Spirit. On board are all the founders of religious orders including St Francis, St Bruno, St Dominic, St Benedict, St Anthony, St Augustine and St Ignatius de Loyola, the central figure of the whole composition.

Typus religionis, painting from the late 17th century. Archives Nationales, Paris.

The art of the Counter-Reformation united didactic, even polemical intentions with a deeply sincere quest for renewed spirituality. Marian piety and the greatness of sacrifice were among the favourite themes of Georges de la Tour.

The Virgin triumphing over Protestantism, painting by Dominiquin, *c.* 1637. Chapel of St Januarius, the Cathedral, Naples.

The Nativity, painting by Georges de la Tour, first half of the 17th century. Musée de Rennes.

St Sebastian by torchlight, painting by Georges de la Tour, first half of the 17th century. Staatsmuseum, Berlin.

Montanès or Murillo. The Protestant denial of purgatory was itself denied in Rubens' *Judas Maccabeus*, le Guerchin's *St Gregory* and Philippe de Champaigne's *Souls in purgatory* among many others. Yet beyond this polemical and apologetic stance iconography witnessed to a search for Christ through the most important moments of his life, a search which was shared by the foremost spiritual leaders of the time, especially in the French school. Often the infancy of Jesus was conceived as a meditation on incarnation and redemption. That spirit is present in the famous *Nativity* of Georges de la Tour (Rennes). Stark, reduced to three people – Jesus, Anne and Mary – the composition invites meditation. It excludes all distraction, drawing the observer in towards the mystery of the Redeemer.

The life of faith

The doctrinal or didactic catechism prepared the faithful in the Roman Church for a fervent and rigorously controlled life. The diffusion of humanism had distanced eastern European thought from the great scholastic constructions and increased its concern for psychological and moral depth. In the process devotion became individualized. An essential part of Christian life became the spiritual director who penetrated the most secret corners of the heart and guided meditation or prayer into personal forms. He decided on 'cases of conscience' and helped the faithful to adapt to a society in the process of change. These new developments affected both forms of prayer and moral conduct.

Liturgical prayer – the only kind in which the faithful of the Middle Ages had participated – far from disappearing, was actually renewed to accompany the beauty in which the sanctuary was adorned, and by the wish to make all ceremonies, especially the mass, even more solemn. But from this time on personal prayer was practised alongside the collective rite – not, strictly speaking, a novelty, since its ancestry went back to the *devotio moderna*, but now it surpassed the strict confines of monastic or scholarly centres to affect the whole body of the faithful. In distinction from liturgical prayer, private devotion took a free and personal turn. Yet the sense of proper order in the seventeenth century gave rise to numerous manuals of direction like the popular *Instructions and Christian prayers for all people* (1646) by Antoine Godeau, Bishop of Grasse. These collections generally reflected the thought of great spiritual leaders like François de Sales or Bérulle, or, later, Bossuet and Fénelon. The fundamental character of such prayer, at least at the beginning of the century, lay in its pastoral direction and its spirit of social awareness. Prayer was suited to each Christian according to his or her rank, profession or simple existence. Thus the *Instructions* of Antoine Godeau contain prayers for a merchant, a servant, a Minister of State, an ecclesiastic, a magistrate and 'fathers and mothers at the death of their only child'. The prayer of a Treasury Official illustrates in a moving and almost dramatic way how personal the supplication could be: 'Let me remember constantly that the money I handle is sacred since it is State finance . . . Let me remember that the preservation of the Kingdom is built on the blood of the people: and if I cannot staunch their wounds at least let me not ride roughshod over public calamity through scandalous expenditure. May I find banquets repugnant while so many people, like me redeemed by the blood of your Son, have no bread to eat . . . If I have already acquired wealth by illicit means, keep me conscious of that and give me courage to emululate Zaccheus in making restitution.'

In Catholic eyes, prayer did not constitute an end in itself. It achieved its true significance and full efficacy only by means of the grace conferred through the sacraments and the spiritual force of devotion. These devotions were founded largely on the ancient Christian cult of intercession. The saints were venerated in many ways, particularly for their protection of earthly goods and their healing of the sick. St Owen was reputed to cure deafness, St Martial blindness and St Maur epilepsy. The cult continued in its earliest form, but often took a more complex turn. St Sebastian was invoked against the plague, but that same saint, an officer in Diocletian's guard who became a Christian and was martyred for his faith, taught the greatness of conversion and the value of sacrifice. The famous engraving by Jacques Caillot carries that apologetic message, and it can be found again in *St Sebastian by torchlight*, the painting by Georges de la Tour. But there the meaning is rather different, more like the 'inner way' of Bérulle. It teaches the cost of self-denial and summons the Christian to lose him or herself through prayer and renunciation. Marian piety also remained faithful to the forms it took in the Middle Ages, which St Bernard had fostered. But another, more elevated form took shape in the seventeenth century in parallel with public devotion which tended to connect the Virgin with the work of salvation. She became in effect the image of the most perfect

Far from limiting itself to a confrontation with Protestantism, the Counter-Reformation engaged in a vast movement for Reform within the Church. A good illustration of this is the work of St Vincent de Paul (1581–1660), founder of the Sisterhood of Charity and protagonist of a solidarity with the poor authentically inspired by the Gospel. Like many others he showed that one could not defeat the Protestant churches without simultaneously attacking the excesses and failures which had made the Lutheran *sola fide* so attractive.

Portrait of St Vincent de Paul, drawing by Daniel Dumonstier, first half of the 17th century. Musée Bonnat, Bayonne.

St Vincent de Paul and the Sisters of Charity, anonymous painting, *c.* 1740. Musée de l'Assistance Publique, Paris.

Christian woman. In her quiet life she incarnated the different 'states' of Jesus; meditation on her mysteries was a privileged means of adherence to the virtues of Christ.

These catechetical and spiritual depths were not simply for contemplation since they demanded that a faithful Christian become a workman in the plan of the Incarnation by converting and sanctifying the world through the exercise of neighbourly charity. Hence the overwhelming necessity to make individual behaviour conform to the principles of the faith. Without doubt the greatest historical achievement of Catholic Reform was to have restored effectively the link between morality and belief. The transformation of conduct was unspectacular but profound.

In the course of the seventeenth century the moralizing character of the catechisms became accentuated, while canonical visitors to parishes sought more and more to discover disorders or predominant vices. A rapid improvement in morality came about among the clergy on account of the seminaries. The same happened – much more slowly – among the laity after 1670: drunkenness, adultery and prostitution – that scourge of the century – were on the wane. Moral prescriptions were generally accompanied by a marked distrust of pleasure. For almost all ecclesiastics of the classical age the quest of pleasure for its own sake was a logical consequence of original sin, since it was the primary form of concupiscence, the *libido sentiendi*. No doubt pleasure itself was not sin, but it led to sin. That conception justified a multitude of scruples running right through Christian life and to the minute 'general review of faults' exposed before the tribunal of penitence. There developed a practice of asceticism, inspired, at least indirectly, by the thought of St Augustine, and sanctioned by all the theologians and Catholic moralists of the time, especially by the greatest of them, Antoine Arnauld.

This basic rigorousness was stressed in every area of life, but particularly in relations between the sexes. Throughout southern Europe everything to do with sexuality, within marriage as much as outside it, came into general disrepute. Thus nakedness, indecent behaviour or obscene talk were seriously reprimanded. The sexual act was regarded as impure and in some places, like the dioceses of western Normandy, the ancient periods of abstinence were revived to contain it. One might almost call this a 'Cathar mentality'. Strict control of the libido was primarily directed towards moral conduct, but its consequences had further implications. Because it led to late marriages it was one reason for a Malthusian demography which lasted until the Enlightenment in spite of the slow disappearance of religious values.

Morality is inseparable from works, of which they are an organic part, since love is expressed primarily by serving the neighbour. So the Catholic Reformation was a time when works of all kinds proliferated. Some were notable for their large-scale achievements, like the missions which maintained the driving power of faith as it was conceived at the end of the fifteenth century in the Franciscan centres of Spain. These missions gave birth to young Christian communities in America with their universities, bishoprics, four hundred monasteries, thousands of parishes, cathedrals sumptuous with the deployment of colonial baroque art – in fact the creation of new civilizations.

But most 'works', to outward view at least, were more modest in scope. They were born of a spiritual intention and in general directed towards the assistance of the poor. Like children, poor people are ambivalent characters. As habitual participants in 'popular disturbances' they are a constant menace to the social order. But at the same time they represent the promise of redemption for they incarnate *par excellence* the Bérullian sense of a 'state' of Jesus who chose to be born, to live and to die far from the riches of this world. In that respect the poor were figures of Christ. To give to the poor was to give to God. Moreover alms were not only an ordinary gesture of solidarity, they were an essential virtue for salvation. But this intention was bolstered by a more pragmatic factor since the seventeenth century was a time of civil and international wars, and thus of increasingly atrocious misery which churchmen – bishops, priests and monastic superiors – judged irreconcilable with Christian faith.

The life of St Vincent de Paul is an eloquent illustration of the complementarity of works and learning. He began by setting himself three essential objectives: the choice of bishops, the formation of priests and the teaching of Christians. In that spirit he founded the congregations of the Mission which came in time to provide professors for the seminaries. But the miseries of the age brought him in spite of himself to the works of charity which still bear his name. Similar adaptations took place in large abbeys like Port Royal des Champs, originally devoted to prayer and contemplation but becoming by necessity involved in the fight against poverty. Less time was given to meditation and more to the distribution of assistance, since they had not only to make the unfortunate welcome but also to send out to the starving

near and far whole convoys of flour or corn. Such acts became common and multiplied. Small convents – houses of Capuchins or Grey Sisters – which had been scattered over the territory for centuries, became centres of charity. In society at that time the sister of St Vincent de Paul was without doubt the most popular person.

It is clear through these initiations and achievements that the Catholic Reformation cannot be reduced to a strictly polemical phenomenon. It was not merely the 'Counter-Reformation', as the German historian von Ranke called it in the nineteenth century. It is true that since it was organically connected with the religious or politico-religious conflicts of the time it could sometimes, like other contemporary Churches, adopt narrowly defensive attitudes with aggressive impulses, but that concession should not hide the positive aspects of its work.

Catholic Reform did not fully attain the objectives set by Trent. How could it be otherwise? The Tridentine ethos may not have explicitly justified theocracy, but it certainly did not exclude the possibility, which implied the existence of a Christian state as the temporal armour of the whole religious system. But instead political evolution led to the predominance of the monarchical State, whose prince came more and more to consider the Church as merely part of the machinery of government. Such secularization was quite the contrary of the Council's ideal. Moreover the stability and vigorous faith of Protestant churches withstood the missionary apostolate of Catholicism. So Christianity remained then, and is now, divided. This is no doubt something to be regretted, yet there does exist an ecumenicity which is not based on compromise and which when practised with mutual respect – as has sometimes been done in the last four centuries – may lead to exchanges between the Churches, giving rise to a positive increase in spiritual life.

The fate of the Reformation

1

2

While Genevan theologians like Louis Tronchin and François Turrettini assured the transmission of Calvinist orthodoxy, others in Germany and elsewhere were tempted by the anti-intellectualism of Pietism or by the mysticism of the Enlightenment.

1. *Portrait of Louis Tronchin*, anonymous 17th-century painting. Bibliothèque Publique et Universitaire, Geneva.

2. *Portrait of François Turrettini*, anonymous 17th-century painting. Bibliothèque Publique et Universitaire, Geneva.

3. *Enlightenment*, engraving by Daniel Chodowiecki, second half of the 19th century.

Who can contest Max Weber's thesis? Who can deny that the map of the Reformation is identical to that of the industrial revolution, including lofty intellectual achievements, flourishing economies, democratic states? But the affirmation of these truths and the apologetic use made of them becomes irritating self-satisfaction unless the other side of the coin is remembered too, which is the great vulnerability of Reformed Christianity.

Success in this world

Of the three great theological debates within Protestant orthodoxy, the least damaging was over the Lutheran doctrine of the ubiquity of Christ. Perhaps it even contributed, through the shrill and mountainous tomes which were written on it, towards deepening the mystery of mysteries that the living God should offer himself to human touch. In 1601 Hoe van Hoeneg trumpeted in Latin from the ramparts of Lutheran Jerusalem his solid, just and orthodox detestation of the Pope and the Calvinists. J. Gebhardt, on the other hand, found it wiser to confine himself to twenty-eight large volumes of *Loci communes*. And as these theologians were married and the fathers of families, the Gebhardts and the Andreaes – like the Tronchins and the Turrettinis in Geneva – succeeded their fathers in professional chairs in the universities of central Germany.

The debates over predestination caused more damage. Double predestination was highly divisive, since it was perceived as an insult both to the glory of God and to human reason. The Gomarians were hated, while the Arminians, whom the Catholics and the philosophers courted, either went in the direction of the Unitarians of Poland and Holland or else joined up with mystical groups which were still flourishing at the Enlightenment. But of all the theological debates the one over exegesis was the most acute.

Yet in the eyes of the world the Reformation had a fortunate outcome: success in this world. If one looks today at a map of the great confessions it is clear that the divisions of 1560 are still in place in the late twentieth century, while the rest of the world takes its character from the geographical extension of the divisions of Christianity in the middle of the sixteenth century. Of those affected by British expansion through America and the Empire, 90 per cent are non-European Protestants. So 90 per cent of those who count Calvin among their ancestors are British, American or people from former colonies or missions.

There is total positive correlation between the Protestant tradition and political regimes of elected representation, e.g. democratic states. A counter-example confirms this: there is total negative correlation between the Protestant tradition and the most tyrranical form of utter socialism in Communism. There is not a single Communist regime which has been able to insinuate itself into a country with a Protestant tradition – except for East Germany, whose political state depends on Soviet military occupation. Yet I am not too fond of this kind of apologetic which has been abused by American Protestants in this century. For instance it sustained the advance of a 'mini-sixteenth century' attitude in Latin America up to the 1950s, but the real breakthrough there was made by Pentecostalism. Between 5 and 10 per cent of Catholics who had been left without a framework of faith, without formation or instruction, joined Baptist or Methodist churches, but most of all the lively, warm Pentecostal churches. This was a total change, but the gains have been

consolidated over the last twenty years. It is now certain that the endeavour which won the approval of the historian E.G. Léonard will not be overthrown.

There is no new sixteenth century. The world map of Christian confessions, eroded from within and hemmed in on all sides, remains. But only Islam at present is growing. In geo-political terms Christianity has been marking time for thirty years, and Protestant churches more than the Catholic Church. Only an ostrich with his head in the sand could deny this.

Yet the map of the Churches, or of Church traditions, shows clearly what Sombart had already hypothesized before Weber advanced his cautious thesis on Protestantism and the rise of capitalism: Protestantism, especially of the Zwinglian and Calvinist traditions, produces the highest income and product per capita, the greatest number of new initiatives, 80 per cent of Nobel prizewinners, the highest percentages of publications, and of adolescents effectively schooled in higher education of proven quality, and 90 per cent of patents for usable inventions. But in limiting himself to the Catholic/Protestant polarity in Wilhelmine Germany, Weber reduced the scope of his explanation. In fact the aptitude for initiative, creativity and investment for the future came from *Christian* education. Protestantism in action is only vigorous, applied Christianity.

The cosmos of creation, freed from the omnipresent sacred, is a lay cosmos, a profane cosmos, an area of liberty in which one may grope one's way without risk of sacrilege. Within the Christian grouping the Protestant sub-group occupies the top of the ladder. Even the exceptions to this are scarcely exceptions. Thus the foothold of Protestantism in southern France is due to the negative factor that the weight of the centralized State precluded the normal pressure of its forces. Note within the Protestant sub-group the better scores of the Reformed against the Lutherans, the dissenters and Methodists against the Anglicans and Episcopalians. In Latin America the standard of living among the Protestant *crentes* is between four and ten times superior to the average. All the factors in Weberian analysis: initiative, literacy, the investment in education of the religions of the Book, predestinarian assurance which is the choice of a small number against a large number, of an élite against a crowd,

3

No one embodies Protestant success better than Albert Schweitzer (1875–1965), who was an influential theologian, an internationally renowned organist, a doctor and the founder of a hospital at Lambaréné in Gabon. The famous Nobel Peace Prize crowned his humanitarian endeavours and his religious convictions.

MARTIN LUTHER KING ASSASSINÉ

HOMMAGE

AU PRESTIGIEUX COMBATTANT ANTIRACISTE
PRIX NOBEL DE LA PAIX

MARDI 9 AVRIL 1968, A 20 H. 30

AU CIRQUE D'HIVER 110, rue Amelot, Paris 10e
- Métro : Filles-du-Calvaire

MOUVEMENT CONTRE LE RACISME, L'ANTISEMITISME ET POUR LA PAIX (M.R.A.P.)
30, rue des Jeûneurs, Paris 2e - C.C.P. : PARIS 14825 85. Tél. : GUT. 09 57

Today more than ever Protestantism is active on the world scene. From the United States to South Africa, from Europe to the Far East, it is directly involved in the great disputes of our time.

Tract distributed in France after the assassination of Martin Luther King in 1968.

Twenty years after Martin Luther King the South African Bishop Desmond Tutu received the Nobel Peace Prize.

point in the same direction while the superimposition of the maps of success and religion indicates a high level of correlation.

In the valley of tears where the road winds between the yawning abysses before and behind, and where every instant is in Christian eyes a moment with eternal meaning, the Christian's lot is good, and from this angle at least, the Protestant lot is better. But I hasten to add that there is no great apologetic weight in that observation and it has no great significance, except that good fortune brings a heavier responsibility in connection with other Christian traditions. Protestants may be fortunate Christians, may be 'purified', 'reduced to essentials', 'uncluttered' in their faith and their practices, but they are also fragile Christians. Reformed Christianity is both fragile and robust.

Amama, Cameron and Cappel

Reformed Christianity is fragile because it is basic and has nothing more to sacrifice. It cannot follow the strategy of *reculer pour mieux sauter*. For instance *sola Scriptura* opposes Scripture alone, Scripture as it were naked, against the delegated *dominium* of a fallible great Church. In that case everything centres on the exegesis of the Bible. Throughout the history of the Church exegesis has played an essential part, but in Christianity based on *sola Scriptura* it is everything.

In 1556 Theodore de Beza, Calvin's designated successor, denounced those who had believed that they had uncovered some Semitic vocabulary in the Greek of the New Testament. What horror to suppose it could contain barbarisms and solecisms, like faults in the Greek! Was the Holy Spirit open to a charge of carelessness? Absolutely impossible! For Theodore de Beza God dictated the very words. One would certainly suppose in that case that he had consulted a good grammar! The fascination of the inspired text at the heart of everything was responsible for that regression in understanding. For it had been grasped long before de Beza that inspiration was not dictation and that 'God, stirring up the intelligence and will of the writer whom he inspired', respected and used the personality of the author. In that case how could one refuse to observe the particularity of that strange and often awkward Greek full of semitisms? In order to justify the Holy Spirit, eminent philologists went on to invent a 'Hellenistic language' which was nothing other than the semitic Greek of the gospels.

But the New Testament was protected from scrutiny for a long time by having Christ at its centre and thus producing respect. The Old Testament was therefore the first object of a long scholarly tradition of separating meaning from the demythologized letter of the text. Protestants, the newcomers, were proud of their ability in Hebrew, championing the Massoretic text against the Septuagint which had usually been enough for the ancient Church, or against the Vulgate which had sufficed for Catholics, more from its usefulness than from any deliberate decision.

François Laplanche has described three honest Reformed men at the beginning of the seventeenth century who experienced the effects of Protestant orthodoxy's unconscionable lapse from the thought of the Reformers, which was evidence of rupture and hardening in the movement and was bound to have dangerous repercussions. These men who wished to free the Holy Spirit from a new straitjacket were the Dutchman Sixten Amama (1593–1629), Professor of oriental languages at the University of Francker in Frisia, the Scotsman Cameron – born in Glasgow in 1579, he died at Montauban on 27 November 1625, a victim of his fidelity to the King of France – and Louis Cappel (1585–1658), the great theologian and linguist from Saumur. All three cast the same critical gaze on the hardening of Protestant orthodoxy, a phenomenon perfectly illustrated by the works of Lambert Daneau (1530–95).

Having to leave France after the St Bartholomew's Day massacre (1572) Daneau, with his twenty-seven large volumes, was appointed to the prestigious chair of dogmatic theology in Leyden. As Olivier Fatio has shown, he surmounted all barriers to the construction of a 'theological dogmatic' for the second time round – almost as complex as the old medieval scholastic variety. In 1568 Bullinger, the successor to Zwingli in Zurich, and the friend and confidant of Calvin, expressed in a letter to de Beza his anxiety at a development which seemed to him a retrograde step. 'If philosophical minds continue to examine all the dogmas of our religion with Aristotelian methods, we shall have a new scholasticism again and several new Seraphic Doctors like Aquinas, Duns Scotus and Albertus Magnus . . .' Curiously de Beza, who had been so closely allied with Calvin during his lifetime, favoured Lambert Daneau rather than Bullinger. When the controversial *Isagoras* of Daneau was published de Beza gave him the greatest support from Geneva. As Olivier Fatio

observes: 'In a surprising manner (de Beza) finds the sign of the renewal of Christianity not in the preaching of the pure word of God . . . but in the restoration of Stoic peripatetic logic in the schools!' This could be traced back to Lefèvre d'Étaples in France and the incomparable Melanchthon in Germany. Certainly de Beza, like Daneau, maintained the primacy of Scripture, but he expected logic, intelligence and reason to order the message of revelation into a logical, intelligible, convincing and coherent whole.

The appearance of Daneau's *Isagoras*, the large dogmatic treatise endorsed by de Beza, the greatest Calvinist authority in Europe, marked a decisive development. The Thomist tradition was renewed even in the structure of the discourse. Since the treatise began with a *De Deo* concerning knowledge of God in himself rather than God's saving work to us, Daneau had put himself without realizing it in opposition to one of the fundamental principles of the Reformation, namely the principle that God does not reveal himself except in what concerns our salvation. Paradoxically that unexpected and radically anti-Calvinist step was taken by those of the Lutheran persuasion who were suspected of being crypto-Calvinist. Certainly there was some curious cross-fertilization less than fifty years after the Reformation. It came about because Latin remained the international language and because men and books circulated freely among Lutheran and Calvinist universities. The disciples of Philip Melanchthon, the 'Philippists', were suspect to the hyper-Lutherans, these hard pure souls encamped in their systematic and exegetic ultra-orthodoxy. Since the Philippists respected traditional Christology they were to that extent in Calvin's camp. It is understandable that Melanchthon, who had enjoyed Calvin's friendship, should be treated almost with veneration by rigorously orthodox Calvinists, who could see the danger, at the very least a political danger, in departing from the solid Lutheran path.

It can scarcely be denied that orthodoxy itself represented the renewal of Aristotle's 'first philosophy', a gesture towards Erasmus and Aquinas with reason promoted from the rank of 'God's whore' to that of the humble servant of God, since it is the gift of God to man made in his image. Although people were once again in touch with the tradition of the first centuries with respectful and prudent enjoyment, and with the inheritance of the most gifted and intelligent of honest pagans, they yet regressed in their exegesis. Naturally, however, when there were only two or three thousand literate people in society everything could not be done, and in any case intellectual effort is subject to changing fashion. It took time to construct the new exegesis, just as it took time to build the great temple of orthodoxy. Just as later Antiquity stopped reading the book of Nature to concentrate on the written word, so these new systematicians required an immobilized Bible. No more new meanings were to be found in the sacred text. In his *Antibarbus Biblicus*, which appeared in Amsterdam in 1628, Amama wrote the history of Scriptural study in oppositions of black and white, just as Protestants habitually described the history of the Church. 'In every age barbarians have sullied the sacred Scriptures.' Fortunately the Reformers and humanists in alliance chased out the barbarians. But after Luther, Erasmus, Reuchlin, Melanchthon, Calvin, Zwingli, Oecolampadius, Bucer and Carlstadt even Reformed Christianity returned to the fleshpots of Egypt. Protestants had come to venerate their translations just as Catholics idolized the Vulgate; they abandoned the study of languages and like the good old days of ancient scholasticism wanted to impose on critics and grammarians their imaginary meanings instead of the obvious meaning of the canonical text.

For Amama, Cameron and Cappel, the liberal successors to Sebastian Castellio, Erasmus remained the master. They were pious, sincere liberals, convinced that God in the willed condescension of his incarnation had not intended those texts which carried his Word to be treated differently from any other human material. Nor did they believe that God had protected the Scripture which carried his word from all other human frailty. To think otherwise was to betray the incarnation. But one may preserve nothing out of the desire to preserve too much, just as the fear of losing a single crumb may risk spoiling the whole loaf. Certainly God willed that his Apostles should be men like us, guilty of negligence, exposed to errors, inattention and fatigue. After all, God did not will that his Son should live in a palace. So one must admit that in creating God granted freedom, including the possibility of going astray, making mistakes and being ruined, just as in the incarnation God abased himself utterly. In such weakness the glory of God abounds for those whose eyes are opened, whose hearts are softened and whose intelligence is enlightened by the Holy Spirit.

That is not an easy affirmation to make, and it is not always made in the heat of polemic. In the rage to convince and the desire to conquer their adversaries,

Louis Cappel (1585–1658) was one of the forerunners of liberal Protestant critical exegesis. This pioneer of biblical criticism was first a pastor, then Professor of theology and Hebrew at the Saumur Academy.

Portrait of Louis Cappel, 17th-century engraving. Bibliothèque Nationale, Paris.

The programme of studies at the Saumur Academy, 1680. Archives Nationales, Paris.

systematic theologians of the new voracious orthodoxy and the exegetical theology often lacked charity and even elementary mutual respect. That is why the incautious hypersacralizing of Holy Scripture to the point of idolizing it led to desacralization and the treatment of Scripture as a secular book, to be followed in time by its demythologization which was attacked as a denial of faith. That point was not yet reached with Amama, Cameron and Cappel, for the shadows of the nineteenth and twentieth centuries were not then discernible. To begin with it seemed necessary to go to Jewish sources to learn Hebrew. Yet Johannes Reuchlin, Melanchthon's uncle, aroused the enmity of the Dominicans who could not bear his philosemiticism. But then it became difficult to resist the seduction of the Cabbala, which treated the sacred text as if each Hebrew letter had a hidden significance. With Cabbalistic exegesis the Bible grew imperceptibly more and more like the Koran. So the Cabbala exercised both good and bad influences since it encouraged the study of Hebrew but led in the direction of idolatry over the letter of the text.

A fatal reduction

The Massoretic text of the Old Testament had been knocked from its pedestal even before Spinoza had expressed anti-revolutionary tenets in his *Tractatus theologico-politicus* (1670). Then, on the road which led to the great demolition of Scripture by nineteenth-century German university hyper-criticism, Jean Leclerc (1657–1736) and Jean Astruc (1684–1766) separated the historical person of Christ from the New Testament canon, for reasons deriving from philosophical presuppositions which Spinoza had had the honesty to declare. Yet these are presuppositions which contemporary scientific progress (in philology and the treatment of the Dead Sea Scrolls) demonstrate to be hypothetical and hence revisable. What true science discovers matters little to neo-theologians with their impersonal deaf and dumb God whose decrees have nothing to do with the direction of history.

Clearly, if the New Testament canon is only the imaginative product of small church communities over 150 years, Holy Scripture is nothing but an ancient tradition quite arbitrarily elevated by the Church. The Virgin Birth, the divinity of Christ and the resurrection are instances of myth-making imagination. If Christ's resurrection happened only in the imagination of small groups of slaves living eighteen or nineteen centuries ago, of course resurrection and all life beyond time is a ridiculous myth which the arrival of the classless society on earth will in any case render useless. This Hegelo-Marxist reduction of Christianity, which is officially taught and demonstrates complete ignorance of the science which it invokes, may coexist in its extreme form with an illegitimate version of post-Vatican II Catholicism rejected by both Pope John Paul II and Cardinal Ratzinger. Since the Church is everything one may just conceive that as the interpreter of historical direction she may disavow her parentage of other human groups whose interpretation is derived from the historical dialectic.

Although these weapons were polished within one of the Reformed traditions, they were even more effective when turned against the Reformation tradition itself. To make the secret knowledge of obscure hidden meaning coexist with the double intuition of *sola fide* and *sola Scriptura* is incredible enough. To insinuate that radical profanation into the heritage of the Reformation is such an enormous joke played on reason that it falls rapidly flat. Anyway, this disease is mortal. Just as a corpse retains for a few days the features of the living man, so there may still be some resemblances to Christianity for a little while in a few Catholic backwaters, but on the Protestant side the disease is spreading alarmingly. In less than a generation nothing will be left. That could have been foreseen even in the nineteenth century in the neo-liberalism of Edmond Scherer and Félix Pécaut. Protestant individualism, which requires a personal relationship with a personal God, should have nothing to do with that religion designed for past needs – needs, perhaps, of the Stone Age.

The greatness and fragility of the heritage

Exegetical disintegration is slowly but surely killing Protestantism. Yet in any overview of history the Reformation appears as the cradle of all kinds of human achievements. There are some free societies with respect for the human person which have not arisen from the Protestant tradition, but every country in the Protestant tradition has given rise to, and is governed by, legal authorities. The industrial, scientific and technological revolution, the greatest change to occur in the nineteenth and twentieth centuries, exploded from a nucleus in England, Scotland, North America, Holland, Germany, a French fringe, Scandinavia and Switzerland,

all overwhelmingly Protestant in tradition. The impetus is lessening, certainly, but it has been maintained. For the last two centuries, from 1780 to our own day, the Protestant world on every conceivable count has had the lion's share of success. And yet, although the Protestant world has been characterized by calm political evolution and rapid change in economics, science and technology, so that it has been a world where the biblical vale of tears has been well under control (grow, multiply, dominate), and where one may await, perhaps too comfortably, the Kingdom of God, for all that the Protestant world is in perpetual flux on the religious level.

No one could live comfortably through the Reformation, which was divisive in its resemblance to a new Pentecost and brought to life the hard core of the Word of God. The Reformation tradition floats on a sea which is always troubled by turbulent waves. Thus *sola fide* meant direct relationship with God, face to face without mediation, while *sola Scriptura* referred to the ancient biblical tradition which could be neither changed nor rearranged, and could be used at any time to challenge the institution of the Church through personal reading of the Bible. From that point several paths were possible, especially the choice between Scripture alone or Scripture officially interpreted. The large churches chose interpreted Scripture, and Protestantism has shown an inexhaustible capacity to construct beautiful, ornate but ephemeral orthodoxies which were so perfect that they were fragile and short-lived.

Orthodoxy does not burn with the ardour of faith for long. It soon becomes an intellectual game, the delight of an ecclesiastical technostructure. Orthodoxy appeals primarily to reason, having been waylayed by rationalism: hardened orthodoxy makes the Church into a stuffy ghetto. So free churches have escaped from established orthodoxy. Arminians and Socinians would not accept the heavy predestinarianism of the Synod of Dordrecht and they disapproved of Calvin's execution of Servetus. So they formed free churches of ardent souls who could not be contented with the cold conformity of State churches. For that reason Pietism flourished, such as the German pietism of Spener (1638–95), the pietism common in the University of Halle at the time of Francke and the vision espoused by Zinzendorf and the Moravians. It concentrated on a pious life and emotional transports of mysticism. The Protestant tradition has not been without its mystics, from Jacob Boehme (1575–1624), who with Meister Eckhart and Teuler renewed the *Philosophia Teutsch*, to Friedrich Christopher Oetinger (1702–82) and Franz von Baader (1765–1841). It has also had its theosophists, of whom Swedenborg (1688–1772), 'the Buddha of the North', is the most famous.

A heated exodus from the Church could also take the concrete form of piety and practical works for the glory of God. Thus the Methodists developed a practical, factual, Anglo-Saxon form of religion, preaching the resurrection of Jesus Christ outside the churches on open ground, and evangelizing prostitutes and ruffians. But the exodus from the established Church could be done quite simply in an orthodox way. The structures of established churches which had been infected by rationalism were soon contested by systematic theologians and by rigorous and faithful exegesis. Then a free church could develop, free to live a more authentic orthodoxy and faithful to the spirit of the Reformation in opposition to the illegitimate official Church. A typical example of this development comes from Holland where the *Hervoormde Kerk* had thrown out its Reformed and Calvinist identity. Abraham Kuyper (1837–1920), a Protestant historian and counter-revolutionary, set up in opposition the Free University of Amsterdam and the powerful, lively, coherent and rigorous Re-reformed Church of Holland. In 1985 its three million strict Calvinists could be distinguished from the ethically disordered mass of the population by their high productivity, the test of a practical, concrete meaning in life.

After the orthodox drift and the liberal stampede came the Revival, like a new Reformation. César Malan, Louis Gaussen, Alexandre Vinet and Adolphe Monod staked out the Revival in the nineteenth century. What may become the Revival of the twentieth century is already visible in the western states of mid-America. As the nineteenth and twentieth centuries have progressed, so too has the tension between orthodoxy, which means fidelity to perennial doctrine and an exegesis which respects the inspiration of Scripture, and liberalism which preserves, somehow, a few things in the midst of its negations and abandonment. The great and noble figure of liberalism is Friedrich Ernst Schleiermacher (1768–1834), who retained only a sentimental attachment to the man Jesus (denying the Virgin birth, the Resurrection and the Ascension) and a quasi-Catholic sense of the Church, the meritorious cult of an empty shell. In reaction to this minimal liberalism arose the fundamentalist movements which in America have powerfully opposed Darwinism, neo-Darwinism and all the vicious forms of dogmatic scientific materialism. Their exegesis is very formal, attached in understandable reaction to the letter and the

1

From the common trunk of the Protestant tradition grew very different branches such as the mystical doctrines of the Swede Emmanuel Swedenborg (1688–1772) or the pragmatic philanthropy of the Swiss Henri Dunant (1828–1910), a moving force behind the Geneva Conference of 1863 and the creation of the Red Cross.

1. *Portrait of Emmanuel Swedenborg*, 18th-century engraving. Bibliothèque Nationale, Paris.

2. Portrait of Henri Dunant.

2

details, making little use of the great Reformation principle of the analogy of faith.

The ambition of Karl Barth (1886–1968) was to reconcile and transcend the opposition between orthodoxy and liberalism. Since he began in a traditional way with a re-reading of the Epistle to the Romans after the manner of the Reformation, one might have expected his *Church dogmatic* to have inclined towards orthodoxy, as his *bêtes noires* were Schleiermacher and his contemporary Bultmann, who elegantly emptied Scripture of all content. But that is an error. By insidiously loosening the Reformation principle that Scripture is the Word of God in itself and not only in its announcement of Christ, by sacrificing the indispensable natural theology of orthodoxy which preserves a dialogue with secular knowledge, and by concealing under a historical sophism his political engagement with the broad left, Karl Barth opened the way for the liberal-marxism which has infiltrated the World Council of Churches and has won the loyalty of a section of the churches who are holed up in a cul-de-sac.

Conclusion:
What is the fate of the Reformation today?

We are in a cul-de-sac from which only the Holy Spirit can rescue us.

Truly, although Geneva has just been celebrating four and a half centuries of the Reformation which was a new Pentecost, we have everything to (re)learn. If you will accept a biblical image in the tradition of the good pupils of Mathurin Cordier or the Council of Trent, we must now take the bitter path for forty years at least, as in the time of Moses — or even for four hundred years, for the consumables with which we are gorged are less digestible than those with which the Israelites were obsessed in the consumer society of brilliant Egypt (Numbers 11.5). We must in our own turn walk behind today's invisible Ark of the Covenant, which is still in place since God is faithful, studying its opening words right from the beginning, from *Bereshith bara Elohim*, whose meaning has scarcely been penetrated after twenty-five brief centuries of meditation. So stop taking yourself for a Pilgrim Father landing at Cape Cod, do not speak this language of Canaan which we no longer know.

There is a crisis of values which even politics and the media have got hold of because the customer is worried about his security, his privacy and his death — which is all the more unacceptable because it has been deferred. This crisis of values, which even the rationalists have called by its proper name, is the crisis of the churches, or, better, the crisis of the Church. The Church crisis is not the crisis of Protestantism or Catholicism, it is a crisis common to all churches. Protestant churches, faithful, unfortunately, to their vocation of being the vanguard, have only been affected sooner and more deeply than the others, especially the Catholic Church which is rudely shaken in its European domains. To the extent that the Reformed tradition sees itself as purifying the approach to and reception of the ancient tradition, it carried within itself the promise of new reformations. Thus churches which issued from the Reformation soon found themselves called to produce a new reformation, a new Apostolic age — we have witnessed it — called the Revival.

A look at our churches makes obvious the expectation of a revival — something scarcely reasonable in human terms. Hope remains intact by the light from the written Word of God understood by the analogy of faith as it has been throughout Christian history. Indeed, it is when there is no more hope that hope rises again. Calvin's *Institutes* begins with a proposition from the *Imitation of Christ*, that knowledge of God and knowledge of ourselves are related. Our self-knowledge is grievous and could lead us to that terrible point of utter self-despair. *Denial of life* and *capitulation before death* have become incontestable, statistically-calculable facts.

Denial of life has caused the whole industrial world to reduce family sizes for simple collective survival, even when infant mortality has been reduced almost to zero. This paradoxical behaviour has come about at the time and in the part of the world where the accumulation of economic means and the collection of global information has attained levels which were inconceivable yesterday and even today are hard to imagine. Since 1960 we have had painless and convenient means for dissociating from procreation the pleasure of the sexual act in a satisfying interpersonal relationship. So it is clear that human life, on the level of control of one's destiny, will not be reproduced unless it is recognized to have some meaning. Yet life involves a necessarily wretched knowledge of oneself as between the abyss before and the abyss behind. It will have no meaning, therefore, unless it is not entirely trapped in the vectorial passage of time, unless there really exists elsewhere a

beyond which is not mere appearance, a true beyond which gives meaning, which gives some definition to our sketchy lives. From the first entombment men have groped for this idea which Christ brought, as Peter proclaimed with the Apostolic Church. It is these words, creative of eternal life, which give to transience and inconstancy the eternal solidity of the Kingdom which God has created out of our stammering and repentance.

In a survey taken among Catholics and Protestants in Europe and America in the early 1960s, subjects were asked about life after death – the only worthwhile question on the meaning of life – and two-thirds responded in terms of the Christian belief their churches had taught them.

A slight sociological difference was perceptible between Catholics and Protestants (beyond the nuances of vocabulary and imagery). In Protestant countries, fundamentalists and mystics apart, fewer affirmed belief in life after death. So it had come to this, that the purifying rigour of Protestant beginnings had led to the very feebleness of commitment it had reacted against in the first place. Fewer Protestants would commit themselves to a belief in heaven and, appropriately enough, they had fewer children than the Catholics. Likewise, in its modernizing way, the Reformation had encouraged individuality. Reformed Europe and its American extension are more

Every year thousands of Protestants gather for an 'Assembly in the Wilderness' at Mas-Soubeyran, the centre of resistance in the Cevennes. It was the birthplace of Roland, one of the leaders of the camisards, those Calvinists constrained to take up arms after the Revocation of the Edict of Nantes.

The Assembly in the Wilderness at Mas-Soubeyran (Gard) in September 1976.

287

modern, more industrial and technical on the Weberian model, but also more fragile.

This is one indication that, confronted with death (that most natural occurrence) the Reformation followed the Old Testament line of dismissing it as a merely cultural phenomenon. Everything which could have made a natural theology of death out of that universal experience was rejected, even the ancient tradition in 2 Maccabees (admittedly an apocryphal book) where there is prayer for the dead in view of judgement, thus maintaining the healthy distinction between time and eternity. There was endemic fear of anything which might detract from the absolute, immeasurable, incomprehensible sovereignty of God. And now that diabolical exegesis murders Scripture, refusing to recognize the hand of God in the canonical text, nothing is left.

Earlier differences have disappeared since over the last two decades huge numbers of Catholics in Europe and America have joined the Protestants in abandoning natural theology and doubting the inspiration of Scripture. The French, of whom 70 per cent, when questioned on death in 1969, confessed themselves saddened by their inability to believe, were mostly from the Catholic tradition.

We who have denied so much, dying a little each time, must we abandon all hope – even, like the damned in *The Divine Comedy*, all hopefulness? Complacency can be bought too cheaply by denying the importance of empty churches, the quest for pleasure, immersion in the present, capitulation before nothingness (which Bergson described so well in a still-relevant passage from his *Creative Evolution* of 1907), emptiness and the abandonment of action, discourse and thought. All of these are signs of an absolute rupture which it is absurd to deny. Yet that should not prevent us from uncovering the scarcely discernible signs of a recovery, the time and shape of which we cannot yet recognize.

Western Europe and its offshoots seem to have been by-passed. The debility of the old churches is compensated for by the ardour of the young churches of the Third World. Eastern European churches rally in defiance under the Cross. The fact that Polish Catholics have an attitude to life more like the easterners should give us pause. We in the West are those who are likely to lead them astray.

It is here, in the heart of ancient, betrayed Christianity, that we should look for signs. Life is absurd, but that no longer leads to belief. But it is in the heart of knowledge that the real questions are being raised. Cosmogenesis, for instance, has moved from the 'standard' model to the brilliant new 'expanding' model with its notion of space-time which requires a beginning. So evolution, which caused such distress in the nineteenth century, now appears as the most appropriate background for the biblical representation of the universe. It is extraordinary, and a measure of the crisis in the Churches, especially the Reformed Churches, that so many in their blinkered haste have not noticed this. These signs continue to go unperceived because we have neglected all *theology of creation*.

As in the time of Herod, a star shines in the heavens. God, for whom 'a thousand years . . . are but as yesterday when it is past', waits for the wise men of the new Pentecost. They are still drowsy, but they will rise and teach us to recognize that light, so brilliant already that it pierces through the heavy shutters enclosing our evil thoughts.

Bibliography

General introduction

A bibliography on this subject, even when scientifically selective, would include, I should guess, more than a hundred thousand titles from Europe and America. There is nothing surprising in that. Since the beginning of the nineteenth century almost all books on religious history have been devoted to the Reformation epoch. The miles of books on our library shelves demonstrate what one knows intuitively – that the Protestant and Catholic Reformations lie at the heart of our identity. For this reason, I believe there is space on the shelves for this book, which could equally well have been called: 'A Pilgrimage to the Heart of the Identity of One Branch of the Christian Family'. And since Protestants and Catholics alike are related through the complex time of the Reformation, this could be called a pilgrimage to our roots, to the heart of our common identity.

I owe my thanks first and foremost to Pastor Maurice Graber, organizer of the Reformation's 450th anniversary commemorations in Geneva, whose enthusiasm was infectious and his resolution unswerving. My thanks go also to Éditions Hermé and to Charles Chauvin, as well as to the eminent specialists who at my request, and from a synopsis I suggested to them, accepted the thankless task of condensing into 15, 20 or 25 pages the essence distilled over 20, 30 or 40 years of reading, reflection and research. Their tremendous effort to simplify things is why this book is so tightly packed and yet so clear.

Sixteen of the most eminent scholars responded to my request. We received two texts in German and three in English. I do not believe that the Reformation, that great moment in Church history (*Ecclesia semper reformanda*, as Liebniz wrote), can be separated from a common Christian history to which the Reformation Churches laid claim, as indeed the Catholic and eastern Orthodox Churches do. It seems to me that the radical specificity of the Christian message cannot be understood unless it is included within a religious anthropology, and thus at the heart of the sacred which, pilgrims as we are, we discern intuitively as we grope along the road to death. Someone had to render an account of those forty-five short millenia between the first tomb and that strange new Pentecost fifteen centuries after the appearance of the Divine Master. Thus I somewhat imprudently undertook the risk of writing the Foreword, the general introduction, the major features of Christianity and of the two last centuries of scholasticism.

We asked the greatest Swiss economic historian, Jean François Bergier, Professor at the Polytechnikum in Zurich, to highlight, out of all we know of the well-researched era of Christian society in the fifteenth and sixteenth centuries, characteristics vital to our understanding of it. With such a guide readers can enter, not only with intelligence but also with feeling, into that world where tentative modernity was still hindered by immemorial sluggishness rooted as much in the neolithic age as in the great demographic changes of the twelfth and thirteenth centuries.

The schism had fatal consequences only for those who know the course of history. Guy Bédouelle of the Dominican Order, Professor in the University of Fribourg (author of, among other things, the definitive study on Lefèvre d'Étaples, *Faber Stabulensis*), conveys the world and influence of the humanists. Marc Lienhard, the foremost authority on Martin Luther and author of the magisterial work *Un temps, une vie, un message*, is also a historian, philologist, theologian and Professor of Protestant Theology at Strasburg. Jacques Courvoisier, Honorary Professor at the University of Geneva, an enlightening, sensitive scholar and pastor, brings Zwingli to life and studies the infinite complexity of the Reformation in Switzerland. As for Calvin, traditionally studied with more exactitude and less love than Luther, he is entrusted to Alexandre Ganoczy, a priest and brilliant Catholic theologian. The eminent author of *Calvin, théologien de l'Église et du ministère*, he is a Professor at the Hermann-Schell Institute in the University of Würzburg. Italy and Spain are dealt with by Manfred Welti and Carlos Gilly, both men whose authority is warmly recognized and respected in international intellectual circles.

Georges Livet, Emeritus Professor of the free town of Bucer and the Sturms, masterfully presents an overall picture of the situation in France and the complexity of the Rhineland. Bernard Vogler of the University of Strasburg, author of the definitive study of the Reformation in the Palatinate, guides us through the territories of Germany and Scandinavia.

The English *via media* and the roots of the Puritan 'long English memories' are brilliantly presented by the American scholar Robert Kingdon, an expert on the sixteenth century and Director of the Institute for Research in the Humanities at the University of Wisconsin at Madison. Jean Béranger of Strasburg guides us safely through the maze of eastern Europe with his extensive knowledge and impressive linguistic range. Olivier Fatio of the University of Geneva explains, with the clarity of twenty years' familiarity, the great Christological and ontological debates of the paradoxical and little-loved orthodoxy of the second and third Reformed generations, and of the thorny Formula of Concord of the little Council of Dort.

William Monter, of the University of Evanston, gives a lively account of the effects of the Reformation in daily life. Hans Guggisberg, Professor at Basle, offers a study of the witchhunts. Gabriel Mützenberg, with his knowledge and his pastoral sensitivity, begins with the modest Mathurin Cordier to delineate the enormous pedagogical contribution of the Reformation.

The indispensible counterpoint of Catholic Reform was provided by René Taveneaux, Professor Emeritus of the University of Nancy, who is a specialist in Lorraine Jansenism and a master of all facets of the Tridentine world.

Many intellectuals, historians, theologians and Catholic priests have enriched us with their generous and fraternal co-operation. We have reclaimed our own origins without shame, and have made a modest contribution to *true ecumenism*.

Pierre Chaunu
Institute of France

Bibliographical orientation

One hundred thousand titles, of which nearly five thousand are dedicated to Luther alone: the bibliography of works on the Reformation is an ocean (and often a tempestuous one) of western historiography.

Three books give the titles of 1,745 of the most respected works on the subject : *L'Église et la vie religieuse à la fin du Moyen Age*, by Francis RAPP, *Naissance et affirmation de la Réforme*, by Jean DELUMEAU and, by the same author, *Le catholicisme entre Luther et Voltaire*, Nouvelle Clio, repeatedly reprinted by PUF (Paris).

Three syntheses: *Le temps des Réformes* (Fayard and, in pocket edition, Complexes); *Église, culture et société, Réforme et Contre-Réforme (SEDES)*, by Pierre CHAUNU, and *Histoire générale du protestantisme*, Émile G. LÉONARD, vols. I and II (PUF).

In addition to these, vols. XII, XIII, XV, XVI, XVII, XVIII of the great *Histoire de l'Église* by FLICHE and MARTIN (Bloud & Gay).

The following works must not be forgotten: *Un destin, Martin Luther; Le problème de l'incroyance au XVIe siècle: la religion de Rableais; Au coeur religieux du XVIe siècle*, all by Lucien FEBVRE; *Dieu, la création et la Providence dans la prédication de Calvin* (Peter Lang, Berne) and *Interprètes de la Bible* (Beauchesne), both by Richard STAUFFER; and the irreplaceable *Calvin* by Émile DOUMERGUE (7 vols. in folio).

For economic history, *Genève et l'économie européenne* by Jean-François BERGIER, and his *Histoire économique de la Suisse*, that jewel published by Armand Colin.

Five major theses have been honoured recently in this field of research in France: *Érasme, lecteur d'Origène*, by André GODIN (Droz, 1982); *Église et société, Genève au XVIIe siècle*, by Roger STAUFFENEGGER (Droz, 1984); *Guillaume Briçonnet*, by Michel VEISSIÈRE (published by the Société d'Histoire et d'Archéologie de Provins); and the seminal *L'Écriture, le sacré et l'histoire; le protestantisme français devant la Bible*, by François LAPLANCHE.

Also the brilliant colloquy *Les Réformes, enracinement socioculturel* (colloquy of Tours), presented by B. Chevalier and R. Sauzet in the edition by Guy Trédaniel (Éditions de la Maisnie, 1985).

Several collaborators have judged it indispensable to add a brief bibliography to their chapters. To avoid repetition, they will be in the following order: 1. Lienhard; 2. Welti and Gilly; 3. Vogler; 4. Livet; 5. Bérenger; 6. Livet; 7. Guggisberg; 8. Mützenberg.

1. LIENHARD

Luther and Europe

BENZING, Joseph, *Lutherbiographie. Verzeichnis der gedruckten Schriften Mart Luthers bis zu dessen Tod* (Baden-Baden, 1966).

EBELING, Gerhard, *Luther* (Geneva, 1983).

ELTON, G.R., *Reformation Europe 1517–1559* (London, 1963).

FEBVRE, Lucien, *Un destin: Martin Luther* (Paris, 1928).

JOUTARD, Philippe (ed.), *Historiographie de la Réforme* (Paris, 1977).

LÉONARD, Émile G., *Histoire générale du protestantisme*, vol. I, 'La Réformation' (Paris, 1977).

LIENHARD, Marc, *Martin Luther. Un temps, une vie, un message* (Paris-Genève).

'Luther entre l'Allemagne et la France', in *Positions luthériennes*, no. 32 (1984), pp. 113–136.

LORTZ, Joseph, *La Réforme de Luther* (Paris, 1970).

OLIVIER, Daniel, *La foi de Luther. La cause de l'Évangile dans l'Église* (Paris, 1978).

PESCH, Otto Herrmann, *Hinführung zu Luther* (Mainz, 1982).

STAUFFER, Richard, *Le catholicisme à la découverte de Luther* (Neuchâtel, 1966).

VOGLER, Bernard, *Le monde germanique et helvétique à l'époque des Réformes, 1517–1618* (Paris, 1981).

2. WELTI and GILLY

Italy and Spain: diffusion, failure and survival of Reforming convictions

One could avail oneself of a bibliography published from research among the footnotes of Manfred WELTI's book *Kleine Geschichte der italienischen Reformation* (Gütersloh, 1985); Italian translation: *Breve storia della Riforma italiana* (Casale Monferrato, 1985); the same goes for the text by A. Gordon KINDER, *Spanish Protestants and Reform in the 16th Century* (London, 1983). From these two works, the following should be noted as being of particular value:

For Italy:

The works of Massimo FIRPO, Paul ROTONDÒ, Aldo STELLA, Lech SZCZUCKI, Delio CANTIMORI and Frederic C. CHURCH.

For Spain:

BOEHMER, Eduard, *Bibliotheca Wiffeniana: Spanish Reformers of two Centuries from 1520* (3 vols.) (London, 1874, 1883, 1904).

MENÉNDEZ Y PELAYO, Marcelino, *Historia de los heterodoxos españoles* (3 vols.) (Madrid, 1880–81).

SCHÄFER, Ernst H.J., *Beiträge zur Geschichte des spanischen Protestantismus und der Inquisition im 16. Jahrhundert* (3 vols.) (Gütersloh, 1902).

BATAILLON, Marcel, *Érasme et l'Éspagne* (Paris, 1937).

HENNINGSEN, Gustav, 'El "Banco de Datos" del Sto. Officio. Las relaciones de causas de la Inquisición española (1550–1700)' in *Boletin de la R. Academia de la Historia*, CLXXIV, III (Madrid. 1988) pp. 547–70.

Also the works of William MCPHERSON, José C. BIETO, Augustin REDONDO and José I. TELLECHEA IDIGORAS. Some of our information is published in Carlos GILLY's book *Spanien und der Basler Buchdruck bis 1600* (Basle–Frankfurt-am-Main, 1985), especially in chapter V.

3. VOGLER

The establishment of the Reformation in Germany and the north (1530–1620)

DUNKLEY, E.H., *The Reformation in Denmark* (London, 1949).

HOFFMANN, J.G., *La Réforme en Suède (1523–1572) et la succession apostolique* (Neuchâtel et Paris, 1945).

LAU, F. and BIZER, E., *Reformationsgeschichte Deutschlands bis 1555*, coll. 'Die Kirche in ihrer Gestchichte' (Göttingen, 1964).

MOELLER, B., *Deutschland im Zeitalter der Reformation*, coll. 'Deutsche Geschichte' (Gottingen, 1977).

ROBERTS, M., *The early Vasas. History of Sweden (1523–1611)* (Cambridge, 1968).

SKALWEIT, S., *Reich und Reformation* (Berlin, 1967).

Theologische Realenzyklopädie, articles 'Dänemark', VIII, 1981, pp. 304–7, and 'Finland', XI, 1983, pp. 186–7.

UHLHORN, F., *Geschichte der deutsch-lutherischen Kirche*, vol. I (1517–1700) (Leipzig, 1911).

VOGLER, B., *Le monde germanique et belvétique à l'époque des Réformes (1517–1618)* (2 vols.), coll. 'Regards sur l'histoire' (Paris, 1981).

4. LIVET

France: failure or spiritual heritage?

Proceedings of the colloquy *'L'amiral de Coligny en son temps'*, Paris, 1974.

La controverse religieuse (XVIe–XIXe siècle), 2 vols. (Montpellier, Université Paul-Valéry, 1980).

DELAFOSSE, Marcel (ed.), *Histoire de La Rochelle* (Privat, Toulouse, 1985) (chapter by Étienne TROCMÉ: 'La Rochelle protestante, 1568–1628', pp. 85–154).

Les Églises et leurs institutions au VXIe siècle (Montpellier, Université Paul-Valéry, 1979).

GARRISSON-ESTÈBE, Jeanine, *Protestants du Midi, 1559–1598* (Privat, Toulouse, 1980).

Histoire des protestants en France (Privat, Toulouse, 1977) (chapter by R. MANDROU, J. ESTÈBE, D. LIGOU).

LAPLANCHE, François, *L'Écriture, le sacré et l'histoire: le protestantisme français devant la Bible dans la première moitié du XVIe siècle* (thesis in Literature at the Sorbonne), 1984. C.R. Michel Reulos, BSHPF, vol. CXXX, July–Sept. 1984, pp. 404–7.

LECLER, S.J. (snr.), *Histoire de la tolérance religieuse au siècle de la Réforme*.

LIVET, G., *Les guerres de religion* (Paris, PUF), coll. 'Que sais-je?', no. 1016, 1983 (4th edn.).

PINEAUX, J., *La poésie des protestants de langue française, 1559–1598* (Paris, Klincksieck, 1971).

STAUFFER, Richard, 'Brève histoire de la Confession de La Rochelle', in BSHPF, vol. CXVII, July–Sept. 1971, pp. 355–66.

YARDENI, Myriam, *La conscience nationale en France pendant les guerres de religion (1559–1598)* (Louvain & Paris, 1971).

5. BERENGER

The spread of the Reformation in eastern and northern Europe

BULLINGER, Henry, 'Brève et pieuse Institution de la religion chrétienne', in *Études & documents,* BSHPF, 1975, pp. 241–286.

COURVOISIER, Jaques, ed., *La confession helvétique postérieure* (French text of 1566) (Neuchâtel-Paris, 1944).

The whole form and content of the ecclesiastical ministry . . . by M. JEAN A LACKO, Baron of Poland, translated by Gilles Crematius, s.l., 1556. *Consensus de Sandomierz* ('Consensus mutuus in fide et religione christiana inter ecclesias evangelicas majotis et minoris Poloniac Magnis Ducatus Lithuaniae primo Sandomiriae anno 1570 sanctus') (Heidelberg, 1605).

BENDA, Kalman, 'Calvinism et le droit de résistance des ordres hongrois au commencement du XVIIe siècle', in *Études européenes, Mélanges offerts à V.L. Tapié* (Paris, 1973), pp. 235–43.

'La Réforme en Hongrie', BHSP, 1976, pp. 30–53.

BERENGER, J., 'Caractères originaux de l'humanisme hongrois', *Journal des savants,* 1973, pp. 257–88.

'Strasbourg et l'affirmation de la Réforme en Hongrie', in *Strasbourg au coeur religieux du XVIe siècle. Hommage à Lucien Febvre* (Strasburg, 1977), pp. 391–400.

BINDER, Ludwig, 'Grundlagen und Formen der Toleranz in Siebenbürgen bis zur Mitte des 17. Jahrhunderts', *Siebenbürgisches Archiv,* 1976.

BUCSAY, Mihaly, *Geschichte des Protestantismus in Ungarn* (Stuttgart, 1969).

'Humanismus und Reformation in Ost-und Südosteuropa', in *Brücke zwischen Kirchen und Kulturen,* Barton & Stupperich ed. (Vienna-Graz, 1976).

Der Protestantismus in Ungarn 1521–1978, vol.I (Vienna-Graz, 1977).

JOBERT, Ambroise, *De Luther à Mohila: La Pologne dans la crise de la Chrétienté, 1577–1648* (Paris, 1974).

MAKKAI, Laszló, *Histoire de la Transylvanie* (Paris 1946).

Anfänge und Wandlungen der Reformation in Ost-mitteleuropa (XVI. Jahrhundert), report at the 16th Congress of the Historic Sciences, Stuttgart, 1985 (for which the text was graciously lent by the author).

REVESZ, Imre, *History of the Hungarian Reformed Church* (Washington, 1956).

REVESZ, Laszlo, 'Die helvetische Reformation', in *Ungarn-Jahrbuch,* IV, 1972.

TAZBIR, Janusz, 'La tolérance religieuse en Pologne', in *La Pologne* at the 12th Congress of Historic Sciences, Varsovie, 1965.

6. LIVET

The Rhineland success

Rheinische Geschichte, vol.II, 'Neuzeit'.

PETRI, Franz, *Im Zeitalter der Glaubenskämpfe (1500–1648),* pp. 25–122.

Quellen und Literaturhinweise, pp. 199–217.

SKALWEIT, S., *Reich und Reformation* (1967).

ZEEDEN, E.W., *Das Zeitalter der Glaubenskämpfe (1555–1648)* (1970).

Also many monographs (*Rheinische Geschichte,* pp. 200–201).

CHRISMAN, M.U., *Lay Culture, Learned Culture: Books and Social Change in Strasbourg 1480–1599* (New Haven, Connecticut, 1982).

DEBARD, Marc, 'La Réforme luthérienne et la langue française: le cas de la principauté de Montbéliard du XVe au XVIe siècle', in BSHPF, vol. CXXIX, Jan.–March 1983.

DENIS, P., *Les Églises d'étrangers en pays rhénan (1538–1568),* thesis for doctorate in philosophy (Liège, 1982).

Horizons européens de la Réforme en Alsace. Hommage à Jean Rott (Strasbourg, 1980).

KINTZ, Jean-Pierre, *La société strasbourgeoise du milieu du XVIe siècle à la fin de la guerre de Trente Ans* (Paris, Strasbourg, 1984).

Strasbourg au coeur religieux du XVIe siècle. Hommage à Lucien Febvre (Strasburg, 1977).

VOGLER, Bernard, *La vie religieuse en pays rhénan dans la seconde moitié du XVIe siècle* (Paris, Sorbonne, 1972 and thesis edited at Lille in 3 vols., 1974).

Le clergé protestant rhénan au siècle de la Réforme (1555–1619) (Paris, Ophry, 1976).

7. GUGGISBERG

Men and ideas on the margin of history

BURMAN, Edward, *The Inquisition: The Hammer of Heresy* (Wellingborough, Northants., 1984).

CHAUNU, Pierre, *L'expansion européenne du XIIIe au XVe siècle.* Nouvelle Clio 26 (Paris, 1969).

Conquête et exploitation des nouveaux mondes. Nouvelle Clio 26bis (Paris, 1969).

ELLIOTT, John H., 'Renaissance in Europe and America: A Blunted Impact?', *First Images of America, The Impact of the New World on the Old,* ed. by F. Chiapelli (Berkeley, Los Angeles, 1976), vol. I, pp. 11–23.

FEBVRE, Lucien, *Le problème de l'incroyance au XVIe siècle: la religion de Rabelais* (Paris, 1942, 1968).

GINZBURG, Carlo, *I Benandanti: Ricerche sulla stregoneria e sui culti agrari tra Cinquecento e Seicento* (Turin, 1966).

Il formaggio e i vermi: Il cosmo di un mugnaio del '500 (Turin, 1976).

GUGGISBERG, Hans. R., *Religiöse Toleranz: Dokumente zur Geschichte einer Forderung* (Stuttgart, 1984).

HERSCHE, Peter, 'Unglaube im 16. Jahrhundert', *Schweizerische Seitschrift für Geschichte 34,* 1984, pp. 233–250.

LECLER, Joseph, *Histoire de la tolérance au siècle de la Réforme* (2 vols.) (Paris, 1955).

LIENHARD, Marc, 'Les épicuriens à Strasbourg entre 1530 et 1550 et le problème de l'incroyance au XVIe siècle', *Croyants et sceptiques au XVIe siècle . . .* (published by Marc Lienhard, Strasbourg, 1981), pp. 17–45.

MONTER, William, *Ritual, Myth and Magic in Early Modern Europe* (Athens, Ohio, 1983).

Witchcraft in France and Switzerland: The Borderlands during the Reformation (Ithaca, NY, 1976).

POPKIN, Richard H., *The History of Scepticism from Erasmus to Spinoza* (Berkeley, Los Angeles, 1979).

VICKERS, Brian (ed.), *Occult and Scientific Mentalities in the Renaissance* (Cambridge, 1984).

YATES, Frances A., *Giordano Bruno and the Hermetic Tradition* (London, Chicago, 1978).

8. MÜTZENBERG

The rise of the schoolmaster

BORGEAUD, Charles, *L'adoption de la Réforme par le peuple de Genève* (Geneva, 1923), p. 21.

BUSCARLET, Daniel, *La Réformation à Genève* (Geneva, 1936), p. 22ff.

CIPOLLA, C.M., *Literacy and development in the West* (Penguin Books, 1969), p. 86ff.

LE COULTRE, Jules, *Mathurin Cordier et les origines de la Pédagogie protestante dans les pays de langue française (1530–1564)* (Neuchâtel, 1926).

LUTHER, Martin, *Oeuvres,* vol. IV (Geneva, 1958), p. 91ff, p. 101ff, p. 108, p. 111ff; vol. IX (Geneva, 1961), p. 192ff; vol. II (Geneva, 1966), p. 146.

MESNARD, Pierre, 'Mathurin Cordier (1479–1564)' in *Foi-Éducation,* 29th year, no. 47, April-June 1959, pp. 76–94.

MÜTZENBERG, Gabriel, *Genève 1830. Restauration de l'école* (Lausanne, 1974), p. 147ff.

Registres du Conseil (published by La Société d'Histoire et d'Archéologie), vol. XIII (Geneva, 1940) p. 576ff

VUILLEUMIER, Henri, *Histoire de l'Église réformée du pays de Vaud sous le régime bernois,* vol. I (Lausanne, 1927), p. 31 ff.

Index

Numbers in italic indicate references to illustrations.

Names of people

A

AEBLI 147
AGRICOLA, John 234, 237
AGRICOLA, Mikael 195
ALBA, Duke of 203
ALBRET, Jeanne d' 249
ALCALA 72
ALEXANDER VI 68
ALLEN, William 206
AMAMA, Sixten 282, 283
AMSDORF, Nicolas 234
AMYRAUT, Moses 240, 241
AMDREAE, Jacob 189, 236, 237, 280
ANGOULÊME, Marguerite d' 117
AQUINAS, Thomas 88, 89, 120, 132, 135
ARAGON, Catherine of 69, 207, 209, 210
ARCHIMEDES 66
ARIÈS, Philippe 55, 56
ARIOSTO 69
ARISTOTLE 36, 37, 56, 66, 72, 120, 259
AUBIGNE Agrippa d' 179
ARMINIUS, Jacob 240

B

BACH, Johann Sebastian *192*, 205, 242
BADE, Josse 69
BADUEL, Claude 71
BAIROCH, Paul 44
BALDUNG-GRIEN, Hans *190, 232*
BALTIMORE, Lord 222
BAPST 193
BARTH, Karl 286
BATAILLON, Marcel 77, 160
BATHORY, Stephen 229
BAVARIA, Ernest of 201, *201*
BERQUIN, Louis de 103
BERULLE, Pierre de *80*, 273, 276
BESSARION 66, *68*
BEZA, Theodore de 132, *150*, 152, 153, 178, 179,
   202, 203, 204, 216, 217, 228, 236, 237, 238,
   238, 239, 240, 244, 256, 282, 283
BIFREN, Jachiam 265
BIRO DEVAY, Matthias 106
BLANDRATA 228, 229
BLARER 186
BOCCACCIO 60, 64
BOCSKAY, Stephen 229
BODIN, Jean 43, 256, 259
BOLEYN, Anne 207, 209
BOLSEC, Jerome de 131, 151, 216
BOMBERG, Daniel 72
BORROMEO, Charles *80*, 272, 273,
BOSSE, Abraham *183, 242*
BOURG, Anne du 173
BOVELLES 78
BRANDENBURG, Albert de 104, 200, 224
BRANDENBURG, Jean-Georges de 201
BRANDENBURG, Jean-Sigismund de 191
BRANDENBURG BAYREUTH, Marie de 199
BRENZ, John 186, 236, 237
BRÈS, Guy de 202
BRIÇONNET, Guillaume 75, 103, *103*, 122, 149
BROWNE, Robert 219
BRUCCIOLI 103
BRUCCIOLI, Antonio 104
BRUEGEL 54, *202*, 251, *252*

BRULLY, Pierre de *202*
BRUNO, Giordano 68, 259, 260
BUCER, Martin 12, 78, 95, 98, 99, 116, 119, 123,
   125, 127, 146, 149, 151, 166, 171, 184, 186,
   196, 197, 198, *198*, 200, 202, *223, 226*, 227,
   227, 228, 235
BUD, Guillaume 71, 103, 132
BUGENHAGEN, Johannes 97, *97*, 101, *194*
BULLINGER, Henry *114*, 132, 147, 148, 151, 160,
   166, 191, 198, 211, 215, *215*, 223, 226, 227,
   235, 254, 282
BURES, Idelette de 197

C

CAILLOS, Roger 18
CAJETAN 74, 89, 90, *92*, 132
CALOV, Abraham 238
CALVIN, John 11, 12, 13, *13*, 14, 15, 17, 20, 22,
   24, 31, 38, 75, 98, 99, 110, 112, 116, 117, 118,
   119, 120–136, 137, 143, *145, 148*, 150, *150*,
   151, *151*, 152, *152*, 153, *153, 156, 158*, 166,
   168, 171, 178, *178*, 179, 180, 181, 191, 197,
   198, 199, 202, 203, 204, 206, 211, 212, 213,
   214, 216, 218, 222, 227, 235, 236, 238, 241,
   244, 245, 246, *246*, 247, *247*, 248, *248*, 249,
   250, 254, 256, 261, 263, 264, 282
CAMERON 282, 283
CAMPANELLA, Thomas 68, 259, 260
CANTERBURY 138
CAPITO, Wolfgang 12, 70, 146, 147, 149
CAPPEL, Louis 282, 283, *284*
CARDANO, Girolano 259
CARLSTADT 98, 99, 104, 106
CARPACCIO, Vittore 68
CARRANZA, Bartolomé de *80*, 166, *166*
CARTWRIGHT, Thomas 218
CASIMIR, Jean 199
CASTELLIO, Sebastian 130, 151, 166, 255, 256,
   257
CAJETAN 89, 90, *92*
CASTRO, Alfonso de 164
CERULAIRE, Michel 34
CHARLES V 41, 69, 71, 96, 100, *109*, 138, *140*,
   160, 163, *168*, 184, *184*, 186, 187, 197, 202,
   207, 232, 233, 234, 268, 269
CHARLES IX 171, 195
CHRISTIAN II 104, *104*
CHRISTIAN III 195
CISNEROS, Ximenes de 72, 160, *164*, 267, 268
CLAUDEL, Paul 83
CLEMENT VII 69, *223, 226*
CLICHTOVE, Josse 71, 78
COLIGNY, Gaspard de *172*, 173, 175
COLUMBUS 266
COMENIUS, Jan Amos 265, *265*
CONSTANTINO 164
COP, Nicholas 123
COPERNICUS, Nicholas 68, 182, *259*, 260
CORDIER, Mathurin 71, 120, 152, 263, 264, 265
CORRO, Antonio del 160, 166
CORVIN 195
COTTON, John 221
COVERDALE, Miles 75, 207
CRANACH, Lucas 24, *24, 84, 93, 97, 190, 232*
CRANMER, Thomas, Archbishop of Canterbury 104,
   207, 209, 210, *210*, 213, 227
CROMWELL, Oliver 220, *220*, 233
CROMWELL, Thomas 208
CUSA, Nicholas of 66, 259

D

DANEAU, Lambert 238, 239, 282, 283
DANES 122
DANIELOU, Jean 33
DANTE 56, *57*, 64
DAVID, François 228, 229
DELUMEAU, Jean 17, 85
DENIFLE 11, 83
DEVAO BIRO, Mathias 106
DONAUWORTH, Sebastian Franck de 258
DOOYEWEERD, Herman 29
DOUMERGUE, Émile 14·
DUDLEY, John, Duke of Northumberland 209
DUDLEY, Rober 219
DUMEZIL, Georges 31
DUPLESSIS-MORNAY 179
DÜRER, Albrecht 38, 44, *47*, 54, *69, 100, 190, 232*

E

EBELING, Gerhard 84
ECK, John 89, *94*, 97, 116, 146, 223
EDWARD VI 206, 209, 210, 227
ELIADE, Mircea 17, 18
ELIZABETH I 49, 152, 206, 209, 210, 211, *211*,
   213, *213*, 214, 216, *216*, 217, 219, *219*, 220, 232
ELZ, Jacob III von *200*
EMSER, Jerome 97
ENGELS 83
ENZINAS, Francisco de 103, 166
ERASMUS 54, 58, 65, *69, 69*, 70 *70*, 71, *71*, 72,
   73, 74, 75, 77, 78, 81, *81*, 85, 86, 97, 99, 102,
   111, 112, 116, 123, 132, 146, 147, 160, 164,
   181, 223, 251, 255, *256*, 257, *263*, 273, 283
ERASTUS 216, 217

F

FABER 143, 146
FALK, Peter 70
FAREL, Guillaume 11, 12, *13*, 78, 102, 125, *125*,
   126, 127, *148*, 149, 150, 151, *152*, 198, 261
FARNER, Oskar 112
FEBVRE, Lucien 17, 34, 85, 128, 258
FERDINAND 101, 184
FICINO, Marsilio 66, 156
FLACCIUS ILLYRICUS, Matthias 234, *236*, 237
FLUE, Nicolas de 112, *113*
FOURIER, Pierre 274
FOX, George *220*, 222
FRANCE, Renée de 158, *158*
FRANÇOIS DE SALES, St *80*, 81, *273*, 276
FRANCIS I *41*, 48, 69, 117, 122, 124, *124*, 135,
   138, *138, 168*, 173, 226, *250*, 272
FREDERICK III *190*, 199, 235
FREDERICK IV 199
FREDERICK V 199
FROBENIUS 111
FROMENT, Antoine *148*, 150, 262
FUGGER 50
FUNEL, Baron de 175
FUST, Johann 67

G

GAGLIARDI, Ernest 149, 152
GALILEO 182, *259*, 260, *260*
GAMA, Vasco de *54*
GERHARD, Johann 189, 238
GERHARDT, Paul 242

Names of places

Picture credits

Institutions

ARCHIVES D'ÉTAT, GENEVA: F. Martin: pp. 131 (1), 238, 247.

ARCHIVES NATIONALES, PARIS: pp. 198 (2), 284 (2).

ALLIANCE BIBLIQUE, PIERREFITTE: p. 35 (1–2).

BIBLIOTHÈQUE NATIONALE SUISSE, BERNE: p. 110.

BIBLIOTHÈQUE NATIONALE, PARIS: pp. 15 (1–2), 19 (1), 28, 31, 32 (1), 33, 38, 40, 41, 43 (2), 44 (1), 46 (1–2), 53 (1), 64 (1–2), 67 (1), 70 (1), 72, 73 (1–2–3), 74, 75 (1), 78, 81 (1–2), 98, 103 (2), 125 (2), 132 (2), 134 (3), 146 (1), 171, 174 (1), 178, 179, 182, 183, 187, 200, 201, 215 (1), 216, 219 (2), 227 (1), 239, 240 (1), 256 (2), 258 (1), 262 (1), 265 (1–2), 267, 284 (1), 285 (1).

BIBLIOTHÈQUE PUBLIQUE ET UNIVERSITAIRE, GENEVA: pp. 121, 248–249, 248 (2), Dagli Orti: pp. 13, 153; F. Martin: pp. 118, 130, 148 (1–3), 151, 186, 246, 264, 280 (1–2), 285 (2).

BIBLIOTHÈQUE NATIONALE ET UNIVERSITAIRE, STRASBURG: pp. 23 (2), 191, 198 (1).

ZENTRALBIBLIOTHEK, ZURICH: pp. 114 (1–2), 116 (1), 119 (1–2), 143, 147 (2).

CENTRE REGIONAL DE DOCUMENTATION PEDAGOGIQUE, CLERMONT-FERRAND: p. 231.

OEFFENTLICHE KUNSTAMMLUNG, BASLE: p. 147 (1).

MUSÉE D'ART ET D'HISTOIRE, GENEVA: pp. 12–13, 126 (2), 136, 249.

MUSÉE DE L'HOMME, PARIS: p. 17.

SCHWEIZERISCHES LANDESMUSEUM, ZURICH: pp. 144–5.

MUSÉE CALVIN, NOYON: p. 138.

SOCIÉTÉ DE L'HISTOIRE DU PROTESTANTISME FRANÇAIS, PARIS: pp. 71, 83 (1), 146 (2), 210 (1), 234 (1–2), 236, 258 (3).

Agencies

ARTEPHOTO, PARIS: Acraci: pp. 268–9; Archiv. fur Kunst und Geschichte, Berlin: pp. 11, 70 (2), 82, 84–5 (1–2), 88–9, 92 (1–2), 93, 96–7, 97 (2), 184 (1), 189, 192 (1–2), 194 (1–2), 254, 281 (1); Babey: p. 185; Bildarchiv Preussicher Kulturbesitz, Berlin: p. 241; Bridgeman: pp. 211 (2), 220 (2), 221; Burkard: p. 112; Candelier: p. 101 (1–2); Fabri: p. 30; Faillet: p. 61; Held: pp. 18, 20 (2), 75 (2), 105, 116 (2), 128, 152 (1–2), 176–7, 209 (1), 272, 276 (2), 277; Lessing: p. 253; Nimatallah: pp. 169, 181 (1), 220 (1); Oronoz; pp. 53 (2), 124 (1), 161, 164, 165, 166, 167 (1–2), 203 (2); Schneider, Lindau: pp. 108, 113 (1); Takase: p. 29; Tok: pp. 20 (1), 21.

BULLOZ, PARIS: pp. 22, 42, 47, 52, 55, 58 (2), 94 (2), 104 (2), 112–13, 162–3, 175, 190 (1–2), 202, 209 (3).

EDIMEDIA, PARIS: pp. 12, 23 (1), 50 (1), 56, 86 (1), 88 (2), 94 (1), 98–9, 106, 107 (1), 123, 125 (1), 129, 132 (1), 134 (1–2), 135, 203 (1), 207 (1), 210 (2), 233, 259 (2), 260 (1), 282 (1).

GIRAUDON, PARIS: pp. 19 (2), 34 (1–2), 36, 48, 49, 50 (2), 51, 57 (1), 60, 66, 69 (2), 76–7, 79 (2), 80, 87, 90, 115, 124–5, 137, 150, 158 (2), 159 (2), 168, 170, 172–3, 181 (3), 186, 197 (1), 204–5, 205 (2), 206 (1), 207 (2), 208, 211 (1), 213 (2), 226 (1), 237, 240, 242, 250, 252, 257, 261, 263, 266, 269, 270, 275, 278; Anderson: pp. 65, 174 (2); Bridgeman: pp. 212, 213 (1); Garanger: p. 273 (1); Jurgens: pp. 24, 95, 133, 140–1, 232; Lauros: pp. 44 (2), 172, 180, 184 (2), 256 (1).

MARY EVANS, LONDON: pp. 214, 217, 219 (1), 251.

EXPLORER, PARIS: pp. 67 (2), 69 (1), 102 (2), 130 (2), 186–7, 195, 262 (2), 276 (1).

MAGNUM, PARIS: Lessing: pp. 25, 54, 245; Stock: p. 281 (2).

RAPHO, PARIS: p. 43 (1); Everts: p. 111; Silvester: p. 286.

ROGER-VIOLLET, PARIS: pp. 114 (3), 215 (2), 255 (1–2).

SCALA, FLORENCE: pp. 45, 57 (2), 68, 156 (2), 157, 160, 271.

Photographs

P. ALMASY: pp. 229 (1), 230 (2).

J.-L. CHARMET: p. 41 (2), 58 (1), 59 (1–2), 67 (3), 77 (2), 79 (1), 83 (2), 86 (2), 90–1, (2), 102 (1), 103 (1), 107 (2), 109, 113 (2), 117, 126–7, 131 (2), 148 (2), 156 (1), 158 (1), 159 (1), 188, 196, 204 (1), 223, 224 (1–2), 225 (1–2), 226 (2), 227 (2), 228 (1–2), 229 (2), 230 (1), 246 (1), 258 (2), 260 (2), 274, 279.

J.-P. DUMONTIER: p. 197 (2).

H. SCHWENK: p. 193.

Other sources

ENCYCLOPAEDIA UNIVERSALIS: p. 139
PRESSES UNIVERSITAIRES DE FRANCE: p. 142.
ENDPAPERS: View of Geneva. Patrick Thonnessen.